International Actors, Democratization and the Rule of Law

Do external factors facilitate or hamper domestic democratic development? Do international actors influence the development of greater civil and political freedom, democratic accountability, equality, responsiveness and the rule of law in domestic systems? How should we conceptualize, identify and evaluate the extent and nature of international influence?

These are some of the complex questions that this volume approaches. Using new theoretical insights and empirical data, the contributors develop a model to analyze the transitional processes of Romania, Turkey, Serbia and Ukraine. In developing this argument, the book examines:

- the adoption, implementation and internalization of the rule of law;
- the rule of law as a central dimension of liberal and substantive democracy;
- the interaction between external and domestic structures and agents.

Offering a different stance from most of the current literature on the subject, *International Actors, Democratization and the Rule of Law* makes an important contribution to our knowledge of the international dimensions of democratization. This book will be of importance to scholars, students and policy-makers with an interest in the rule of law, international relations theory and comparative politics.

Amichai Magen is W. Glenn Campbell National Fellow, Hoover Institution, and Lecturer in Law, Stanford Law School, Stanford University, USA.

Leonardo Morlino is Professor of Political Science at Istituto Italiano di Scienze Umane, Florence, Italy.

UACES Contemporary European Studies Series

Edited by Tanja Börzel *Free University of Berlin,* **Michelle Cini,** *University of Bristol and* **Roger Scully,** *University of Wales, Aberystwyth,* on behalf of the University Association for Contemporary European Studies.

The primary objective of the new Contemporary European Studies series is to provide a research outlet for scholars of European Studies from all disciplines. The series publishes important scholarly works and aims to forge for itself an international reputation.

1. **The EU and Conflict Resolution**
Promoting peace in the backyard
Nathalie Tocci

2. **Central Banking Governance in the European Union**
A comparative analysis
Lucia Quaglia

3. **New Security Issues in Northern Europe**
The Nordic and Baltic states and the ESDP
Edited by Clive Archer

4. **The European Union and International Development**
The politics of foreign aid
Maurizio Carbone

5. **The End of European Integration**
Anti-Europeanism examined
Paul Taylor

6. **The European Union and the Asia-Pacific**
Media, public and elite perceptions of the EU
Edited by Natalia Chaban and Martin Holland

7. **The History of the European Union**
Origins of a Trans-and supranational Polity 1950–72
Edited by Wolfram Kaiser, Brigitte Leucht and Morten Rasmussen

8. **International Actors, Democratization and the Rule of Law**
Anchoring democracy?
Edited by Amichai Magen and Leonardo Morlino

International Actors, Democratization and the Rule of Law

Anchoring democracy?

Edited by Amichai Magen
and Leonardo Morlino

Routledge
Taylor & Francis Group
LONDON AND NEW YORK

First published 2008 by Routledge

2 Park Square, Milton Park, Abingdon, Oxfordshire OX14 4RN
52 Vanderbilt Avenue, New York, NY 10017

Routledge is an imprint of the Taylor & Francis Group, an informa business

First issued in paperback 2018

Typeset in Garamond by Keyword Group Ltd

British Library Cataloguing in Publication Data
A catalogue record for this book is available from the British Library

Library of Congress Cataloging in Publication Data
A catalog record has been requested for this book

ISBN 13: 978-0-415-45102-4 (hbk)
ISBN 13: 978-0-415-49295-9 (pbk)

Contents

List of Figures

List of Tables

Notes on Contributors

Elena Baracani is Deputy Director of the Interuniversity Research Centre for European Studies (CIRES) at the University of Florence (Italy), and is Lecturer of European Political Organization at the University for Foreigners in Perugia (Italy). Her research interests focus on the EU's foreign policy and democracy promotion.

Ali Çarkoğlu is Associate Professor of Political Science at Sabancı University, Istanbul. His areas of research interest include party politics in Turkey, political economy of the Middle East, voting behaviour, public opinion, formal modelling and research methods. His most recent books include: *Greek-Turkish Relations in an Era of Détente*, (London, 2004), *Religion and Politics in Turkey* (London 2006), *Politics of Modern Turkey* (London, 2007), *The Rising Tide of Conservatism in Turkey* (London, 2008).

Cristina Dallara is Research Associate at the Center for Judicial Studies (CESROG) of the University of Bologna. She holds a PhD in Political Science (University of Florence), with a thesis entitled 'European Union Rule of Law promotion in Romania, Serbia and Ukraine'. Her research interests include judicial reforms in Eastern Europe and the Balkans, EU enlargement, democracy and rule of law promotion.

Ana Demsorean is a member of the Bucharest Bar and has been involved in a number of research projects and publications conducted by Stanford University and Freedom House including the 2005 Freedom House *Assessment Report of the Anticorruption Policy of the Romanian Government*. She received a Master's degree in European and International Business Law from the Université de Paris I Panthéon-Sorbonne and is currently concluding her PhD on 'Risk management policies'.

Senem Aydin Düzgit is completing her PhD in Political Science at the Free University of Brussels (VUB) and is an Associate Research Fellow at the Centre for European Policy Studies (CEPS) in Brussels. Her recent publications include 'Europeanization, Democratisation and Human Rights in Turkey' (with E. Fuat Keyman) in Esra Lagro and Knud Erik Jorgensen (eds.), *Turkey and the European Union: Prospects for a Difficult Encounter* (Palgrave, 2007). Her main research interests are: EU enlargement, politics of identity and democratization.

Amichai Magen is Lecturer in Law, Stanford Law School, and a Fellow at the Center on Democracy, Development and the Rule of Law (CDDRL), Freeman Spogli Institute (FSI), Stanford University. His research interests are in EU and International Law, the law and policy of international development, democratization theory and rule of law reforms in transitional countries. His writings have appeared in, among others, the *Stanford Journal of International Law*, the *International Studies Review*, the *European Foreign Affairs Review*, and the *Columbia Journal of European Law*.

Leonardo Morlino is Professor of Political Science at the Istituto Italiano di Scienze Umane (Florence, Italy). His present research interests are focused on the analysis of the 'qualities' of democracy in Europe and the processes of democratization. His most recent books include *Assessing the Quality of Democracy* (Johns Hopkins, 2005, with Larry Diamond), *Party Change in Southern Europe* (Routledge, 2007, with Anna Bosco) and *Democracias y Democratizaciones* (CIS, 2008).

Sorana Parvulescu is Analyst for Central and South Eastern Europe at Control Risks, an international business consultancy. She has previously worked on several research projects and publications conducted by think tanks such as the Romanian Academic Society and Freedom House. Her current research focuses on political and security risks, as well as the general business environment, in the Central and South Eastern European region.

Roman Petrov is Jean Monnet Lecturer in EU law at the Donetsk National University (Ukraine). Currently, he is Max Weber Fellow at the European University Institute (Italy). His research and publications are in the field of EU external relations law, particularly, the European Neighbourhood Policy.

Oleksandr Serdyuk Vasylyovych is Associate Professor at National Law Academy of Ukraine (Kharkiv) and Director of Analytical Center at the Research Institute of Applied Humanities. His most recent publications include: *Sociological Approach in Science of Law: Cognition of Social Nature of Law* (Pravo, 2007); *Social and Legal Problems of Prevention of Crime in the Field of Migration* (Yashma, 2004); and 'Law and Economy': Social Nature of Legal Phenomena in the Theory of Rational Choice' in *Yurydychna Ukraina* (6, 2007). His main fields of research are sociology, philosophy of law and comparative research in law.

Bogdan Vetrici-Soimu is a member of the Bucharest Bar Association, and has been participating in several research projects and publications conducted by Stanford University and Freedom House, including the 2005 Freedom House *Assessment Report of the Anticorruption Policy of the Romanian Government*, as an internal expert on Romanian legislation. He also graduated in Political Science at Bucharest University. At present he is an associate in an international alliance of law firms.

Preface

The objective of spreading liberal democracy and the rule of law abroad has, particularly since the September 11th attacks on the United States, entered the very heart of the foreign policy discourses of the leading western powers, most notably the US and the European Union (EU). The National Security Strategy of the United States issued by the White House in March 2006 opens with the following words:

> *It is the policy of the United States to seek and support democratic movements and institutions in every nation and culture, with the ultimate goal of ending tyranny in our world. In the world today, the fundamental character of regimes matters as much as the distribution of power among them. The goal of our statecraft is to help create a world of democratic, well-governed states that can meet the needs of their citizens and conduct themselves responsibly in the international system.*[1]

Even more striking than this extraordinary statement about the presumed relationship between the institutions and norms of democracy, on the one hand, and a host of domestic and international goods – security, peace, economic development, and environmental protection – on the other hand, is the fact that fundamentally the same conception is shared by Europe. Indeed, more than two years prior to the US statement the first European Security Strategy, formulated by Javier Solana and unanimously endorsed by the European Council in Brussels, declared that:

> *The quality of international society depends on the quality of the governments that are its foundation. The best protection for our society is a world of well-governed democratic states. Spreading good governance, supporting social and political reform, dealing with corruption and abuse of power, establishing the rule of law and protecting human rights are the best means of strengthening the international order.*[2]

In other words, despite squabbles over a host of international issues, the view that liberal democratic government is the sole legitimate form of socio-political organization and model to be promoted globally is shared, as perhaps never before, by both sides of the Atlantic – underlined by the erosion of state sovereignty and principles of non-intervention, as well as a growing appreciation of the links between substantive democracy and economic development, peace and security.

Nor is this all empty talk. World Bank (WB) figures indicate a tenfold increase in international support for promoting democracy, from 0.5 percent of Official Development Assistance (ODA) in 1991 to five percent in 2000 – an annual increase of approximately US$3 billion.[3] By 2006, institution building for democratic governance accounted for 40 to 45 percent of the United Nations Development Programme (UNDP) worldwide budget (Dervis 2006, 153). In the US, funds allocated specifically to the promotion of democracy and good governance rose from US$128 million in the 1990s to US$817 million in 2003, with spending on human rights, judicial development and anticorruption programs amounting to a full 47 percent of expenditure.[4] A similar trend has emerged in Europe (Burnell 2006, 361). All in all, western democracies and the international organizations they lead now spend billions of taxpayers dollars and euros each year with the explicit aim of building the rule of law in underdeveloped and transitional countries. Many more are spent through the WB and other multilateral development institutions, whose 'good governance' agenda is fast expanding and converging with overt democracy promotion – integrated peacekeeping missions under the auspices of the United Nations (UN), as well as multiple efforts to establish minimal conditions of law and order in conflict zones from Afghanistan and Gaza to Iraq, from Haiti to Liberia.

What struck us most powerfully about this evolving reality, and what has been the original driving impetus that gave birth to this book, is the fact that despite growing western investment in promoting democratic development abroad – an investment increasingly paid in blood as well as treasure – the dynamics of international influence on democratic development remain poorly understood. In particular, our understanding of the causal impact of international instruments on domestic outcomes is still woefully under-theorized and under-researched. Do international factors, including the conscious efforts of western actors, play a significant role in encouraging or discouraging transition to and consolidation of liberal democracy? If so, when and how do external incentives, financial and technical aid, socialization techniques, diplomacy or demonstration effects influence domestic decision-makers to adopt, implement and internalize the values and practices of liberal democracy? What combination of domestic conditions and foreign interventions is most likely to lead to the successful growth of effective, accountable democratic government that respects the rights of citizens and is responsive to their needs? What are the pathways of external influence on domestic change and what does the nexus of interaction between external and domestic variables look like in reality?

In deciding to confront these complex issues, we were all too conscious that we could not provide definitive answers to all of them, yet we both sensed that the experience of EU engagement with its neighbors over the last decade and a half – first in the context of eastern enlargement, and later in the Stabilization and Association Process (SAP) in the Balkans and in the European Neighbourhood Policy (ENP) more broadly – held the key to at least some of the most meaningful insights into the puzzle. To be sure, a relationship between Europeanization and democratization has long been assumed, but it is only with the proliferation of enlargement and nonenlargement engagement strategies over the last decade that a varied empirical canvas has emerged which can now be systematically explored – with important lessons not only for Europeanists, but for scholars and practitioners in the area of international security, development and democratization theory. By defining the democratic outcome we were most interested in – the rule of law – proposing an integrated conceptual framework for thinking about external influence on domestic change, and testing our concepts using both enlargement and non-enlargement cases of EU engagement, we hoped to gain a better understanding of external influence on domestic democratic development dynamics, and to provide a better guide to future academics and policymakers interested in promoting democracy abroad.

At the more prosaic level, this book is the result of the animated corridor debates between us (how else for an Israeli and an Italian) on the nature of democratization, its international dimensions, and the limits of western influence on its development in autocratic or transitional countries. The opportunities for our initial discussions arose, courtesy of our sharing adjacent office space in the Center on Democracy, Development and Rule of Law (CDDRL) at the Freeman Spogli Institute for International Studies (FSI), Stanford University. However, the ideas that eventually grew into this book would have likely remained only ideas, had it not been for the initial warm support of Coit Blacker, Director of the FSI, and the continued encouragement of CDDRL directors Stephen Krasner and Michael McFaul, as well as Stanford University President (Emeritus) Gerhard Casper, and Director of CDDRL and Stanford Law School's Rule of Law Program, Thomas Heller. To these colleagues we owe our deepest gratitude. Our warm thanks go to Robert Fishman for his interest and a number of very useful comments on several chapters of the book. We are also grateful for the generosity shown to us in the form of financial support which came initially from CDDRL, and then from the Italian Ministry for University and Research, the Jean Monnet Action and International Social Science Council (ISSC). We are also deeply indebted to our Routledge/UACES Contemporary European Studies Series Editor, Tanja Börzel, whose expert advice and meticulous editorial work helped us make the final steps towards completion of this manuscript.

Conducting comparative research in Romania, Serbia, Turkey, and Ukraine has had its own special rewards, allowing us to obtain first hand at least a glimmer of the daily struggle for freedom, decent government and opportunity being fought by extraordinary men and women in emerging democracies in Europe and beyond. Some of the colleagues we met in the process of designing the research which would eventually turn into this book, became the natural choices for authors of our case study chapters. Among the others who contributed generously of their time and knowledge to the project, we would like to thank Srjdan Darmanovic, Boris Begovic, Dragor Hiber, Jovan Jovanovic and

Stanislav Shevchuk. Special thanks to Fondazione Eunomia (Florence, Italy) for helping us with the paperback edition of the book. We enjoyed exploring an uncharted path – a journey that is surely the highest reward for a scholar. More than informing, perhaps, we hope this book will stimulate and provoke both theoretical and empirical inquiry into one of the central questions of our time: how to encourage not only more democracies, but better, higher quality ones.

Notes

1 See The White House, The National Security Strategy of the United States (available at: http://www.whitehouse.gov/nsc/nss/2006/), p. 1.
2 A Secure Europe in a Better World: European Security Strategy, European Council in Brussels, December 12, 2003 (available: http://www.consilium.europa.eu/uedocs/cmsUpload/78367.pdf), p. 10.
3 World Bank, *World Bank Development Report* (2004) cited in Burnell (2005, 361).
4 These figures do not take into account the enormous costs of post-conflict reconstruction and attempts to build state institutions in Afghanistan and Iraq. See Steven Finkel, Anibal Perez-Liñan and Mitchell Seligson, *The Effects of U.S. Foreign Assistance on Democracy Building*, 1990–2003 (draft article manuscript, on file with author).

1 Hybrid regimes, the rule of law, and external influence on domestic change

Amichai Magen and Leonardo Morlino

Introduction

At the beginning of the twenty-first century, two sets of phenomena are challenging our understanding of democracy and democratization. First, transition from authoritarian regimes into some form of democracy is no longer understood to constitute the most prevalent or important change in worldwide democratization processes. Second, contemporary processes of domestic political change are unfolding within a radically transformed international environment compared to even two decades ago (Gershman 2005; Whitehead 2004).

As the *Freedom House* organization has been underlining in its reports over the last decade,[1] the stable, closed authoritarian regime has become something of a rarity. While in 1974 – the year that heralded the launch of the 'third wave' of global democratization with the Portuguese *Revolução dos Cravos* (Huntington 1991) – the number of democracies on the planet stood at a mere 39, at the end of 2006, out of 193 independent countries, 123 ranked as electoral democracies (Freedom House 2006). Thus, for the first time in human history, democracy had become not only a universal aspiration, but the predominant form of government in the world, and the only form enjoying broad international legitimacy (McFaul 2004; Gershman 2005; Sen 1999). The triumph of democracy, moreover, has (so far at least) proven steadier than many would have expected, with cases of outright breakdowns and reversions to autocracy, and fears of a 'reverse wave' to autocracy, largely held at bay (Diamond 2000; 2005).

Yet a serious reservation is attached to this seemingly sanguine story. For as overtly authoritarian regimes have disappeared from many parts of the world, they have typically been replaced – particularly since the end of the Cold War – not by high-quality, liberal democracies, but by hybrid regimes that combine democratic and authoritarian elements. Sandwiched on a continuum between liberal democracy, on the one side, and closed authoritarian regimes, on the other side, these 'grey zone' entities (Carothers 2002) – which today number as many as 58 countries, roughly a third of the world's total – represent both the new frontiers of democratization theory and a novel challenge for local and international reformers concerned to promote the consolidation of free and effective government in transitional countries. The uncomfortable co-existence in so many countries around the world of, on the one hand, formally democratic procedures and, on the other hand, abuse of fundamental civil and political rights, high levels of criminality and violence, endemic corruption, and floundering socioeconomic structures, in other words, is beginning to motivate scholars to consider explicitly the substantive, non-electoral dimensions of democracy. Indeed, some of the most salient contemporary questions for students of democratization, development and international affairs – whether academics, aid practitioners or policy-makers – no longer have to do with electoral breakthroughs, or the consolidation of the bare procedural rules necessary for the existence of electoral democracy. Rather, the new questions are focused on the content of democratic government, understanding the nature of hybrid regimes, the dynamics of their endurance or change and, from a more practical perspective, the conditions and dynamics that could encourage the transformation of hybrid regimes into substantive democracies of reasonably high quality (Diamond and Morlino 2005).

These new questions in democratization studies, moreover, are today addressed against an international backdrop radically different from the one that guided the transitologists of the 1970s and 1980s and, to a lesser degree, the consolidationists of the 1990s. Indeed, with the hindsight of two decades at most, our analytical models of democratization have been challenged not only by the proliferation of hybrid regimes – a phenomenon that highlights the absurdity of conceptualizing democratization as a short, unidirectional interval between two clearly defined, stable regime types – but by a radically transformed international environment, and a parallel recognition of the importance of the international dimensions of democratization (Pridham 1991; Whitehead 1996a; Burnell and Calvert 2005).

Twenty years ago democratic transitions were relatively infrequent, bipolarity discouraged the risk of instability inherent in democratic experimentation, and the notion that steady authoritarian rule helped to foster the conditions of stability necessary for economic modernization still carried a substantial following (Whitehead 2004). The end of the Cold War not only expanded democratic practices into the former Communist world, it also eliminated a chief rationale for tolerating autocracies in the non-Communist one, as the withdrawal of western support for Apartheid South Africa demonstrated. With the number of new democracies growing rapidly in the 1980s and 1990s, democratization not only began to be perceived as the international norm rather than the exception, it also precipitated an unprecedented surge in democracy promotion activity by the main western powers (Smith 1994; Carothers 1999; Youngs 2004). At the hard edge of the spectrum of intervention – in countries from Haiti to Sierra Leone, from Bosnia-Herzegovina to East Timor and Afghanistan – weakening norms of state sovereignty, coupled with the growing linkage made by the United States (US) in particular between freedom and security, have led to the proliferation of the use of military force and the establishment of new forms of international trusteeship to remove authoritarian rulers and install democratically elected and run governments, even under the most difficult post-conflict conditions. The deployment of non-coercive mechanisms to protect and promote democracy has also exploded over the same period. World Bank figures indicate a tenfold increase in international democracy promotion expenditure between 1991 and 2000 – an annual increase of approximately US$3 billion (World Bank 2004). Institution building for democratic governance now accounts for 40 to 45 percent of the United Nations Development Programme (UNDP) worldwide budget (Dervis 2006), and more regional organizations, NGOs and transnational networks now wield more resources than ever before in order to protect and promote good governance and democracy through sanctions and positive incentives, socialization techniques, monitoring and reporting (Slaughter 2005; Russett and Oneal 2001).

Not surprisingly, contemporary democratization scholarship displays a growing interest in both Western democracy promotion policies and the international dimensions of democratization more broadly (Burnell 2005; Levitsky and Way 2005; Pevehouse 2005; Carothers 2004; Youngs 2004). Still, critical questions of theory, conceptualization and measurement abound in the field. Do international factors, including the democracy promotion policies of western actors, play a significant role in encouraging or discouraging democratic development in domestic systems? If so, when and how do different strategies – external incentives, financial and technical aid, socialization techniques, diplomacy or demonstration effects – influence domestic decision-makers to improve freedom, democratic accountability, equality and responsiveness? How can the influence of external actors be conceptualized and evaluated? What combination of domestic conditions and foreign 'interventions' is most likely to lead to the transformation of illiberal, ineffective and corrupt procedural democracies into freer, fairer and better governed democracies? What are the pathways of external influence on domestic change, and what does the nexus of interaction between external and domestic variables look like in reality?

This volume approaches these complex questions using new theoretical insights and empirical data. To engage with the themes outlined above in a conceptually and methodologically informed manner, we trace the dynamics of change in a central dimension of liberal, substantive democracy – the rule of law – and on the interaction between external and domestic structures, agents and processes shaping such change. In order to get as near as is possible in social science to tracing causal links between domestic and external factors, we consciously focus on the interaction between a defined international actor that seeks to promote rule of law reforms in third countries, the European Union (EU), and four countries with a different, yet comparable, history of structured interactions with the EU and basic domestic political transformations – Romania, Turkey, Serbia and Ukraine – in the period since the end of the Cold War (see below). Empirically, the volume presents the results of original research on the influence of externally driven rule of law promotion strategies in a group of subject countries where: (1) the strategies deployed emanate from the same external actor; (2) similar reform goals are sought; but (3) the strategies differ substantially in key features – the force of conditionality, opportunities for elite socialization and immediacy of incentives for compliance. Thus, we supersede the existing literature on EU influence on candidate countries (Kelley 2004a; Linden 2002, Pridham 2005; Sadurski, Czarnota and Krygier 2006; Schimmelfennig and Sedelmeier 2005a; Vachudova 2005), going 'beyond enlargement' to compare membership with non-membership EU strategies. In doing so, we seek to unpack the still poorly conceptualized and poorly understood notion of external influence on domestic democratic reform processes; to ascertain where and to what extent, if at all, such influence has in fact occurred; under what conditions external influence is more likely, and with what consequences for democratic quality in the case study countries. By asking these questions vis-à-vis four examples of 'hard cases' targeted by the EU for transformative engagement (Youngs 2005), we seek to derive lessons of broader application for scholars (of democratic development, comparative politics, international relations theory and international legal studies), as well as practitioners (in national aid agencies, NGOs, security and multilateral development organizations).

The remainder of this chapter addresses the notion of hybrid regimes, drawing on O'Donnell's insight that a major factor missing from flawed democracies is the 'democratic Rule-of-Law' (O'Donnell 1998; 2005). Having laid these conceptual foundations, we identify the gaps in existing analyses of external influence on democratic development in national systems, explain our focus on the EU as a rule of law promotion entity, and justify our case study selection. Chapter 2 of this volume then sets out in greater detail the analytical framework uniting this comparative study.

Hybrid regimes: definition and challenges

That the distinction between non-democracy and democracy could be conceptualized in terms of gradations, rather than as a dichotomy, and that in reality there always existed a gray area between non-democratic stable regimes of different sorts (see e.g. Linz 2000, and Brooker 2000) and consolidated, liberal democracy, was already evident to political comparativists in the late 1960s (Finer 1970; Dahl 1971) and later (Collier and Adcock 1999). The magnitude and spectrum of that gray area, however, have both greatly expanded since the advent of the 'third wave' of democratization in 1974 (Huntington 1991). At that time democracies were few, but they were largely liberal democracies – characterized not only by free, fair and competitive elections, but by protection of civil and political freedoms, a reasonable degree of accountability and responsiveness to citizen needs, and the rule of law. Democracies were concentrated in western Europe, North America and a number of their former colonies; they were a clear minority, but they were nearly all 'good democracies' (Morlino 2004; Diamond and Morlino 2005).

One of the most striking characteristics of the third wave, particularly in its late period in the 1990s, has been the unprecedented growth in the number of hybrid regimes: political regimes that adopt the form of electoral democracy (with regular, seemingly or actually competitive, elections), but fail to fulfill the substantive content of consolidated, liberal democracy, or do so only ambiguously (Karl 1995; Diamond 2002; Levitsky and Way 2002). As Diamond (2002) observes, the term 'hybrid regime' is itself a generic category containing at least four distinct subtypes of regimes. The category of non-democratic regimes that contain some form of electoral competition can itself be divided into competitive (variously described as 'competitive authoritarian' or 'electoral authoritarian') or uncompetitive ('hegemonic authoritarianism') (Diamond 2002; Schedler 2006). This leaves electoral (illiberal or minimal) democracy as a third subtype of diminished forms of democracy, and a residual category of 'ambiguous regimes' positioned on the fuzzy border between electoral authoritarian and electoral democracy.

Whereas recent scholarship has focused primarily on conceptualizing and explaining the proliferation of electoral authoritarianism (Brownlee 2007; Schedler 2006), we are chiefly concerned with the latter two subtypes of hybrid regimes. Clearly, these partial democracies are morally and practically pernicious. They give democracy a bad name by failing to deliver on people's legitimate expectations for effective participatory government, blur the distinction between genuinely free societies and authoritarianism, and help bad rulers endure in power by semi-legitimizing them. Their democratic content is at best weak, and at worst they display serious problems of corruption, inequality, abuse of civic and political freedoms, and state ineffectiveness. But it is the sheer rapidity and scale of their proliferation that has brought the problem of hybrid regimes to the forefront of policy and academic attention:

> While the 'transitologists' of the 1970s and 1980s investigated the conditions and modes of transition from dictatorship to democracy, the 'consolidologists' of the 1990s concentrated on inquiring into causes, conditions and models of the consolidation of young democracies. Most recently, the questions of whether democracy is working, how 'good' or 'bad' a democracy is, and of the conceptual issue of diminished sub-types of democracy (illiberal democracies, defective democracies and so on) have begun to become the new predominant trend in democracy theory and democratization studies.
>
> (Merkel and Croissant 2004, 1).

If we now know what hybrid regimes are, and how widespread they have become, the next question is: what determines whether such regimes evolve into fuller, higher quality democracies, remain stuck in a gray zone of illiberal, minimal electoralism, or backslide into outright authoritarianism?

What, in other words, is the 'democratic substance' missing from what has been variously referred to as 'democracy with adjectives' (Collier and Levitsky 1997) - 'illiberal' (Zakaria 1997), 'delegative' (O'Donnell 1994), 'clientelist' (Kitschelt 2000), or simply 'pseudo' (Diamond 2002) democracy? What accounts for the emergence, retardation or wilting of such substance? And finally, from a democracy promotion point of view, what action can and should be taken by domestic and external reformers to best encourage transitions from hybrid regimes to substantive, higher quality democracy?

In approaching these questions we encounter a gap in knowledge that we hope, at least in part, to fill in this volume. As Epstein *et al.* assert:

> [Partial democracies] account for an increasing portion of current regimes and the lion's share of regime transitions ... [but] ... we have little information as to the factors that would lead partial democracies to either slide down to autocracy or move up to full democracy ... the determinants of the behavior of the partial democracies elude our understanding ... the factors affecting transitions out of partial democracy remain poorly understood.
>
> (Epstein *et al.* 2006, pp. 556 and 564–5).

To approach the double conundrum of understanding the dynamics of change away from hybrid regimes, and the role that external actors may play in such transformation, we first identify a key dimension of democratic substance that is missing from hybrid regimes – the 'democratic Rule-of-Law' – and then proceed to begin addressing the topic of international influence on domestic democratic development.

Democratic substance and the rule of law

Transitions from hybrid regimes to more substantive, higher quality democracy can be explored along several theoretical axes (Morlino 2003, Whitehead 2002). Impressed by the violence, inefficiency, ineffectiveness, inequality, corruption and frequent violation of civil freedoms that characterize many formally democratic states – in Latin America, Asia, Africa and the former Soviet bloc – scholars have recently shifted the focal point of democratic theory in an attempt to identify what is missing from such regimes. At the same time, the growing interest of development economics over the last decade in issues of public voice and accountability, political stability, government effectiveness, the rule of law, regulatory quality and control of corruption (all under the notion of 'good governance', rather than the more overtly political 'democracy') are also focusing new attention on the non-electoral dimensions of democracy (Kaufmann, Kraay and Mastruzzi 2006; Jomo and Fine 2006; Drury, Krieckhaus and Lusztig 2006). The quest has led democratic theory to expand the discussion of democratic substance, or quality, and to critique older conceptualizations for confusing 'real' democracy with mere electoralism (Karl 1995; O'Donnell 1998).

At a bare minimum democracy requires: sovereign elected institutions; universal adult suffrage; free, competitive, fair and recurring elections; multiple serious political parties and a plurality of sources of information (Dahl 1971; Schmitter and Karl 1993). The basic conditions for democracy, in other words, involve institutionalized guarantees for participation in public contestation for power. In contrast, when we approach the issue of democratic substance – what makes a good democracy – we can identify eight dimensions on which an empirical determination of quality can be made: (1) the rule of law; (2) Participation (3) Competition; (4) Electoral Accountability; (5) Inter-institutional Accountability; (6) Responsiveness to the needs, interests and expectations of citizens; (7) Freedom (consisting of political, civil and socioeconomic rights); (8) Equality/solidarity (Diamond and Morlino 2005).

Prima inter pares among the dimensions of democratic quality is the rule of law (O'Donnell 1998; Bratton and Chang 2006; Thier 2007). As Linz and Stepan's seminal work on democratic consolidation indicates, the degree to which the rule of law exists in a given polity reflects the entire democratic quality of that regime (Linz and Stepan 1996). Indeed, the rule of law may be understood as the foundation upon which every other dimension of democratic quality ultimately rests (Diamond and Morlino 2005). Hence, the study of rule of law reform dynamics reflects deeper and broader processes of domestic democratic development, and an inquiry into the influence of international actors on changes in the quality of the rule of law moves the research agenda beyond the procedural, macro-democracy nexus of inquiry which characterizes so much of contemporary democracy promotion literature.

Anyone concerned to uphold the rule of law at home or to promote it abroad, however, is confronted with an a priori challenge of conceptualizing the term. Conceptualization involves the identification of the attributes that are constitutive of the concept under consideration. Such definition is a critical task, since the specification of the meaning of the concept forms the epicenter around which all subsequent decisions regarding theory, data collection and analysis are taken. Accordingly, the attributes that are constitutive of the concept under consideration have to be defined carefully, which means neither minimally nor with such overburdened detail as to make the concept synonymous with 'all things bright and beautiful', thus rendering it of little analytical use.[2]

Yet, to a degree perhaps unparalleled in social science phraseology, the term 'rule of law' is vulnerable to overreaching and abuse. More so than the term 'democracy' even – which itself has gained hegemonic international endorsement – the ideal of the rule of law is advocated nearly universally and, just as importantly, never seriously rejected. Amidst a host of deep cleavages – between east and west, north and south, Islamic and non-Islamic, liberal and non-liberal societies – as Tamanaha observes: 'there appears to be widespread agreement, traversing all fault lines, on one point, and one point alone: that the "rule of law" is good for everyone' (Tamanaha 2004, 1). Notwithstanding its pervasiveness as an ideal, however, the term is afflicted by an extraordinary divergence of understandings. Often, it seems 'there are almost as many conceptions of the rule of law as there are people defending it' (Taiwo 1999, 152).

Does this mean, as some theorists would have it, that the concept of the rule of law has been rendered meaningless by ideological abuse and general over-use? (Shklar 1987, 1). We submit that it does not. But neither does it mean that anything goes, and that any given definition is as good as another. Rather, because conceptualization is both intimately connected with theory and is a legitimately open-ended, evolving activity that is ultimately assessed in terms of the usefulness of the theory it helps to formulate, scholars are at liberty to determine what attributes must be included in a definition of the rule of law, while observing the methodological sensibility of avoiding the extremes of including too little, or too much, relative to their theoretical goals (Kaplan 1964, 51–3).

Identifying the constitutive attributes of the rule of law represents a challenge, less so because of the term's 'essentially contested' nature than by virtue of its evolving one, and the loose use made of it by practitioners and scholars from different disciplines (Radin 1989).[3] For Dicey, who coined and popularized the phrase, the concept represented one of the two legs upon which the constitutional order of England consistently rested since the Norman Conquest of 1066 (Dicey 1908). For Neumann, a Weimar Republic jurist and member of the Frankfurt School writing in the 1920s, it stood for one of the two defining characteristics of the modern nation-state; the rule of law being in perpetual, irreconcilable struggle with the modern state's other basic characteristic – sovereignty (Neumann 1986). Whereas in the middle of the twentieth century Hayek (1944) perceived the rule of law as the essential safeguard against the totalitarian tendencies of state socialism, by the late 1980s Hayek's disciples invoked the rule of law in their assault on Keynesian economics and as part and parcel of their calls for the US and the International Financial Institutions (IFIs) to pursue liberal market economy and development policies.[4]

In contemporary use, as Kleinfeld (2006) observes, the phrase is commonly brandished by politicians, practitioners and scholars to imply at least five meanings that are in fact distinct, but seldom clearly differentiated by those who invoke the term: (1) government bound by law; (2) equality before the law; (3) law and order; (4) predictable, efficient justice, and (5) public power respectful of fundamental rights. The definitional challenge is further compounded by the deep disconnection between the different communities now making use of the phrase, and the intellectual contexts from within which they operate.

Taking a step back from this confusion, we can divide conceptions of the rule of law into two broad types: thin and thick. This basic typology corresponds roughly to what Craig (1997) calls 'formal' and 'substantive',

Selznick (1999) 'negative' and 'positive', and Dworkin (1985, 11–13) terms 'rule-book' versus 'rights' conceptions of the rule of law.

Thin, formal, or negative conceptions of the rule of law demand the essential separation of law from politics (or 'autonomous law'), and focus on the minimal conditions necessary for law to restrict sheer arbitrariness in the ruler's use of power.[5] Restraining, if not actually taming, Leviathan has been the historically original context within which the concept of the rule of law emerged. Hence for Dicey: 'the rule of law is contrasted with every system of government based on the exercise by persons in authority of wide, arbitrary, or discretionary powers of constraint', so that no individual could be lawfully punished by the state 'except for a distinct breach of law established in the ordinary legal manner before the ordinary courts of the land' (Dicey 1908, 188). Restraining discretionary use of power is similarly at the heart of Hayek's definition of the concept. 'Stripped of all technicalities' as Hayek's powerful formulation puts it:

> this means that government in all its actions is bound by rules fixed and announced beforehand – rules which make it possible to foresee with fair certainty how the authority will use its coercive powers in given circumstances, and to plan one's individual affairs on the basis of this knowledge.
>
> (Hayek 1944, 54).

Such a conception – sometimes dubbed 'government by law, not by man' – stems from the historic struggle to curb the coercive force of the fiercest in human society, and is thus chiefly concerned with the 'negative' goal of shackling coercive authority. The constitutive attributes of a thin conception, therefore, stress formal or procedural aspects of the rule of law: laws must be open and public so that they can act as a guide to people (there should be no secret laws); the meaning of laws must be reasonably clear so that ordinary people can be guided by them; laws should be relatively stable, so that people can plan their lives by them; laws must be prospective, not retroactive; and the making of laws themselves must be governed by known, clear and relatively stable rules.

In contrast, a thick, substantive or positive (though anti-positivist) conception of the rule of law, accepts all the constitutive attributes of the thin definition, but at the same time insists that the rule of law cannot be divorced from fundamental elements of political morality and institutional practicality. In a substantive conception, laws enshrine and protect political and civil liberties, as well as procedural guarantees. It assumes that all those wielding public power must themselves be embedded in a comprehensive legal framework, so that individuals can enforce their rights against the state as a whole. Since government itself is ruled by law, political corruption and other forms of illegality are prohibited. The requirement that rights should be actually defendable means that the central institutions of the justice system, including lawyers, courts, the police and prosecution are at least reasonably fair, competent and efficient. This assumes a reasonably effective structure of state institutions, wielding a degree of administrative capacity adequate to carrying out the functions of the state. It further means that judges ought to be impartial and independent of the remainder of the state apparatus – otherwise the ability of individuals to uphold their rights before them would be endangered by political dependence and manipulation.

A substantive democracy, accordingly, is characterized by the presence of a democratic rule of law, which itself embodies five main dimensions: (1) protection of civil freedoms and political rights; (2) independent judiciary and a modern justice system; (3) institutional and administrative capacity to formulate, implement and enforce the law; (4) effective fight against corruption, illegality and abuse of power by state agencies; and (5) security forces that are respectful of citizens rights and are under civilian control.[6] These five dimensions, accordingly, are our main indicators of changes in democratic quality.

Though the two concepts are not synonymous, the affinity between the democratic rule of law and liberal democracy is clearly profound and multidimensional. Even a minimal, electoral democracy cannot exist unless rulers comply with at least one rule – that which regulates who should occupy the position of ruler given the outcome of general elections. More broadly, the virtues of the rule of law are substantially the same as those of the democratic process, in three key respects: the rule of law upholds the political rights of a democratic regime; it protects the civil liberties and rights of the entire population (including minority and other disadvantaged groups); and it establishes 'horizontal accountability' – networks of responsibility 'which entail that all public and private agents, including the highest state officials, are subject to appropriate, legally established controls on the lawfulness of their acts' (O'Donnell 2005, 7). Indeed, as Carothers suggests, properly conceived the interrelation between the rule of law and liberal democracy goes beyond democratic processes to permeate institutions and spheres across society:

> The rule of law makes possible individual rights, which are at the core of democracy. A government's respect for the sovereign authority of the people and a constitution depends on its acceptance of law. Democracy includes institutions and processes that, although beyond the immediate domain of the legal system, are rooted in it.
>
> (Carothers 2006, 4–5).

At the turn of the twenty-first century, in sum, the rule of law is most appropriately conceptualized not merely as a check on naked tyranny, an elixir for sustainable economic growth, or a set of institutional attributes, but as a key dimension (arguably *the* key dimension) of democratic quality. Such a conception taps into advances in legal philosophy, development economics, and democratic theory, in a manner that facilitates an analytically useful understanding of the rule of law as democratic substance, and its development as indicative of progress in democratic quality.

External influence on domestic democratic development

From their inception in the late 1960s through to the immediate aftermath of the Cold War, the predominant explanatory models of democratic development perceived the process of democratization as essentially a domestic drama, took the individual nation-state as the unit of analysis, and largely screened out international factors.[7] Indeed, until the early to mid-1990s, the role of the international context was correctly described as the 'forgotten dimension' (Pridham 1991; Burnell 2005) in the study of democratization. While some political comparativists continue to examine processes of political, institutional and legal reform at the national and sub-national levels in isolation from the broader international environment (Elster, Ofee and Preuss. 1998; Geddes 1999), since the end of the Cold War growing attention is being placed on the tasks of identifying, conceptualizing and, most recently, evaluating the role of external factors in domestic democratization processes. Along with rising recognition of the role of international factors in democratic transitions and consolidation, moreover, we have been witnessing growing interest – particularly in the US and Europe after the 11 September 2001 attacks – in examining the deliberate promotion of democracy abroad (Burnell 2005; Carothers 2004; Crawford 2003; Cox, Ikenberry and Inoguchi 2000; Ottaway 2003; Youngs 2004; Fukuyama and McFaul 2007). Still, as a five-year, joint American–European research project on the state of the art regarding international democracy promotion concluded, although democracy promotion has become an increasingly prominent feature of the foreign policies of leading western actors, the 'international dimension of democracy promotion nonetheless remains at best understudied and poorly understood' (Schraeder 2003, 22). We identify four main gaps in knowledge as follows.

First, the study of international democracy promotion necessitates piercing the domestic–international membrane, opening up the 'black box' of the state and developing both theoretical and empirical knowledge on external–internal linkages of democratization. In practice however, for a variety of historical, intellectual, methodological and institutional reasons, theories of comparative politics, international relations, institutionalism and international law have constructed largely separate, independent and self-contained spheres of inquiry, with distinct actors and research questions. Just as political comparativists have screened out international factors, international relations theorists concentrate on international outcomes and have been insufficiently prepared to research causal linkages between international agents and domestic actors.[8] Researching external dimensions of democratization, moreover, must involve the insights of both academics and practitioners. Yet the separation between the two worlds remains profound. In attempting to explain exogenous influences on domestic political developments, academics have tended to gravitate towards history (often going back several centuries) (Moore 1966; Tilly 1975, 1990; Greif 2005, 2006) rather than grapple with the messy history of the present. For their part, practitioners borrow few insights from academics, and the two groups are generally 'engaged in dissimilar enterprises' (Carothers 1999, 94).

Second, the existing literature on international democracy promotion tends to be descriptive, focusing on the democracy promotion motives, strategies and instruments (the 'supply side') of individual countries, primarily the US, rather than attempting to get at the experience of countries targeted for change or, even more so, the interaction between external actors and domestic change processes.[9] In reality, it is never the case that international factors alone, whether a single actor or a host of them, play an independent causal role in the development of democratization within a given domestic setting. If until the mid-1990s international actors were screened out altogether, in the more recent literature it appears that the pendulum has swung to the opposite extreme, whereas what is required is more empirical knowledge regarding when and how external actors have managed to promote internal reforms, as well as far greater attention to understanding the interactions between external and domestic factors.

Third, just as democracy promoters have tended to adopt a 'one size fits all' template to their work (Carothers 1999; Boerzel and Risse 2004), evaluators of domestic democratic change tend implicitly to homogenize external influence on domestic reform processes. In reality, however, the same set of independent variables (whether internal or external) may have a different influence on democratization outcomes depending on the kind of outcome being analyzed. The mix of independent variables that generate political liberalization in an autocratic regime, for instance, may not be the same forces that trigger a successful transition. Likewise, the factors that cause an electoral breakthrough may be of little relevance to the flow of democratic content post-transition – the protection of political and civic rights, accountability, responsiveness and effective rule of law – necessary for high-quality, liberal democracy. Countries trying to build democratic institutions after a war or a collapse face a different set of challenges than democratizing regimes with effective states. Since to date there has been little contiguity between scholars of democratic transitions, consolidation and post-conflict state-building, it is less surprising perhaps that we have not yet differentiated between what are in reality radically different contexts and processes of change, and the varying roles of external actors in each category. Historically, scholarly and policy emphasis has gravitated towards dramatic events of transition from authoritarian rule and, more recently, post-conflict political reconstruction efforts. By exploring the nature and limits of external influence on the quieter processes of shifts in the quality of democracy, we hope to draw attention to the phenomenon of variety, where external factors play different roles in different types of domestic political outcomes.

Indeed, our need to attend to the less visible, messier travails inherent in efforts to improve democratic quality in flawed democracies, is explained, in part at least, by the intellectual history of democratization studies as a field. Whereas the 'transitologists' of the 1980s (focusing on southern Europe and Latin America as their case studies) saw democratization as a short interlude between one stable regime type and another – non-democracy to democracy – we have come to understand democratization as a more complex, multilayered, long-term and open-ended process. Especially where the goal is the eventual establishment of a high-quality democracy, democratization has come to be understood as a multi-faceted, potentially reversible process lasting decades rather than years (Whitehead 2004). Accordingly, new analytical models are required to conceptualize international actor influence on regime development in the spheres spanning the aftermath of electoral breakthrough, all the way to the entrenchment of high-quality democracy. Instances of reversals, hurdles and even outright failure, must be included in the analysis not only to avoid selection bias and to isolate the causal mechanisms that were ultimately necessary for democratic change, but equally to capture the ebbs and flows that characterize ongoing, often non-linear, processes of democratic development.

Finally, the strong incentive for multilateral development banks, state aid agencies and other donor organizations, is to document success stories, where the wisdom of investment in aid for democracy can be showcased before budget allocating legislatures and taxpayers reassured that democracy promotion 'works'. This is partly a reflection of the political economy of the growing post-Cold War, post-9/11 democracy promotion 'industry'. Thus, for example, a large cross-national quantitative report on the effects of US foreign assistance on democracy promotion – compiled with the participation of the United States Agency for International Development (USAID) and published in 2006 – contends that US$10 million invested in USAID democracy assistance between 1990 and 2003 produced, on average, a 0.25 point improvement in the Freedom House score of the recipient state (Finkel, Perez-Linan and Seligson 2007). Are these felicitous findings matched by the experience of transitional countries struggling to improve the quality of accountability, clean government, and protection of civil and political rights? Does this aggregate level, quantitative report and others like it – which can tell us very little about causality or the pathways of connections between external influence and domestic change processes – reflect the reality of post-Cold War international actor influence on democratic development? Or does the picture that emerges from a close qualitative examination of external influence on domestic change suggest a different conclusion? Chapter 2 in this volume sets out an analytical framework specifically addressing these puzzles. But before that, we need to justify our focus on the EU as an agent of rule of law promotion, and explain our case study selection.

Why the European union? Why these cases?

The EU is not the sole international actor currently engaged in the promotion of rule of law reforms in developing and transitional countries (Carothers 2006; Jensen and Heller 2003). Neither was it the first to have become involved in this field of international activity. Indeed, although since the end of the Second World War four main 'waves' of rule of law promotion movements have taken place – where leading Western states have sought, either directly or through multilateral development organizations, to promote legal and judicial reforms in transitional countries – the EC/EU can only be said to have become a significant promoting actor in the last wave, which commenced in the immediate aftermath of the Cold War (Jensen 2003; K. Smith 2003a; Youngs 2001).

The fact that the EU has been a relative latecomer to an area of activity historically shaped primarily by the Americans (Ikenberry 2000; T. Smith 1994) has in several respects hampered both theoretical and empirical inquiry into its role as an international democracy and rule of law promotion actor. Since the institutional and intellectual prism within which EU thinking about democracy promotion originally developed in the post-Cold War era has primarily been the enlargement of the regional organization itself (K. Smith 2003a) – a prism radically different from that of the US, or the World Bank and the UN for that matter (Jomo and Fine 2006; Newman and Rich 2004) – the American-dominated democratization literature has long neglected the European experience. In reality, EU enlargement processes in the Central and Eastern European countries (CEECs), and later Turkey and the Balkans, have been, as Whitehead (2001a, 415) observes: 'a major, but under-theorized, component of the post-cold war drive for "democracy promotion" in those parts of the world that were until recently not organized into liberal democratic regimes', yet even in the case of post-Communist transformations, as Dimitrova (2002, 174) laments, the enlargement and democratization literatures have until very recently tended to 'not only pass each other as ships in the night, but they rarely even sail in the same sea'. Indeed, until the turn of the Millennium, studies on Eastern enlargement were almost entirely either descriptive or focused on accounting for individual Member States' policy preferences, as well as the EU's collective decision to assume the risks and costs of expansion (Maresceau 1997; Mayhew 1998; Henderson 1999; Ott and Inglis 2002).

The dearth of careful attention to the external influence on domestic change puzzle imbued in pre-accession processes can be explained with reference not only to the lingering insularity of European studies from broader questions in comparative politics and international relations theory, but to a number of additional factors including: the wider screening out of international dimensions from earlier generations of democratization scholarship; the incremental and fragmented manner in which EU policies have developed since the inception of the first pre-accession process in 1994; the highly technocratic, often cryptic nature of accession negotiations, which made the topic inhospitable to non-EU experts; and finally, the perception among scholars of democratization and democracy promotion that the EU's *sui generis* nature as an international actor, as well as the temporally and spatially limited nature of enlargement, offered few lessons of broader utility to the field (Magen 2004).

This latter point deserves further elaboration, since the focus on enlargement as a self-contained phenomenon has also afflicted to a considerable extent those scholars who did eventually turn to examine the EU expansion–democratization nexus of inquiry (Dimitrova 2002; Haughton 2007; Kelley 2004a; Kubicek 2003; Pridham 2005; Sadurski 2004; Schimmelfennig, Engert and Knobel 2003; Schimmelfennig and Sedelmeier 2004 and 2005a; Vachudova 2005). Although a number of commentators have pointed out that the dynamics created by EU expansion in the last decade constitutes a set of conditions as close to a laboratory experiment in external influence on domestic democratic development as is likely to occur in social science (Falkner 2000; Pridham 2002), rigorous comparative analysis on the EU expansion–democratization nexus has remained sparse and fragmented. Studies in the area typically analyze single enlargement rounds (Kelley 2004a; Pridham 2005; Vachudova 2005), single country cases, or single policy areas (Jacoby 2004; Linden 2002; Schimmelfennig and Sedelmeier 2005a). Within this picture, several studies are dedicated to democracy generally (Kubicek 2003; Pridham 2005; Sadurski, Czarnota and Krygier 2006) and human rights (Fierro 2003), but the subject of rule of law has attracted little systematic attention, remaining to a great extent the 'forgotten Copenhagen Criteria'.[10]

Moreover, it is now high time for scholars and practitioners alike to look beyond enlargement and onto a broader canvas of EU engagement strategies meant to exercise transformative power abroad and in particular to undertake systematic, comparative studies of enlargement and non-enlargement strategies so as to gain a better understanding of the nature, extent and limitations of external actor influence. Evidence of what a number of observers variously describe as 'external Europeanization', 'EU external governance', 'transformative engagement' and 'transformative power' (Grabbe 2006; Lavenex 2004; Schimmelfennig and Wagner 2004; Youngs 2005) – all involving the projection of EU rules, institutions and governance processes to non-member, non-candidate states and other international organization – can be found globally (Grugel 2004; Horng 2003; Szymanski and Smith 2005), but the phenomenon is most pronounced in the European peripheries. Regions surrounding the EU 'attract attention from policy-making institutions of the EU and, over time, become targets of significant 'policy export' from the Union' (Christiansen, Petito and Torna 2000, 410).

EU efforts to affect transformation in neighboring regions have not been confined to the hope that the Union's liberal-democratic example would somehow infect neighboring regions through some passive form of diffusion (Kopstein and Reilly 2000; Simmons, Dobbin and Garrett 2006; Skrede Glenditsch and Ward 2006). On the contrary, the perception that enlargement has been the most successful foreign policy instrument the EU has ever wielded, new security imperatives, path dependence, and turf battles over the making of EU foreign policy have, over the past several years, prompted EU actors – notably the Commission and the European Council – to adapt the methodologies used to promote democratization and marketization in the CEECs and apply these first to Turkey, the Balkans, and later to Ukraine, the South Caucasus, North Africa and the eastern Mediterranean (Magen 2006).

EU efforts at transformative engagement, exercised through bilateral agreements and regional frameworks – notably the Stabilization and Association Process (SAP) in the western Balkans, the Euro-Mediterranean Partnership (EMP) and now the European Neighbourhood Policy (ENP) – involves the establishment and progressive development of formal comprehensive ties incorporating regularized cooperation, dialogue and monitoring (bolstered by financial assistance, technical aid and conditionality) on a broad range of subjects (trade, competition, standards, transport, environment, justice and home affairs, human rights, democracy and so forth) with the aim of affecting far-reaching economic, political and social change in targeted countries.[11]

As chapter 3 in this volume explains in detail, the incentives deployed by the EU in an attempt to affect such changes in the CEECs, Turkey, the Balkans and the ENP countries vary in certain critical respects, and are comparable in others. Most importantly, the 'golden carrot' of full EU membership credibly present in the case of Romania, has, at different times over the last decade been less or more uncertain in the case of Turkey. In a third category, western Balkan countries included in the SAP, such as Serbia, have since 2000 been made 'potential candidates' – offering a more distant and tenuous prospect of full inclusion – whereas ENP countries, such as Ukraine, have so far been completely excluded from a membership horizon, and instead offered the prospect of a still vaguely defined form of partial integration into the EU system (Magen 2006).

At the same time, the methodologies used by the EU in an attempt to affect democratic rule of law development across these different categories of engagement share common assumptions about modes and instruments of external influence, creating new opportunities for comparative analysis. In essence, all four categories are characterized by: (1) a top-down mode of engagement, focusing on intergovernmental bargaining and bureaucratic exchange rather than more diffuse, bottom-up support for civil society; (2) a legalistic, technocratic approach to reform-promotion, drawing on the *Acquis Communautaire* for standards and benchmarks of reform; (3) the use of 'reinforcement by reward' type of conditionality, rather than punitive measures or *ex ante* conditionality;[12] (4) regular monitoring and reporting on progress in meeting reform benchmarks; (5) financial and technical assistance to help fund reforms; and (6) the progressive establishment and development of 'socialization forums' – such as technical committees and subcommittees, secondment of bureaucrats in 'twinning' programs, and selective third-country participation in EU programs and agencies.

Table 1.1 shows the universe of possible cases and the ones selected (in bold) by giving priority in the presentation of criteria to the first one, i.e. the status of relationships with the EU. In this perspective we may have a *prospective member*, when there is already a decision on accession, a *negotiating candidate*, when that decision has still to be made but negotiation has begun, a *potential candidate*, when there is no negotiation but there is the possibility of membership, and a *neighbor country* where the prospect of membership is absent, but the prospect of looser ties is available.[13]

Table 1.1 Relationships of selected regimes with the EU

Category	*Countries in category/**Case Study***
Prospective/new members	Bulgaria, **Romania**
Negotiating candidates	Croatia, **Turkey**
Potential candidates	Albania, Bosnia-Herzegovina, Macedonia, **Serbia**
European neighboring countries	Armenia, Azerbaijan, Belarus, Georgia, Moldova, Russia, **Ukraine**

In our choice of the countries, by going beyond enlargement and examining the interaction between EU strategies of transformative engagement, on the one side, and domestic dynamics in Romania, Turkey, Serbia and Ukraine, on the other, we can derive more general lessons regarding the mechanisms, pathways and limitations of international influence on domestic change than would have been possible where the canvas of inquiry involves candidates alone. What are our theoretical expectations concerning the scope and depth of potential EU influence across these different categories of engagement? Where, if at all, do we find evidence that EU attempts to export its rules, institutions and norms have had an influence? If we do identify evidence of such influence, where do we find it and what actually constitutes that 'influence'? Where we can trace EU influence in particular, rather than the involvement of other actors such as NATO, the Council of Europe, USAID or the World Bank, how does that influence sit with our theoretical expectations about the variable power of conditionality, financial and technical aid, and socialization techniques deployed by the EU in an effort to encourage rule of law reforms across these different categories of engagement? What confluence of domestic considerations and external mechanisms are more likely to achieve compliance with EU reform demands? Does influence, where it exists, appear random, or can we identify clear patterns which can then inform future policy in Europe and beyond? By posing these questions in relation to both enlargement and non-enlargement cases, we break away from the self-contained constraints of existing inquiries into the enlargement–democratization nexus, and seek lessons of broader interest to scholars and practitioners in the fields of comprehensive security, democracy and rule of law promotion and development economics.

Useful inquiry into the role, actual and potential, of the EU as an international democracy and rule of law promotion actor in its near abroad has also suffered from generalizations and a dearth of empirical study. Commentators writing on the effects of European integration on the improvement of democracy in the CEECs, from both the supply and receiving ends of the relationship, have tended to oscillate rather wildly between awe and dismissal.[14] Where it has been declared to be found, moreover, EU transformative power has largely been assumed, rather than demonstrated, and although a number of recent studies have began to formulate finer-grained hypotheses about conditions and modes of influence, as well as trying to locate particular influences (Haughton 2007; Kelley 2004a; Pridham 2005; Sadurski, Czarnota and Krygier 2006; Schimmelfennig and Sedelmeier 2005a; Vachudova 2005), large gaps in knowledge persist over critical questions – where, how and to what degree has the EU managed to influence rule of law conditions in enlargement versus non-enlargement countries; through what modes of interaction with domestic decision-makers and other constituencies, and with what consequences?

This study addressed these questions through qualitative empirical analysis, using structured, focused comparison of case studies (George and Bennett 2005). The method is 'structured' in that it identifies a set of questions that reflect the objectives of the research and then poses these questions to each of the four case studies under consideration in order to standardize data collection, thereby making the systematic comparison and cumulation of the findings of the cases possible. The method is 'focused' in that it is concerned with certain aspects of the cases examined (rule of law reforms) within a given period of time (from 1991 to 2006). These methodological requirements of structure and focus apply equally to all individual cases under consideration.[15]

This involved a two-pronged research strategy. First, detailed 'country reports' were compiled on each one of the case study countries. These covered the long-term domestic economic, historical and political legacies of the country, constitutional and governmental systems; as well as a host of shorter-term indicators relating to levels of economic development, political party constellation and elections, media freedom, civil society, civil liberties and political rights, state capacity, judicial independence, organized crime, civilian control of the police and armed forces, due process, corruption and governance. In addition, each country report mapped the country's international linkages, both with the EU and other international actors in order to identify antecedent conditions, as well as domestic and external independent variables.

Second, using a detailed, structured questionnaire we posed a common set of questions to the case study authors and required that answers to the questions posed be backed by reliable data – including interviews with officials, official reports, local media materials and commentary. Using the questionnaire as a shared analytical framework, allowed case study authors to trace domestic changes in the five dimensions of rule of law conditions over the applicable period, and to analyze when and how international factors have impacted such reforms across the three levels of analysis studied – formal rule adoption, internalization and implementation. In order to minimize the risk of privileging EU impact over both domestic variables and other international actors, country experts were asked to first trace domestic rule of law reforms in the five dimensions identified, and only then zoom out to examine external influences, identifying both EU and non-EU influences.

How were the case studies selected in the first place? The first step towards specific case study selection involved a clear identification of the applicable universe of cases. This universe was shaped by three broad criteria. First, we were interested in those states that were subject to some type of EU regional transformative engagement strategy (either enlargement or non-enlargement bound) and who were, by the time the research was launched in 2004, non-EU Member States (see Table 1).[16] The pool of countries falling within this category covered a total of twenty-five countries: the remaining candidates negotiating accession (Bulgaria and Romania); the only country that was then officially recognized as a candidate but with whom accession negotiations were not yet opened (Turkey); the western Balkan countries covered by the SAP policy (Albania, Bosnia-Herzegovina, Croatia, Macedonia, Montenegro, and Serbia); and the fifteen states (and one non-state entity) covered by the ENP (Algeria, Armenia; Azerbaijan; Belarus; Egypt; Georgia; Israel; Jordan; Lebanon; Libya; Moldova; Morocco; Syria; Tunisia; Ukraine, and the Palestinian Authority).

Second, whereas recent scholarship has chiefly focused on transition to democracy (Bunce 2003; McFaul 2004; 2007) or the endurance of authoritarian regimes (Brownlee 2007; Schedler 2006), we were concerned with the dynamics that facilitate or hinder the transformation of these ambiguous or minimalist, electoral democracies, into more substantive, higher quality democracies, with a genuine rule of law. This meant that those countries falling within the nominal universe of cases but which were either fully consolidated liberal democracies (Israel) or, more typically, clear non-democracies (Albania, Algeria, Azerbaijan; Belarus; Egypt, Jordan, Libya, Moldova, Morocco; Syria, and Tunisia) were excluded from the pool of cases. And thirdly, we avoided cases of territories lacking full state sovereignty, thus excluding Bosnia-Herzegovina, Kosovo, and the Palestinian Authority from the pool of cases.

Apart from isolating the explanatory factor it wishes to vary – i.e. relations with the EU – and carefully defining the relevant universe of cases, the study controls (to the extent possible in country-level structured, focused comparisons) for the key independent variables that may impact rule of law development in the domestic systems of the subject countries. The choice of specific case studies, therefore, was informed by the two main explanatory theories of democratic development – the actor-based, agency-driven approach, on the one hand, and the structuralist, socioeconomic approach, on the other hand.

For more than two decades now, the dominant (perhaps even hegemonic) theoretical approach to explaining the success or failure of democratic transition and consolidation has emphasized the role of agency, strategic-bargaining calculation, and institutional power dynamics, particularly among ruling and opposition elites. Departing from what they saw as the overly deterministic, pessimistic bent of modernization and dependency theories in the 1960s and 70s, scholars of the third and fourth 'waves' of democratization emphasize the role of state and societal actors in determining the outcomes of democratic development (Bermeo 1990; Berins Collier 1999; Fish 1999; McFaul 2002; Bunce 2003). Most importantly, the presence or absence of meaningful political contestation and the party constellation of hybrid regimes, represent independent variables that could strongly influence domestic dynamics of rule of law reforms, determine conformance with international norms, and so should be standardized as far as possible in comparative case study research. As Schimmelfennig argues, in a study of the effects of membership incentives on compliance with EU demands in Central and Eastern Europe, the most important factor for successful external influence on domestic policy reforms is the constellation of political parties (Schimmelfennig 2005a). Medium- to long-term prospects of what Schimmelfennig calls 'international socialization' with EU norms, not only depend on the incumbent regime but on the calculations of their major political competitors, and the ability of those competitors to gain power through elections. In those CEECs where all major parties are pro-Western and reform-minded (or 'liberal party constellation') 'international socialization has been smooth and has produced stable, consolidated democracies'. (Schimmelfennig 2005a: 828). In countries with an 'anti-liberal' constellation of political forces (such as Belarus, Moldova and Russia), at the other end of the spectrum, attempts at external influence by liberal international actors will fail. In contrast, all four case study countries selected for this study fall into a third category of 'mixed constellation' – where the major political parties in the country are split between reform-oriented and nationalist/communist-authoritarian oriented parties. Schimmelfennig contends that the 'lock-in effects' of EU integration led nationalist-authoritarian parties in those countries engaged by the EU in the enlargement process to adapt to the requirements of the West so that membership incentives have been ultimately successful. By examining hybrid regimes with mixed-party constellations, across different types of EU engagement, this study helps isolate the explanatory factor we wish to vary.

Secondly, the socioeconomic requisites, or 'structuralist' approach, which dominated theorizing about regime outcomes in the 1960s, has remained influential throughout the past four decades (and is recently enjoying a degree of resurgence) essentially views democratization processes as most likely to take place in countries displaying higher levels of economic and social development. Strongly influenced by modernization theory, the notion that there exists a positive relationship between a society's level of economic development and its likelihood to be a democracy was intuited for millennia, but first explicitly articulated by Lipset in 1959, and is now one of the few general and uncontroversial facts to have emerged from the study of democratic development processes (Geddes 1999). Higher levels of socioeconomic development (typically measured by the Human Development Index (HDI)) makes transition to democracy more likely, helps democracies endure (Przeworski *et al.* 1996; Przeworski *et al.* 2000; Boix and Stokes 2003), and is also associated with higher levels of civil liberties and political rights as measured by Freedom House (Rowen 1995). Accordingly, case studies were also selected from among the universe of cases, based on their similar ranking on the HDI score, to standardize levels of socioeconomic development (Table 1.2).

Comparative standardization is also increased by the fact that the study has opted for case study countries that are relatively large in terms of both geographical and population size. In order to avoid allegations of 'cherry picking', moreover, the study deliberately focuses on 'hard cases', where problems of legacy – post-communism in Romania, Serbia and Ukrainian, and religious-nationalist fissures in Serbia and Turkey – entrench anti-liberal

Table 1.2 Human Development Index (HDI) rankings of case study countries[1]

Case study country	*HDI rank 1990*	*HDI rank 1995*	*HDI rank 2000*	*HDI rank 2004*
Romania	0.775	0.770	0.778	0.805
Turkey	0.706	0.729	0.747	0.755
Serbia[2]	–	0.729 (1999)	0.772 (2002)	0.786
Ukraine	0.800	0.748	0.755	0.774

Sources: for 1, see United National Development Program, Human Development Report: http://hdr.undp.org/hdr2006/statistics/indicators/15.html); for 2 see http://www.undp.org.yu/tareas/reports/details.cfm?id=91).

Notes:

1 The HDI is a composite index measuring levels of socioeconomic development in a given territory. The index is a combined score of three indices: (1) Life expectancy at birth; (2) Combined primary, secondary and tertiary education, and; (3) Gross Domestic Product per capita (PPP US$). All case study countries rank in the upper–medium human development countries range.

2 The lack of internationally recognized data collected by the Serbian authorities has meant that the UNDP has started publishing National Human Development Reports on Serbia, including the calculation of the HDI, only since 1996, and that figures were published on Serbia in 1999, 2002 and 2004. Despite the impossibility of guaranteeing the full compatibility of data on Serbia with the general HDI, the UNDP is confident that a close level of approximation exists between the Serbian human development picture and the general index.

political and bureaucratic actors in the domestic system, posing comparable challenges to democratic rule of law reforms promoted by a liberal international actor.

In order better to understand the political situation of the chosen countries, some data from the World Bank on the state of rule of law can be recalled in Table 1.3. If the minus sign means that a country is still in a poor condition as to rule of law, the situation of the four countries during the last decade is fairly gloomy. But the notion of rule of law according to the World Bank tries not to include aspects related to democracy.[17] When we include our dimensions of a democractic rule of law (DRoL) the outcome is demonstrated in Table 1.4.

Table 1.3 Rule of law in the four countries 1996–2005 (World Bank)

Country	*1996*	*1998*	*2000*	*2002*	*2003*	*2004*	*2005*
Romania	–0.34	–0.35	–0.32	–0.23	–0.22	–0.23	–0.29
Serbia	–1.26	–1.06	–1.14	–0.99	–0.97	–0.78	–0.81
Turkey	–0.02	–0.01	–0.07	–0.15	+0.02	+0.02	+0.07
Ukraine	–0.73	–0.88	–0.80	–0.87	–0.84	–0.83	–0.60

Source: World Bank, *A Decade Measuring the Quality of Governance. Governance Matters 2006 Worldwide Governance Indicators*. (http://siteresources.worldbank.org/INTWBIGOVANT COR/ Resources/ 17404791150402582357/26booklet_decade _of_measuring_ governance.pdf)

Notes:

The indicator of rule of law adopted by the World Bank refers to 'the extent to which agents have confidence in and abide by the rules of society, and in particular the quality of contract enforcement, the police, and the courts, as well as the likelihood of crime and violence'. Its range is from –2.5 (worst governance outcomes) through 2.5 (better governance outcomes). Until the 2006 referendum, Serbia was grouped together with Montenegro.

Table 1.4 Measures of democratic rule of law in the four countries

(A) Civil and political rights

Country	*89-90*	*90-91*	*91-92*	*92-93*	*93-94*	*94-95*	*95-96*	*96-97*	*97-98*	*98-99*	*99-00*	*00-01*	*01-02*	*02- 03*	*03-04*	*04-05*	*05-06*
Romania	7	5.5	5	4	4	3.5	3.5	2.5	2	2	2	2	2	2	2	2.5	2
Serbia	4.5	4.5	5.5	5.5	6	6	6	6	6	6	5	4	3	2.5	2.5	2.5	2.5
Turkey	3	3	3	3	3	5	5	4.5	4.5	4.5	4.5	4.5	4.5	3.5	3.5	3	3
Ukraine			3	3	4	3.5	3.5	3.5	3.5	3.5	3.5	4	4	4	4	3.5	2.5

(B) Judicial independence and capacity

Country	*1997*	*1998*	*1999*	*2001*	*2002*	*2003*	*2004*	*2005*	*2006*
Romania	4.25	4.25	4.25	4.25	4.25	4.25	4.25	4.00	4.00
Serbia	5.00	5.75	5.50	4.25	4.25	5.00	4.25	4.25	4.25
Turkey	n/a	n/a	n/a	n/a	n/a	n/a	n/a	n/a	n/a
Ukraine	3.75	4.00	4.50	4.50	4.75	4.50	4.75	4.25	4.25

(C) Institutional and administrative capacity

Country	*1996*	*1998*	*2000*	*2002*	*2003*	*2004*	*2005*
Romania	–0.88	–0.63	–0.67	–0.32	–0.16	–0.11	–0.03
Serbia	–0.71	–1.11	–0.08	–0.61	–0.50	–0.12	–0.31
Turkey	+0.10	–0.07	–0.36	–0.45	–0.27	–0.25	+0.08
Ukraine	–0.79	–0.97	–1.03	–1.01	–0.94	–0.96	–0.63

(D) Reform to combat corruption, illegality and abuse of power

Country	*1996*	*1998*	*2000*	*2002*	*2003*	*2004*	*2005*
Romania	–0.88	–0.63	–0.67	–0.32	–0.16	–0.11	–0.03
Serbia	–0.71	–1.11	–0.08	–0.61	–0.50	–0.12	–0.31
Turkey	–0.16	–0.38	+0.11	–0.05	+0.09	+0.07	+0.27
Ukraine	–0.87	–1.00	–0.76	–0.73	–0.58	–0.63	–0.42

(E) Police reform and civilian control over military

Country	*Trend 2001–06*
Romania	6
Serbia	6
Turkey	6
Ukraine	6

Sources: They are respectively: for (A) *Freedom in the World*; for (B) *Freedom House Nation in Transit*; for (C) and (D), *World Bank*, *A Decade Measuring the Quality of Governance. Governance Matters 2006. Worldwide Governance Indicators*; for (E), *Bertelsmann Transformation Index 2006. Political Management in International Comparison.*

Notes:
For (A) the ratings are based on a scale of 1 to 7, with 1 representing the highest level of democratic progress and 7 the lowest. For (B) the set of indicators are: 1. highlights constitutional reform, 2. human rights protections, 3. criminal code reform, 4. judicial independence, 5. the status of ethnic minority rights, 6. guarantees of equality before the law 7. treatment of suspects and prisoners, and 8. compliance with judicial decisions. For (C) 'Government effectiveness' is composed of 4 specific dimensions: 1. the quality of public services, 2. the quality of the civil service and its degree of independence from political pressures, 3. the quality of policy formulation and implementation and 4. the credibility of the government's commitment to such policies. For the range see Table 1. For (D) 'Control of Corruption' refers to 'the extent to which public power is exercised for private gain, including both petty and grand forms of corruption, as well as 'capture' of the state by elites and private interests'. For the range see Table 1. For (E) the indicator is 'Penalties for abuse of power ' and the related question is: 'are there legal or political penalties for officeholders who abuse their position?'. The rating is: 0-worst outcome in guaranteeing penalties for abuse of power; 10-best outcome in guaranteeing penalties for abuse of power.

While this basic data can provide some sense of the existing situation in the four countries along our definition of DRoL, there are at least two evident problems. The first is the heterogeneity of the sources – here, Freedom House, World Bank and Bertelsmann Transformation Index – and the different spans of time we have data for. But for us there is a much more relevant problem: what those figures actually say. To understand something that helps us to reply to the research questions addressed above, we need to go in depth into the qualitative analysis of those five dimensions in the four countries. But to do that we need to review and assess the existing hypotheses in the literature and then to develop a theoretical framework for the empirical analysis. The next chapter is devoted to this task, before the analysis of what have been the policies of the EU in terms of DRoL vis-à-vis those four countries (see Chapter 3), and the subsequent discussion of what has happened inside the countries (see Chapters 4–7).

Notes

1 See Freedom House 'Freedom in the World' surveys (available at: http://www.freedomhouse.org).

2 The identification of the attributes of the Rule of law has always been a contested issue. Indeed, because the conceptualization of the Rule of law is inherently linked with theory of the Rule of law (itself an open, evolving concept) there is no point in arguing about 'the correct' definition. We therefore follow the sage advice of Gerardo Munck and Jay Verkuilen not to insist that there exists one correct definition of a concept, but to avoid the extremes of including too little or too much in a definition relative to our theoretical goals (see Munck and Verkuilen 2002, 7–9).

3 In fact, the term is contested along several axes. Linguistically, the term 'rule of law' is often equated with the concepts of *l'Etat de droit*, in the French legal tradition, *Rechtstaatlichkeit* or *Rechtstaat*, in the Germanic legal tradition, and *Estado de derecho*, in the Spanish and Portuguese traditions, including in Latin America. However, the concepts are not synonymous. Grote (1999) concludes that the term belongs to the category of open-ended concepts which are subject to permanent debate. Substantively, too, the concept of the Rule of law has been subjected to liberal, feminist, socialist critiques. See: Sypnowich (1999); Horwitz (1977). It has also been subjected to claims that it is impossible to achieve (see: Endicott (1999); Hutchinson and Monahan (1987); McCormick (1999). We do not contend with these various critiques here, since we essentially agree with Peerenboom's point that the fact that there is room for debate about the proper interpretation of the term '*should not blind us to the broad consensus of its core meaning and basic elements*' (Peerenboom 2002, 472).

4 See Ungar (1976), who argues for a strong affinity between liberal market reforms and the rule of law, and McAuslan (1997). But see also the social-democratic defence of the Rule of law in Scheuerman (1994).

5 Nonet and Selznick (1978) used the term 'autonomous law' to denote the idea of law in modern legal culture, which is distinguished from 'repressive law'.

6 The development of those five aspects involves the achievement to different extents of: the equal enforcement of the law toward everyone, including all state officials; the implementation of the principle that no one is above the law; the supremacy of legal state throughout the country, leaving no areas dominated by organized crime, local oligarchs, or political bosses who are above the law; the minimization of corruption, and where it does exist, its detection and punishment in the political, administrative, and judicial branches of the state; the development of efficiency and competency of a state bureaucracy at all levels that

applies the laws and assumes responsibility in the event of an error; the achievement of a professional and efficient police force that is respectful of individuals' legally guaranteed rights and freedoms, including rights of due process; the equal and unhindered access of citizens to the justice system to defend their rights and to contest law suits between private citizens or between private citizens and public institutions; the hearing and expeditious solution of criminal cases and civil and administrative lawsuits; the independence of the judiciary at all levels from any political influence; the respect for and enforcement of rulings of the courts by other agencies of the state; the supremacy of a constitution that is interpreted and defended by a Constitutional Court.

7 In the conclusions of their well-known seminal study, for example, O'Donnell and Schmitter (1986, 5) asserted that: '[O]ne of the firmest conclusions that emerged ... was that transitions from authoritarian rule and immediate prospects for political democracy were largely to be explained in terms of national forces and calculations. External actors tended to play an indirect and usually marginal role ....'

8 For a detailed discussion of the divide see Moravcsik (1993, 5–9); Yilmaz (2002). For the divide between international relations theory and international law see Slaughter, Tulumello and Wood (1998).

9 Leading examples include: T. Smith (1994); Carothers (1999 and 2000); Cox, Ikenberry and Inoguchi (2000); Youngs (2001 and 2004).

10 A partial exception is found in Sadurski, Czarnova and Krygier (2006), which contains several papers relating to the influence of EU enlargement on constitutional and judicial systems in several post-Communist countries.

11 For a detailed discussion of the origin and evolution of these strategies, as well as the instruments deployed by the EU to facilitate rule transfer and internalization, see Ott and Inglis (2002); Grabbe, (2002); Phinnemore (2003); Magen (2007), Hillion (2000); Adler and Crawford (2004); Hilpold (2002).

12 This involves granting tangible benefits *ex post* where the targeted government complies with the conditions, and withholding the benefits where it does not. See Schimmelfennig, Engert and Knobel (2003, esp. 496).

13 See ch. 3 for the main features that characterize the different status of each country vis-à-vis the European Union.

14 Whitehead (2001, 19), for instance, asserted that the pre-accession process: 'generates powerful, broad-based, and long-term support for the establishment of democratic institutions because it is irreversible, and sets in train a cumulative process of economic and political integration that offers incentives and reassurances to a very wide array of social forces. In other words it sets in motion a very complex and profound set of mutual adjustment processes, both within the incipient democracy and in its interactions with the rest of the Community, nearly all of which tends to favour democratic consolidation.'. A different, though similarly general and positive, view is presented by Schmitter (1995, 524), who argues that: 'more than any other international commitment, full EU membership has served to stabilize both political and economic expectations. It does not directly guarantee the consolidation of democracy; it indirectly makes it easier for national actors to agree within a narrower range of rules and practices.'. For a similarly sanguine view from the CEECs see Pehe (2004). For examples of negative views see Kochenov (2007) and Raik (2004).

15 On structured, focused comparisons see George and Bennett (2005, 67–72).

16 This criteria excluded those Central and Eastern European Countries that became full EU Member States on 1 May 2004 (The Czech Republic, Estonia, Hungary, Latvia, Lithuania, Poland, Slovakia, and Slovenia) as well as Cyprus and Malta.

17 Whether this is possible or not is a different issue. See Hiil (2007) for a position in favor of a definition of 'a democratic' Rule of law. Here we contend that today in these countries is empirically impossible to disentangle Rule of law from aspects such as civil rights and some political rights. In fact for our purposes we proposed to consider and analyze a democratic Rule-of-law.

2 Methods of influence, layers of impact, cycles of change

A framework for analysis

Leonardo Morlino and Amichai Magen

Introduction

How should we conceptualize and evaluate the extent and nature of international influence, if any, on democratic rule of law (DRoL) developments in domestic systems? Throughout history, most studies in democratization have been characterized by a puzzling lack of systematic thinking about these fundamental questions. From the inception of modern democratization studies in the 1960s until the end of the Cold War, scholars of democratic transitions and consolidation largely conceived the outcomes of domestic political processes as being driven by national forces and calculations, at both elite and mass levels, and were reluctant to venture beyond the demos in search of the causes of democratization. What was true of studies regarding the development of democracy reflected a broader malaise in which research into international impact on domestic change was largely neglected for many decades by historians, political scientists and lawyers. The dominant paradigm of political sociology from Marx to Barrington Moore, for one, has stressed the importance of internal social structure and culture in the shaping of politics and the state, sidelining the calls of such eminent scholars as John Robert Seeley, in the late nineteenth century, and Otto Hintze, in the 1960s, to remedy the neglect of international factors in the explanation of domestic political developments (Almond 1989, 239–41). Indeed, the intellectual progeny of the same tradition continues to wield considerable influence (and yield meaningful insights) by emphasizing the importance of inherited cultural, ideological, socioeconomic, and institutional legacies to defining post-transition outcomes of democracy, attitudes to liberal values, as well as national and ethnic identities (Ekiert and Hanson 2003).

Several additional factors have conspired until fairly recently to suppress both theoretical and empirical research into international influence on domestic democratic development. When preoccupation with the international-national linkages arose in the aftermath of the Second World War – notably in the work of American diplomatic historians, political scientists and international relations theorists such as Almond (1950), Dahl (1950) and Waltz (1967) – the prism adopted first was a 'bottom-up' one, in which it was the impact of national factors on international politics that was the nexus of inquiry, not the other way around (Haas 1964; Keohane 1984; Krasner 1976). Normative judgments further stifled inquiry in this field. The dependency movement of the 1970s and 1980s, for instance, while drawing attention to the importance of external conditions on internal economic and political developments, perceived the influence of international factors to be wholly debilitating, rather than enabling (Wallerstein 1979; Cardoso and Faletto 1979). Developing countries, so the Marxist inspired theory proclaimed, were condemned to wallow in backwardness or suffer developmental retardation, by virtue of an international class system dominated by western capitalist institutions. The narrative of exploitation and damage infliction, on the part of the international system, discouraged open-minded analysis of the possible role of external actors in supporting or promoting democratic change in developing countries.

From the opposite side of the domestic/international divide, theories of international relations and international law have traditionally focused on horizontal outcomes at the supranational level (notably interstate balance of power, conflict, and cooperation), rather than the more vertical, 'outside-in' linkages between international agents and domestic factors (Pevehouse 2002, 516). Even more so than their international relations peers, international lawyers have historically, and mostly remain, chiefly occupied with categorizing, analyzing and debating the rules of state responsibility, interstate relations and international organizations, largely shunning questions of domestic regime characteristics and the potential influence of international rules on national and sub-nation level systems (Fox and Roth 2000).

Although this lack of analytic attention has begun to be rectified, with increasing intensity and sophistication in the last two decades, important gaps in theoretical and empirical knowledge persist. Building on Charles Tilly's studies on the role of international competition in modern state formation (Tilly 1975), Peter Gourevitch's insights on the circularity of national–international interaction (Gourevitch 1978), as well as Robert Putnam's two-level international bargaining games (Putnam 1988), scholars working from within different theoretical traditions (neoliberal internationalism, sociological and historical institutionalism, and social constructivism) have, particularly since the end of the Cold War, contributed important insights on the impact of international conditions, organizations and networks, domestic security, economic, political, institutional, regulatory, legal and normative behavior (Busch and Milner 1994; Checkel 2002, 2005; Finnemore 1996; Goldstein 1998; Greif 2006; Ikenberry and Kupchan 1990; Kahler 1992; Keohane and Martin 1995; Pevehouse 2002; 2005; Pridham 1994; Risse, Ropp and Sikkink 1999; Russett and Oneal 2001; Whitehead 1996a). One body of literature focused on democracy in particular has began to theorize the mechanisms and pathways by which international factors may facilitate democratization in transitional states, invoking notions such as diffusion, contagion, gravity, demonstration effect, complex interdependence, convergence, emulation, socialization, learning, conditionality and even *zeitgeist*

(Gleditsch and Ward 2006; Grugel 1999; Huntington 1991; Kopstein and Reilly 2000; Kubicek 2003; Linz and Stepan 1996; Pridham 1991; Simmons, Dobbin and Garrett 2006). These notions are of variable analytic usefulness. While Pevehouse's work on the linkages between membership of international organizations and transitions to democracy identifies important potential causal mechanisms of International Organization influence on regime change (Pevehouse 2002 and 2005), discussions of democratic diffusion (Gleditsch and Ward 2006; Kopstein and Reilly 2000; Simmons, Dobbin and Garrett 2006) fail to address causality or operationalize methods of external influence on domestic change (Kubicek 2003, 4).

EU Cycles and Layers of International Democratic Anchoring (EUCLIDA)

This chapter outlines an analytical framework designed to approach these questions; a framework which is subsequently put to the test with reference to each case study country, and which therefore provides the remainder of the volume with a cohesive structure for comparative analysis. In approaching this topic, we are consciously avoiding theory testing *per se*. Rather, since we are seeking to conceptualize and explain phenomena involving complex linkages between power, interests, norms, human agency and legal-institutional change, we engage in 'analytical eclecticism' (Katzenstein and Okawara 2002), drawing selectively on the different theoretical traditions and insights we view as necessary to advance clearer, finer-grained and more reliable knowledge regarding the external–internal dynamic of democratization processes and, more instrumentally, enabling environments for successful DRoL developments in domestic systems. More precisely, the 'analytical ecleticism' we engage is, first of all, problem-driven and aimed at finding a framework to analyze in an empirically effective way several cases within a similar system comparative design. Thus, the traditional agency dominant literature on democratization (Morlino 1998; Whitehead 2001c) is complemented by the rationalist approach and the constructivist one in the way Fearon and Wendt (2005, 68) suggest: 'the most fruitful framing of 'rationalism v. constructivism' is a pragmatic one, treating them as analytical lenses for looking at social reality', as do Checkel (2005, 801–26) as well as Risse and Ropp (1999, 272–3) when adding strategic calculations or instrumental reasoning to role playing or persuasion and to normative suasion or institutionalization and habitualization.

The overarching notion we propose as a means of conceptualizing external influence on domestic DRoL change processes, and the interaction between the two is democratic anchoring. At the highest level of analysis, anchoring affirms an essentially dichotomous, two-level prism according to which in the contemporary international system nation-state regimes are subject to variably dense external (international, transnational and supranational) linkages, pressures and stimuli influencing internal conditions of democracy, yet democracy and processes of democratization exist solely within national systems, so that the proper level of analysis of democratization processes remains essentially domestic and the correct nexus of inquiry ought therefore to focus on identifying empirically discernable external–internal agency interaction.

Any analysis of international influence on domestic democratic change, in other words, must begin with the recognition of an overarching, structural constraint regarding the role of external factors. Since, by definition, democratization involves processes of change in the governing of a demos – a self-defined community based on citizenship and distinguishing the 'us' from the 'them' – such processes always are, in a fundamental sense, an essentially 'domestic drama' (Whitehead 1986). Even in the most extreme cases of external intervention therefore (such as long-term control by an occupying power), democratization in any meaningful sense must entail the free exercise of rights of citizenship in a sovereign entity, all of which depend on domestic actors, institutions and procedures. As such, it is difficult to view international factors as truly independent variables, since democratization processes (unlike modernization, for instance) are ultimately always carried through domestic actors, institutions and procedures. It is external–internal interactions, rather than external factors *per se*, which are more accurately said to shape domestic outcomes. The effects of international factors are, thus, only apparent in changes occurring within national and sub-national systems where the concept of a demos has any real meaning.

This does not mean that the notion of democratic anchoring falls into the trap of 'methodological nationalism' (Wimmer and Glick Schiller 2002). Although democratization processes are now unfolding within a radically transformed international environment compared to two decades ago (thus challenging our existing models), this does not mean, as Grugel (1999) suggests, that it is no longer legitimate to maintain a basic analytical distinction between domestic and external levels of analysis in democratization studies. A more accurate conception, we submit, is to embrace the nation/state/society as the proper sociopolitical context of inquiry into democratization processes – recognizing the inescapability of the primacy of the domestic in democratization processes – and begin to address the various parts of the external-influence-on-domestic-change puzzle in an integrated manner. This involves three primary, interrelated components: firstly, identifying the different methods of possible external influence and different modes by which these interact with domestic factors; secondly, conceptualizing the extent and nature – or what we call 'layers' – of external impact, and; thirdly, tracing temporal and spatial sequencing – or what we call 'cycles' – of such an impact.

Methods of influence, modes of interaction

We identify four main categories of methods of influence – control, conditionality, socialization, and example – each involving different modes of interaction with domestic systems and drawing on different theoretical traditions.[1]

Democratic control

At the hardest edge of the spectrum of intervention tools available to the most powerful Western state actors (US), regional organizations (NATO, EU) or global fora (UN), is the use of military force directly to overthrow an authoritarian regime and attempt to install a viable democratic regime in its place or, more commonly, attempt to build basic conditions of public security and legality as part of a post-conflict state reconstruction effort.[2]

In instances where elected governments have been forcefully removed by military coup and have requested the intervention of external actors to restore conditions of public order and democracy – as in Haiti (1994) and Sierra Leone (1998) – virtually the entire international community has accepted the use of coercive power as a legitimate means to reinstate the ousted democratic regime (Stromseth Wippman and Brooks 2006). Where military intervention took place without domestic invitation, the legality of invasion pacts has been disputed, notably in cases of unilateral action (such as the US invasion of Panama in 1989 and Iraq in 2003) or where no UN Security Council authorization was obtained by external actors prior to the initiation of military action (such as the above or NATO's action against Serbia in 1999).[3]

Nevertheless, since the end of the Cold War, the erosion of non-intervention principles, coupled with a strengthening of human rights and humanitarian intervention norms, have resulted in a proliferation of instances of 'imposed democratization' (see Whitehead 2004, 137). These have involved a range of 'neo-trusteeship' arrangements (Fearon and Laitin 2004), extending from full military occupation led by a handful of states (Iraq) or a broader coalition (Afghanistan), to variably robust UN peacekeeping and peace-building missions (Liberia, East Timor) and long-term transitional administrations (such as Bosnia-Herzegovina and Kosovo) – all with substantial post-conflict state-building and rule of law promotion dimensions (Chesterman 2001; 2004b; Hysa 2004; Peceny 1999). Indeed, a focus on the establishment of conditions of personal security and a popular perception that leaders respect and are subject to the law, is increasingly identified as being perhaps the single most important factor in determining the success or failure of democratic state building (Bratton and Chang 2006).

What unites the various forms of these interventions is a common method of influence, namely control – or what Ikenberry and Kupchan have called 'internal reconstruction' (Ikenberry and Kupchan 1990, 58). Transformation of domestic institutions and laws is achieved through direct intervention in which the international/domestic membrane is pierced, often in the aftermath of war. Though highly costly, often controversial, and of mixed success, taking control of a country's political institutions and processes, has historically been one method by which international actors can facilitate democratization, or hamper it, as in the case of Soviet policy towards Central and Eastern Europe during the Cold War. Owen (2002) lists no fewer than 198 cases (between 1555 and 2000) of forcible efforts by individual or groups of states to create, preserve or alter the political institutions – including constitutions and laws – within a third state, with post-World War II instances of such imposition dominated by western great powers efforts to promote liberal democracy. As a method of influence, control can be 'heavy' or 'light' – the latter involving efforts to avoid local dependency through the early and/or gradual transfer of control functions to indigenous authorities. It may extend over the entire territory of a state, or be limited to seizure of strategic posts, notably the capital city and the state's borders. It may exist for a relatively short period of time, as in the case of the Allied occupation of Japan and Germany, or involve open-ended, long-term control by a succession of controlling agents, as in the case of Bosnia-Herzegovina.[4]

Democratic conditionality

Short of deploying coercive intervention, powerful external actors manipulate threats of punitive measures and promises of positive rewards to alter the costs and benefits of domestic decision policy choices. Exogenously generated sticks and carrots act either directly, by altering the instrumentalist calculations of governing elites, or indirectly, through the relative weakening of veto players and the differentiated empowerment of domestic change agents (Tsebelis 2002; Schimmelfennig and Sedelmeier 2005a).

Methods of democratic conditionality fall into two broad categories: negative and positive. The first refers to non-military, coercive political, diplomatic and economic measures used to induce policy change in a targeted country (Hart 2000; Hufbauer, Schott and Elliott 1990; A. Smith 1995). Although the efficacy and preferred design of sanctions are hotly debated, serious violators of democratic principles are now far more likely to suffer punitive measures than was the case even 20 years ago.[5] Indeed, since the end of the Cold War, it is difficult to find cases where political, diplomatic or economic sanctions of some sort were not imposed in reaction to a breakdown in democracy, as is evident from the imposition of sanctions on: Belarus (in 1997 and 2005), Cambodia (1997), Fiji (2000 and 2007), Guatemala (1993), Haiti (1991 and 1994), Niger (1999), Pakistan (1999), Paraguay (1996), Peru (1992), Thailand (2006), Venezuela (2002) and Zimbabwe (2002). Worldwide, as Marinov (2004, 7) shows: 'an illiberal state ran about 21% risk of being subject to foreign pressure over its lack of political pluralism in the year 2000. This compares to only about 3% in 1983'.[6]

Still more marked has been the increased deployment of positive conditionality in the democracy promotion policies of leading western states and the international organizations they dominate in the post-Cold War period (Dimitrova and Pridham 2004; Kelley 2004b; Woods 2005).[7] Since the collapse of Soviet communism in particular, Western international actors have generated a wide range of policy instruments to link progress in democratization to the receipt of various international entitlements. These have included making collective recognition of new states and governments dependent on their adherence to democratic practices (Murphy 1999), bundling the conferment of security, trade and aid benefits with acceptance of democracy and human rights clauses in contractual agreements, and sanctioning existing member states for conduct deviating from collective norms (Halperin and Lomasney 1998; Horng 2003; Piccone 2004).

Moreover, democratic conditionality assumes two broad forms: the first, and historically by far the more common of the two, has been *ex ante* conditionality. Here benefits are provided prior to confirmation of compliance or as a simple matter of reinforcement. Despite a recent, gradual shift away from it, *ex ante* conditionality still characterizes the bulk of aid expenditure policies practiced by multilateral development banks and leading donor states (Mosley, Hudson and Verschoor 2004; Svensson 2000). The democracy and rule of law promotion policies of some regional organizations, such as the Organization for Security and Cooperation in Europe (OSCE), and human rights and democracy clauses inserted by the EU into its regular free trade agreements with third countries, similarly follow the *ex ante* model (Horng 2003). Overall, studies in the last two decades have shown a meager, though not entirely negligible, systematic relationship between this variety of positive conditionality and policy changes in targeted states. However, as Collier argues, failures of conditionality may be at least partially attributable to perverse incentives within and among donor institutions, resulting in donors being insufficiently motivated to punish recipients of aid for non-compliance (Collier 1997; Collier and Dollar 2004).

The second form of democratic conditionality involves 'reinforcement by reward', in which material and symbolic goods are provided only *ex post* in cases where the targeted government complies with the conditions, and the benefit is withheld where it does not.[8] Governments that fail to respond to incentives to adopt and implement prescribed reforms are neither coerced nor rewarded, but are left to bear the costs of exclusion (from aid allocation, favorable trade and investment conditions, security guarantees, membership in organizations or other forms of linkages to benefit-granting international regimes) until such a time as they, or a successive government, decide to comply. Until recently, the number of international actors able and willing to deploy this type of external pressure has been very small. In Europe, where the practice of *ex post* conditionality has assumed the most advanced, institutionalized forms, there have been glaring cases of 'wasted leverage' (K. Smith 2001, 43). Most notably, the Council of Europe has largely opted to forego stringent membership conditionality in favor of a policy emphasizing post-accession socialization into western liberal practices. Its pre-accession procedures, therefore, have been slack, a reality epitomized by the controversial acceptance of Albania (1995), Russia and Croatia (1996), the southern Caucasus countries (1999 to 2002) and Bosnia-Herzegovina (2003). Indeed, even in Europe, as Schimmelfennig (2005, 832–3) argues, 'reinforcement by tangible punishments and rewards has been limited to the two organizations capable of providing material incentives and disincentives in the areas of security and welfare: the EU and NATO.' Outside Europe, the World Bank's growing disappointment with the results of its traditional *ex ante* conditionality policies, has spurred it, over the last several years, to shift to a concept of what it calls 'selectivity' – where aid agreements are only concluded with those states whose policy choices already demonstrate a prior commitment to reform (World Bank 2001, 193–6). This shift does not reflect any truly new insights into external influence methodology since 'to an extent selectivity is no more than ex-post conditionality.' (Mosley, Hudson and Verschoor 2004, 220). In essence, the same logic underlies the Millennium Challenge Corporation (MCC) initiative, launched by the Bush administration in March 2002. The MCC preconditions the receipt of aid by targeted governments on a demonstrated 'commitment to policies that promote political and economic freedom, investments in education and health, control of corruption, and respect for civil liberties and the rule of law by performing well on 16 different policy indicators.'[9]

Unlike coercive interventions that rely on a method of control, the mechanisms of influence underlining punitive and positive external incentives assume (a) that domestic actors retain a degree of autonomous choice and (b) that those actors respond to a 'logic of anticipated consequences and prior preferences' (March and Olsen 1998, 949). All strategies of conditionality, in other words, follow an actor-based, rational bargaining logic of influence, emphasizing a utilitarian calculation where domestic decision constituencies are affected by the costs and benefits of compliance. In this latter sense, conditionality is linked to example since domestic costs will be higher where there is a weaker cultural match between the externally driven rule and domestic norms. The potency of conditionality varies and can be shaped along several axes, including: the relative bargaining power of the actors (including the availability of realistic alternatives for the targeted state); size and speed of rewards; the credibility of conditionality; the size and distribution of domestic costs of compliance; and the determinacy of conditions applied.[10] Determinacy (or specificity) also plays an important role in shaping the effectiveness of conditionality (Schimmelfennig and Sedelmeier 2005a). Determinacy refers to (a) the clarity and (b) the formality of the rule – what some have called the 'density of norms' (Jacoby and Cernoch 2002, 320). The more specific and formal the rule, the higher its determinacy value. High determinacy serves an informational role, acting as a road map for the targeted government, and at the same time enhances the credibility of the conditionality, as it narrows the scope for interpretation and therefore manipulation of the rule and aids monitoring of compliance. Moreover, conditionality allows other methods of influence, such as the exercise of normative pressure and persuasion, to be pressed by the promoter with greater confidence, since these rhetorical actions are then made in the shadow of material incentives for compliance (Kelley 2004a). Conditionality can influence the target government either directly, through bargaining, or indirectly through the differential empowerment of domestic actors. In the latter sense, conditionality changes the domestic power dynamics in favor of domestic actors with incentives to adopt EU rules and norms, and strengthening their position in relation to opponents in government and society.

Democratic socialization

If incentive-based instruments rely on the superior leverage external actors can wield, what may be termed 'international democratic socialization' represents a distinct method of external influence which aims to facilitate internalization of democratic norms, policies and institutions through the establishment and intensification of linkages between liberal international fora and state actors in transitional countries (Checkel 2001; 2005; Johnston 2001; Kelley 2004a; Levitsky and Way 2005; Schimmelfennig 2005a; Schimmelfennig and Sedelmeier 2005a).

International democratic socialization – defined as a process of inducting individuals and states into the democratic norms and rules of a given regional, international or transnational community – involves variably intrusive linkages, with the socialization potential and practices of different international actors ranging on a continuum of intensity. As Levitsky and Way assert, at the highest level of abstraction there exist at least five dimensions of such linkages: (1) economic ties, which include trade, credit, investment and assistance; (2) geopolitical ties, which include membership in, or other forms of association with, regional or global governance institutions and alliances; (3) social linkage, including migration, diaspora communities, technical and professional epistemic communities and elite education; (4) communication linkage, including cross-border telecommunications and media; and (5) transnational civil society ties, including involvement with international NGOs, multilateral corporations, social entrepreneurship organizations, party foundations, bar associations, and churches (Levitsky and Way 2005).

Focusing on a narrower, though still vast category of international factors, Slaughter (2004) has flagged the importance of 'government networks' (information networks, enforcement networks and harmonization networks, operating across regulatory, legislative and judicial functions of governance) to western efforts to transform bad governments, or partially replace them in failed, weak or transitional states. Horizontal regulatory networks of national officials interacting in their respective issue areas range from anti-money laundering and anti-corruption regulation, to law enforcement, and human rights protection. Information networks involve judges, legislators, regulators and enforcement agents coming together in a myriad fora, such as the Organisation for Economic Co-operation and Development (OECD) and the Commonwealth, to discuss, collect and distill professional best practices; while horizontal enforcement networks (such as INTERPOL and EUROPOL, at the global and regional levels) are increasingly compelled to interact due to the growing activity in transnational illegal activities (Slaughter 2004, 135–44).

Many of the horizontal networks, as well as some of the modes of linkage identified above (social, educational, technological, and cultural), represent diffuse, non-institutionalized mechanisms of potential influence. These may be understood as situated closer to the soft end of the intervention spectrum, adjacent to the dispersed modern world society scripts identified by Meyer and others as having been influential in the spread of a host of 'administrative rationality' features in transitional countries.[11]

International actors also deploy a range of tools intended to 'name and shame' states into compliance with democratic practices, with little or no institutionalized engagement and attempts at deliberative induction into community practices and norms. Normative pressure can take the form of informal verbal pressure where a prominent leader of a democratic country, international institution or NGO makes use of the bully pulpit to laud certain practices, berate others, or place a targeted phone call to a foreign leader at decision-making junctures, with specific demands.[12] Normative pressure can, and increasingly does, assume more formal, structured shape. Observation of national elections, plebiscites and referenda to monitor procedural fairness, violations of basic political and human rights tied to electoral contestation, and even campaign financing in countries claiming to be democratic, has become the international norm, and has reached a high degree of institutionalization (Carothers 1997; Santa Cruz 2005). Governments, international organizations and leading NGOs – such as Amnesty International, Transparency International and Human Rights Watch – issue regular declarations, reports and demarches, openly criticizing countries on a host of rule-of-law issues, from corruption, to abuse of rights, to detention and prison conditions. The Bureau of Democracy, Human Rights, and Labor of the US Department of State, for example, is mandated under the Foreign Assistance Act (FAA) to submit to Congress annual country reports on human rights practices and democratic government. The first reports, compiled in 1977, covered 82 countries sreceiving US aid, whereas in 2006, 196 reports were presented to Congress. Among the 46 members of the Council of Europe, similarly, a number of intergovernmental committees monitor and report on the state of compliance with Council of Europe conventions and non-binding guidelines on a broad range of rule of law issues.[13]

The post-Cold War explosion of interest in the quality of domestic governance has, in the last decade, generated an unprecedented proliferation in the compilation and dissemination of democracy and governance indicators.[14] Based on the maxim that you can only monitor what you measure, a plethora of international actors – from private investors and corporate risk analysts, to multilateral development agencies and academics – now generate dozens of governance indicators and databases, that provide ready, quantitative canon fodder for business, policy and academic audiences to critique practically every country in the world on a broad range of democracy, human rights and rule of law issues.[15]

At the harder, more heavily institutionalized edge of the linkage category, furthermore, we locate what Slaughter calls 'vertical networks' – global or, more commonly, regional organizations and their deliberative processes, which perform two related functions of international socialization. First, international institutions, such as the United Nations Development Program (UNDP), United Nations Education, Scientific and Cultural Organization (UNESCO), the World Bank, International Labour Organization (ILO) and OECD, function as norm entrepreneurs and teachers of norms – generating and disseminating information about appropriate templates of policy, institutional design and administrative conduct (Finnemore 1996; Finnemore and Sikkink 1998; Keck and Sikkink 1999). Second, international organizations and the processes they foster act as social environments that shape domestic policy choices, behavior and possibly even the identity of governmental, bureaucratic and broader societal actors who interact with them (Grigorescu 2003; Johnston 2001; Simmons, Dobbins and Garrett 2006).

Liberal international actors can, and do, shape the fora they control in an effort to reconfigure the preferences and identities of targeted states. Since the end of the Cold War, regional organizations in particular have defined the international democratic socialization of transitional states as a new core task for themselves (first, in post-Communist countries and Latin America, extending gradually into Africa), and devised an increasingly institutionalized set of instruments to support and promote, *inter alia*, rule of law reforms by fully or partially anchoring targeted countries in pre-existing international liberal communities.[16] Beyond Europe, international democratic socialization mechanisms have so far been less robust, but present nonetheless. In 1990, for example, the Organization of American States (OAS) – in which all 35 independent states of the Americas are members – established a Unit for the Promotion of Democracy, to encourage members 'to renew, preserve and strengthen democratic institutions.'[17] The Inter-American Juridical Committee of the OAS, similarly, polices the implementation of the Inter-American Democratic Charter (adopted on 11 September, 2001), and provides an institutionalized platform for regular deliberation and the promotion of legal integration in a range of rule of law topics, such as administration of justice, measures to combat crime, drug trafficking, terrorism and corruption, police standards, judicial cooperation, access to justice, and protection of fundamental rights.[18]

There is some evidence, too, that the use of international socialization mechanisms is proliferating geographically and thematically. It remains to be seen, for instance, whether the African Peer Review Mechanism – established under the auspices of the African Union (AU) in 2002 as part of growing international donor pressure for better governance – would or would not evolve into a useful collective peer pressure mechanism capable of inducting states into the AU's formal commitment to 'promote and protect human and people's rights, consolidate democratic institutions and culture, and ... ensure good governance and the rule of law.'[19] In an attempt to ensure that emerging powers buy into the core tenets of the US-led international order, moreover, Washington has been in the last several years striving to include countries like

China, India and Brazil in a diverse set of regional and global fora ranging from G-7 meetings and the Inter-American Development Bank, to the International Monetary Fund (IMF), the World Health Organization (WHO) and the World Trade Organization (WTO) (Drezner 2007).

Whereas external incentives modes of influence follow rational choice expectations of state behavior, theoretically mechanisms of state/agent socialization sit more comfortably with norm-based, social constructivist and social psychology explanations for individual and collective action. The notion of international democratic socialization, in other words, assumes that domestic decision-makers are themselves cognitive-social actors that respond, at least in part, to a 'logic of appropriateness', where ideas, norms and identity shape compliance with and internalization of rules and institutions (March and Olsen 1998, 951). According to this method of influence, external impact on domestic democratic development is not reducible to materialist, cost-benefit balancing of predetermined interests. Rather, those interests themselves are best understood as the product of social structures and interactions. Since 'actors who enter into a social interaction rarely emerge the same' (Johnston 2001, 488), processes of rule of law change occur through deliberative, communicative processes of habituation, argumentation and persuasion (Checkel 2005; Risse 1999).

Socialization may take more than one form. Agents may change their domestic institutions and policies by virtue of having their choice of modes of behavior bounded by external organizations, networks and rules (Jacoby 2004; Jones 1999) – complying with rules and norms expected of them by virtue of their belonging to a certain community, irrespective of whether they internalize these rules and accept them as their own. Alternatively, following a logic of appropriateness may extend beyond ordering from a circumscribed menu of socially acceptable policy choices, and involve agents internalizing community or organizational norms as appropriate, legitimate and correct in their own right.[20]

Moreover, the 'influence density' of different international socialization mechanisms (whether horizontal or vertical) would differ depending on a variety of factors, including the duration and intensity of interaction, the perceived legitimacy of the socializing actor, the determinacy of the rules it seeks to have internalized, and the financial and technical resources it can muster to encourage socialization. Thus, unlike the more passive democratic example method of influence, democratic socialization involves an active, deliberative aspect where impact on domestic systems is assumed to be enhanced by the intensification of opportunities for complex learning, deliberation and shifts in identity. In institutional terms this can happen through the development of political dialogue, bureaucratic and professional collaboration and academic networks, as well as mass exchanges through popular media, movement of persons, youth, education and cultural exchanges. Socialization will be eased where externally driven reforms are seen as legitimate and the demand for compliance deemed by domestic constituencies to be substantively and procedurally fair.

Democratic example

Finally, the fourth method of external influence on domestic rule of law development is captured in the notion of democratic example, or demonstration. According to this model, state and societal actors in transitional states accept new rules, institutions and policy choices not as a result of external incentives or socialization, but through sheer emulation of a successful external model. The prosperity, security, freedom and eunomia of leading democratic states serve as exemplars, a 'city upon the hill' which others are inspired by and seek to mimic (Haveman 1993).

A number of causal processes have been suggested for emulation of a successful democratic example. Voluntary lesson drawing (Dolowitz and Marsh 2000; Rose 1991; Schimmelfennig and Sedelmeier 2005a) – which can assume straightforward copying or loose imitation – can take place as the result of internal dissatisfaction with the policy status quo, coupled with the transferability of external norms, policies and institutions. This assumes certain capacities and a sequence of policy decisions: domestic policy-makers are dissatisfied with the existing state of affairs; they define the problem and mark it as potentially solvable, or at least improvable, through the adoption of new rules, institutions or policies; they look outside their domestic system to an external source identified as a potential model for emulation; form the perception that the external practices, rules or institutions are successful in solving difficulties identical, or at least comparable to those at home; determine that the external rules are not only technically transferable, but politically acceptable (Schimmelfennig and Sedelmeier 2005a, 22–4). A second main approach to emulation relies on insights from group theory in social psychology. Free of control, conditionality or active induction, some scholars suggest that geographic (Kopstein and Reilly 2000; Whitehead 2001c) and psychological proximity (Rose 1993) facilitates emulation, a phenomenon which helps explain the temporal and regional sequencing of democratization processes (Lankina and Getachew 2006). From this perspective, actors emulate the conduct of their self-identified peer group, with which they identify and strive to be associated. World society scholarship and literatures on epistemic communities offer additional strands on the causal processes of emulation. Meyer and others suggest that countries establish institutions and sign up to various international obligations for diffuse, 'world social' reasons, acquiring a sense of belonging and identification with modernity by rhetorically and legally embracing human rights, labor, environmental and public health standards, even where they lack both the capacity and intention to put them into effect (Meyer *et al.* 1997a; Hathaway 2002). These processes of emulation may be catalyzed by the presence of epistemic communities, where professional, technocratic and academic groups influence governments to adopt new rules and policies by setting agendas, defining problems and formulating policy solution options in a manner that makes them accessible to domestic decision-makers (Simmons, Dobbin and Garrett 2006, 800).

Democratic anchoring, in sum, may involve four main methods of influence, ranging on a spectrum of measures, from deliberate, highly institutionalized, intrusive (occasionally coercive) mechanisms, to the type of diffuse scripts identified by world society scholars. In practical, policy-oriented terms, the most promising and potentially malleable methods of anchoring are represented by the two mid-range methods of influence: conditionality[21] and socialization, since anchoring through control usually involves highly costly (sometimes in blood as well as money) instruments of engagement that Western actors are generally reluctant to expend, whereas democratic examples entail culture, ideas and norms the construction and controlled use of which policy actors are generally ill prepared for. Moreover, in a strictly empirical perspective, while control is very easy to be proved because its same characteristics, emulation is very elusive and in the best case can be indirectly suggested. At the end, however, as Chapter 3 demonstrates, it is largely through the gradual development and deployment of the conditionality and socialization type methods of democratic anchoring that the EU has sought to transform neighboring countries. All in all, these are the reasons why we decided to focus on those two mechanisms and leave out control and democratic example or emulation.

Layers of impact, cycles of change

If we now have a clearer understanding of the types of external methods of influence that exist and their different logics of persuasion, the next step is to develop an integrated framework for an empirical analysis of external actor impact on domestic change processes, which involves asking what that impact actually consists of, how it occurs, and in what sequences.

Academic engagement with these questions, where it exists at all, has tended to remain rather evasive. Lawyers approaching the topic of external influence on domestic legal reforms have sought to avoid the methodological challenges of looking beyond formal compliance with international rules, into genuine implementation of commitments (Hathaway 2002). The problem of implementation and internalization is also central in the 'spiral model', proposed by Risse and Sikkink (1999, esp. 17–35) and in the 'membership conditionality' model developed by Schimmelfennig (2005a), who set as their dependent variable formal and informal 'rule adoption' involving the transposition of EU law into domestic law, the restructuring of domestic institutions according to EU standards, and the change of domestic political practices according to EU practices (Schimmelfennig and Sedelmeier 2005a, 7).

Here we propose that democratic anchoring involving external actor efforts to promote legal, institutional and behavioral change should be conceptualized as potentially involving three related, but analytically distinct 'layers' of impact, namely, rule adoption, rule implementation, and rule internalization.

Rule adoption (RA)

Following Schimmelfennig and Sedelmeier's formulation (2005a), RA involves the transposition of EU mandated rules and standards into domestic laws, the restructuring of domestic institutions according to EU rules and the changing of domestic political practices in line with EU standards. With regard to the DRoL, rule adoption concerns five main substantive domains. The first two, that is, (1) protection of civil freedoms and political rights and (2) institutional and administrative capacity to formulate, implement and enforce, refer to the moment when the decision to have a democracy is made and implemented. In fact, they substantiate that decision. The other three domains to include in the analysis are: (3) the independence of the judiciary and a modern justice system; (4) the fight against corruption, illegality and abuse of power by state agencies; and (5) effective civilian control of the police and other security forces.

Within those domains RA means the formal passage of domestic legislation, the establishment of domestic institutions, as promoted by the relevant external actors. The scope and intensity of RA may vary extensively. Adoption may be limited to harmonization of legislation in specific, functional, 'low-politics' areas. At the other end of the spectrum, insertion can involve fundamental constitutional provisions that go to the heart of national sovereignty, and may involve massive *en bloc* acceptance of external laws. RA may also entail a commitment to ongoing, even future, adjustment of domestic rules – as is the case in the European Economic Area (EEA) countries with regard to Single Market rules.

Rule implementation (RIm)

Here, we are considering preliminarily the development or improvement of the rules, governing institutions, administrative structures that are necessary to implement the required and possibly adopted changes. That is, to have any implementation process there has to be prior development of institutional and administrative capacity (IAC). In our view this is one of the key factors explaining the institutional 'decoupling' (Meyer *et al.* 1997a, esp. 154–6) or 'institutional hypocrisy' (Katzenstein and Iankova 2003) those and other authors suggested. That is, the gap between formal rule adoption and implementation. Our hypothesis here is that if we have poorly developed institutions and bureaucracy that decoupling becomes very obvious. Furthermore, we should be ready to observe deliberate emptying of reform content by governmental actors who feel compelled (by domestic or external pressures) to assume formal legal or institutional commitments, but who then act to minimize, retard or completely block the intended effects of those commitments.

The difference, here suggested, between institutions and administration is a classical one where the key institutions, such as cabinet, parliament and magistracy are differentiated from bureaucracies, local and central. The necessity of such a development has already been a crucial point of debate in western European countries when a reformist government comes to office and tries to implement the changes that made possible its victory in political elections. Likewise, there can be the strongest elite commitment to rule adoption and rules can be approved, but if there is little or no IAC, then any decision is bound to remain just on paper.

RIm goes in the same five directions as RA: (1) protection of civil freedoms and political rights; (2) additional institutional and administrative structures to formulate, implement and enforce the law; (3) judicial independence and a modern justice system; (4) fight against corruption, illegality and abuse of power by state agencies; (5) police reform and civilian control of the security forces.

Rule internalization (RI)

RI means the acceptance of transferred rules, beyond formal adoption among state bureaucracy, political elites, relevant groups and the wider public, that is, a slower and gradual sub-process of legitimation of both the adopted rules and the institutions that were set in motion, making the RA and the development of IAC more than a superficial result without actual meaning. We can assume that only when RI gradually takes place does the implementation, which is relevant for the growth of DRoL, actually take place as well.

The entire framework with its three layers may be better presented by answering three related questions: how rule adoption is achieved; how the implementation is carried out; and how some degree of rule internalization is achieved. The reply to these questions also allows us to present our main hypotheses, but before moving on in this direction the basic lines of our reasoning can be clarified by making explicit the underlying matrix (see Table 2.1). The matrix also helps to stress and clarify an important theoretical feature. The dimension we call 'institutional, administrative structures' refers to the development of institutional and bureaucratic capacity and entails the three processes of RA, RIm and RI. But here, actually, two different moments in time are conflated for analytical reasons, although the time difference has to be maintained for a correct reading of the process. In fact, only when that capacity begins developing in at least the first and second processes (RA and RIm) (see the third column in Table 2.1, i.e. the vertical direction of the matrix), can the real process of RI actually begin; this is relevant for the development of that entire process (see the third row in Table 2.1, i.e. the horizontal direction of the matrix).

Before going on to propose conditions and pathways under which the three layers of change occur, it may be useful to add the dimension of temporality and sequencing to the equation. It is proposed that democratic anchoring involves 'cycles', as well as layers of change. Indeed, as also proposed in the 'spiral model' by Risse and Sikkink with the 'boomerang throws' (1999a, 18), anchoring is a long iterated process, where the different events and moments,

Table 2.1 The matrix of EUCLIDA

Relevant dimensions / *Sub-processes*	*Civil and political rights*	*Judiciary and justice system*	*Institutional, administrative capacity*	*Combat of corruption, illegality, abuse of power by state* agencies	*Civilian control of army, police and security forces*
Rule adoption					
Rule implementation					
Rule internalization					

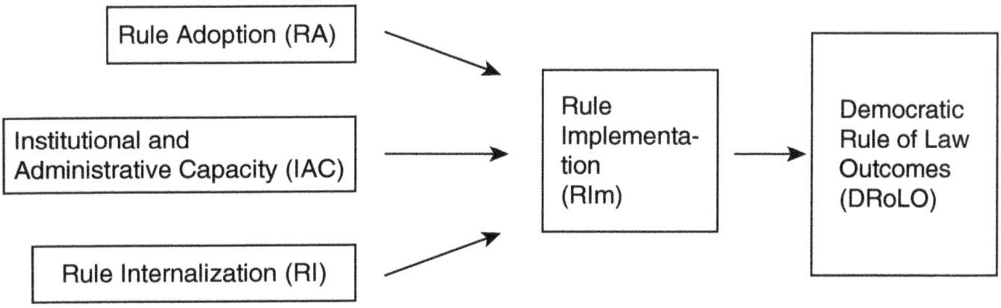

Figure 2.1 The outcomes of EUCLIDA

occasionally close in time, in one sector follow the same direction. Prolonged stops, delayed effects and reverse of direction may be anticipated before the DRoL becomes genuinely internalized and entrenched. Thus, within those cycles there is a different pace of possible changes in the various aspects involved in the development of rule of law conditions. The three main layers of change, which may well develop at different – even extremely different – paces, are rule adoption, rule implementation and rule internalization. The connections between the first two components of the process (RA and RIm) lie in the fact that RA is a condition for RIm and in this way to the development of DRoL when RI is added and considered (see Figure 2.1).

When does rule adoption take place? To disentangle the sub-process that brings about RA we begin with the actions of international actors (IAs), which is part of the anchoring mechanism, to meet the actions of domestic actors, some of whom are change agents. Action of IAs, be they EU officials or representatives, IMF officials, western government representatives, or others, has to be credible. That is, there have to be the commitments and the resources for those actions by the involved actors, otherwise the entire process is bound to fail. A key point in this is what goals are set out by the IAs. If the EU is the actor, then may membership or virtual membership, that is, the involvement in different policies with similar integrative effect, have a similar impact? This is a more specific, but very important question that our research addresses and answers.

Change agents (ChAs)

Here we borrow this notion from social-constructivist theory, which points to such an additional domestic variable which should be accounted for when seeking to explain rule adoption in the subject states – namely the degree to which change agents are present in the domestic system. According to this notion, change agents or 'norm entrepreneurs' (Finnemore and Sikkink 1998) not only mobilize to pressurize decision-makers to adopt democratic rules by increasing the costs for reform-recalcitrant elites, but they also engage domestic decision-makers in processes of persuasion and social learning to redefine their interests and identities. We can distinguish between two main mechanisms by which this process occurs – a structural mechanism and a more agency-centred mechanism.

The first account focuses on institutional isomorphism. Domestic institutions that frequently interact with other institutions (both domestic and external) and private actors (such as private NGOs) are more open to being influenced by change agents and over time converge with the influencing agents in their formal organizational structures, practices, meaning structures and reform patterns (DiMaggio and Powell 1991; Scott and Meyer 1994). The degree of exposure and openness will therefore determine the propensity for social learning and rule adoption. The second, agency-centered mechanism focuses on socialization processes, whereby domestic actors (either governmental or informal) internalize norms and practices in order to become members of international society 'in good standing' (Finnemore and Sikkink 1998). They are socialized into appropriateness through processes of persuasion and social learning which redefine their interests, creating momentum for change (Checkel 1999).

In this context, we would take into account the proposition that these processes are facilitated by dense interaction between domestic and external 'epistemic communities' – actors with an authoritative claim to knowledge and a normative agenda (Haas 1992) – such as elite decision-makers, bureaucracies, professional associations, NGOs, think-tanks and academics. In practical terms, therefore, the presence or absence of such epistemic communities and the density of their interaction with the external promoter should influence rule adoption and, later on, internalization as well.

Shift in costs and benefits balance (CBB)

This key notion of costs and benefits of adjustments draws upon a neo-institutional approach that assumes a 'logic of consequences' (March and Olsen 1988; 1989), whereby domestic leaders respond to external democracy promotion according to their calculations of the benefits and costs of compliance. A target state will adopt the rules advanced by an external promoter if and where the benefits of reward exceed the domestic costs of adoption or, if at some point there is an actual shift in the balance between costs and benefits. This general proposition contains several features that need to be unpacked.

First, we need to take account of the degree of 'misfit' or basic differences between the domestic norms, rules and policy willingness, on the one hand, and the norms and rules promoted by the EU, on the other hand. These differences represent 'adaptation pressure' (Borzel and Risse 2000). Clearly, some adaptation pressure must exist for change to occur – a perfect fit between the domestic and external rule obviates the need for rule transfer. The greater the misfit, the greater the adaptation pressure will be. Second, according to this notion the size of domestic compliance costs and their distribution among domestic actors will greatly influence the decision whether to accept or reject the rule promoted. Thus, the costs will be higher and not acceptable, or lower and acceptable, depending on: (1) the differences between the domestic and external rule; (2) whether the rule advanced by the external promoter relates to a matter of 'low politics' or a matter of 'high politics', that is, at the core of national power arrangements; and (3) the strength of the domestic opposition to its adoption. Adoption costs can have different sources: (1) they may take the form of opportunity costs of foregoing alternative rewards offered by adopting rules other than those promoted by the external actor; (2) they may entail the constraining of autonomous behavior by the target state; (3) they may produce welfare or power costs for public or private actors in the domestic system.

The preferences of the government and other 'veto players' – i.e. actors whose agreement is necessary for a change in the status quo – are a critical component here (Tsebelis 2002). We will therefore need to account for the veto players with significant net costs of rule adoption, as well as the relative strength of veto players in different policy contexts. On the basis of the literature related to Europeanization and the central and eastern European countries (Borzel and Risse 2000; Dimitrova 2002; Schimmelfennig, Engert and Knobel 2003), we can hypothesize that rule adoption will be easier and more effective in countries and policy areas where the veto players incurring costs are weaker and can be overcome.

A key aspect is the shift in the CBB in the perception of decision-makers as a result of the interaction between international actors (IAs) and change agents (ChAs). In fact, because of this interaction there may be changes in opportunity structures, empowerment of ChAs or other governmental elite, or civil society groups, and relative weakening of veto players. If some of these partially or largely take place, then there is a shift in the CBB. This shift may bring about a policy reassessment and the actual subsequent rule adoption when there is domestic fluidity, or the opposite situation, that is, domestic stability, but with a diffuse perception of legitimacy of the RA. Moreover, no real alternative is present.

Domestic fluidity posits that external democracy promotion is more likely to be effective in uncertain (or 'fluid') political environments, when state actors will be more open to new solutions and the possibility of substantial domestic change. According to this hypothesis, in situations of political fluidity – such as following the collapse of an ideological regime or in the aftermath of deep internal crisis or conflict – where there are elite and popular pressures for a re-orientation of state direction and state leaders may themselves be new and lack entrenched directions, the domestic system will be more open to international influence.

The presence of alternatives

If regimes have (or, more accurately, perceive themselves to have) economic and political alternatives, they will be less likely to be influenced by pressures from a given international actor. Put differently, we need to ask what is the subject country's 'best alternative to inclusion' within the promoting international actor's economic/political system. EU conditionality of any kind, in particular, would not be effective if the target government had other sources offering comparable benefits (Killick 1996, 221–4). Hence, a hypothesis to be tested is that EU influence will be weakened where a neighboring state finds affiliation and support from other powerful international actors – Turkey (US), Ukraine (Russia), Morocco (the Arab world), for example. If, on the other hand, the persuader is seen as authoritative – i.e. the EU is viewed as vital to the state's economic and political wellbeing – whereas the influence of other actors is limited, then EU promotion efforts are likely to be more effective.

On the whole, the sub-process of rule adoption is as follows: when credible actions of IAs are complemented by actions of committed change actors, then there are changes in opportunity structures, empowerment of change agents or of governmental elite or of civil society groups and relative weakening of veto players; if so, there is the possibility of a shift in CBB for decision-makers; if there is domestic fluidity and no presence of domestic or international-related alternatives, then the shifts bring a policy reassessment; if there is a policy reassessment, then there can be rule adoption. But there is also the opposite possibility at every step, of course, especially if no policy reassessment occurs. Figure 2.2 summarizes our hypotheses.

When does rule implementation take place? The presence of effective formal institutions provides actors with material, human and ideational resources to undertake rule adoption. We must account, therefore, for situations where domestic actors are willing to adopt and internalize rules promoted by external actors, but where they are unable to undertake the whole or parts of this process by virtue of lacking the necessary action capacity.

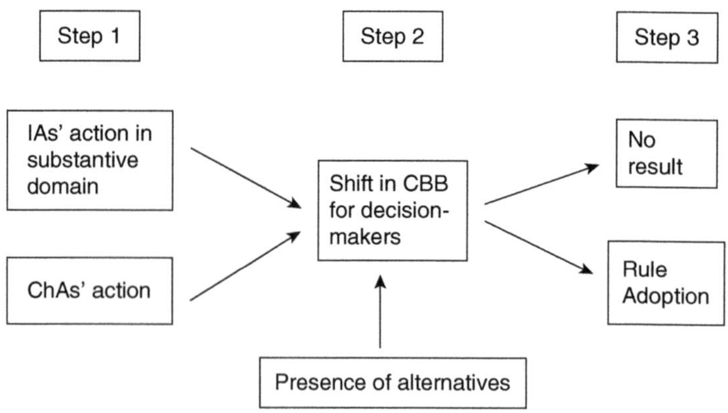

Figure 2.2 The path to rule adoption

All other factors being equal, the presence of formal facilitating institutions determines whether reform-oriented actors are able to achieve domestic processes of rule implementation.

Again with this second sub-process there is a point of departure when the credible actions of international actors are complemented by the commitment of change agents with regard to: the setting up of an institutional and administrative capacity to formulate, implement and enforce the law; the development of an independent judiciary and a modern justice system; a police reform and civilian control of the security forces. If this happens, then there is a growth in knowledge resources, material resources and learning opportunities inside the country. Such a growth is filtered and occasionally stopped and distorted by bureaucratic inertia and the non-commitment of decision-makers. If this happens to a high degree, then there is no improvement in IAC and even the rule adoption is seriously undermined. If bureaucratic inertia and non-commitment are successfully overcome by the complementary commitments mentioned earlier of international and domestic actors, then an improvement in IAC is achieved and rule implementation is possible. Figure 2.3 summarizes the path of a part of this second sub-process, where special attention should be devoted to step 2.

When does rule internalization take place? The fabric of each of our subject countries is, to a considerable degree, unique. Differences in legacy, socioeconomic conditions and national culture can be neither ignored nor controlled for with any scientific rigor – but they can, indeed must, be recognized and accounted for as fully as possible. Achieving a deep contextual understanding of domestic conditions is very important.[22] However, the third sub-process of RI has its own path, which can be applied to each of the case study countries under scrutiny.

The starting point is similar to the previous one, but on the whole the subprocess of RI is actually a distinct one, since it concerns essentially cognitive processes at both elite and mass levels. To be effective, this layer of change

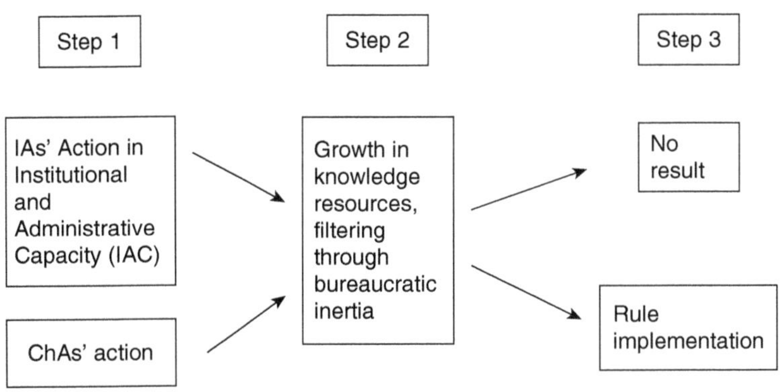

Figure 2.3 The path to rule implementation

requires some a priori value commitment of change agents to democracy, better if complemented by the presence of similar values in civil society. This means a commitment to pluralistic liberal values, notably the rule of law, tolerance of opposition, respect for different opinions, civil and political freedoms. If this happens there is the possibility of a diffusion of those values as an effect of rule adoption. Ironically, perhaps, formal rule adoption will take place first, with normative commitment to it coming only later. This is where we can see at work the core of a socialization process that, as happens in other domains when socialization is involved, results in a sort of chain where we find previous existence of rules, protracted implementation of them, absorption and education. If there is no presence of domestic alternatives, then such diffusion is more likely to take place. If there is democratic value diffusion, then the democratic constituency becomes larger and larger, and to different extent rule internalization is a consequent result. If there is an absence, or scant diffusion of democratic values, no diffusion occurs and no enlargement of the democratic constituency, with a consequent lack of rule internalization. The key element, however, is the elapsing of time that brings about that 'habituation phase' Rustow (1970) was recalling or that 'habitualization' process Risse and Sikkink (1999a, 33) developed in the final phase of their spiral model: 'whereby international human rights norms are fully institutionalized domestically and norm compliance becomes a habitual practice of actors'. In an empirical perspective this usually implies an analysis in the middle run and situations of stronger or weaker socialization. All this will be seen in the empirical chapters and reconsidered in the conclusions. Here, figure 2.4 displays this sub-process and its related hypotheses, and Figure 2.5 the entire model with its different hypothesized connections. The whole model presents an already complex set of connections, steps, dimensions and variable involved. From a strictly theoretical point of view it could have been even more complex, but the purpose was to sketch an empirical model that could be useful in setting the guidelines for sound empirical analysis. This is the challenge we confront in the empirical chapters and in the conclusions.

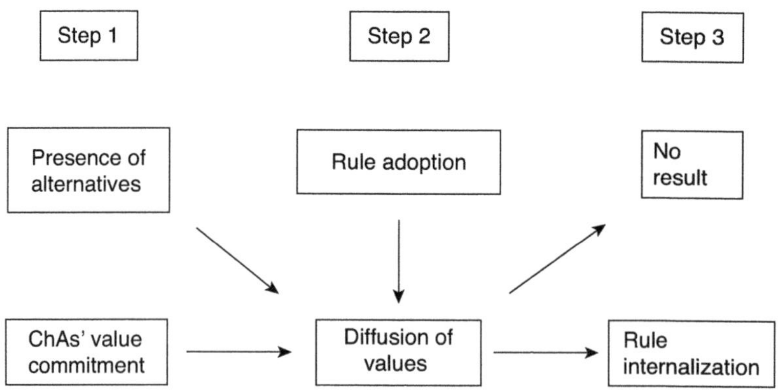

Figure 2.4 The path to rule internalization

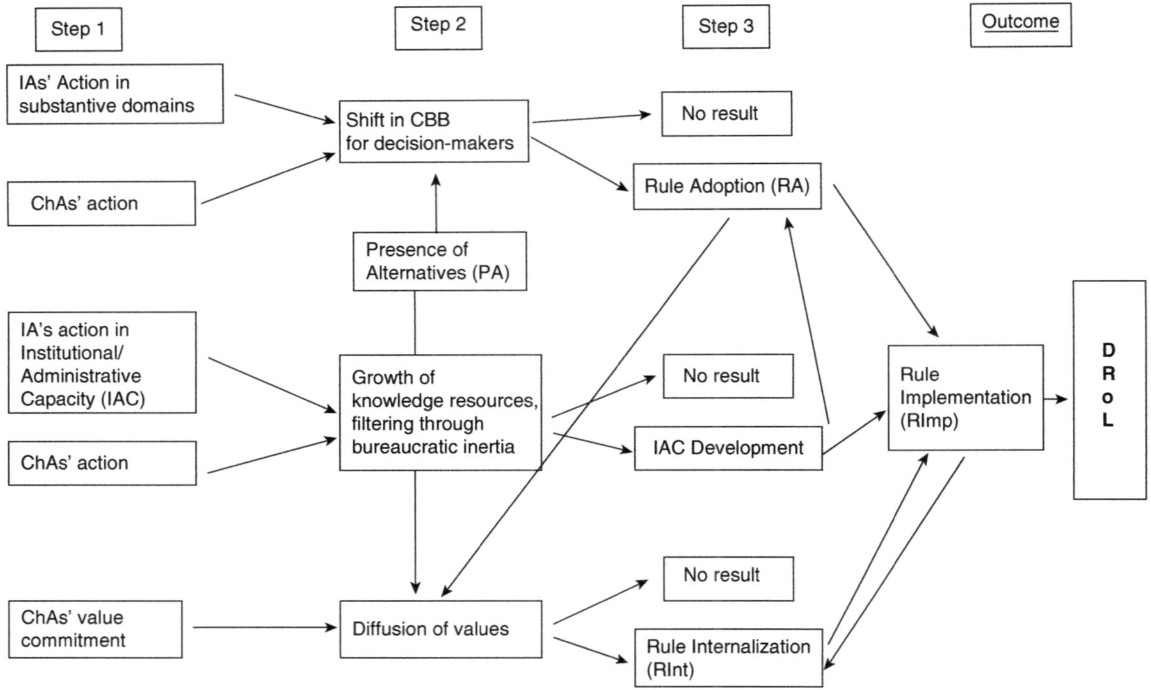

Figure 2.5 EU cycles and layers of international democratic anchoring (EUCLIDA)

IAs = international actors; ChAs = Change agents; ChA's Value commitment = commitment to values such as the rule of law, tolerance of opposition, respect for different opinions, civil and political rights; IAC = Institutional and Administrative Capacity; CBB = Cost-Benefit Balance; shift in CBB is related to change in opportunities structures, empowerment of ChA or other governmental elite, or civil society groups, relative weakening of veto players; PA = Presence of Alternatives; RA = Rule Adoption: RA concerns approval of domestic legislation, domestic establishment of institutions; RInt = Rule Internalization; RImp = Rule Implementation; DRoL = Democratic Rule of Law

Note: The three layers present differences in the timing of the steps.

EUCLIDA does not come out of the blue, but in part develops and integrates components of earlier insights drawn from both interest-based and norm-based theories of compliance. Thus, likewise the 'spiral model' (Risse and Sikkink 1999a) and the conditionality model (Schimmelfennig 2005a), first, the attention is not only on rule adoption, but also rule implementation and internalization, the three layers mentioned above; second, as the other two, it aims to be a dynamics model where different cycles are singled out. But differently from the 'spiral model', EUCLIDA focused on rule of law in its five dimensions and not on human rights alone; had analytic purposes rather than causal ones, that is, it was aimed at developing an integrated analytical framework in the effort of capturing better the reality of different cases; rather than to the impact of principles and ideas on domestic political change, it pays specific attention to the interactions of institutions and people and the shifting of balance that made domestic actors push in the direction of rule of law; consequently, the main focus is on inside-out rather than on outside-in. Differently from other models, such that on conditionality (see above), here another basic mechanism will also be considered, that of socialization, as both conditionality and socialization are indeed the most recurrent ones when the European Union as actor is involved. Finally, differently from any other previous model, EUCLIDA is not a model for every empirical case, but for the cases of hybrid regimes where democratic or quasi-democratic domestic elites are present (see chapter 1). The main consequent asset of this choice should be the possibility of a more precise, in depth analysis as it can be done at a lower level of abstraction when also some of the main notions of the literature of democratization is applied.

Notes

1 Several earlier studies offer their own typologies as to how international factors may shape processes of democratization. Kubicek (2003, 4–7) offers four categories which partly overlap with our own – (1) Control; (2) Contagion; (3) Convergence; and (4) Conditionality. In a typology that similarly tries to conceptualize external influence on domestic change, Schimmelfennig and Sedelmeier (2005a, 10–25) outline three competing explanatory models: (1) the 'external incentives model'; (2) the 'social learning model'; and (3) the 'lesson-drawing model'. An earlier, influential conception is Ikenberry and Kupchan's (1990) hegemonic power and socialization thesis. These typologies do not, however, make the distinction between methods of influence and modes interaction, or address the latter in any systematic manner.

2 Military intervention itself ranges from full military occupation to more limited paramilitary intervention, support for one side in an internal conflict, or various types of covert involvement. See Chesterman (2001); Forsythe (1992); Hendrickson (1994); Peceny (1999); Schraeder (1992).

3 See Reisman (1995), supporting military intervention in certain circumstances, versus Roth (2000), arguing against the legality of such interventions.

4 As part of international efforts towards successful implementation of the 1995 Dayton Peace Agreement, an international High Representative has effectively ruled Bosnia-Herzegovina since 1997, with NATO, EU, OSCE and UN involvement. The High Representative's mandate was significantly strengthened at the Peace Implementation Council (PIC) meeting in Bonn in late 1997. Since 2002 the High Representative has 'double-hatted' as the EU's Special Representative (EUSR), reflecting a shift in strategy in which the EU has assumed

greater responsibility to managing the trusteeship and intending to steer Bosnia-Herzegovina into eventual EU membership. See Recchia (2007).

5 The general thrust of the literature is that sanctions are rarely effective in promoting domestic reforms. See: von Hippel (2000); A. Smith (1995); Hufbauer *et al.* (1990). In contrast, several recent studies assert that the effectiveness of sanctions has been underestimated, partly because of a problem of selection bias, since the bulk of successful coercion episodes end with sanctions threatened but not actually imposed. See, in particular, Drezner (2003); Blake and Klemm (2006). On choices in the design of sanctions regimes, particularly the use of 'smart sanctions' see Shagabutdinova and Berejikian (2007). As Marinov (2004, 2) observes: 'Since 1977, the use of economic pressure to further liberalization has increased dramatically. Between 1985 and 2000, the number of countries subject to such pressure increased fourfold ... the United States and European Union (EU) member states in particular, have been especially prominent in this rising trend. More than 85% of all sanctions for democracy have been levied with the participation of either Europe or the U.S'.

6 While all regions (with the exception of the Middle East) have experienced a marked rise in the risk that autocracy will be sanctioned, substantial regional variation in the likelihood of sanctioning exists. A Latin American country which experienced a lapse in democracy in 2000, Marinov writes, had a greater than 80% risk of being sanctioned by outsiders.

7 As Judith Kelley (2004b, 425–6) observes, the body of theoretical and empirical research on the use of democratic conditionality by international actors (as opposed to the structural adjustment conditionality policies of the IFIs) is sparse and until recently the strategy had not been subjected to close analysis. See also Svensson (2000), showing that the voluminous literature on foreign aid and development has generally not dealt with incentive problems in the donor–recipient relationship, and credibility and institutional design issues in foreign aid policy, in particular.

8 The notion of 'reinforcement by reward' is articulated by Schimmelfennig, Engert and Knobel (2003, 496).

9 For the Millennium Challenge Corporation (MCC) selection criteria see: http://www.mcc.gov/selection/index.php. For commentary on the MCC see the series of papers published by the Center for Global Development: http://www.cgdev.org/nv/features_MCA.html. On the MCC see also: Soederberg (2004); Radelet (2003).

10 For an excellent summary of the literature on external incentives see: Schimmelfennig and Sedelmeier (2005a). International lawyers have approached similar questions, but from the point of view of compliance with international rules and norms. See, in particular, Hathaway (2002); (2005).

11 Including corruption control, prominent court systems, civil service professionalization, modern administrative practices, as well as environmental, educational and scientific policies. See, in particular, Meyer *et al.* (1997a); Ramirez *et al.* (2003).

12 See Schraeder (2003).The international community's swift and decisive verbal condemnation of General Oviedo's attempted military coup in Paraguay in April 1996, for instance, played a pivotal role in castigating the military's insubordination against civilian control as normatively unacceptable, and bolstered the weak elected government, effectively saving the country's fragile democracy from collapse. On this case see Valenzuela (1997).

13 These include: The Committee of Legal Affairs and Human Rights (CLAHR); The European Committee on Legal Cooperation (CDCJ); The European Committee on Crime Problems (CDPC); The Group of States Against Corruption (GRECO); The Committee of Experts on Terrorism (CODEXTER), and the European Commission on Democracy Through Law (Venice Commission). Many of these activities are coordinated by the Directorate General of Legal Affairs of the Parliamentary Assembly of the Council of Europe (see: http://www.coe.int/t/dg1/default_en.asp).

14 For a summary of existing indicators and the reasons for their rapid emergence in the last decade see: The World Bank: A Decade of Measuring the Quality of Governance: governance matters 2006 (2006) (available at: http://siteresources.worldbank.org/INTWBIGOVANTCOR/Resources/1740479-1150402582357/266182 911580); Arndt and Oman (2006); Munck and Verkuilen (2002).

15 The privately-owned International Crisis Risk Guide (ICRG), for example, provides a political risk assessment of 161 countries comprising, inter alia, contract viability and risk of property expropriation, corruption, civilian control of the military, bureaucratic quality, as well as strength and impartiality of the legal system. The ICRG is compiled by the PRS Group (see: http://www.prsgroup.com/). Similarly, from the non-profit, NGO sector, Transparency International (TI) and Freedom House (FH) produce the widely cited Corruption Perceptions Index (CPI) and Freedom in the World index, respectively; ranking the vast majority of countries in the world on comparative scales, covering, inter alia, rule of law dimensions. Freedom House's measure of the degree to which 'civil liberties' are protected in 192 countries, for instance, includes four specific questions under the title 'the rule of law' – asking whether there is an independent judiciary, whether the rule of law prevails in civil and criminal proceedings, if the police operates under civilian control, and if individuals are protected from police terror, unjustified imprisonment, torture or exile. Among international institutions, the World Bank produces two major sets of influential governance indicators, partly dedicated to assessment of rule of law conditions in the monitored countries. The Country Policy Institutions Assessments (CPIAs) – published by the Bank annually since 1977 but only publicly disclosed from 2006 – cover 16 criteria, including business regulatory environment, property rights, rules-based governance, quality of budgetary and financial management, quality of public administration, and transparency-accountability-corruption in the public sector. More importantly still, since 1996 the World Bank Institute has produced the Worldwide Governance Indicators (or 'KKZ' indicators), which have become the most widely quoted governance indicators by the media, academia, and the broader donor community. For a critique of the way in which governance indicators are compiled and used see Arndt and Oman (2006).

16 The EU has not been the sole example of this phenomenon. In a series of large-scale, ongoing processes, the main international organizations of the transatlantic community – the EU, NATO, the Council of Europe and the OSCE – have actively sought to transmit their rules, institutions and norms, by combining membership conditionality and financial assistance with engagement in a long-term, multilevel set of deliberative processes of varying content and density. Through the establishment of permanent links (such as the Partnership for Peace, PFP, policy), joint training operations and monitoring, NATO, for instance, has played an increasingly structured role in socializing military leaders in Central and Eastern Europe to the idea of civilian control of the military, transparent security budgets and other modern regulatory standards. Foregoing the EU's rigorous architecture of membership conditionality, similarly, the Council of Europe and the OSCE have opted primarily for a post-accession model of influence through socialization.

17 OAS General Assembly, Resolution 1062.

18 For the text of the Inter-American Democratic Charter see: http://www.oas.org/OASpage/eng/ Documents/ Democractic_Charter.htm. See the annual reports of the Inter-American Juridical Committee (available at: http://www.oas.org/cji/eng/ reports_iajc.htm).

19 Preamble to the Constitutive Act of the African Union (2000) (text available at: http://www.au2002.gov.za/docs/key_oau/au_act.htm). Article 4(m) of the Constitutive Act also states that the African Union shall act in accordance with the principle of: 'Respect for democratic principles, human rights, the rule of law and good governance'.

20 Checkel (2005, 804) calls these two types of socialization 'Type I' and 'Type II', respectively.

21 On this mechanism Schimmelfennig and Scholtz (2007) developed a very effective empirical analysis on 36 cases to show its salience.

22 To reach such an understanding a detailed 'country report' has been prepared on each country. The template of the report is standard, covering: key facts and figures; historical and political background with detailed post-Cold War coverage; an analysis of governmental structure and practice (executive, legislative and judiciary); an analysis of democratic conditions (electoral processes, economic conditions, civil society, legacy and conflict issues, protection of freedoms); as well as international factors (membership in variety of international and regional organizations and fora, subscription to international treaties and relationship with other major promoters, where applicable).

3 EU democratic rule of law promotion

Elena Baracani

Introduction

This chapter analyzes the action of the European Union (EU) to promote democratic rule of law in Romania, Serbia, Turkey and Ukraine, that is, the independent variable of the EUCLIDA model (see Chapter 2). After a brief description of the origins of the EU's activity of democracy and rule of law promotion, I explain how the EU favors the adoption, implementation and internalization of norms concerning the five aspects of the democratic rule of law, i.e. civil and political rights, judicial system, institutional and administrative structures, anti-corruption policies and civilian control of the army and police in our case studies. My explanation is based on the assumption that the international actor's (IA's) action of the EUCLIDA model (see Chapter 2), and in particular the EU's strategy to promote democratic rule of law is based on a supply of institutional ties and economic assistance to non-member countries, complemented by the demand to comply with certain political conditions. Moreover, the analysis shows that EU economic assistance is implemented through the realization of different projects, also in fields close to our dimensions of democratic rule of law. On the whole, the unique feature of this strategy is the combination of two main different modes of influence for an international actor, i.e. democratic conditionality and democratic socialization (see Chapter 2).[1] Finally, the chapter compares the strategy of the EU to promote democratic rule of law with similar activities of other international actors, such as the United States Agency for International Development (USAID), the Council of Europe (CoE), the Organisation for Security and Cooperation in Europe (OSCE), the United Nations (UN), and the World Bank (WB).

The origins

In the original founding treaties there was no mention of 'democracy', 'human rights', and 'rule of law'. It was only with the creation of the EU, at Maastricht in 1992, that these terms were incorporated into treaty language with two references concerning the Union's Common Foreign and Security Policy (CFSP) and the Community's development policy. In particular, it is stated that the development and consolidation of democracy, the rule of law, and respect for human rights and fundamental freedoms is one of the objectives of the CFSP, and that the Community development policy shall contribute to develop and consolidate democracy and the rule of law, and to respect human rights and fundamental freedoms (Magen 2007). On this basis, it is not surprising that it was only with the beginning of the end of the Cold War that the European Community (EC) started to adopt in its policy documents the objective of promoting democracy, human rights, and the rule of law towards third countries.

However, it should be recalled that in the framework of the Mediterranean enlargements, as early as 1962, the Birkelbach Report set out the first standards on democracy among prospective members, even though the literature has underlined that the role played by the EU in the democratic consolidation of Greece, Spain and Portugal during the 1980s was only an indirect one (Whitehead 1996b, 261; Morlino 1998, 166; Kubicek 2003, 9).

Indeed, the EU started to play a direct role in the democratization process of accession candidate countries only in the case of those from central and eastern Europe. Initially, the relationship in the 1990s between the central and eastern European candidates and the Union was characterized by euphoria over the 'return to Europe'. But this euphoria vanished with the first association agreements of 1991, which did not affirm membership as the aim of the Union. In fact, they were perceived by the EU more as alternatives to, rather than a preparatory instrument for, accession. It was only at the 1993 Copenhagen European Council that the heads of state and government of the EU agreed that those associated countries of central and eastern Europe desiring membership could become members of the EU, even though, for the first time, the promise of membership was accompanied by a statement of formal membership conditions – democracy, rule of law, and protection of human and minority rights, a functioning market economy, and implementation of the *acquis*. However, only with the Luxemburg European Council of December 1997, which launched the enhanced pre-accession strategy to be applied to all central and eastern European applicants, did the EU move from indirect influence to direct leverage. This is first of all because the Copenhagen political conditions started to be translated by the EU into the demand for specific reforms from each candidate. Moreover, the progress of each candidate in complying with these demands began to be monitored annually by the European Commission in specific reports. Finally, the EU started to reward, in terms of institutional links and economic assistance, those candidates that complied with its requests. In line with its treaties' provisions, at the beginning of the twenty-first century, the EU is seeking to replicate this strategy not only with the current candidate countries (Turkey, Croatia and the Former Yugoslav Republic of Macedonia), but also with the remaining potential candidate countries of the western Balkans (Albania, Bosnia-Herzegovina, Montenegro and Serbia), and with those countries of eastern

Europe, the south Mediterranean and the south Caucasus that fall under the European Neighbourhood Policy (ENP) launched in 2003.

Institutional links

Institutional links, together with economic assistance, are the main incentives the EU offers to third countries. Institutional links refer to the status of contractual and non-contractual relations between the country and the EU, to the final objective of this relationship (association or membership), and in some cases when accession is expected to take place. Indeed, membership is a stronger incentive than association, as it means that the country that joins the Union can participate, at the same level as the other member states, in the EU process of decision making, and that it can benefit, as the other member states, from redistributive polices of the EU.

Table 3.1 shows the current status of the relations between the EU and each of the countries studied here. Romania became a new member of the Union after signing the Accession Treaty, Turkey has started accession negotiations, Serbia has started negotiations with a view to sign a Stabilization and Association Agreement (SAA), and Ukraine is starting negotiations for a new association agreement to replace the Partnership and Cooperation Agreement (PCA) that is about to expire.

Only the EU contractual relationship with Turkey dates back to the 1960s, when the Ankara Agreement came into force.[2] In the case of Romania and Ukraine there were no relevant contractual relations until the 1990s. In fact, relationships between the EU and Romania date back to the beginning of the 1990s, after the end of the Cold War and the dissolution of the Soviet Union. In the same international context, Ukraine signed the PCA with the EU in 1994 that came into force only in 1998, as it took four years for EU member states to ratify it, reflecting the low priority given to Ukraine in those years by the EU (Kuzio 2003, 14). Serbia still has no contractual relationship with the EU, as no agreement has been signed or is in force. However, as soon as the Milosevic regime ended, in October 2000, the Federal Republic of Yugoslavia (FRY) became a full participant in the Stabilization and Association Process (SAP).

It is important to note that relations between the EU and Romania, Serbia, Turkey and Ukraine have developed in the framework of different external policies of the Union, of the last few years, namely, the pre-accession policy for Romania and Turkey, the SAP for Serbia, and the new neighborhood policy for Ukraine. Only in the case of the pre-accession policy is membership the final objective of the process, although Turkey might turn into an exception. Indeed, the accession negotiating framework for Turkey establishes that negotiations are an 'open-ended process, the outcome of which cannot be guaranteed beforehand'. Moreover, it specifies that '[w]hile having full regard to all Copenhagen criteria ... if Turkey is not in a position to assume in full all the obligations of membership it must be ensured that

Table 3.1 The process of getting closer to the EU

Country	*First negotiations for an agreement*	*Signing of an agreement*	*Formal application for membership*	*Grant of candidate status*	*Start of accession negotiations*	*Signing of the Accession Treaty*	*Membership*
Romania	1990	1991*	June 1995	July 1997	Feb. 2000	April 2005	Jan. 2007
Serbia	Oct. 2005						
Turkey	1960	1963	April 1987	Dec. 1999	Oct. 2005		
Ukraine	1991	1994					

Notes:
*This year refers to the Trade and Cooperation Agreement, which was superseded by the signing of the Europe Agreement in 1994. However, in 1974 an Agreement already included the country in the Community's Generalized System of Preferences.

Turkey is fully anchored in the European structures through the strongest possible bond'. This means that in the case of Turkey it is uncertain what the end of pre-accession process will be; it might be membership but also possibly something different.

The most important steps in the pre-accession process are the formal application for membership, the granting of accession candidate status by the European Council, the European Council's decision to open accession negotiations with the country, and the signing of the Accession Treaty. A precondition to applying for membership is to have an Association Agreement with the EU. In the case of Romania, after the signing of the Europe Agreement, the country applied for EU membership in 1995, accession candidate status was granted in 1997, accession negotiations opened in 2000, in 2002 the Copenhagen European Council established 2007 as the target date for Romania to join the Union, the Accession Treaty was signed in 2005, and finally the country joined the EU in January 2007.

In the case of Turkey, the association agreement, the so-called Ankara Agreement, dates back to 1963, but the country applied for membership of the EC only in 1987, after the Mediterranean enlargements to Greece, Spain and Portugal. Differently from Romania and the other central and eastern European countries that joined the Union in 2004, Turkey became in 1995 the first country to establish a customs union with the EU in anticipation of subsequent full membership.[3] After an initial rebuttal by the Luxemburg European Council in December 1997, the Helsinki European Council made a great leap forward in EU–Turkish relationships two years later, deciding that 'Turkey is a candidate state destined to join the Union on the basis of the same criteria as applied to the other candidate states'.[4] But the Turkish process of getting closer to the EU seemed to slow down after the Copenhagen European Council of 12–13 December 2002, which decided to enlarge the Union from 15 to 25 member states. Indeed, according to the presidency conclusions, it was agreed to postpone the decision for opening accession negotiations with Turkey until December 2004, because the government still had 'to address swiftly all remaining shortcomings in the field of political criteria, not only with regard to legislation but in particular with regard to implementation'. However, in October 2004 the European Commission recommendation concluded that Turkey had sufficiently satisfied the political criteria and suggested opening accession negotiations. The following European Council of December 2004 confirmed the recommendation of the Commission and decided to open accession negotiations with Turkey on 3 October 2005.

The ultimate objective of the SAP for the western Balkan countries is not membership, but the signing of an SAA with the Union. This process was launched in May 1999 in order to stabilize the area and provide a framework for relations between the EU and the western Balkan countries for the entire period prior to the possible future accession. The SAAs for western Balkan countries are similar to the Europe Agreements for central and eastern European countries, as they both ask the third country for a commitment to the EU's values in exchange for the creation of a free trade area with the Union. A year after launching the SAP, the Feira European Council affirmed, for the first time, that western Balkan countries are potential accession candidates, and thus that their future should be inside the EU. The Federal Republic of Yugoslavia became a full participant in the SAP as soon as the Milosevic regime ended. However, until October 2005 the EU would not open negotiations for the SAA because of the delays in the implementation of the new Constitutional Charter and of major deficiencies in the implementation of the country's international obligations.

In 1994 Ukraine was the first one of the Commonwealth of Independent States (CIS) to sign a PCA with the EU. But differently from the association agreements, PCAs do not foresee the possibility of membership of the Union. For this reason, since its adoption, Ukraine has insisted that relations should be upgraded to the level of an association agreement. Furthermore, in March 1998 Ukraine declared its intention to seek EU membership. The EU's response was an update of its relationship with Kiev, through the promulgation of a Common Strategy on Ukraine, but this may be considered a 'consolation prize' given in lieu of offering membership to Ukraine (Kubicek 2003, 161). In fact this document states on the one hand that 'the EU acknowledges Ukraine's European aspirations and welcomes Ukraine's pro-European choice', but on the other hand that 'the main responsibility for Ukraine's future lies with Ukraine itself'. Its main objective is limited to strengthening cooperation between the EU and Ukraine. Since the creation of the ENP in 2003, Ukraine has become a partner of this new policy. But as in the case of the SAP for the western Balkan countries, the final aim of the ENP is not to grant its partners membership, but in the short term 'reinforced relations', through the possibility of participating in EU activities and greater political, security, economic and cultural cooperation, and in the long term a 'closer relationship' which involves 'a significant degree of economic integration and a deepening of political cooperation' (Council of the EU 2004a). However, as officially designed, this new policy should ask all its partners of eastern Europe, southern Caucasus, northern Africa and the Middle East for the same commitments to the Union's common values that it demands of accession candidates or potential candidates. Therefore, even though the EU did not offer Ukraine the incentive of full political integration, the Union asked it to make the same commitments in terms of democracy, human rights, the rule of law and minority rights of accession candidates or potential candidates. From the Ukrainian perspective, the ENP was an improvement on the PCA and the Common Strategy, but Ukrainian reactions were negative as the country expected to be offered accession. In the framework of this policy, the Council of the EU has recently adopted negotiating directives for a new agreement – known as the 'enhanced' agreement – that should replace the PCA between the EU and Ukraine that expires in March 2008. From the point of view of Ukraine, this agreement could be the occasion to establish the possibility for the country to become a member of Union in the future. But, the Council and the Commission have reaffirmed that 'through this Agreement, the European Union aims to build an increasingly close relationship with Ukraine, aimed at gradual economic integration and deepening of political co-operation', even though at the same time it is declared that the new agreement 'shall not prejudge any possible future developments in EU–Ukraine relations'.

Economic assistance

Economic assistance is the other main benefit that third countries are given by the EU. In this section, I compare the total Official Development Aid (ODA)[5] with the same aid provided by only the EU.[6] This allows me to evaluate whether Romania, Serbia, Turkey and Ukraine are the main recipients of only EU aid or also of non-EU aid, and consequently to assess whether the EU is the principal donor for these case studies. Later on, I look at the allocation and distribution in different sectors of EU economic assistance for each case study, through different programs or agencies.

Official development aid

Unlike other countries, Serbia is at the moment among the top recipients not only of EU development aid but also of non-EU development aid. In 2004 Serbia-Montenegro was the twenty-third largest recipient of total aid per capita amounting to US$144, and was the eighth country with the largest EU aid per capita, amounting to US$83 (EU Donor Atlas 2006, 16 and 17), which means that non-EU aid per capita was US$61, mainly from the United States and from the WB (OECD 2006b). Therefore, the EU share of total ODA to Serbia-Montenegro in 2004 was only 58 percent (EU Donor Atlas 2006, 22). For instance, in 2004 Serbia-Montenegro benefited from a total aid of US$1170 million (see Table 3.2), million US$675 of EU aid and US$495 million of non-EU aid (European Commission and OECD 2006, 26 and 28). However, EU aid should be separated into the Union's aid, amounting to US$366 million in 2004 (see Table 3.3), and EU member states' aid, mainly from Germany, France, Switzerland, Norway, Sweden, Greece and the Netherlands (OECD 2006b). If I consider EU aid per capita, Serbia-Montenegro has been the top recipient among our case studies.

Again, considering EU aid per capita, Romania is, among our cases, the second largest recipient after Serbia. In the case of Romania, the largest donors, after the EU, are Japan, Germany, the United States, France, Switzerland, Hungary, the United Kingdom, Greece, and the Netherlands (OECD 2006a). In comparison with Serbia and Romania the total aid given in recent years to both Turkey and Ukraine is much smaller. As in the case of Serbia and Romania, also for Turkey, the EU is the first donor, followed by Japan, Germany, Spain, France, Austria, the Arab countries, the United States, the United Nations High Commissioner for Refugees (UNHCR), and

Table 3.2 Total aid by all donors, net disbursement (million US$)

Country	*1994*	*1995*	*1996*	*1997*	*1998*	*1999*	*2000*	*2001*	*2002*	*2003*	*2004*
Romania	154.39	297.85	230.92	219.23	366.96	396.82	432.23	647.68	419.44	601.12	914.25
Serbia-Montenegro	49.22	95.06	69.51	97.36	107.93	676.22	1133.63	1305.56	1929.68	1317.63	1169.87
Turkey	147.33	312.74	245.06	6.64	28.81	10.98	326.84	168.66	410.32	164.74	285.7
Ukraine	289.91	319.22	397.62	267.93	464.74	569.07	541.2	518.79	482.52	323.37	357.55

Source: Data extracted on 2007/01/17 from IDS Online-DAC Database – Destination of Official Development Assistance and Official Aid – Disbursement, OECD. Stat (my compilation).

Table 3.3 EU aid by recipient (million US$)

Country	*1994*	*1995*	*1996*	*1997*	*1998*	*1999*	*2000*	*2001*	*2002*	*2003*	*2004*	*2005*
Romania	74.18	193.87	112.63	125.37	172.61	243.7	264.17	497.07	220.26	330.05	694.8	–
Serbia-Montenegro	–	8.9	0.09	19.76	12.56	–	470,91	614.7	–	341.76	365.93	157.5
Turkey	−23.32	−13.08	5.93	60.78	81.92	20.34	186.68	142.59	150.78	140.37	303.05	391.98
Ukraine	23.57	155.52	16.06	5.71	97.82	70.82	71.65	97,35	58.51	48.62	75.42	102.14

Source: Data extracted on 2007/01/17 from IDS Online-DAC Database – Destination of Official Development Assistance and Official Aid – Disbursement, OECD. Stat (my compilation).

Greece (OECD 2006c). Indeed, the EU share of total ODA to Turkey in 2004 was 75 percent (European Commission and OECD 2006, 22 and 27). However, a comparison of EU aid per capita to Turkey shows that the country receives much less assistance than Serbia and Romania.

Unlike Serbia, Romania and Turkey, the EU is not the first donor in the case of Ukraine. The United States comes first, followed by the EU, Germany, Israel, Canada, the United Kingdom, France, Sweden, the European Bank for Reconstruction and Development (EBRD), and Switzerland (OECD 2006d). For instance, in 2004 of the total aid received by Ukraine, which amounts to 357 million US$, only 75 million come from the EU. Then, comparing the EU aid per capita given to Ukraine with that given to Serbia, Romania, or Turkey, it is clear that Kiev receives a very small amount of aid.

Allocated assistance and effective distribution

The only aid provided to Serbia from 1993 to 2000 by the EU was humanitarian aid, delivered through the European Commission's Humanitarian Aid Office (ECHO), for victims of the conflicts, socially vulnerable groups, independent media, and the civil society sector. In addition, from the end of 1999 onwards, heating oil was donated by the EU to the 34 municipalities then in opposition to the Milosevic regime. To help Serbia get through the winter of 2000–01, the Union launched a special program of emergency aid, worth 180 million euros, designed to help the country back on its feet. In order to implement this program rapidly and efficiently, the EU decided that the mandate of the European Agency for Reconstruction (EAR),[7] initially limited to Kosovo, should be extended to cover the whole of the country. The Agency accordingly opened offices in Belgrade and Podgorica and since the beginning of January 2001 it has been officially responsible for implementing all the main programs of EU aid in Serbia and Montenegro, as well as in Kosovo.

This is the reason why I concentrate here only on the assistance to Serbia managed by the EAR, even though Serbia also benefits from other minor forms of assistance not managed by the Agency, which include macro-financial, humanitarian, democratization, customs and fiscal planning aid, support for higher education cooperation programs, a western Balkans' regional program, and support for the EU pillar of the UN administration in Kosovo. From 2001 to 2005 EAR managed for Serbia an average each year of assistance amounting to 185 million euros.[8]

In those years the main sector of assistance to Serbia was energy, with an average between 2001–05 of about 63 million euros per year (see Table 3.4). As regards those sectors related to democratic rule of law (public administration reform, support to municipalities and administrative decentralization, justice and home affairs, civil society and media, returns/reintegration of refugees and internally displaced persons), the larger amount of assistance was given to support municipalities and the administrative decentralization, and the reform of the public administration.

Table 3.4 Main sectors of EU assistance allocated to Serbia 2001–05 (million €)

Sector	*2001*	*2002*	*2003*	*2004*	*2005*	*Total*	*Average*	*Average 2002–05*
Public administration reform	0	12	26.5	31	6.7	76.2	15.24	19.05
Support to municipalities and administrative decentralisation	4	0	37.8	21.5	19.7	83	16.6	19.75
Justice and home affairs	0	3.5	13	12.5	13.8	42.8	8.56	5
Civil society and media	2	3.5	7	7.2	4.5	24.2	4.84	5.55
Return/reintegration of refugees and IDPs	0	0	0	9	12.5	21.5	4.3	5.37
Energy	108	66.5	74.5	43.6	25.5	318.1	63.62	52.52
Infrastructure and transport	0	44	4.5	16	15	79.5	15.9	19.87
Health	31.5	5	9.5	8.5	8.5	63	12.5	7.87
Agriculture/rural economy	19	6	7.3	7.1	8	47.4	9.48	7.1
Environment	0	0.5	10.4	14	9.5	34.4	6.88	8.6
Enterprise	16	15	14	13	16.6	74.6	14.92	14.65
Vocational education and training	0	2	13	8.4	3.5	26.9	5.38	6.72
Other	5	9.7	0.2	6	0	20.9	4.18	3.97

Source: European Agency for Reconstruction, Annual Report 2005, 12 June 2006 (my compilation).

From 1964 to 1995 EU assistance to Turkey was given through financial protocols that accompanied the Ankara Agreement. According to the Turkish General Secretariat for EU Affairs, even though in this period Turkey was allocated 453 million euros of assistance, only 78 million euros were paid, which amounts to 2.4 million euros each year. Then, from 1995 Ankara became a partner of the Barcelona Process and received EU assistance through the MEDA Programme, which is the principal financial instrument for the implementation of the Euro-Mediterranean Partnership. Under MEDA I (1996–99) Turkey was allocated 376 million euros for 55 projects on economic transition, on the strengthening of socioeconomic equilibrium and on democratization and civil society. But according to the same Turkish General Secretariat for EU Affairs, only 52 million euros were paid, which amounts to 13 million euros each year. After the Helsinki decision to recognize Turkey as a candidate for accession (1999), financial assistance to the country has been pre-accession oriented. This means that such an assistance has been granted since 2000 according to the priorities listed in the accession partnership for Turkey. On the whole, during 2000–06 Turkey received each year an average of 232.8 million euros.[9]

In the five years 2002–06 the main sectors of EU assistance to Turkey were economic and social cohesion, followed by approximation to the *acquis*, public administration, political criteria, civil society dialogue and support for European integration, and justice and home affairs. In terms of assistance for the political criteria, it was very low in 2002, but it increased in 2003 and 2004, and in 2005 reached a peak of 48.24 million euros (see Table 3.5).

After the signing of a Trade and Cooperation Agreement in 1991, superseded by the coming into force of the Europe Agreement in 1995, Romania started to be granted financial assistance through PHARE, the EU's program to assist central and eastern European countries in their economic and political transition.[10] In 1998, with the beginning of the pre-accession process, assistance was increased[11] and pre-accession oriented, that is, granted in order to satisfy the priorities listed in the Accession Partnership for Romania. On the whole, between 1999–2006 Romania was allocated each year an average of about 279 million euros.[12]

In the eight years 1999–2006, the main sectors of EU assistance to Romania were economic and social cohesion, followed by meeting the obligations of the *acquis*, political criteria, Community programs, economic criteria, and strengthening administrative capacity. Assistance for the political criteria increased significantly after 2003, reaching a maximum in 2006 of 57.90 million euros (see Table 3.6).

In the case of Ukraine the EU provided its assistance from 1991 to 2006 under the TACIS[13] Programme, as well as under thematic budget lines such as the European Initiative for Democracy and Human Rights (EIDHR) and humanitarian assistance provided by ECHO.[14] The TACIS Programme was created after the end of the Cold War to support the process of transition to

Table 3.5 Main sectors of EU assistance allocated to Turkey 2002–06 (million €)

Sector	*2002*	*2003*	*2004*	*2005*	*2006*	*Average*	*Average 2002–05*
Political criteria	2.04	9.5	21.02	48.24	9.79	18.11	20.2
Approximation to the acquis	0	22.6	31.8	63.67	53.91	34.39	29.51
Public administration	44.66	25	49.54	0	0	23.84	29.78
Justice and home affaires	12.20	5.02	11.4	0	0	5.72	7.15
Economic and social cohesion	40	45.3	77.5	91.35	16.8	54.19	63.53
Civil society dialogue, and support for European integration	0	0	0	55.43	24.85	16.05	13.85

Source: Directorate General Enlargement of the European Commission (my compilation).

Table 3.6 Main sectors of EU assistance allocated to Romania 1999–2006 (million €)

Sector	*1999*	*2000*	*2001*	*2002*	*2003*	*2004*	*2005*	*2006*	*Average*	*Average 2002–05*
Political criteria	28	13	27	19	34.90	50	44.59	57.90	34.29	37.12
Economic criteria	10.5	40.90	5.60	2.50	11.40	4.5	0	8.02	10.42	4.6
Meeting the obligations of the acquis	15.7	73.12	18	83.73	56.40	155.4	136.69	140.33	82.95	108.05
Economic and social cohesion	1	88	109.25	106.52	112	160.1	175	187.01	117.23	138.4
Strengthening administrative capacity	0	0	18	33.55	27.21	0	0	0	3.40	15.19
Community programs	0	0	21.44	20.14	23.40	24.10	0	0	11.13	16.91

Source: Directorate General Enlargement of the European Commission (my compilation).

market economies and democratic societies of countries in eastern Europe, the south Caucasus and central Asia. It was composed of four components: (1) national assistance that has focused on support for institutional, legal and administrative reform, on private sector and economic development, and on the social consequences of transition; (2) regional assistance that has addressed issues related to increased inter-state cooperation in transport, energy and sustainable management of natural resources; (3) support for cross-border cooperation that has focused on economic and social development of border areas, efficient border management and people to people contacts; and (4) support in the area of nuclear safety to upgrade and modernize Ukrainian nuclear power plants to internationally recognized safety standards. The following analysis of EU assistance to Ukraine focuses only on the national component of the TACIS Programme, as it is the most significant component in terms of the amount of assistance allocated.[15]

Funding under the TACIS National Programmes has increased in the period (2004–06) in comparison with the previous period (1991–2003).[16] Indeed, while the annual average of EU assistance allocated in the last period amounts to 86 million euros, the annual average in the previous period amounted to about 48 million euros. Moreover, Table 3.7 indicates that the main sector to which EU assistance was allocated in the period 2002–05,[17] through the TACIS National Programmes, was institutional, legal and administrative reform, which is a very important sector for the democratic rule of law, with an annual average of about 27 million euros that has constantly increased.

Table 3.7 Main sectors of EU assistance allocated to Ukraine, through TACIS National Programme 2002–05 (million €)

Sector	*2002*	*2003*	*2004*	*2005*	*Average*
Institutional, legal and administrative reform	21.5	22	31	35	27.37
Support to the private sector and assistance for economic development	8	8	15.5	41	18.12
Support in addressing the social consequences of transition	6	7	13.5	5.5	8
Small projects programs and reserve	11.5	13	10	6.5	10.25

Source: EuropeAid Cooperation Office of the European Commission (my compilation).

Conditionality and required reforms

Developing what has been said in Chapter 2, EU political conditionality can be analyzed at two different levels: formal or 'proclaimed' conditionality, which may be both positive and negative, and 'applied' conditionality, which refers to the implementation or concrete application of formally declared political conditionality and in particular to the level of determinacy of political conditions, to the monitoring of the country's compliance with the political conditions, and to reward or punishment in case of compliance or non-compliance. The hypothesis is that only if conditionality is applied, it can contribute to making the country comply with the democratic rule of law requirements of the Union.

In 1993, the Copenhagen European Council complemented the promise of membership for the associated countries of central and eastern Europe with a statement of the political, economic and *acquis*-related conditions for membership. More precisely, it stated that

> [m]embership requires that the candidate country has achieved stability of institutions guaranteeing democracy, the rule of law, human rights and respect for and protection of minorities, the existence of a functioning market economy as well as the capacity to cope with competitive pressure and market forces within the Union.

Moreover, '[m]embership presupposes the candidate's ability to take on the obligations of membership including adherence to the aims of political, economic and monetary union'. This is a positive conditionality, as the Council affirms that '[a]ccession will take place as soon as an associated country is able to assume the obligations of membership by satisfying the economic and political conditions required' (European Council 1993, 13), which means that the more the associated country satisfies the conditions required, the more it will become closer to the Union.

Positive political conditionality has been declared by the EU not only in the case of accession candidate countries, but also for potential candidates of the western Balkans and new ENP partners. In the case of Serbia and the other western Balkans countries the Zagreb summit of 24 November 2000 emphasized the connection between progress in the countries of the region towards democracy, rule of law, regional reconciliation and cooperation on the one hand, and the prospect of possible accession to the EU, on the other hand. In a similar way, the EU offers ENP partners increased political, security, economic and cultural cooperation in return for political and economic reforms (European Commission 2003a, 16). In particular, in the case of Ukraine, and the other ENP partners, it is the first time that the Union has declared its intention to base its strategy of democracy export not only on negative conditionality, but also on positive conditionality. Indeed, before the ENP, EU conditionality, both in the framework of the Euro-Mediterranean

Partnerships for southern Mediterranean countries and in the context of the PCAs for the former Soviet Republics, was only negative. Consequently, it has been observed that the principle of positive conditionality in the framework of this new policy, if implemented, could encourage reform-willing states to pursue their reform agenda further, and, conversely, reform-reluctant states would at least not benefit from increased aid or trade concessions (Emerson 2004, 15; Schmid 2004, 416; Del Sarto and Schumacher 2005, 22).

However, since the experience of accession of central and eastern European countries, formally declared EU conditionality has been not only positive, but also negative, which means that the EU may penalize a country that does not respect the required conditions by suspending economic assistance or accession negotiations. Indeed, in the case of both Romania and Turkey, the Accession Partnership contains a negative conditionality clause, according to which EU economic assistance is conditional on satisfying the Copenhagen criteria and meeting the specific priorities of the Accession Partnership, and a failure to respect these conditions can lead to a decision by the Council to suspend this financial assistance (Council of the EU 1999a, 13; Council of the EU 2001, 10).

The negative conditionality clause is present not only in Accession Partnerships for candidate countries, but also in European Partnerships for potential candidates, even if in this case the failure to respect the Union's general conditions can lead the EU to take more general 'appropriate measures' instead of the suspension of financial assistance as in the case of accession candidates.[18] In fact, in the European Partnership for Serbia, it is declared that '[c]ommunity assistance under the stabilisation and association process to the Western Balkan countries is conditional on further progress in satisfying the Copenhagen political criteria' and that '[f]ailure to respect these general conditions could lead the Council to take appropriate measures ...' (Council of the EU 2004a, 3).

In the case of the ENP, the EU's positive conditionality has also been complemented by a negative conditionality clause, already present in the MEDA regulation for Community assistance to Middle East and north African countries, and in the TACIS regulation for Community assistance to former Soviet Republics. In the 2006 European Neighbourhood and Partnership Instrument (ENPI)[19] Regulation, the relevant clause reads as follows:

> where a partner country fails to observe the principles referred to in Article 1 [liberty, democracy, respect for human rights and fundamental freedoms and the rule of law], the Council, acting by a qualified majority on a proposal from the Commission, may take appropriate steps in respect of any Community assistance granted to the partner country under this Regulation
>
> (Council of the EU and European Parliament 2006, article 28).

As mentioned above, EU conditionality for the associated countries that wish to become members of the Union was proclaimed at Copenhagen in 1993, but only in 1997, when the Luxemburg European Council launched the enhanced pre-accession strategy, did the EU start to apply this conditionality. In fact, the enhanced pre-accession strategy was based on three new key components that have allowed the European Commission and the Council of the EU to implement this proclaimed conditionality: Accession Partnerships, annual assessment of the progress achieved by the candidate country; and accession-driven economic assistance.

The main idea behind the new concept of Accession Partnership is that specific priorities or required reforms concerning the Copenhagen criteria are set out in these documents for each candidate country. Therefore, for the first time, formal political conditions – democracy, human rights, minority rights and rule of law – are translated into much more specific political priorities that should address the main democratic challenges of each country. It is also worthwhile observing that, even though Accession Partnerships are the result of consultations with candidate states, they are not agreements, but unilateral acts decided by the Council of the EU on the basis of a proposal from the European Commission. This means that, after consultations with the authorities in the candidate country, it is the Commission that decides what specific priorities the country has to fulfill.

Another important feature of the enhanced pre-accession strategy is the monitoring of compliance in the framework of the Europe Agreement bodies and the annual review by the European Commission of the candidate's progress in fulfilment of the Accession Partnership's priorities. The monitoring of compliance by the European Commission is the way chosen by the EU to assess, once political priorities have been listed, whether they have been satisfied or not. But this is also a way for the Commission to make sure the country has understood what reforms are necessary to fulfill the priorities indicated in the Accession Partnership. Finally, all the various forms of EC assistance become accession-driven, that is, economic and technical assistance is designed to help candidates satisfy the priorities set by the EU in the Accession Partnerships.[20] This means that for each priority it should be possible to assess what assistance the country has been given by the EU.

In the framework of the SAP, the EU implements the conditionality through the same instruments. First of all, as in the case of Accession Partnerships, European Partnerships list the specific conditions that the country has to satisfy to become closer to the Union, and they are adopted by the Council of the EU upon proposal of the Commission. Then, as in the case of pre-accession, progress in complying with those priorities is monitored annually in the Commission reports and the various forms of assistance are designed to help potential candidates to satisfy the same priorities.

As regards the implementation of the EU's political conditionality in the case of Ukraine, and all other ENP partners, it should be observed that the ENP method is based on three components that are very similar to those identified for the pre-accession strategy. These components are Action Plans, incorporating a set of priorities for ENP partner countries; monitoring of progress in meeting the priorities listed in the Action Plans; and assistance programs to help partners satisfy the priorities listed in the Action Plans (European Commission 2004b, 3). In the case of Ukraine, the ENP Action Plan was negotiated by 2004. However, the EU did not sign the Action Plan before the outcome of the presidential elections at the end of 2004. As a result, the EU–Ukraine ENP Action Plan was signed only after the convincing victory of the 'Orange Revolution' on 21 February 2005, thereby marking the EU's full support for the 'Orange government'.

As regards the implementation of political conditionality, there is an important difference between the pre-accession policy or the SAP and the ENP. Indeed, unlike the Accession or European Partnerships, Action Plans are not unilateral acts decided by the Council on a proposal of the Commission, but have to be jointly agreed upon with the partner and approved by the respective Cooperation or Association Council. This might mean that if a certain ENP partner does not want some specific priorities to be included in the Action Plan, the Commission and the Council cannot oblige the partner to add them (Baracani 2007, 339).

In order to evaluate the level of determinacy of the EU's political priorities for Romania, Serbia, Turkey and Ukraine, the actual content of these required reforms has to be analyzed, for each dimension of the democratic rule of law. Moreover, in order to establish a temporal link between the requirements of the EU and the reforms of a country, it is important to take note of when the Union formulated a certain demand. Table 3.8, which summarizes this information, shows that all dimensions[21] of the democratic rule of law were the object of the EU political conditionality for our case studies. All cases were asked to improve the functioning or the efficiency of the judiciary and its independence, and to strengthen the fight against corruption. Required reforms to improve the institutional and administrative capacity mainly concerned implementation of the Constitution, reform of the electoral law and democratic conduct of elections, reform of public administration (and in particular the reform of the civil service and the creation of European integration structures), decentralization of power to local government, and strengthening of the Parliament and of the policy formulation process. Among our cases, Serbia and Romania were those most affected by the EU's demands to strengthen their institutional and administrative capacity. As regards civil freedoms and political rights, it is worth noting that only in the case of Romania were there no demands from the EU. For the other countries, the most common requirements have concerned the prevention of torture and ill-treatments, the protection of freedom of expression and media freedom, the protection of freedom of association and peaceful assembly, and also the prevention of discrimination. Moreover, other requirements have addressed the abolition of death penalty and freedom of religion, in the case of Turkey, and the protection of property rights in the case of Serbia. It is not surprising

Table 3.8 EU democratic rule of law priorities

Priority		*Romania*[1]	*Turkey*[2]	*Serbia*[3]	*Ukraine*[4]
Civil freedoms and political rights	Death penalty	Not present	2001	Not present	Not present
	Torture and ill-treatment	Not present	2001, 2003 and 2006	2004 and 2006	2005
	Freedom of expression (and media freedom)	Not present	2001, 2003 and 2006	2004 and 2006	2005
	Freedom of association (and peaceful assembly)	Not present	2001, 2003 and 2006	2004 and 2006	2005
	Freedom of religion	Not present	2001, 2003 and 2006	Not present	Not present
	Property rights	Not present	Not present	2004 and 2006	Not present
	Discrimination	1999, 2002 and 2003	2001, 2003 and 2006	2006	2005
Judicial system	Independence	1999, 2002 and 2003	2003 and 2006	2004 and 2006	2005
	Efficient functioning	1999, 2002 and 2003	2001, 2003 and 2006	2004	2005
Institutional and administrative capacity	Constitution	Not present	Not present	2004 and 2006	Not present
	Election	Not present	Not present	2004 and 2006	2005
	Public administration (civil service, European integration structures, etc.)	2002 and 2003	2006	2004 and 2006	2005
	Policy formulation process	2002 and 2003	Not present	Not present	Not present
	Local government	2002 and 2003	2006	2004 and 2006	2005
	Parliament	2002 and 2003	Not present	2004	Not present
Fight against corruption	Policies against corruption	2002 and 2003	2006	2004 and 2006	2005
Civil control of the military	Civil control of the military	1999, 2002 and 2003	2001, 2003 and 2006	2004 and 2006	Not present

Source: Official documents listed in the notes (my compilation).

Notes:

1 For the five dimensions of the democratic rule of law, see Council of the EU 1999a, 7, 8 and 11; Council of the EU 2002, 3 and 4; Council of the EU 2003a, 7, 8, 11 and 12.

2 For the five dimensions of the democratic rule of law, see Council of the EU 2001, 4 and 7; Council of the EU 2003b, 3-5; Council of the EU 2006a, 2-6.

3 For the five dimensions of the democratic rule of law, see Council of the EU 2004b, 3, 4, 8 and 9; Council of the EU 2006b, 5–12.

4 For the five dimensions of the democratic rule of law, see EU/Ukraine ENP Action Plan 2005: 5–8.

that, among our cases, the country most affected by the EU's demand of reforms to protect civil freedoms and political rights was Turkey. Finally, with the sole exception of Ukraine, civil control of the military has been another fundamental dimension of the EU's political conditionality in the case of Turkey, but also Serbia and Romania.

Analysis of the specific content of the EU's political priorities for Romania and Turkey in the Accession Partnerships, for Serbia in the European Partnership, and for Ukraine in the ENP Action Plan, has shown that within the EU perspective it was sufficiently determinate in all cases. This means that the EU has informed governments as to what objectives they have to reach, even though each country has been left autonomous in deciding how to reach these goals. Only in the case of civil freedoms and political rights was there constant reference to European and international democratic standards in order to let the government know exactly what it has to do to comply with the conditions of the Union. Specifically, the most common of these standards are the European Convention for the protection of Human Rights, protocols number 1 and 6 of the same Convention, the case law of the European Court of Human Rights, the European Convention for the Prevention of Torture, and the United Nations Covenant on Civil and Political Rights and its protocols. A partial exception is the case of Turkey, as far as the judicial system is concerned, as there are two reports by two legal experts, asked by the EU to visit the country twice to evaluate the progress made in satisfying the Accession Partnership's priorities, which list very detailed recommendations to satisfy the Union's priorities and refer to specific European and international standards, in order to help the Turkish authorities to comply with those priorities (Björnberg and Richmond 2004 and Björnberg and Cranston 2005). For instance, as far as judicial independence is concerned, the standards quoted are the UN Basic Principles on the Independence of the Judiciary and Recommendation No. R (94) 12 of the Committee of Ministers of the CoE. Finally, the level of determinacy of the EU's political priorities has been reinforced through annual monitoring of the political situation of the Commission, which informs the countries whether they met the specific requests and what further steps are required (on this last point, see also Schimmelfennig 2005b, 119–20).

As regards the European Commission monitoring of the progress accomplished or not by the country in satisfying the Union's priorities, there is usually annual monitoring, which started in the case of Romania in 1998, in the case of Serbia in 2002, in the case of Turkey in 2001, and in 2006 in the framework of the ENP for Ukraine. This activity is fundamental to enable the EU to reward or sanction the country that has fulfilled, or failed to fulfill, the Union's political conditions.

Both in the case of central and eastern European countries that joined the Union in 2004, and Romania and Turkey, but also of Serbia and Ukraine, the EU has never implemented the negative conditionality clause, with the suspension of economic assistance, in order to sanction a country which has not sufficiently fulfilled the Copenhagen political criteria. However, in the case of Serbia and Turkey the EU has sanctioned these two countries in terms of institutional links, and in particular suspending negotiations for the SAA in the case of Serbia in May 2006, and deciding not to open accession negotiations on some specific chapters with Turkey in December 2006. In the case of Serbia, the reason was the insufficient cooperation with the International Criminal Tribunal for Former Yugoslavia (ICTY). Indeed, from the opening of SAA negotiations, no indictees were transferred to The Hague and at the same time the Belgrade authorities did not cooperate with the Tribunal to arrest war crimes suspect Ratko Mladic. In the case of Turkey, it was the lack of full implementation of the Additional Protocol to the Ankara Agreement, and the restrictions on the free movement of goods, that made the Commission recommend that the Intergovernmental Conference on Accession with Turkey should not open negotiations on chapters covering policy areas relevant to Turkey's restrictions as regards the Republic of Cyprus,[22] and that no chapter could be provisionally closed until the Commission had confirmed that Turkey had fully implemented its commitments with respect to the Additional Protocol (European Commission 2006b).

Progress in fulfilment of political priorities was rewarded – in terms of institutional links – in the case of Romania with the decision to grant the country candidate status in 1997, and with the decision to start accession negotiations in 2000. Similarly, Romania's progress was rewarded in terms of EC assistance allocated to the country. For instance, in 2000 assistance allocated to Romania was 215 million euros, while in 1999 it was only 55 million euros. In the case of Turkey the progress in satisfying the requested priorities was rewarded in 1999 with the decision to grant the country candidate status and also in October 2005 with the decision to open accession negotiations. Moreover, the decision to open accession negotiations with Turkey was accompanied by the decision to allocate this country 500 million euros of economic assistance for 2006 (the same assistance allocated for 2005 had been 300 million euros). Serbia was rewarded for its partial progress in complying with the political priorities, deciding in October 2005 to start negotiations for an SAA. Finally, in the case of Ukraine information on institutional links and economic assistance are not yet sufficient to evaluate whether the EU has rewarded the progress of the country in satisfying the political conditions indicated in the ENP Action Plan for Ukraine.

Socialization through projects to develop democratic rule of law

At the domestic level of political leaders and high bureaucrats, institutional links with the EU and the Union's implementation of political conditionality can favor the process of democratic socialization. Differently, at a lower level of state officials and civil servants, it is the implementation of the EU's economic assistance through the realization of different projects in fields close to our dimensions of democratic rule of law that should favor socialization with the EU's democratic values. Indeed, EU projects in the fields close to those dimensions are implemented mainly through twinning and technical assistance contracts, which are forms of social interaction between state officials of the third country and of the EU member states, and which should persuade domestic actors of the legitimacy of EU members' democratic rule of law principles and practices. To explain how this democratic socialization can be favored by the EU at the lower level of state officials and civil servants, it is important, first of all, to look at what should be, according to the EU, the main beneficiary and the amount of assistance allocated for each project that might strengthen the democratic rule of law.[23] Then, for each project its concrete realization should be analyzed to assess its impact in terms of socialization with the EU's democratic values.

In the case of Serbia, there are EU projects that can be related to democratic rule of law in the sectors of assistance for public administration, municipalities and administrative decentralization, justice and home affairs, media, and civil society NGOs. For the public administration sector, the analysis shows that the most important projects, in terms of amount of assistance allocated, dealt with the support for public administration reform and assistance to public finance reforms, amounting to about 50 million euros in the period 2002–05, and were followed by minor projects to reinforce the process of integrating with the EU. Moreover, in the sector of municipalities and administrative decentralization, the analysis indicates that an average of about 16 million euros was allocated annually, in the period 2001–05, for projects intended to contribute to an efficient and coherent decentralization process and to enhance the delivery of municipal services. In the sector of justice and home affairs, EU data show that the main beneficiary of projects in the period 2002–05 was to be the Ministry of Justice, in order to improve the efficiency of the judicial process and court management systems, and to upgrade court facilities. In the same period the other main beneficiary of justice and home affairs projects was to be the police to modernize their professional capacities. Finally, as regards the other sectors of EU economic assistance close to the dimensions of democratic rule of law, it can be observed that different EU's projects were designed, in the period 2000–05, to strengthen independent and state media and also to support civil society NGOs.

In the case of Turkey, there are projects that can be related to democratic rule of law in the sectors of assistance for political criteria, public administration, justice and home affairs, and civil society dialogue and support for European integration. The analysis of assistance for the political criteria shows that the most important projects in this sector involved the support for the construction of courts of appeal amounting to 22.50 million euros, support for the implementation of human rights reforms (12.45 million euros), and the strengthening of civil society through a NGO Grant Facility (10.50 million euros). The institution that was to benefit from the larger amount of assistance for the political criteria was the Ministry of Justice, followed by the Secretariat General for EU affairs. Data on assistance for public administration show that it was very high in 2002 and also 2004, but from 2005 it was no longer a priority sector. However, it can be observed that such assistance was given for very different purposes, not always strictly related to public administration and closer to alignment with the *acquis*. Beneficiaries of such assistance, were to be, for example, the Ministry for Environment, the Ministry for Agriculture and Rural Affairs, the Ministry of Energy and Natural Resources, the Ministry of Transport, the Ministry of Health, and also the Faculty of Mechanical Engineering of Istanbul Technical University, the Petroleum Pipeline Corporation, and the Turkish Electricity Transmission Corporation. Then, it can be observed that the larger amount of assistance was distributed to projects dealing with the modernization of Turkish customs administration (22.58 million euros), and to a project on capacity building in the field of the environment (15.55 million euros). In the field of justice and home affairs, assistance was given only during the period 2002–04. The main beneficiary of such assistance should have been the Ministry of the Interior and in particular the national police. However, the largest project dealt with the strengthening of the fight against money laundering (7.75 million euros) and the beneficiary was the Ministry of Finance. The 'civil society dialogue and support for European integration' sector has been present only since 2005 and deals with projects aiming at the continuation of the Jean Monnet scholarship program, at the participation in Community programs and agencies, to support activities to strengthen the European Integration Process, and to promote civil society dialogue between the EU and Turkey. The main beneficiary of such assistance was to be the Secretariat General for the EU Affairs and the larger amount of assistance was allocated to participation in Community programs and agencies (36.71 million euros), and to promote civil society dialogue between the EU and Turkey (21.50 million euros).

In the case of Romania, there are projects that can be related to democratic rule of law in the sectors of assistance for the political criteria and for administrative capacity. As far as assistance on the political criteria is concerned, the analysis shows that between 1999 and 2003 the most important projects dealt with the support for the protection of children and since 2004 they have concerned the judiciary system, public administration reform, and the fight against corruption. The institution that was to benefit from the larger amount of assistance for the political criteria was the Ministry of Justice. In the years 2001–03 the strengthening of administrative capacity was not included in the projects related to political criteria, as it was from 2004 onwards. Therefore, it is noticeable that before 2004 the EU gave special attention and a larger amount of its economic assistance to projects aiming at strengthening administrative capacity. Indeed, while in the period 2001–03 assistance for such projects was about 30 million euros on average each year, in the period 2004–06 it decreased to an annual average of about 13 million euros. Moreover, it can be observed that, while in the first period (2001–03) assistance to improve the administrative capacity was allocated mainly to support the strategic plan of the Ministry of Public Finance, and to strengthen the Romanian administration capacity to manage pre-accession funds, in the second period (2004–06) such assistance was allocated to support civil service reform by developing a professional body of civil servants, to support local public administration reform through continuation of the decentralization process, and to support central government reform through improvement of the policy formulation process.

In the case of Ukraine, projects that can have an impact in terms of democratic rule of law are those on institutional, legal and administrative reform. In 2002 projects on institutional, legal and administrative reform for Ukraine focused on four main areas: border management improvement, assistance to the State Treasury of Ukraine in promoting effective management of the state budget, support in the area of civic education, and support for municipal services – in particular, improving water service levels in medium-sized cities.[24] Again in 2003, key priority areas of assistance for institutional, legal and administrative reform were border and migration management and reform of municipal administration. However, for the first time, new areas of assistance included were the implementation of the PCA between the EU and Ukraine, reform of the judicial system, development of civil society, and support for independent media. In particular, the specific objective of the project to reform the judicial system was to assist the court administration in strengthening an institutionalized system of training for judges of all courts of the Ukrainian judiciary, and the creation of a system of alternative dispute resolution to improve access to justice and to decrease the number of cases submitted to the courts. Key priorities in EU assistance in 2004 were support for legal and administrative reform, justice and home affairs, and support to the development of civil society. However, it should be noted that projects related to legal and administrative reform dealt only with support to the TACIS national coordinating unit, support to PCA implementation, accession of Ukraine to international conventions and agreements on transport, and support for the implementation of the ENP Action Plan with Ukraine. In a similar way, projects related to justice and home affairs dealt only with international cooperation in criminal matters with judicial bodies and law enforcement agencies, the fight against and prevention of corruption, support to border surveillance along the Transdniestrian sector of the border with Moldova, and reconstruction of the Jagodin border point.[25] For these years – 2002–04 – it is not possible to say which area or project was given priority, as the data do not show the amount of EU economic assistance allocated to each project. However, on the basis of our analysis, it is possible to state that most projects in the sector of institutional, legal and administrative reform dealt with border management. Finally, data on 2005 projects in the sector of institutional, legal and administrative reform again show that border management was given priority, together with media, electoral, and civil service reform, followed by projects related to fair access to justice and Ukraine's integration into the Trans-European Transport Network.

Table 3.9 Top ten donors of gross ODA, 2003–04 average (millions of US$)[a]

Donor	*Romania*	*Serbia-Montenegro*	*Turkey*	*Ukraine*
1st donor	EU (512)	EU (354)	EU (232)	United States (112)
2nd donor	Japan (53)	United States (196)	Japan (129)	EU (62)
3rd donor	Germany (49)	IDA[b] or World Bank Group (133)	Germany (104)	Germany (46)
4th donor	United States (41)	Germany (119)	Spain (46)	Israel (22)
5th donor	France (36)	France (108)	France (26)	Canada (17)
6th donor	Switzerland (13)	Switzerland (57)	Austria (19)	United Kingdom (11)
7th donor	Hungary (9)	Norway (40)	Arab countries (9)	France (10)
8th donor	United Kingdom (9)	Sweden (37)	United States (8)	Sweden (8)
9th donor	Greece (5)	Greece (36)	UNHCR (5)	EBRD (7)
10th donor	Netherlands (4)	Netherlands (24)	Greece (5)	Switzerland (6)

Source: OECD 2006a, 2006b, 2006c, 2006d.

Notes:
a Gross refers to commitments, rather than disbursements.
b International Development Association.

The role of other international actors

This final section analyzes the role played by other international actors to help Romania, Serbia, Turkey and Ukraine in their reform processes, the most important sectors of assistance from these actors, and their relevance for the democratic rule of law. As has already been underlined, the following table shows that, among our case studies, it is only for Ukraine that the United States has been the first donor, rather than the EU (see Table 3.9). Moreover, Table 3.10 shows that in the period 1993–2005 Ukraine received from the United States an amount of assistance more than twice that from the EU, underlining the importance of Ukraine for the United States, but not for the EU.

In particular, since 1992 the USAID Mission to Ukraine has been implementing the United States' foreign economic and humanitarian assistance programs for Ukraine focused on the areas of democracy and governance, economic growth, and social assistance. The following table shows that for the period 2004–07 the first sector of USAID assistance has been democracy and governance, with an annual average of US$35 million, while human rights has been allocated an annual average of only about US$1 million (see Table 3.11).

The United States has also given a considerable amount of assistance to Serbia, and has been the second donor for this country after the EU. As in the case of Ukraine, since 1997 the USAID Office of Transition Initiatives has supported pro-democracy elements in the country. Table 3.12 shows that for the period 2004–07 the first sector of USAID assistance for Serbia has been

Table 3.10 Official development assistance to Ukraine from the United States and the EU (millions of US$)

	1993	*1994*	*1995*	*1996*	*1997*	*1998*	*1999*	*2000*	*2001*	*2002*	*2003*	*2004*	*2005*	*Average*
US	66	99	45	256	72	139	319	244	246	255	104	102	113	158.46
EU	2	23	155	16	5	97	70	71	97	58	48	75	102	63

Source: Data extracted on 2007/04/20 from IDS Online-DAC Database – Destination of Official Development Assistance and Official Aid – Disbursement, OECD. Stat (my compilation).

Table 3.11 USAID program budget for Ukraine by sector (millions of US$)

Budget sector	*2004*	*2005*	*2006*	*2007*	*Average*
Agriculture and environment	34.11	47.51	35.11	34.31	30.20
Higher education and training	0	0.4	0	0	0.1
Economic growth	17.76	18.77	13.04	14.92	16.12
Human rights	1.35	0.72	1.21	1.19	1.11
Democracy and governance	32.78	57.34	24.93	25.49	35.13
Conflict management/humanitarian assistance	1.33	2.01	0.99	1.01	1.33
Family planning/reproductive health	0	2.46	0	0	0.61
HIV/AIDS	1.75	2.19	2.17	2.17	2.07
Child survival and maternal health	2.9	1.64	3.67	2.35	2.64
Other infectious diseases	1	3.49	1	1.40	1.72
Other					
Total	99.78	143.76	85.33	87.17	104.01

Source: USAID.

Table 3.12 USAID program budget for Serbia by sector (millions of US$)

Budget sector	*2004*	*2005*	*2006*	*2007*	*Average*
Agriculture and environment	2.3	2.47	2.38	2	2.28
Economic growth	11.6	49.88	53.71	45.15	40
Human rights	1.3	0.3	0	0	0.4
Democracy and governance	75.55	20.76	12.70	14.84	30.96
Conflict management/humanitarian assistance	6.71	0.17	0.5	0	1.84
Family planning/reproductive health	1.5	0	0	0	0.37
Total	98.96	73.6	69.30	62	75.96

Source: USAID.

democracy and governance, with an annual average of US$31 million. But other European and international organizations have also promoted democracy in Romania, Serbia, Turkey and Ukraine. While in the case of European organizations this analysis focuses on the activity of the CoE and of OSCE, in the case of international organizations I briefly summarize the strategy of the UN, and of an international financial institution such as the WB.

Romania, Serbia, Turkey and Ukraine have been members of the CoE since 1993, 2003, 1949 and 1995, respectively. However, as Dimitrova and Pridham have emphasized, the CoE's approach to democracy promotion is not based on strict membership conditionality but on post-membership socialization into western democratic practices (2004, 99). In 1993 the CoE set out membership conditions that included free and fair elections, freedom of expression (especially of the media), minority rights, and signing up to the European Convention on Human Rights. But until then these membership conditions had only been implicit, as the CoE was not rigorous in applying these democratic criteria to aspirant member states. Therefore, the main contribution of the CoE to democratic rule of law in its members and candidates has been and still is in terms of socializing them into Western democratic norms and practices through its activities or programs.[26] It is important to emphasize that the CoE democratic norms and practices affect many different areas such as the judicial system, legal training, cross-frontier crime, corruption, organized crime and money laundering, trafficking in human beings, protection of children, legislative reforms, constitutional issues, police and internal security services, protecting individual rights and freedoms, and local and regional democracy, to mention only some of them. In particular, socialization with these legal standards and practices is developed through three main types of activity or strategy: (1) intergovernmental activity programs, (2) cooperation programs, and (3) joint programs between the CoE and other international organizations. Intergovernmental activity programs refer to the drafting of legal instruments as Conventions, which are binding instruments for member and non-member states that ratify them, and Recommendations, which establish non-binding but important guidelines. Cooperation programs are all those activities carried out to support candidate states and members in their democratization process. Joint programs may be between the CoE and the European Commission, or between the CoE and the OSCE. The common aims of the CoE and the European Commission, in terms of protection of democracy, respect for human rights and fundamental freedoms and the rule of law, have led them to develop cooperation links. In particular, since 1993 a number of joint programs have been set up in order to facilitate legal and institutional reform of countries that have joined the CoE since 1989. The countries involved in these programs have included Ukraine since 1995, and Serbia and Turkey since 2001. The activities of these joint programs between the CoE and the

European Commission have been training courses, for instance on human rights protection, expert reports and advice to governments, and conferences, workshops, seminars and publication and dissemination. In terms of the cooperation between the CoE and OSCE, in 2005 the organizations decided to establish a Coordination Group to ensure complementarities and avoid unnecessary duplication of activities.

Like the CoE, the OSCE's influence on the democratic rule of law of post-socialist reforming countries, such as Romania, Serbia and Ukraine, which are all members of the OSCE,[27] has also been in terms of socialization and not of membership conditionality. In fact, the OSCE has never used conditionality that would require countries to take certain clearly defined actions before they are allowed to become members, and even though the OSCE has the power to suspend the membership of countries that are in flagrant violation of its principles, it is very reluctant to do so (Merlingen and Ostraukaité 2005, 135). But notwithstanding this similarity, there are some differences with the CoE. First of all, it seems that the OSCE is perceived by third countries as an organization with a lower status than the CoE. The reason for this seems to be that, while the CoE is based on a constitutive treaty, the OSCE was created by a political accord, and its norms therefore lack the prestige of law (Merlingen and Ostraukaité 2005, 130). But there are more important differences between the activity of the CoE and of OSCE, in terms of both its objective, and its socializing strategies. OSCE activity aims at promoting 'human security' (Merlingen and Ostraukaité 2005, 128).[28] The OSCE has concretized the notion of human security in the form of prescriptions for action in a wide range of policy areas covering, among other issues, human rights, elections, inter-ethnic relations, gender equality and criminal justice. To promote these norms, the organization has created new organs, such as the High Commissioner on National Minorities (HCNM), the Office for Democratic Institutions and Human Rights (ODIHR), and long-term field missions. The main socializing devises used by the OSCE are technical or expert assistance projects through long-term missions on the ground, social influence or normative pressure, training projects, normative intermediation, and awareness raising campaigns. With regard to normative pressure, the organisation is able to exert some social influence through its statements and reports on the compliance of post-socialist states with international norms, as governments want to avoid the material disadvantages that are, indirectly, linked to social punishment by the OSCE. These material costs come from the fact that the EU, in its political or assistance-related decisions, takes into consideration the views expressed by the OSCE.[29] Training project are usually small-scale training projects aimed at grassroots actors as well as junior- and mid-level state officials.[30] Normative intermediation is a hallmark of the OSCE, and it seeks to change the deeply held beliefs, norms and values of socializees through argumentative reasoning. Finally, the objective of awareness raising campaigns is to familiarize countries with OSCE norms before expecting them to internalize them. On the whole, the particular feature of the socializing strategies of the OSCE, in comparison with the EU and the CoE, seems to be the fact that it pays great attention to the socialization of grassroots actors and that it is based on a teaching philosophy intended to empower local knowledge and values, insofar as they do not violate fundamental OSCE beliefs (Merlingen and Ostraukaitė 2005, 145).

The promotion of human rights, rule of law and democracy also has a prominent place on the agenda of the UN, of which Romania, Serbia, Turkey and Ukraine are all members. But in the case of this international organization, too, the impact of its different activities on the democratic rule of law reforms of its member states can only be in terms of socialization and not of membership conditionality. The efforts of the UN in this field are manifold and multifaceted, and they are based on the main consideration that human rights, rule of law and democracy are strictly interlinked and mutually reinforcing. Notably, socialization with UN legal standards in this field is promoted through three main strategies: (1) the development of international legal standards, i.e. UN conventions; (2) technical assistance and advisory services to member states upon request, in order to implement the UN legal standards; and (3) *ad hoc* judicial bodies, such as ICTY. Moreover, these activities are carried out at the headquarters level as well as in the field. Many offices, departments and programs of the organization are actively engaged in this endeavor, as the Office of the United Nations High Commissioner for Human Rights (OHCHR), the United Nations Office on Drugs and Crime (UNODC), the United Nations Development Programme (UNDP), the Department of Peacekeeping Operations (DPKO), and the International Tribunals, to mention only a few.

According to Dimitrova and Pridham, in the 1990s international financial institutions – like the WB – started to exercise a more overt political conditionality. However, they affirm that it is a loose conditionality rather than democracy promotion. In particular, it is noticeable that political principles have always been subordinated to economic considerations, and that no benefited country has ever had its loans suspended on political grounds. Therefore, negative political conditionality is not effectively implemented, but the authors argue that the increasing tactic of linking loans with demands placed on 'governance' might have the potential to increase the impact of these international financial institutions on democracy (Dimitrova and Pridham 2004, 100–01). All our cases are members of the WB and there is a WB mission in each of them, but only in the case of Romania does at least one of the landmark projects deal with governance.[31] The WB started its activities in 'governance' in 1991 and it is of particular relevance to understand the meaning of 'governance' for the Bank, in order to describe its activities in this field. The Bank's work on governance was designed to take into consideration the prohibition against intervention in countries' internal political affairs laid down in the Bank's Articles of Agreement. Therefore, those aspects of governance consistent with the Bank's mandate were found in the meaning of 'good order' understood as a system, based on abstract rules which are actually applied, and on functioning institutions which ensure the appropriate applications of such rules. In particular, it was emphasized that this system of rules and institutions is reflected in the concept of the rule of law (Shihata 2000, 272–3). Thus, the WB definition of governance does not associate the rule of law with democracy or with any particular type of political system or government. Only a system of rules and institutions is considered an important prerequisite for developing market economies (Shihata 1991, 87). Finally, it should be recalled that the activity of the WB to strengthen governance in developing countries is financial and technical assistance through a variety of lending instruments.

Conclusions

This chapter confirms that the EU adopts a single strategy of democracy promotion towards accession candidate countries, potential candidates and ENP partners. The same strategy however is adapted to each case along four main dimensions, with institutional links and economic assistance as incentives to be offered, and conditionality and socialization as key mechanisms of democratic anchoring. The existing differences can be explained taking into consideration: (1) the different degrees of acceptance by each case of EU principles and practices; and (2) their prospects for membership.

The analysis of the institutional links has shown that the promise of membership to Romania, Turkey (from 1999[32] until 2005), and Serbia (since 2000) should have been more powerful than the promise of association to Ukraine, to make Romania, Turkey and Serbia comply with the EU's requirements to strengthen the democratic rule of law. However, the date of accession has been close in time only in the case of Romania (2007), as for Turkey the envisaged year has been at least 2014, while Serbia still has to negotiate a SAP. Therefore, on the basis of the analysis on institutional links done in this chapter, it can be expected that the promise of membership was more powerful in removing domestic obstacles to the adoption of democratic rule of law reforms only in the case of Romania, as it was granted a date of accession much closer in time than Turkey or Serbia.[33]

The section on economic assistance has shown that the EU is the main donor for three of our four cases, with the exception of Ukraine – for whom the main donor is the United States – and that Serbia has been since 2000 the country allocated the largest amount of EU assistance per capita. This means that in order to sanction a country that has not complied with the EU's political conditions, a decrease in terms of the EU's economic assistance allocated should be much more effective in the case of Romania, Serbia and Turkey than in the case of Ukraine, for whom the EU is not the first donor. However, it should be that noted that, unlike the Romanian case, Serbia and Turkey can also count on other significant amounts of economic assistance from the United States and Japan, respectively. As far as the distribution of EU's

Table 3.13 First three sectors of EU assistance 2002–05 (million € per year)

Sector	*Serbia*	*Turkey*	*Romania*	*Ukraine*
1st sector of EU assistance	Energy (52.52)	Economic and social cohesion (63.53)	Economic and social cohesion (138.4)	Institutional, legal and administrative reform (27.37)
2nd sector of EU assistance	Infrastructure and transport (19.87)	Public administration (29.78)	Approximation to the *acquis* (108.05)	Private sector and economic development (18.12)
3rd sector of EU assistance	Local administration (19.75)	Approximation to the *acquis* (29.51)	Political criteria (37.12)	Small projects programmes (10.25)

Source: Data from previous tables (my compilation).

economic assistance is concerned, it is possible to state that only in the case of Ukraine was the first sector of EU economic assistance linked to the dimensions of the democratic rule of law. For Serbia, Turkey and Romania, sectors of EU assistance close to the dimensions of the democratic rule of law come only in second or third position (see Table 3.13). Indeed, for Serbia the first sector of EU assistance was energy, and for both Turkey and Romania it was economic and social cohesion. However, it should be observed that, in the same period (2002–05), while in the case of Ukraine the amount of EU assistance allocated for 'institutional, legal and administrative reform' was only 27.37 million euros each year, assistance allocated to Serbia for 'energy' was 52.52 million euros each year, and that to Turkey and Romania for 'economic and social cohesion' was 63.53 and 138.4 million euros each year, respectively.

It has been assumed that in order to have a positive impact on third countries, the EU's democratic conditionality has to be concretely applied, which means that conditionality has to be determinate, monitored, and rewarded or sanctioned. In all our cases, democratic conditionality has been sufficiently determinate, as political priorities have been listed in the Accession Partnerships for Romania and Turkey, in the European Partnerships for Serbia, and in the ENP Action Plan for Ukraine. Moreover, in the field of human rights, the Union has made constant reference to democratic European and international standards, and the requirements of the EU have been further clarified through the annual monitoring of progress by the European Commission. In fact, the European Commission has started to monitor the progress accomplished by each country in satisfying the EU's democratic conditionality – since 1998 for Romania, 2001 for Turkey, 2002 for Serbia and 2006 for Ukraine. Then, it has been shown that respect for the political conditionality has been rewarded by the EU, advancing the process of becoming closer to the Union and allocating a larger amount of EU economic assistance, and that lack of respect for the democratic conditionality has been sanctioned, through total suspension of SAA negotiations in the case

Table 3.14 Total of EU assistance allocated to sectors relevant for the democratic rule of law 2001–05 (million € per year)

Sector	*Serbia*	*Turkey*	*Romania*	*Ukraine*
Institutional, legal and administrative reform	Not present	Not present	Not present	27.37
Political criteria	Not present	20.2	37.12	Not present
Local administration	19.75	Not present	Not present	Not present
Public administration	19.05	29.78	15.19	Not present
Justice and home affaire	5	7.15	Not present	Not present
Civil society and media	5.55	Not present	Not present	Not present
Civil society dialogue and support for European integration	Not present	13.85	Not present	Not present
Return/reintegration of refugees and IDPs	5.37	Not applicable	Not applicable	Not applicable
TOTAL	54.72	70.98	52.31	27.37
TOTAL per capita	6.84 euro	1.01	2.37	0.57

Source: Data from previous tables (my compilation).

of Serbia, or partial suspension of accession negotiations, in the case of Turkey. On the basis of these findings, it is possible to conclude that – with the sole exception of Ukraine[34] – the EU's implentation of democratic conditionality for Romania, Serbia and Turkey should have contributed to removing domestic obstacles to the adoption of democratic rule of law reforms.

Table 3.14 shows that Serbia is the country that has been allocated, per capita, the largest amount of EU assistance in the sectors close to the dimensions of democratic rule of law, with an annual average between 2002–05 of about 7 euros, followed by Romania, with about 2 euros, Turkey, with about 1 euro, and Ukraine with about half a euro. On this basis, it could be concluded that the EU's assistance should have had a more relevant impact, in terms of socialization with democratic rule of law, in the case of Serbia, as it was allocated the largest amount of EU assistance for projects concerning the dimensions of the democratic rule of law, and in the case of Romania, for projects aiming at strengthening its democratic rule of law date back to 1999, rather than 2001 or 2002. However, it has to be underlined, firstly that the amount of EU assistance allocated to projects dealing with the five dimensions of democratic rule of law can be different from the amount of assistance actually paid, and secondly that only impact evaluations for each single project can really assess the influence of the projects financed by the EU on socialization with democratic rule of law.

The final section has demonstrated that, unlike other international actors, the EU's strategy of democratic rule of law promotion in Romania, Serbia, Turkey and Ukraine is based not only on socialization with the EU's democratic rule of law principles and practices but also on applied conditionality.

Notes

1 Indeed, control and democratic example or emulation are less applicable than conditionality and socialisation to the anchoring of the EU, as the Union does not impose democracy – at least with the use of force – and as the dynamic of example and emulation may also occur without the activity of democracy promotion of an external actor. This is the basic reason why in this chapter I focus on conditionality and socialization, and leave out control and democratic example or emulation.

2 This is an association agreement. Its main feature is the creation of a customs union, and it foresees the possibility of membership of the Community (see art. 28 of the Ankara Agreement).

3 It seems that the establishment of the customs union with Turkey has led to misunderstandings about membership, on both sides. On the one hand, the EU hoped that Turkey would have started to commit itself to the implementation of the customs union, without pushing for the moment on membership. On the other hand, the Turkish authorities thought that the customs union was a fundamental step towards membership, which should have occurred within two years (Arikan 2003, 82).

4 It seems that the Helsinki decision to extend the status of candidate country to Turkey was the result of a series of diplomatic compromises to avoid a crisis with the United States (Dorronsoro 2004, 50).

5 Official Development Assistance (ODA) is defined as those flows of funds to developing countries and multilateral institutions provided by official agencies, including state and local governments, or by their executive agencies, each transaction of which meets the following tests: (i) it is administered with the promotion of the economic development and welfare of developing countries as its main objective; and (ii) it is concessional in character and conveys a grant element of at least 25 per cent.

6 In this chapter we adopt the term EU economic assistance or aid, even though when not differently specified, we refer only to the European Community's economic assistance or aid.

7 The European Agency for Reconstruction is an independent agency of the EU, accountable to the Council and the European Parliament and overseen by a Governing Board composed of representatives from the 25 EU Member States and the European Commission. The Agency works within the Community Assistance for Reconstruction, Development and Stabilisation (CARDS) Programme, a wider EU commitment, which also includes Albania, Bosnia & Herzegovina and Croatia, and which is part of the EU's SAP. The EAR also manages the EU's main assistance programs in the former Yugoslav Republic of Macedonia.

8 According to the European Agency for Reconstruction Report of 12 June 2006 Serbia was allocated, in million euros, 185.1 in 2001, 167.7 in 2002, 231.9 in 2003, 197.8 in 2004, and 143.8 in 2005.

9 According to the Directorate General Enlargement of the European Commission, EU pre-accession assistance allocated to Turkey was, in million euros, 177 in 2000, 147 in 2001, 126 in 2002, 144 in 2003, 235.6 in 2004, 300 in 2005 and 500 in 2006.

10 Total commitments for the period 1990–96 were 731 million ECU.

11 Moreover, alongside the PHARE Programme, it comprises, from the year 2000, aid for agriculture, through SAPARD, and a structural instrument to give priority to measures similar to those of the Cohesion Fund for environment and transport, through ISPA.

12 According to the Directorate General Enlargement of the European Commission, Romania was allocated, in million euros, 55.2 in 1999, 215.02 in 2000, 248.89 in 2001, 265.5 in 2002, 265.5 in 2003, 405.3 in 2004, 372.29 in 2005, and 408.63 in 2006.

13 Programme for Technical Assistance to the Independent States of the former Soviet Union and Mongolia.

14 In the period 1991–2006 Ukraine was allocated total assistance under the EIDHR of 5.95 million euros, and under the ECHO of 20.5 million euros.

15 In particular, while in the period 1991–2006 Ukraine was allocated a total of 891.6 million euros under the TACIS National Programme, in the same period Ukraine was allocated 621.2 million euros under the TACIS Nuclear Safety component, 40.2 million euros under the TACIS cross border component, and 50 million euros under the TACIS regional component.

16 According to the Directorate External Relations of the European Commission, EU assistance allocated, through TACIS National Programme, to Ukraine was, in million euros, 407 in the period 1991–98, 38.6 in 1999, 48 in 2000, 43 in 2001, 47 in 2002, 50 in 2003, 70 in 2004, 88 in 2005, and 100 in 2006.

17 Data on the TACIS national programmes for Ukraine before 2002 are not available on the website of the EuropeAid Cooperation Office of the European Commission.

18 Appropriate measures instead of the suspension of financial assistance could make a difference. For example, Africa, Caribbean and Pacific countries, as former Soviet Republics, have fiercely opposed a suspension clause in their agreements with the EU, while they could accept the 'appropriate measures' clause.

19 It is the new instrument for Community assistance to ENP partners.

20 The PHARE Programme used to be at the beginning 'demand driven', that is, assistance was provided according to the needs of the transition, as established by the recipient (Rupnik 2000, 125).

21 With the only exceptions of civil freedoms and political rights in the case of Romania, and of civil control of the military in the case of Ukraine.

22 Free movement of goods, right of establishment and freedom to provide services, financial services, agriculture and rural development, fisheries, transport policy, customs union, and external relations.

23 Sources of data on these EU's projects were, for Serbia, the Annual Report 2005 of the European Agency for Reconstruction (12 June 2006), for Romania and Turkey the website of the Directorate General Enlargement of the European Commission, and for Ukraine, the website of the EuropeAid Cooperation Office of the European Commission.

24 Available data do not show the amount of EC assistance distributed for each project, so it is not possible to state what area was given priority.

25 The Jagodin border crossing post is of strategic importance for trade and human flows between Ukraine, Poland and the rest of Europe.

26 However, the CoE can also postpone or suspend membership and these would be clear instances of strict conditionality. For example, Belarus has been strongly criticized by CoE officials, who have repeatedly stated their demand that Belarus show a more convincing record of political reforms before membership can be considered. Then, in 1997 Ukraine was warned that the CoE might suspend its membership of the organization if it failed to abolish capital punishment. But in 1999 the CoE decided to delay its proposed moves to suspend Ukraine's membership over its failure to abolish death penalty, and finally in 2000 the Ukrainian Parliament abolished the death penalty.

27 Romania has been a member of the OSCE since 25 June 1973. Ukraine has been a member of the OSCE since 30 January 1992. In the case of Serbia, the former Yugoslavia was suspended from the organization in 1992. However, after the downfall of Slobodan

Milosevic, in November 2000, the country was readmitted to the organization. Turkey has been a member of the OSCE since 25 June 1973. There is an OSCE mission in Serbia and also an OSCE Project Coordinator in Ukraine (which is the second OSCE field operation to have been established in Ukraine, preceded by the OSCE Mission to Ukraine, which began its work on 24 November 1994). There have been no such permanent field missions of the OSCE in Romania and Turkey.

28 In general, human security entails emancipation from oppressive power structures and the promotion of institutions and practices that embody respect for human rights, fundamental freedoms, democracy and the rule of law.

29 Moreover, the Europe Agreements contain a statement in the preamble reaffirming the commitment of the signatories to the full implementation of all provisions and principles in the OSCE documents. Similar provisions are also included in the SAA and the PCAs, and the ENP, too, requires countries to show commitment to OSCE international norms.

30 Moreover the OSCE values experimental learning which incorporates local values and knowledge.

31 In fact, the main projects of the WB's mission in Romania concern social inclusion, knowledge society, municipal services, but also judicial reform. The main projects of the WB's mission in Serbia dealt with pension reform, energy community of southeast Europe, irrigation and transport rehabilitation. The main projects of the WB's mission in Turkey involve agriculture reform, seismic risk mitigation, and renewable energy. Finally, the main projects of the WB's mission in Ukraine are in export development, cadastre development and hydropower rehabilitation.

32 In the case of Turkey, it has already been affirmed that while following the decision of the Luxemburg European Council of December 1997 the EU's leverage over Turkey diminished (Smith 2003b, 132). Two years later the Helsinki European Council decision represented the external impetus which has encouraged the subsequent process of domestic reforms (Sozen and Shaw 2003, 115; Ugur 2003, 177; Müftüler Bac 2005, 21).

33 Of course, only the empirical analysis of each specific country can either confirm or falsify such an expectation.

34 In the case of Ukraine, the EU's political conditionality has been sufficiently determinate, but periodic monitoring by the European Commission of progress in complying with these conditions has not yet started. Thus, it has not yet been possible to reward the progress achieved by Ukraine or sanction the lack of progress.

4 Romania

Vetoed reforms, skewed results

Ana Demsorean, Sorana Parvulescu, Bogdan Vetrici-Soimu

Introduction

Romania became an EU member in January 2007. While this is a notable success – considering the country's situation back in the late 1980s – accession implied a very slow process of internal transformations and democratic rule of law reforms. The continuous predominance of former Communist elites and their reluctance to promote significant reforms during the first years of transition led to the emergence and consolidation of strong veto players that opposed any meaningful reform for years. Consequently, Romania remained a laggard in its transition to democracy and EU integration, compared with other post-Communist countries that joined the EU in 2004.

The objective of this chapter is to assess the mechanisms through which democratic rule of law reform was eventually introduced and implemented in Romania in the five main areas studied by this project: protection of civil freedoms and political rights, judicial independence and capacity, institutional and administrative structures, reforms to combat corruption, and police reform. The analysis will focus on the interplay between international and domestic factors in promoting or obstructing democratic rule of law reform in these five key areas, and test the EUCLIDA model described in the second chapter of this book. In particular, the chapter will try to assess the impact of the EU in promoting such reforms in Romania as a former candidate country for EU accession. The conditionality imposed by other external actors, such as the Council of Europe or the United States will also be highlighted in those areas of reform, in which their influence has been significant.

As expected, there is no single configuration of internal and external actors that have facilitated rule of law reforms in all the areas under study. On the contrary; progress, stagnation or backlash of reforms occurred at specific moments in time as a result of different patterns of interaction between international and domestic factors. This chapter will try to illustrate the variety of such mechanisms by showing how different pockets of reforms have been enacted under different sets of conditions. Given the strong influence of initial conditions derived from Romania's cumbersome Communist legacy on most of its transition, the time span of the analysis will spread from 1989, the year of the collapse of the Communist regime until the end of 2006, when some reforms are still being pursued and the country has become a member of EU.

In order to design a framework for discussion, the chapter will start by drawing a brief general picture of domestic politics and EU accession, as the two main factors accounting for Romania's transition since 1989. Based on these two dimensions, the rest of the chapter will explain how democratic rule of law reforms have been enacted throughout this period and will test the accuracy of the EUCLIDA model against the reality of Romania's recent track record of rule of law reforms.

Domestic politics

Post-1989 Romanian politics have long been seen as 'exceptional' (Linz & Stepan 1996) compared with the other post-Communist countries in Central and Eastern Europe. Indeed, Romania was the only country in the accession process to have had three post-Communist governments out of the first four full cabinet terms after 1989. Despite the violent revolutionary events in December 1989, regime change in Romania occurred more through 'bridging' than through 'breaking' with the Communist past, as Bunce (1998) would put it: despite changing names and faking a pluralist democracy, former Communist elites – including parts of the former secret services (*Securitate*) – managed to hold on to power throughout the transition and gained a disproportionate power over the society (Mungiu-Pippidi 2006).

The early stage of reforms for establishing the rule of law was significantly distorted by the violent political crisis in June 1991, when thousands of miners came to Bucharest at President Iliescu's request to 'restore order', storming the headquarters of opposition political parties and universities and beating up the youngsters demonstrating in the Universitate square against the Iliescu regime. International reactions were strong: the European Community immediately froze economic assistance and postponed the signing of a trade cooperation agreement; Romania was also refused membership of the Visegrad group (Pridham 2007a). Iliescu eventually understood the importance of foreign assistance and the disadvantage of being internationally isolated and appointed pro-reformist Petre Roman as prime minister. However, as soon as Roman's Western-oriented ministers announced sweeping economic reforms, miners returned to Bucharest to oust the Roman government in September 1991 (Gallagher 2005). These clear breaches of rule of law and democratic order dismissed any hopes that reforms in Romania would be quick and successful. Romania was thrown into international isolation until 1996.

During those years post-Communist institutions operated within the framework of procedural democracy, but, in practice, the rules and norms accepted in the West as attributes of liberal democracy were often broken. Public opinion was either too weak, too divided, or simply too indifferent to demand more accountability. The Vacaroiu government (1992–6) constantly delayed any meaningful economic and political reforms. Slow and partial economic reforms led to the continuing impoverishment of the poorest groups (Hellman 1998),[1] but allowed a small group closely connected to the government to enrich themselves and gain control over both politics and the economy, by benefiting from the lack of clear and impartial laws.[2]

After Iliescu and his party lost elections in 1996 due to rampant corruption and poor economic performance, a loose and ineffective anti-Communist coalition (CDR – Romanian Democratic Convention[3]) entered office in 1996. Given its inner fragmentation, the CDR proved incapable of finalizing almost any reform, although it started several of them. The coalition was weak in combating corruption even among its own members[4] and the 1997 economic crisis, which brought the country on the verge of bankruptcy, put an end to any realistic hope that Romania may still catch up with other post-Communist candidate countries in its efforts to join the EU.

Four years later, Ion Iliescu and his renovated party (renamed the Social Democratic Party – PSD) returned to power. By that time the country had already clearly entered the accession path, since accession negotiations had started in spring 2000. The PSD was thus left to put through the needed reforms in the shortest time possible. This was not the case, however, and many of the legislative packages initiated by the former government were put aside. The progress registered due to EU pressure, as well as due to the government's need to keep the appearances of progress towards integration, remained limited to passing formal legislation, while avoiding or delaying implementation. As an example, the government created in 2001 a special Ministry for European Integration. One of the main attributions of this ministry was to coordinate the relations between the other ministries and institutions, on the one hand, and European institutions, on the other hand. It was also in charge of leading and coordinating the activity of the National Delegation for the Negotiation of Romania's accession; of submitting to the Government periodical reports regarding the negotiations; and, generally, of all issues regarding Romania's accession. However, apart from its formal coordination role, the newly created ministry was unable to play a decisive role in designing or implementing reforms.

Meanwhile, corruption was again on the rise and the PSD was capturing state institutions, sparing no effort to strengthen its position with regard to future elections.[5] These efforts included recruiting local mayors and local council members from other parties[6] and exercising tight control over the media[7] and over the judiciary. This attitude continued to encourage the consolidation of a powerful informal anti-reformist structure within the Romanian administration at all levels, which obstructed the implementation of any important legislation. The government was ticking off issues on the list of the European Commission by issuing laws and regulations, but failed to create the mechanisms needed to enforce those laws.

Consequently, a general mistrust ensued in Brussels with regard to promises made by government officials, as it became clear that the *acquis* negotiations and conditionality had not been sufficient to promote democratic rule of law (Pridham 2006). In 2004, before general elections, the Commission added in the Accession Treaty a postponement safeguard clause, which threatened to delay accession by one year unless serious progress with the reform of the judiciary and the anti-corruption fight was registered.[8]

The November 2004 elections, though highly criticized for serious breaches of laws and allegations of electoral frauds (Parvulescu 2004), brought an alteration in power. The Justice and Truth Alliance (DA) (the National Liberal Party – PNL and the Democrat Party – PD) managed to form a fragile coalition together with the Hungarian party (Democratic Alliance of Hungarians in Romania – UDMR) and the small Romania Humanist Party (PUR).[9] After the DA coalition took office, the situation in terms of rule of law reform significantly improved, despite continuous bickering among governing parties. The strong commitment to EU accession of some of the ministers, coupled with the threat posed by the postponement safeguard clause, convinced politicians to go ahead with necessary reforms. Nevertheless, despite its goodwill, the government continued to face serious obstacles in passing and implementing necessary reforms, as these have stumbled in a fierce resistance of the Parliament, which acts today as the most serious veto power against reform.

EU accession

During the early transition period, president Iliescu and his acolytes expressed resistance to the idea of joining Europe and promoted an alternative model of an 'original democracy' and a social market economy. However, it soon became clear that their project was badly failing as people were growing impatient with the lack of economic performance. At the same time, the international isolation, in which Iliescu had thrown the country as a result of his nationalist and undemocratic behavior, was not paying off, as the government needed Western money in order to maintain political legitimacy.

Consequently, the Romanian political establishment gradually switched towards EU accession. Accession was presented to the public as the ultimate goal of transition and the reward for all sacrifices required to that end. The general public mistrust in all that was Russian played in to enforce this ideal and legitimize it, and so did reiterated promises of economic prosperity and prestige. EU integration thus became the most prominent national interest; the idea was gradually embraced by all political parties (Pridham, 2007b); and no other alternative for the future of the country has been seriously considered ever since.

Civil freedoms and political rights

By 1989, the personalistic regime of Ceausescu had turned Romania into a closed centralized system, in which civil freedom and political rights remained completely foreign concepts. While in other countries of the

Communist block, such as Hungary or Poland, some forms of civil society or private ownership were already in place by the collapse of the regime, in Romania the Communist Party maintained complete control over the society, and civil and political rights were blatantly disregarded.

The fall of the Communist regime in 1989 triggered some immediate changes in this respect by making possible (*ad hoc*) freedom of speech and freedom of association, the opening up of the political competition and free elections. However, these immediate changes needed to be enforced by adequate legislation, complemented by a complete overhaul of the relations between the citizen and the state. This proved to be a long and complicated process. In some areas, such as the abolition of the death penalty, sweeping reform was possible during the very early transition, without any international pressure. Other issues, such as that of minority rights, albeit raised by domestic forces, were impossible to settle internally, and were developed through piecemeal reforms under international pressure, rather than through the socialization of relevant stakeholders. Lastly, issues such as child adoption were both raised and settled mainly through strict international monitoring and European conditionality.

Today, the Romanian legislation is largely in line with European standards on civil and political rights, although the enforcement of such legislation remains inadequate in certain areas.

No more death penalty

One of the few instances of genuine domestically driven change in the history of post-Communist transition in Romania was the abolition of death penalty.[10] This was done on 7 January 1990 – just a couple of weeks after the former dictator Ceausescu and his wife were sentenced to death by a military court after a short and superficial trial. Amid the power vacuum created by the toppling of the regime, i.e. in the absence of any government or parliament in charge, the law was adopted as the expression of a general desire to symbolically break with the Communist past, but also possibly thanks to the eagerness of the new elite to ensure that they would not face Ceausescu's fate in case something went wrong.

Ethnic minority rights: different standards for different minorities

Solving the question of minority rights has been a long and difficult task for post-Communist Romania. Discrimination of almost all minority groups, from ethnic groups to women or homosexuals was widely practiced in Romania during early transition by a society, which had not yet developed into a fully tolerant and open one. Moreover, the political class was itself marked by pronounced nationalist and xenophobic rhetoric, as political parties found it easy to capitalize on the Romanian electorate on such grounds (Linden, 2000). Former president Iliescu was famous for his nationalistic speeches and was one of the fiercest opponents of any law that might have broadened the rights of minority groups, especially those of Hungarians in Romania. Hence, the Romanian society and political elite were not ready to promote minority rights and these have been advocated ever since the early 1990s by a wide range of international actors, especially the Organisation for Security and Cooperation in Europe (OSCE), the Council of Europe, Hungary, and the European Union (Kelley 2004b).

The story of granting and enforcing ethnic minorities' rights is perhaps the most telling in this respect. There are two important ethnic groups in Romania: the Hungarian community – estimated at 6.6 percent of the population of Romania by the 2002 Census; and the Roma community – roughly estimated at 2.5 percent of the population.[11] Although at first sight one might expect similar developments in the case of both groups, this was clearly not the case. On the one hand, Hungarians in Romania managed to gradually obtain significant minority rights and even created a strong ethnic party that has been part of all government coalitions since 1996.[12] On the other hand, the Roma population is still subject to serious discrimination on the part of both public institutions and the society in its own. As such, the situation of the Roma remained on the agenda of international actors – especially the EU – until today.

The causes of such divergent developments may be traced by looking at both domestic and international actors that have played a role in the matter. Domestically, the Hungarian community has always been much more mobilized than the Roma population. Early on during transition the Hungarian community organized itself into an ethnic political party (UDMR), which has been actively involved in promoting its rights and interests at the level of central government ever since. At international level, neighboring Hungary raised the issue on the Western agenda by voicing concerns about the preservation of the rights of their kinsmen in Romania and backing the UDMR whenever necessary (Linden, 2000). In 1990 the UDMR had already started to demand greater cultural freedom, including the re-establishment of Hungarian-language schools. The catalysts for attracting huge international attention on the issue were the ethnic clashes in March 1990 between Romanians and Hungarians in the Transylvanian city of Targu Mures (HRW World Report 1990). The Council of Europe went as far as to delay Romania's membership due to concerns, among others, about how minorities' problems were solved by the Romanian government.[13] The OSCE was also highly critical on this issue (Jackson Preece 1998). By December 1993, the UDMR had forwarded to the Parliament a draft law on minorities, but the general political opposition to the idea of granting minority rights made the adoption of the law impossible for years, despite strong international criticism. On the contrary, the PDSR (Party of Social Democracy in Romania) government in early 1995 signed a protocol with two extremist nationalist parties (Kelley 2004b). Only after the 1996 change in government, when the UDMR became part of the government coalition, certain legal aspects related to minority rights were gradually passed. By 1998, the European Commission stated in its first regular report that 'In general terms, the protection of minorities in Romania remains satisfactory, with the major exception of the Roma.' (European Commission Report 1998). Furthermore, in 2000, the EU managed to push the newly elected PSD in a coalition with the UDMR, making it clear that any association with extremist parties would be detrimental to the country's accession perspectives (Gallagher 2005).

Altogether, it might be argued that the Hungarian minority was sufficiently organized – and received considerable external support – to fight for its own rights. The UDMR was able to use linkage strategies and negotiate its priorities within subsequent government coalitions. At the same time, the Hungarian minority benefited from the relative geographical concentration of members of their community in certain regions in Romania. This made the enforcement of adopted laws less difficult, as local authorities in areas with a Hungarian majority were often themselves of Hungarian nationality and thus more inclined to enforce minority rights legislation.

The case of the Roma minority did not follow a similar pattern. Roma were much less organized, were geographically spread throughout the territory of Romania and lacked resources to fight for their rights on a scale similar to those of Hungarians.[14] More than that, members of the Roma community were relatively less educated and had no support from an outside patron. Therefore, the role of international actors (both intergovernmental and nongovernmental) has been much more pronounced in this case, but success remained rather limited to this date. In terms of rule adoption, the Roma community benefited from the pressure of the Hungarian community, as most minority-related laws referred to all ethnic groups, not only the Hungarian one. However, the biggest problem remains the low level of implementation and internalization of such legislation with respect to the Roma community, as its members continue to be discriminated against by both ordinary people and civil servants, while their integration in the society remains very low (UNDP Report 2006). This situation remained almost unchanged over the years, despite continuous EU pressure. Throughout all its monitoring reports, from 1998 to 2005, the Commission has criticized Roma discrimination and advocated measures to improve the situation. Subsequent governments designed national frameworks and created institutions to deal with the matter, but progress was limited (Romani Crisis Report 2006). This was due to both weak administrative capacity and lack of political will to empower such institutions and make them effective, but most essentially, to the widespread anti-Roma sentiments among the Romanian society at large. According to a survey conducted in Romania by Center for Urban and Regional Sociology (CURS) in December 2005 for the Anti-Discrimination National Council, 81 percent of the interviewed people consider that 'most of the Roma population break the law', 61 percent agree that 'Romania is ashamed with the Roma' and about 50 percent of the interviewed people say they are afraid when they meet a group of Roma on the street.[15] It follows from this that EU conditionality was ineffective when it came to altering recurrent behaviors and mentalities, as formal laws and institutions were unable to address such problems overnight.

The parallel process of socialization of the key stakeholders involved in improving the situation of ethnic minorities has had only limited success: indeed, increased levels of donor funds since 1998–2000 led to the launch of numerous programs aimed at integrating the Roma population within the Romanian society, but assessments of the effectiveness of such programs show that success was only partial, at best. In many cases, the benefits of these programs, as well as of the general improvement of the legislative framework promoting the rights of Roma as an ethnic group, have been distributed unevenly, with some sections of the Roma community taking the lion's share of the advantages of these programs and laws.[16] Given that donor funds for stopping discrimination of Roma are widely available, local councils have learned to present themselves as having troubles with discrimination in order to become eligible to access this rich pool of funds (Bunescu 2007, 16).[17]

Moreover, it appears that those Roma who are the most educated, urbanized and financially independent often identify themselves as Romanians, and do not see themselves as Roma anymore. (See National Democratic Institute for International Affairs 2003, 4).

In conclusion, these two cases show that international pressures were effective when complemented by strong domestic change agents that were able to tilt the cost–benefit balance in favor of their interests; but less effective in the absence of change agents and when the problem was more a matter of structural societal issues, rather than political will; while socialization did not manage to significantly tilt the balance in favour of these groups or raise the level of rule internalization.

To stop or not to stop international adoptions

The international adoption of children from Romanian orphanages remains a highly controversial issue, which sets the country at the center of contradicting pressures coming from different international actors. From 2000 onwards, the EU has put serious pressure on Romania to ban international adoptions, which were seen as being against the interest and wellbeing of orphan children. The European Parliament, through its then-*rapporteur* for Romania, Baroness Nicholson of Winterbourne, raised the loudest voice in this respect. In May 2001 the Baroness issued a very critical report pointing out to the poor treatment of children in Romanian orphanages, as well as to the risks associated with inter-country adoptions of these children. The report accused Romanian officials of making financial gains by selling children on the international black market and warned with the suspension of accession negotiations. The report placed the issue at the top of the agenda of European institutions in their dealings with Romania. As a reaction to these pressures, the Romanian government imposed a moratorium in 2001 banning international adoptions. In 2004 the pressure coming from Brussels reached its peak when Enlargement Commissioner Guenther Verheugen warned Bucharest that it might not be considered as fulfilling the political criteria for accession unless it solves the issue of international adoptions satisfactorily (Tomiuc 2004). Consequently, in 2004 a law on child adoption was voted by the Parliament and entered into force in 2005.[18] The law makes internal adoptions a priority and allows international adoptions only in those cases where internal adoption is not possible. The EU requirements have thus been fully met.

The crisis continued, nevertheless, since EU pressures were counterbalanced by protests against this law, coming mostly from the US and Canada, but also from some European states such as Italy, Spain and France.[19] Moreover, the European Parliament in 2006 issued a resolution, which advocated for resuming international adoptions, based on the improvement of adoption mechanisms in light of the new legislation. The government has refused acceptance of this request.[20]

The case of international adoptions shows therefore that international actors can sometimes yield opposing influences and send contradictory signals to national governments. Responding positively to EU conditionality induced considerable costs for Romania in terms of its relationship with the US and other countries interested in adoptions. Nevertheless, this was a clear case of successful international pressure, where the EU forced the Romanian authorities to weigh the costs of not taking such a measure and risk accession against the costs of worsening other bilateral relations and possibly cutting the benefits they received through questionable international adoptions. The fact that the EU directly linked the issue of child adoption to the possible suspension of accession negotiations is likely to have been crucial in convincing the government to make the required decision.

Judicial independence

The reform of judiciary was, and to some extent still is, one of the most controversial and lengthiest reforms in post-Communist Romania. Before 1989 the legal system was completely politicized, as both prosecutors and judges were subject to political commands. The judiciary was mostly used as a mechanism for the repression of ordinary citizens, rather than for defending their rights, while the entire activity of the judiciary was enveloped in a culture of secrecy and arbitrariness. Moreover, since private property and businesses did not exist, entire bodies of legislation, such as commercial law or intellectual property were non-existent as well. This also meant that ordinary people had little contact with the judiciary, and thus no exercise of challenging their rights in courts. As expected, the effect of such a politicized and opaque system on the broader society was a complete lack of public trust in the institution of judiciary and rule of law in general.

The task of reforming the judiciary proved exceptionally difficult in Romania, due to a general lack of political will to promote reform. Subsequent governments were reluctant to reform the system, since they used the judiciary to control the society, intimidate political opponents, and keep silent about their Communist past. Apart from minor procedural changes concerning the organization of the judiciary, there were no significant efforts towards a radical reform during this period. It was only as late as 1998 that the centre-right coalition government drafted a more comprehensive legislative package on the reform of judiciary, but no significant progress was made. Reforms only resumed during the PSD government in 2003–04 under strong pressure from the EU, but even then formality remained the norm, while rigorous implementation never occurred. The most comprehensive package of judiciary reforms was put in place only in 2005–06 by the newly elected, pro-reformist centre-right government, under the pressure of the EU postponement safeguard clause and thanks to the commitment of the new minister of justice.

Nobody's against increased salaries …

The increase of magistrates' salaries might be portrayed as a success story in terms of judicial reform in Romania. During early transition, magistrates and the judiciary were seen as integral part of the Romanian civil service and were thus paid meager salaries. This situation made magistrates vulnerable to corruption and also generated a brain drain of skilled people to other legal professions. The EU had actively advocated for the increase of their salaries in order to offset such trends (European Commission Report 1998; 2003). As a result, salaries were increased in several stages, starting with 1996 and until today.[21] At this point, magistrates are by far the best remunerated personnel working for a public institution in Romania.

In this case, conditionality worked for two reasons. On the one hand, the determinacy of requirements was rather high and the effects were easily measurable. On the other hand, and most importantly, the magistrates did not oppose these measures, since they were the main beneficiaries of the salary increases. In terms of cost–benefit analysis, the government was ready to offer such increases in order to meet both the EU requirements and get the support of certain groups within the judiciary, even if this was sometimes done at the expense of reduced funds allocated to other reform areas.

But when it comes to serious reform …

The issue of judiciary independence has haunted Romania for more than a decade after the fall of Communism. During most of the early transition, the judiciary was formally kept under the control of government, i.e. the Ministry of Justice, which directly influenced judicial appointments. Moreover, the General Prosecutor had the right to file extraordinary appeals against final judgments in both criminal and civil cases, at his/her own initiative or if requested by the Minister of Justice.

The European Commission raised serious concerns on these matters and asked for substantial reforms aimed at granting independence to the judiciary, not least because this situation seriously affected another essential area of reform – the fight against corruption. Since reform had been slow and inconsistent, in 2004 the Commission included this requirement as a top priority in the postponement safeguard clause.[22] This reinforced the credibility of conditionality and made the national government understand that accession might be delayed unless substantial reform was implemented.

At the same time, elections took place in 2004 and a new centre-right pro-reform government took office. The new minister of justice, Monica Macovei, a former civil society activist and human rights lawyer for the Council of Europe, was supported by an important section of civil society, as well as by the President of Romania, who had won elections on a ticket of fighting corruption and getting Romania into the EU by 2007. Despite the corroboration of all these change agents and external conditionality, reforms were not an easy matter, as veto players mobilized themselves very efficiently to maintain the status quo. The most important opponents to reform proved to be the PSD – the main Communist successor party, and conservative magistrates from within the Superior Council of Magistracy and the Constitutional Court.

Rule adoption in itself was difficult. In July 2005, the government revised the three-law package on the reform of justice: the Law on the Supreme Council of the Magistracy (SCM), the Law on the Organization of the Judiciary and the Law on the Statute of Magistrates.[23] These revisions were aimed at clearly defending the judiciary from government interference and transforming the SCM into an independent body, capable of administering the judiciary on its own. The package had received the approval the European Commission. Although the government had a deadline from the EU for May–June 2005 to pass the laws, the SCM postponed discussing the legislative package and then rejected two out of the three revised laws.[24] In response, the government took the package to the Parliament and assumed responsibility for it. The process was delayed again for one and a half month, as several actors blocked the passing of the laws. Firstly, the opposition PSD filed a motion against the government and then attacked the procedure in front of the Constitutional Court. Secondly, members of the High Court of Cassation and Justice attacked the contents of the laws before the Constitutional Court. Four articles of these laws were contested, and all four were related to the status of members of the SCM and especially to those older members holding key positions in the judiciary.[25] All four articles were declared unconstitutional by the Constitutional Court, although there were no clear grounds for the decision. This did not come as a big surprise, however, considering that the composition of the court was clearly conservative and consisted mainly of close PSD allies.[26] The respective articles would have directly affected some of the people that attacked the laws, since they were members of the SCM, while holding management positions in courts. Eventually, the laws were passed without the four controversial articles.

The European Commission and the Minister of Justice continue to argue that holding dual mandates as full-time members of SCM and court presidents or heads of prosecutor's offices might lead to conflicts of interests (European Commission Report 2005).

This was a clear showcase of forces at work when reform incurs costs for strong interest groups within the society. On the one hand, the EU as an international actor – as well as the Justice Minister, the President and the civil society – as change agents, actively promoted rule adoption, arguing that the costs of failing to reform and having accession delayed were too high. On the other hand, veto players whose privileges were at stake, including the former ruling party and the older echelon within the magistracy, did not hesitate to oppose reform and use any institutional instruments at hand to that aim. Rule adoption was, therefore, problematic in itself and a very lengthy process. Due to this uneven process of rule adoption, implementation only occurred gradually (e.g. the SCM was created in 1992 through the Law 92/1992 on the organization of the judiciary, but was only granted independence in 2005). At the same time, the internalization of the independence of the judiciary appears to lag behind considerably among all layers of the society, but especially so among politicians. The larger public continues to show low level of trust in the judiciary, considering it corrupt and under the influence of politics – according to the 2006 Eurobarometer for Romania, only 26 percent of the country's population trusts the judiciary, which is much lower than the average level for the new member states (34 percent) and that of the EU-15 (48 percent).[27] Magistrates, on their part, do not seem to be much more convinced of the independence of the judiciary either according to two consecutive surveys conducted by the Romanian chapter of Transparency International in 2005 and 2006 among Romanian magistrates.[28] 24 percent of the magistrates interviewed in 2005 (and 30 percent in 2006) admitted there had been attempts to influence their decision on court cases, which serves as a good indication that the belief by which magistrates should be left to do their job independently is not yet widely internalized with public institutions. These attempts were made mostly by political parties, the head of a superior court, local authorities, and the Ministry of Justice. According to the same survey, over 60 percent of the magistrates interviewed in 2006 said that there were still political pressures on magistrates on how to rule on specific cases.

It is interesting to note from the same studies that the socialization of magistrates at international conferences of training sessions is not viewed as a source of increasing the independence of the judiciary. Quite on the contrary, 15 percent of the magistrates interviewed in 2005 said that they have encountered situations in which the independence of certain magistrates was (negatively) affected by participation in such programs abroad. According to focus groups conducted during the same surveys, magistrates view the participation at such events as a sort of compensation to certain magistrates who were willing to 'cooperate' and let themselves be influenced in certain court rulings.

In conclusion of these first two sections, one can argue that Romania has remained for a long time at halfway between a true democracy and a state of incipient democracy in terms of human rights and judicial independence. While most civil and political rights were enshrined in the constitution and subsequent legislation, they often remained dead letter, as nobody cared to enforce it. Although rule adoption had occurred in most cases, implementation remained behind due to lack of political will to enforce rights and weak administrative capacity to implement legislative changes. Moreover, rule internalization remained very poor, due to a general lack of public awareness about human rights, public mistrust of the judicial system, and the weakness of civil society throughout most of the first decade of transition.

A positive trend is emerging, however. Romania seems to be moving towards a more consolidated democracy, as improvements in the enforcement of human rights, as well as the quality of the judicial act, have accelerated during the past two years. In terms of human rights, pressures coming from international organizations (EU, Council of Europe, OSCE), transnational NGOs (Human Rights Watch, Amnesty International), as well as the efforts of the administration and the civil society, have started to bear fruit: minority relations have improved, anti-discrimination mechanisms have been put in place, the number of police abuses has decreased, and the treatment of children has significantly improved. In terms of granting independence to the judiciary and making it effective, the results of recent reforms are still to be seen in the near future. Consequently, Romania is on its way to escape the quasi-democratic regime, in which it has been trapped for a decade, and establish a more comprehensive democratic regime.

Institutional and administrative capacity

Building accountable, democratic institutions and reshaping the administration in post-Communist Romania was a difficult task given the highly politicized system put in place by the previous regime. Two main Communist legacies affected in a negative way the development of new democratic structures during early transition.

First, the overlap between the party and state machinery characteristic for Communist bureaucratic systems had created a completely politicized bureaucracy, which mainly served the interests of the Communist party and not those of the citizen. This went hand in hand with a culture of secrecy and opacity, directly opposing the principle of transparency in public life. Further on, the outdated human and technical resources available in the public administration during the early 1990s were incompatible with developing a modern and efficient civil service. Civil servants lacked adequate training to face the new challenges of managing a democratic and capitalist society. They had no foreign language knowledge, no computer literacy and no access to modern management techniques, while technical facilities were rather poor. At the same time, no fair and transparent recruitment and promotion mechanisms were in place and no clear incentives for efficiency were set to encourage initiative and increase attractiveness of such jobs. Therefore, the body of civil servants not only failed to improve until the mid-1990s, but was even worsened by the substantial brain drain of skilled civil servants towards the private sector.

Second, no professional political class existed before 1989, and the highly centralized political regime of Ceausescu did not allow for any divergence of opinions related to the general party line. Furthermore, most of the interwar political elite, which had some parliamentary experience, were decimated during the Communist oppression in the 1960s. This meant that Romania had no experience whatsoever in terms of having an independent and effective Parliament. As a direct consequence, the Parliament has been criticized for its ineffectiveness for most of the transition period.

Reform on these two essential issues was rather slow and had limited success throughout transition. A civil service reform was enacted very late and with significant shortcomings, while the Parliament remains to this day very slow in passing legislation.[29]

Rule by decree or don't rule at all

The lack of Parliamentary efficiency resided essentially in the lengthy procedure of passing laws[30] and the poor quality of legislation. The large size of this institution, complemented by its cumbersome bicameral structure, has made the Parliament unable to keep up with the pace of reforms needed. Moreover, the shortage of qualified support staff has reduced the Parliament's ability to scrutinize legislation. Nongovernmental organizations funded by both the United States and the EU (through the PHARE program) held training sessions and workshops with members of parliament, aiming to improve the quality of the legislative output, but results were rather modest.

Successive governments have blamed the Parliament for not being able to react in due time to legislative initiative and consequently resorted to the practice of 'rule by decree', which has in time become a recurrent pattern. While this practice did speed up the legislative process on many occasions, at the same time it made governments all too powerful, by blurring the separation between the legislative and the executive. This threat placed the issue high on the agenda of the EU throughout accession negotiations.

However, EU conditionality proved contradictory to some extent when asking the government to give up the practice of 'rule by decree'. On the one hand, its concerns regarding excessive use of 'rule by decree' was understandable, since legislative power should be the main responsibility of Parliament in a consolidated democracy. On the other hand, however, meeting conditionality and adoption of the *acquis* required a sustained legislative effort, of which the Parliament was clearly incapable even when the government enjoyed a strong majority. Therefore, the government had to choose between continuing to operate on the basis of a significant number of ordinances in order to meet requirements for accession negotiation or give up this practice and wait until the Parliament would be able to pass all the necessary legislation. The situation got even more complicated under the current legislature. Because of the fragile majority held in Parliament, the new pro-reformist government soon realized that MPs constituted a serious obstacle in passing the legislation required by the EU. The solution was again to rule by decree and assume governmental responsibility for such laws.[31]

Despite the high determinacy of EU conditionality in this case, no solution could be found to address the situation due to the low institutional and administrative capacity of the Parliament. Rule adoption was not a problem in this case, as the Constitution already provided for the separation between the executive and legislative. The problem arose, however, when it came to implementation and, more importantly, internalization: on the one hand, the parliament lacked the institutional and administrative capacity to perform effectively; on the other hand, neither the MPs, nor the governments proved capable to operate efficiently and, respectively, to give up the practice of rule by decree.

The myth of civil service reform

Although the task of civil service reform was enormous after 50 years of Communism during which the party and the bureaucracy were one and the same, reform started very late. Moreover, the government that ruled Romania between 1990 and 1996 managed to transform the civil service into a useful instrument in the hands of those in power by appointing acolytes in key positions and politicizing the public administration even further.

At the same time, international actors did not seem too preoccupied with civil service reform during early transition, so no serious pressure was put on governments in this respect. In the case of EU conditionality, civil service reform did not account for any of the negotiation chapters of the *acquis communautaire*. In the Commission's monitoring reports, the issue of civil service reform was discussed under the broader heading of the Copenhagen political criteria.[32] However, given that Romania has been considered to have fulfilled the political criteria since 1998, no additional emphasis was put on these issues, except in the context of guaranteeing sufficient administrative capacity to absorb EU funds.

In the absence of strong conditionality, rule adoption was very slow and the quality of passed legislation was poor. The first legislative change came as late as November 1999, when a Civil Servants' Statute – Law no. 188/1999 – was finally adopted, after having been blocked in Parliament since 1997. The law had been drafted in 1997, soon after the centre-right coalition took office, in a bid to improve Romania's stance in front of the EU and NATO. Despite good intentions, the law remained stuck in Parliament for two years, due to opposition from politicians on both sides. The law was eventually passed on 8 December 1999, just days ahead of the European Council in Helsinki, which decided upon the beginning of accession negotiations.

Rule adoption, albeit late, was incomplete and brought little progress in terms of rule implementation. The law entered force in 2000 amid election preparations, followed by a change in government during the same year, and later on the government failed to create adequate institutional and administrative capacities to enforce the legislation. The National Agency for Civil Servants (ANFP), which was designed by the law as a guarantor of the Statute, was given only a formal, insubstantial role[33] and remained *de facto* ineffective due to inadequate staffing, unclear responsibilities and because it could not enforce decisions on other state agencies. The 1999 law also failed to address important problems, such as the lack of transparent recruitment mechanisms, poor wages for civil servants and lack of fair and clear rules for promotion and performance monitoring. Perhaps most important, the law failed to set clear limits for the hierarchical subordination within the civil service, which practically meant that civil servants would not benefit from legal protection if they refused compliance with unlawful orders.[34] Despite the European Commission's strong criticism, the revision of the Statute came only as late as 2003.[35] The revised law was included in a broader Anti-corruption Package,[36] for which the government assumed responsibility in Parliament. This package was probably the single most important set of legislation passed by the PSD government under EU pressures during its mandate (2000–04) and included the regulation of conflicts of interest and asset declarations. The revised law failed however again to look into the problems of remuneration and career structures, which required the adoption of other pieces of secondary legislation one year later. Moreover, although the revised statute redefined the responsibilities of the ANFP, it failed to give it enough power to guarantee the observance of the statute[37] and its efficiency remained limited.

A new revision of the Civil Servants' Statute was passed by the Parliament in July 2006, as part of the government program and in line with EU recommendations. The law addresses the shortcomings of previous legislation by clarifying the status, rights and obligations of the civil servants. It also creates a special independent panel to appoint high-level civil servants to assure the depoliticization of appointments.[38]

All these legislative changes have been adopted eventually under serious EU pressure: the 1999 law was adopted under the direct threat of the Helsinki European Council; the 2003 law was part of the long-awaited anti-corruption package lobbied for by the Commission; and the 2006 revisions came just two months before the EC report was to decide whether Romania would join in 2007 or be delayed for one year. Rule adoption was not easy, however, because no government was willing to give up its control over public administration. The balance of costs and benefits was not clearly tilted in favor of reform, since granting the independence of public administration meant losing government control over the bureaucracy. As a result, each party in government delayed reform as much as possible and opted for the reshuffling of the entire establishment once it took office (Romanian Academic Society 2003a). The 2004 Romanian

Civil Service Barometer shows that a 'spectacular renewal of the public administration' occurred after the 2004 local elections, despite the fact that legislation had protected in principle the office of civil servants ever since 1999 (Moraru and Iorga 2004).

Furthermore, rule implementation was made difficult by institutional inertia and vested interests within the system, since the fear of losing their positions made managers reluctant to implement the newly established criteria of recruitment, assessment and promotion. The same 2004 Barometer of Civil Service showed that 70 percent of the civil servants considered that both their managers and colleagues were resistant to change, while 40 percent of them argued that personal connections were essential when looking for a job in the public service. Besides, the lack of adequate administrative capacity, coupled with poor legislative design, made newly created institutions mostly ineffective. An opinion poll conducted in February 2006 by the Alliance of Civil Servants' Unions stated that 90 percent of civil servants believed that the Romanian legislation was generally incoherent, while 86 percent of them said they lacked confidence when applying legal provisions.[39]

Rule internalization was also poor during most of transition, because the mentality of civil servants was difficult to change over night, especially when clientelism and informality remained the norm within the society. Moreover, the wider public remains uneducated regarding the new legislation and is largely unaware of its rights in the relationship with the public administration. According to a study conducted in 2006 by the National Agency for Civil Service (NACS), only 10 percent of Romanians know what to expect from a civil servant and 38 percent of them believe that civil servants include clerks working for private companies.[40]

Consequently, civil service reform is not fully implemented. EU pressure eventually managed to induce rule adoption, despite the lack of political will within subsequent legislatures. However, rule implementation was not that successful due to veto players – embodied by political parties; bureaucratic inertia within the system; and low internalization within the wider public. Furthermore, the low determinacy of conditionality in this area allowed successive governments to pass incomplete laws to check the Commission's list of requirements, but did not specify any clear indicators to assess progress with rule implementation.[41]

In 2004, the government created a series of fast-track career paths, for people working in civil service areas. Among these modalities was the scholarship given by the Romanian Government, for people to study abroad in Western universities for a few years and then return to work in Romania as clerks. Another benefit for these people was the possibility of becoming a Public Manager[42] and to be promoted rapidly and with increased salaries, after completing the public administration Masters studies through the 'Young Professionals Program' (a Master's degree financed by the EU and coordinated by INA, the National Institute of Administration). The program was applauded in the beginning, but difficulties soon ensued with regard to the modality of integrating these people into the Romanian public administration, and paying them the promised salaries. Eventually, many were left out of the system or just employed in lower-grade clerks' positions.

Reform to combat corruption, illegality and abuse of power

Anti-corruption has been a controversial *high politics* issue always and everywhere. This is particularly true for post-Communist countries, where the burden of Communist legacy made this task even more difficult. Widespread corruption plagued Romania after 1989. On the one hand, this was the result of 50 years of Communism, when informality was the rule within a society based on status, and where people close to the power centre were above the law and benefited preferential treatment. On the other hand, the partial character of reforms promoted during early transition led to the creation of a class of initial 'winners' (Hellman 1998), or predatory elites, who managed to gain control over the resources of the state and use them to their own profit. This class of initial winners cut across political ideologies and parties and constituted itself in a group of vested interests capturing the state and opposing any significant reform which would have threatened the status quo.

Although the issue of combating corruption was on the top of the agenda of the EU requirements and was flagged as the priority of future governments in successive rounds of presidential and legislative elections, no significant progress was made until as late as 2005, after the postponement safeguard clause had been introduced into the Accession Agreement. Even then, launching an effective fight against corruption proved exceptionally difficult, as this section will show by analyzing a few episodes of reform.

Stricter asset declarations: A test case for political ideologies in Romania

The history of asset declarations in Romania is a story of veto players fighting for maintaining the status quo. Adoption of legislation regarding asset declarations has proved fairly simple as long as no mechanisms for the actual implementation of the laws were put in place. The first law introducing these declarations was passed in 1996,[43] but had little effect, since it failed to make clear whether asset declaration were to be classified or opened to the public. In 2003 and then 2004 new legislation was passed in this respect and the files were opened to public scrutiny.[44] However, the mechanisms for checking these declarations and eventually taking action against those officials who seemed to have made unlawful gains while in office was poorly designed and completely ineffective, and responsible agencies proved very reluctant in performing this task.[45] Overall, until 2004, rule adoption was smooth, but implementation was deliberately kept to a minimum.

The situation suddenly changed in spring 2005, when the new Ministry of Justice proposed to the Parliament a stricter asset declaration, which included information on spouses and close relatives of officials, as well as information on goods such as jewelry or art collections. The imperativeness of passing such a law, as one of the conditions set out by the European Commission in its postponement safeguard clause for Romania, was clear. Moreover, most of the civil society, as well as the media, had expressed its support for the new declaration forms. Despite all these pressures, just a few members of the Parliament seemed willing to vote for the law. Senators tried to amend almost every strict provision of the law, while members of all political parties, regardless of being in opposition or a part of the governing coalition – which had actually won elections by promising to fight corruption – voted against such a strict asset declaration, as it ruled against their personal interests. It was only when the heads of the governing coalition managed to restore discipline within their parties that the Senate voted in favor of the law and sent it back to the Chamber of Deputies for approval.[46] This episode proved that EU pressure and domestic change agents impersonated by the Minister of Justice, the Prime Minister and the civil society, were hardly able to promote rule adoption, when vested interests cutting across political parties coalesced to oppose reform.

Furthermore, the story was not over with the passing of this law. In order to make these asset declarations an effective instrument in the fight against corruption, and as part of Romania's commitments to the European Union following accession in 2007, the government has submitted to the parliament a law on the so-called National Agency for Integrity (ANI). The Agency was supposed to monitor and investigate asset declarations of the members of parliament against their real wealth, as well as investigate any possible conflicts of interests and incompatibilities of MPs. The draft law had been agreed by the ruling coalition but has met fierce support within the Chamber of Deputies. After a few days of consultation, the Chamber's judicial commission introduced several amendments to the draft law, through which it managed to deplete the future agency of all its responsibilities.[47] Under the amended law, the Agency was not independent any more and was only allowed to verify the existence of asset declarations, without being allowed to check them against the actual wealth of dignitaries. The amendments were introduced by four political parties – the opposition PSD and PRM (the far-right Great Romania Party – *Partidul Romania Mare*) and the two smaller parties of the ruling coalition UDMR and PC (the Conservative Party – *Partidul Conservator*, formerly PUR) that had previously agreed upon the law. Interestingly enough, the four parties that opposed the law chose to massacre it rather than outright reject it, though they mustered a sufficient majority to do that. This showed that they preferred to adopt their traditional stance of passing a law required by the EU, but only after depleting it of any meaningful contents.

This episode reflected once again the power of vested interests cutting across political parties. The government's resolution to pursue the reform, coupled with the strong EU requirements and the civil society's criticism were not able to offset the power of such vested interests. While preparing this chapter, rule adoption had, therefore, been partly undertaken, while implementation and internalization lagged far behind, with public officials only starting to fill in their asset declarations, while no clear institution is in place to enforce this obligation.[48]

Sunshine laws: The long way from theory to practice

The first law on freedom of information access (FOIA law), Law 544/2001, was passed by the Parliament as a result of the cooperation between a number of Liberal MPs and the Ministry of Public Information, as well as some NGOs in one of the rare successful cooperation stories between the government and civil society. Following an impressive lobbying campaign conducted by a coalition of Romanian NGOs, Law no. 52/2003 on transparency in public administration was adopted in 2003. GRASP, a USAID-financed program, assisted the government in drafting the law. Together with the law on free access to public information, the FOIA law provides today a relatively adequate legislative scheme. The EC Regular Reports welcomed this law, but expressed concerns about its actual implementation.

Indeed, while domestic change agents successfully promoted rule adoption, the two laws have been only formally and sporadically implemented and are seldom used by citizens, who are not fully aware about the existence of such provisions – a clear expression of poor rule internalization. The Romanian Academic Society, a Bucharest-based think-tank, in 2003 conducted a study on 500 public institutions to assess the implementation of the Freedom of Information Act (FOIA) provisions one year after the law went into effect (Romanian Academic Society 2003b). By the beginning of 2003, out of the 500 public institutions interviewed, 74.6 percent of them had appointed a FOIA officer, while 68 percent of them had created a FOIA office. However, only a third of the institutions declared they had drafted a list of documents of public interest – the most basic requirement of the law beside the creation of the respective offices. Even worse, when operators asked to see those lists, only 16 percent of the institutions were able to produce one. Therefore, even if around three-quarters of the institutions surveyed had created the formal structures required by the law, only a very small minority of them had actually made the very first step towards rule implementation. Since the offices had been created and special officers had been appointed, this was not any more a question of adequate institutional capacity, but rather of lack of rule internalization, since civil servants were still not able to see the utility and importance of such a law.

This claim was supported by the results of a more recent, similar study conducted by the Romanian Academic Society, aimed at measuring the progress of FOIA implementation since 2003 (Romanian Academic Society 2006). The study showed that the performance of institutions had improved in formal terms, but that compliance with legislation remained low in terms of the quality of implementation. The percentage of institutions appointing a FOIA officer had increased from 75 percent to 97 percent and 73 percent of the institutions were now able to produce the list of documents of public interest (from 16 percent in 2003). However, quality of implementation remained very low according to the study, as 25 percent of the institutions surveyed had failed to issue an annual activity report, as requested by the law. Moreover, these reports – where produced by the respective institutions – were often inconclusive and incomplete and failed to comply with the requirements of the law. Despite such shortcomings in terms of quality of implementation, the report highlighted a positive sign in terms of rule internalization on behalf of the general public, as the percentage of institutions that received information requests under the FOIA law from the public had increased from 22 percent in 2003 to 82 percent in 2006. This illustrated that the public was becoming increasingly aware of its rights and had started applying the legislation. Therefore, rule internalization does occur, though with a considerable time lag behind rule adoption.

PNA: Playing with institutions

Under serious EU pressures to combat corruption, the National Anti-corruption Prosecutor's Office (PNA – now called the National Anti-corruption Department (DNA)) was created in 2002 as an independent organism to fight high-level corruption. Since its creation and until 2005, PNA has not been able to investigate and convict any high level official as a result of continuous political subordination and administrative changeovers.

PNA became operational in September 2002, but remained understaffed and mostly inefficient due to its subordination to the General Prosecutors and the Minister of Justice – the only people who could order the investigation of high-level officials. In April 2004 a governmental ordinance extended the scope of PNA activity by lowering the financial threshold for cases under PNA jurisdiction, which overloaded the PNA with cases of petty corruption. This decision was reversed in March 2005 by the new government, which increased the threshold in order to restrict PNA competencies to cases of high-level corruption. However, just a few days after former Prime Minister Adrian Nastase (the then PSD leader) was cited for a hearing in front of PNA, the PSD-controlled Constitutional Court suddenly ruled that PNA could no longer investigate corruption allegations regarding MPs, because the General Prosecutors' Officer attached to the High Court of Cassation and Justice (HCCJ) was the only competent institution in this respect. This practically left the PNA with no scope of activity and caused serious delays of those investigations at a time when the Commission was expecting clear signals that Romania was finally dealing with grand corruption cases.

During the second half of 2005 the government managed to pass the judicial reform legislative package and was thus able to change PNA's top management. In order to offset the decision of the Constitutional Court, PNA was reorganized into the National Anti-corruption Department (DNA), which now functions as a department within the General Prosecutors' Office attached to HCCJ, but maintains its financial, human resources and operational independence. The competencies of the DNA were further narrowed in order to cover only high-level corruption cases and the institution is now able to investigate (again) members of parliament.[49]

The evolution of this institution is a perfect showcase of the interplay of different factors in promoting or hindering reform. EU pressure had been there all the time, but apparently to no effect. While rule adoption was rather easy and was pointed to in Brussels as progress in fighting corruption, veto players within the government and the Parliament deliberately kept development of institutional and administrative capacity very low. What tilted the balance eventually were change agents and the empowerment of a pro-reformist government, as well as the introduction of the postponement safeguard clause by late 2004. As these two factors came about at almost the same time, it is difficult to say which one had more weight in pushing for reform. Given the high politics aspect of this reform, it would be reasonable to say that political will was essential for its success, and thus the changes in government, as well as the personal dedication of the Minister of Justice were mainly responsible for breaking the deadlock. The introduction of the postponement safeguard clause, which threatened to delay accession, made conditionality more credible and this is likely to have contributed furthermore to the eventual success of the reform by empowering domestic change agents.

Police reform and civilian control of security forces

Terror and repression: those were the tasks of Romanian police during the Communist regime. The then-called *Militia* was part of the repressive apparatus of the state, and, as such, its essential task was to defend the state *from* the citizens. The entire philosophy of its organization and functioning was therefore contrary to the main objective of any police force within a democracy, i.e. guaranteeing the rights of citizens. Moreover, during Communist times the Romanian Militia was a highly centralized and militarized body, strictly subordinated to the structures of the Communist Party. Acquiescence and connections to the *nomenklatura* were the main criteria for promotion within the system, while any legal case involving a policeman was to be trialed by military courts.

This situation has been preserved for a long time even after the fall of Communism, as reform was very slow and the government was not particularly interested in this matter. The essential factor driving reform was the pressure coming from international actors, be it the Council of Europe, Amnesty International, domestic civil society or the EU. Eventually, it was only under serious EU pressure related to accession negotiations within the negotiation chapter on Justice and Home Affairs and it was as late as 2002 that the first significant reform of the police has been enacted.

Demilitarization: From state militia to public politia

Clearly, initial conditions were not favoring reform, but the political establishment has not shown any rush in promoting radical changes either. With a Communist successor party in government and strong groups within the police interested in maintaining the status quo – as well as their offices, no reform was pursued until the pressures coming from international actors made it imperative. The first post-Communist law regarding – albeit indirectly – the police was Law No. 40/1990 on the organization of the Ministry of Interior, which was adopted as a condition imposed by the Council of Europe to Romania's membership. Neither the 1991 Constitution, nor this law made much of a difference in terms of police reform, however, since the institution continued to operate according to the Communist 1969 law on the organization of the police and on the basis of a Criminal Code, criminal procedures and a statute of policemen unchanged since Communist times. A new law on the organization of the police was passed in 1994, but this again failed to introduce serious reform, as the police remained under the control of the executive, while the law did not aim specifically to the demilitarization and decentralization of the institution.

Despite continuous lobbying from domestic NGOs to place the Romanian police under civilian control,[50] the first laws mentioning the civil character of the police were only passed in 2002,[51] as part of Romania's commitments within the accession negotiations related to the Chapter on Justice and Home Affairs. The two laws stipulated that policemen were public servants and finally passed responsibility for judging on crimes involving policemen from military courts to civilian ones, a measure which had been advocated by the EU for years already (European Commission Reports 1998–2001).

While rule adoption was difficult by itself, building the institutional and administrative capacity needed for the implementation of reforms and rule internalization proved even more difficult. After passing the required legislation, the development of institutional capacity has been slowed down by three main factors. Firstly, due to the rather poor quality of the law, the police force has not been completely transferred to the responsibility of local city halls, and remains partly under the control of the Ministry of Interior. Secondly, limited internal and external financial resources and know-how translated into institutional weakness and did not allow for the rapid and radical changes required. Furthermore, decision-making, funds and human resources are still highly centralized, leaving little space for the development of local institutional capacity. And last, but not least, well-consolidated interest groups within the police have played as active veto players in slowing down the implementation of reform and trying to offset its effects in order to preserve their control and privileges. During early stages of reform such groups have tried to delay rule adoption as much as possible using their leverage over the political class. When rules were finally adopted, they showed very reluctant to creating the new structures needed for a proper implementation of the law, and delayed it as much as possible.

Even now, when rule adoption and development of institutional capacity are almost completed, there still remains the problem of rule internalization, since changing the mindset of both policemen and the public is of vital importance for the success of the reform. There are certain signs that the situation is improving. The pressure of public mistrust in the police forces seems to have made a difference within the institutions ranks. Younger and more skilled policemen have grown tired of being pointed out as one of the least trusted institutions in Romania and are starting to constitute themselves into real change agents, willing to improve this image through sincere reform, efficiency and transparency. According to a Gallup survey conducted in 2005, the population appears to see the outcome of police reform as increasingly positive: more than 50 percent of the respondents said that the police was heading in a good reaction, as opposed to healthcare (23 percent), judiciary (38 percent) or education systems (47 percent) (Romanian Academic Society 2005). Such a trend might well become the driving force into changing people's mindsets and leading to full rule of law in this area.

Sanctioning police abuses: Policemen are not above the law!

Another highly contested issue regarding police reform in Romania was the responsibility of trying police officers for abuses committed against civilians. Until 2002, military courts used to hear cases for any allegation related to police abuses, even when these involved civilians. Police officers, prison staff, members of the secret services and members of the Ministry of Defense could thus be investigated and tried only by military prosecutors and military judges, even if their crimes were not related to their official capacity and duties. At the same time, military courts were staffed by military personnel and could therefore be held hierarchically responsible, which severely hampered their independence. Traditionally, these courts have proved rather reluctant in convicting police officers for abuses, although the European Court of Human Rights ruled against such decisions in the few cases brought by abused civilians to Strasbourg.[52] Furthermore, civilians could only appeal the decision of a military court in front of the hierarchical upper military court, while the same military prosecutor that was responsible for the first investigation would conduct the appeal. Chances of success in such cases were thus meager and civilian trust in such institutions was considerably low.

This was mostly a human-rights related issue, but has always been treated as a matter of redefining the responsibilities and accountability of the police as a civil service for the citizen and therefore was an integral part of the police reform. The issue was of great importance, since subsequent reports issued by international human rights monitoring agencies, from Amnesty International, to the UN Human Rights Commission (OHCHR) and Human Rights Watch had warned about the serious infringements of human rights by police officers.[53] As a result, both international actors, such as the EU and the Council of Europe, and domestic

NGOs, such as APADOR-Helsinki Committee, have continuously condemned the practice.

The reform actually comprised two components. On the one hand, existing legal provisions had to be changed to allow for proper trial of police officers abusing civilians, and set examples in order to deter such practices; on the other hand, police officers had to be re-educated in the spirit of respect for human rights. This meant transforming a repressive state agency into an institution which serves the community and guards human rights observance. As expected, police officers had no incentive to support such changes, since the existing situation guaranteed them something close to impunity.

Despite international concerns about this issue, neither of the two required actions was taken during early transition. It was only in 2002, and under serious external pressure, that rule adoption finally occurred with the broader police demilitarization process when the Law on the Statute of the Policemen transferred responsibility for cases of police abuse to ordinary civil courts. While rule adoption was a good development by itself, rule internalization is still far from being achieved. Both domestic and international monitoring agencies continue to report cases of mistreatment by police forces,[54] though a comparison between earlier reports on human rights and police abuses issued by different internal and international monitoring agencies,[55] shows that a smaller number of cases of police abuses was reported in 2005 or 2006, compared with those reported in 2000.

Conclusions: A cross-sectional analysis

This chapter has tried to depict the mechanisms through which democratic rule of law reform was eventually introduced and implemented in Romania in the five main areas studied by this project, focusing on the interplay between international and domestic factors. The table (Table 4.1) displays various factors that inhibit or support the process of rule adoption, rule implementation, and rule internalization of democratic rule of law standards in Romania. The different episodes analyzed here show that there is a great variety of possible combinations that might be conducive to or hamper democratic rule of law reforms. However, a few general conclusions might be drawn from this complex picture.

Firstly, rule adoption was usually much easier to enact compared to the more difficult and time-consuming tasks of rule internalization and implementation. As a result, Romania has to date managed to adopt most of the legislation required to be considered a formal democracy, but rule implementation in key areas lags behind, while the process of rule internalization is just at its beginning.

Second, rule adoption itself proved difficult in those areas of reform concerning high politics issues. In cases such as judiciary reform or the fight against corruption, the mobilization of strong veto players was able to offset

Table 4.1 Summary of issues, actors and mechanisms of change

Key area	*Issue*	*Factors/ Change agents*	*Mechanism/ Problems*
Civil freedom and political rights	Death penalty	(+) Change agents: civil society immediately after 1989	Rule adoption worked
	Minority rights – Hungarians	(+) International actors: Council of Europe, Hungary, EU (+) Change agents: Hungarian ethnic party (–) Veto power: Communist successor party	Rule adoption difficult, but possible Rule implementation worked Internalization problems
	Minority rights – Roma	(+) International pressures: EU, Council of Europe, human rights watchdogs (–) Communist legacy (mentality problems)	Difficult rule adoption Difficult rule implementation Slow rule internalization
	International adoptions	(+) Strong EU conditionality (European Parliament) (–) Contradictory international pressures: EU vs. US	Rule adoption worked Rule implementation worked
Judiciary reform	Increased salaries	(+) EU conditionality (*+) High degree of determinacy (*+) Favors traditional veto players	Rule adoption worked Rule implementation worked Rule internalization not applicable
	Independence of judiciary	(+) EU strong conditionality (+) Change agents: Minister of Justice, civil society, President of Romania, government (–) Strong veto players: the conservative Superior Council of Magistracy, the Constitutional Court, the Communist successor party SDP	Rule adoption difficult and incomplete Weak rule internalization
Institutional and administrative structures	Rule by decree	(+) EU conditionality (*+) High degree of determinacy (–) Reduced administrative capacity of the parliament (*–) Some inherent contradictions between different EU-set objectives	Rule adoption – not the case Difficult rule implementation
	Civil service reform	(+) (late) EU conditionality (–) Veto players: parties in government and opposition (–) Bureaucratic inertia	Slow and difficult rule adoption Difficult rule implementation Slow internalization

Corruption	Asset declarations	(+) EU pressures (+) Change agents: Minister of Justice, NGOs, government (–) Veto players: MPs crosscutting political parties	Very difficult rule adoption
	Sunshine laws	(+) Change agents: NGOs, liberal MPs (–) Bureaucratic inertia	Rule adoption worked Very slow and difficult rule implementation No rule internalization
	PNA-DNA	(+) EU conditionality (+) Change agents: Minister of Justice, NGOs (–) Veto players: Constitutional Court, Communist successor party	Rule adoption eventually worked Rule implementation obstructed as much as possible
Police reform	Demilitarization	(+) EU conditionality (+) Change agents: NGOs (–) Bureaucratic inertia (–) Limited administrative capacity	Rule adoption worked, but late Rule implementation almost completed Slow and difficult internalization
	Sanctioning abuses	(+) International actors: EU, Council of Europe, Amnesty International, Human Rights Watch (+) Domestic Change agents: NGOs (*+) High degree of determinacy (–) Veto players: strong groups within the police	Late rule adoption Low internalization

the action of both the EU and domestic change agents, such as the civil society and pro-reformist governments. In this respect, the mechanism of rule adoption followed closely the EUCLIDA model. During the 1990s, progress with rule adoption was slow and inconclusive. This happened because the action of the EU was not very credible until the mid-1990s. After that, the general domestic view was for a long time that Romania's accession would occur anyway, through a political decision at EU level. Moreover, the civil society was not strong enough to push for reforms. Given these circumstances, subsequent governments were reluctant to give up their gains derived from the maintenance of status quo and enact thorough reforms for the sake of EU accession. As a result, they preferred to delay rule adoption as much as possible. Whenever EU pressures became more credible, as was the case with the law on the Civil Servant Statute passed days before the Helsinki European Council in 1999, minimal legislation was eventually adopted. In such cases, resistance to reform shifted from delaying or opposing rule adoption towards delaying or opposing rule implementation. Consequently, institutional and administrative capacity was developed only to a minimum and new institutions were not given appropriate staffing and independence to function effectively. This situation continued until the emergence of a renewed cycle of increasing EU credibility, which triggered a new process of rule adoption consisting often of amendments to existing legislation.

However, the balance of forces within the society started to tilt by the end of 2004. On the one hand, EU credibility increased significantly with the introduction of the postponement safeguard clause, which threatened to delay accession. On the other hand, a pro-reformist government entered office in December 2004. Meanwhile, the civil society had gradually developed and was now able to play a more visible role on the political stage. The combination of these three forces eventually managed to equilibrate the balance against veto players, but was not able to offset it completely: the laws on asset declarations, or on the Superior Council of Magistracy were indeed passed in 2005–06, but were altered in the process by veto players and their effectiveness was diminished by such intervention.

Third, rule implementation was much less influenced by external pressures, as the EU's leverage on national governments tended to be diluted when it came to pushing for effective institutions and law enforcement. One of the reasons behind this trend was the relatively low determinacy of EU requirements when it called for effective and functional institutions. While the Commission was generally aware that one or the other institution was not functioning effectively due to lack of adequate staffing or funds, it could not indicate precisely how much human or financial resources the Romanian government should allocate to solve the problem. As a result, subsequent governments continued to report minor changes, but kept the institutions largely ineffective, as was the case with the National Agency for Civil Service (NACS). Moreover, bureaucratic inertia often opposed or delayed rule implementation, as people within institutions refused to enforce the legislation, as was the case with police demilitarization or the freedom of information act. Indeed, the only institution discussed here, which was restructured and seems to have become functional, is the National Anti-corruption Prosecutors' Office (PNA/DNA). The exceptionalism of this case has to do with the combination of two essential factors: an increase in credibility of EU conditionality, as the issue was specifically linked to the postponement safeguard clause (i.e. the threat of delaying accession); and the resolution of the new Justice Minister, the president and the civil society to reform this institution. Similar to the EUCLIDA model, the credible action of the international actor, coupled with the strong action of domestic change agents, eventually managed to offset the opposition of veto players and enact the necessary reform.

Fourth, rule internalization has hardly followed rule adoption, at least in the short run, as diffusion of values expressed in the legislation adopted cannot occur over night. Given the totalitarian history of Romania, democratic rule of law reform has been essentially a top-down process, in which very little of the legal and institutional changes implemented were the expression of a local political or legal culture. On the contrary, most changes were often seen as externally imposed and have even triggered resistance, as was the case with apparently simple questions, such as computerizing courts and using aggregate databases of court decisions. Moreover, rule adoption was rarely accompanied by proper information campaigns for raising awareness of the general public relative to their rights and obligations. A good example in this sense is the general unawareness among the general public about the roles and obligations of civil servants. Rule internalization appears thus to be a very lengthy process, which will go far beyond the date of Romania's accession and is likely to be facilitated in the long term by increasing socialization of the public with European norms and values.

Finally, EU membership as the final reward for complying with EU conditionality has been of paramount importance in the whole process of rule of law reform. Reform was very slow, if existent, during the first post-Communist years, as Iliescu and his ruling party promoted the alternative idea of an 'original democracy'. Once his alternative failed, EU membership gradually became the only game in town among both the public and political parties and since then rule of law reform has been increasingly shaped by the prospect of membership. Considering the serious difficulties that these reforms have encountered even in the presence of EU conditionality, there is reason to believe that democratic rule of law reform would have been much slower and even less effective in the absence of such a strong incentive.

Notes

1 Joel Hellman (1998), 'Winners Take All: The Politics of Partial Reform in Post-Communist Transitions', in *World Politics*, 50 (June 1998) 2, pp. 203–34) explains that the outcomes of partial reforms pursued at the beginning of transition created significant groups of vested interests that opposed further reform. The politics of partial reform had

created market distortions which benefited a small group of entrepreneurs (the winners of initial reform). Preserving status quo of partial transition and half-way economic reforms was therefore in the direct interest of these winners.

2 A very useful document listing the connection between different power holders and business in post-Communist Romania is the booklet *A Quest for Political Integrity* published by the Romanian Coalition for a Clean Parliament at Polirom in 2005.

3 The Romanian Democratic Convention (CDR) was an electoral alliance of several centre-right parties, led by PNTCD (National Peasant Christian Democrat Party) and PNL (National Liberal Party). The Democratic Party (PD) joined the CDR later on in the governing coalition.

4 For instance, in August 1997 prime minister Ciorbea dismissed Valerian Stan, the head of the government's control agency, following negotiations with the Democratic Party (PD) – one of the ruling coalition parties, which threatened to walk out of the coalition government, after Stan's agency had issued a report accusing PD members of unlawfully occupying state-owned 'protocol' houses for insignificant rents. [Alina Mungiu-Pippidi (1997), 'Crime and corruption after Communism. Breaking free at last: Tales of corruption from the post-Communist Balkans', in *East European Constitutional Review* 6, 4:85–90.

5 For an extensive account of the 2000–04 PSD rule, see Gallagher, Tom (2005) *Theft of a nation: Romania since Communism*, London: C. Hurst, pp. 308–30.

6 PSD recruited around 800 mayors from the ranks of other parties between 2000 and 2003. (Institute for Public Policy Romania, October 2003, *Dynamics of Mayors' Political Affiliation: the Case of Romania – One Year Before the Local Elections in 2004*, Bucharest).

7 The NIT ratings on independent media in Romania worsened from 2002 (rating 3.50) to 2003 (rating 3.75). [Freedom House, *Nations in Transit 2004*, www.freedomhouse.org] NIT ratings range from 1 to 7, with 1 representing the best possible performance of a country in a given area.

8 Besides the three typical safeguard clauses included by all EU accession agreements in the fifth round of enlargement (the general economic safeguard clause; a specific internal market safeguard clause; and a specific justice and home affairs safeguard clause), the European Commission introduced a fourth postponement safeguard clause in the accession agreements signed with Romania and Bulgaria. The clause stated that the European Council could delay accession for one or both countries until 2008 if 'there is serious risk of either of those States being manifestly unprepared to meet the requirements of membership by the date of accession of 1 January 2007 in a number of important areas'. (Article 39, Protocol concerning the conditions and arrangements for admission of the Republic of Bulgaria and Romania to the European Union, in: *Official Journal of the European Union*, L 157/29, 21.6.2005) The 'important areas' in the case of Romania were home and justice affairs (i.e. border controls), judiciary reform, the fight against corruption, police reform, and competition policy (especially state aid). (Annex IX of the Accession Protocol with Romania)

9 PUR (now called Conservative Party – PC) had been a close ally of the PSD in 2000 elections, than switched sides and ran against social democrats in local elections, than switched sides again and entered an electoral coalition with PSD in 2004 general elections, only to switch sides again and form a governing coalition with the former opposition, as polls were showing that these frequent changes made it loose ground within the electorate, so that it could not reach the 5 percent threshold in case of early elections.

10 Law No. 6/7 January 1990.

11 Some experts estimate the true number of Roma population leaving in Romania at around 10 percent of the population (between 1.8m and 2.5m Roma) much more than the 2.5 percent shown by the census (around 500,000 Roma). [Arno Tarner, 2005 *The Roma of Eastern Europe: Still searching for inclusion,* Migration Policy Institute, retrievable at http://www.migrationinformation.org/Feature/print.cfm?ID=308, last visited 5.11.2006].

12 No matter what coalition or party won elections, the UDMR has managed to secure a place at the government table ever since 1996.

13 The Opinion 176 of the Parliamentary Assembly of the Council of Europe listed several problems related to Romania's capacity to enforce human rights. The list included a request for Romania to sign the European Charter for Regional and Minority Languages as soon as possible. [Opinion No. 176 (1993) on the application by Romania for membership in the Council of Europe, retrievable at http://assembly.coe.int/main.asp?Link=/ documents/ adoptedtext/ ta93/eopi176.htm, last visited 31.10.2006]. On Romania's accession to the Council of Europe, see also Andreescu (2001).

14 See on this National Democratic Institute for International Affairs, *Roma Political Participation in Romania*, February 2003.

15 Survey results (in Romanian) retrievable at http://www.curs.ro/uploads/raport %20sondaj %20discriminare.pdf, last visited 31.10.2006.

16 Bunescu, Ioana (2007) clarifies this in her 'EU Eastern Enlargement 'Conditionality' of Minority Protection as a Political Opportunity for Romanian Roma', *In-Spire*, June 2007, p.6 retrievable at http://www.in-spire.org/articles/ib02062007_Romanian_Roma.pdf, last visited 1.07.2007.

17 See also National Democratic Institute for International Affairs, *Roma Political Participation in Romania*, February 2003.

18 Law No. 274/2004 on the creation, organization and functioning of the Romanian Office for Adoptions.

19 See 'EC issues ultimatum to Romania: stop child exports', the *Telegraph*, February 4, 2004, at www.telegraph.co.uk; and 'Romania pulled two ways over adoption abroad', the *Guardian*, May 6, 2004, at www.guardian.co.uk.

20 'Parlamentarii cer adoptii internationale' [EMPs ask the government to resume international adoptions], Euractiv News, 19.10.2006, retrievable at http://www.euractiv.ro/uniunea-europeana/articles|displayArticle/articleID_8425/Europarlamentarii-cer-adoptii-internationale.html (last visited 30.10.2006)

21 To be precise, we are talking here about increase of salaries in real terms. Salaries were indexed every year since 1990 because of the excessively high inflation that characterized the Romanian economy for most of the early transition. However, increases in real terms were the exception rather than the norm until the mid 1990s.

22 Annex IX of the Accession Protocol with Romania: 'the *development and implementation* of an updated and integrated Action Plan and Strategy for the reform of the judiciary' (authors' emphasis).

23 Law No. 247/2005 on the reform of private property rights and the judiciary.

24 'Reforma justitiei apropie clauza de salvgardare' [The judiciary reform threatens the postponement safeguard clause], daily newspaper *Cotidianul*, 4 May 2005.

25 The contested articles referred to: (1) Any SCM member could not hold at the same time the position of judge or prosecutor. This would constitute a conflict of interest, as one of the main roles of the SCM is to supervise the activity of courts and magistrates. (2) Magistrates who have met their legal retirement age cannot occupy their positions thereafter. (3) Retired magistrates cannot continue their activity by being reinstated in their positions and cumulating salaries and pensions. (4) Mandates for high management positions within the judiciary will be limited to three years. ('Curtea Constitutionala blocheaza reforma justitiei [The Constitutional Court blocked the reform of the judiciary], online news *Hotnews.ro*, 6 July 2005)

26 Out of the nine judges in the Constitutional Court, three were former PSD ministers (A. Gaspar, P. Ninosu, I. Predescu), one was the husband of former PSD Minister of Justice Rodica Stanoiu (S.V. Stanoiu), and one was a former General Prosecutor appointed by the PSD government (N. Cochinescu). See Sabina Fati, 'Curtea Constitutionala – un instrument la indemana PSD' (The Constitutional Court – An Instrument of the PSD), article from the daily *Curentul*, 24 June 2005.

27 Eurobarometrul 66, Toamna 2006, Raport National Romania [Standard Eurobarometer 66/Autumn 2006 – TNS Opinion & Social], retrievable at http://ec.europa.eu/ public_opinion/archives/eb/eb66/eb66_ro_nat.pdf last visited 1.02.2007.

28 Romanian Association for Transparency, *Studiu privind perceptia magistratilor asupra independentei sistemului judiciar 2005* [Study on the magistrates' perception on the independence of the judiciary] and ibidem 2006 (in Romanian), retrievable at http://www.transparency.ro/politici_si_studii/sondaje/2006/index.html, last visited 02.02.2007.

29 On the effectiveness of the parliament and national government, see subsequent *Nations in Transit* reports on Romania, retrievable at www.freedomhouse.org.

30 As an example, during 1999 the Parliament only managed to adopt 99 out of the 453 draft laws, ordinances and emergency ordinances submitted to the Parliament. (2000 Regular Report from the Commission on Romania's Progress Towards Accession).

31 According to the official legislative database of the Chamber of Deputies, the number of emergency ordinances issued by the Romanian government yearly from 2000 until 2007 was: 297 (2000); 195 (2001); 209 (2002); 127 (2003); 142 (2004); 209 (2005); 136 (2006).

32 The Commission introduced however a requirement in the 1998 Accession Partnership that Romania should adopt a civil service law as soon as possible.

33 Indeed, the European Commission welcomed the adoption of the Statute in the 1999 Regular Report (i.e. immediately after adoption), but criticized the inefficiency of this Agency in the 2000 Regular Report and onwards, including in the 2005 report.

34 For the main shortcomings of this law, see Viorescu, Razvan (2004), *The Profesionalising of the Civil Service according to Public Administration Reform (Romanian Case)*, Paper presented to the 12th NISPAcee Annual Conference (Central and Eastern European Countries inside and outside the European Union: Avoiding a New Divide), Vilnius, Lithuania, May 13–15, 2004.

35 Law no. 161/2003.

36 Law no. 161/2003 on Certain Steps for Assuring Transparency in Performing High Official Positions, Public and Business Positions, for Preventing and Sanctioning Corruption.

37 For instance, the Agency can see for the submission of public declaration of wealth and assets, but is not entitled to check their accuracy.

38 Law No. 251/2006 on the modification of Law No. 188/1999 on the Statute of Civil Servants.

39 Amos News, 27 February 2006, *Un sondaj al Sed Lex facut printre functionarii publici ridica semne de intrebare* [SED LEX opinion poll conducted on civil servants raises many questions], retrievable at http://www.informatia.ro/Article163888.phtml, last visited 27 October 2006.

40 Etves, Antoaneta, 'Stapanul din Spatele Ghiseului' [The Master behind the Counter], daily *Cotidianul*, 26 September 2006.

41 For example, the text in the EC Regular Report on Romania 2004 reads as follows: 'Regarding administrative capacity, the credibility of the recruitment and retention schemes delivered by the managing authorities and intermediate bodies may be hampered by the low attractiveness of the civil servant status. In this respect legislation to improve the civil service's status and to ensure adequate remuneration needs to be put in place.' (p. 115).

42 Government Ordinance no. 54/2004.

43 Law No. 115/1996.

44 Law No. 161/2003 and Emergency Ordinance No. 24/2004.

45 In the case of ordinary civil servants, the declarations had to be checked by commissions or inspectors within their own institutions, while the Ministry of Justice, prosecutor offices or the National Anti-Corruption Prosecutor's Office were responsible for checking asset declarations for magistrates and dignitaries. Between 1996 and until 2004 none of them had ever filed any request for the investigation of a declaration. ('Noile declaratii de

avere vor obliga demnitarii sa explice si modul de dobandire a bunurilor' [The new asset declarations will ask dignitaries to explain how they made their wealth], daily *Adevarul*, 1 March 2005)

46 *Evenimentul Zilei* daily newspaper, 'Tariceanu are Probleme cu Alianta PNL-PD' ['Tariceanu faces problems regarding the PD-PNL alliance'], Alina Mihai, April 7, 2005.

47 'Deputatii din Comisia Juridica au macelarit proiectul ANI' [Deputies in the judicial commission have massacrated the ANI project], online news *Hotnews.ro*, 12.11.2006]

48 It is relevant to note in this respect that journalists from *Academia Catavencu*, a weekly magazine and media NGO, in April 2007 have filed a notification to the prosecutor's office attached to the Court of Cassation and Justice, which contains a list with 500 public officials that have either not submitted their asset declarations, have failed to update it, or have provided incomplete information – an indication of the seriousness of public officials in performing this legal obligation. [*Academia Catavencu*, 19(804) from 16–22 May 2007, front page]

49 For a case to fall under PNA competency, it should involve a bribe of over EUR 10,000, or material damages exceeding EUR 200,000.

50 See subsequent Annual Reports of APADOR-Helsinki Committee at www.apador.org/en/index.htm, last visited 5.11.2006.

51 The Law No. 218/2002 on the Organization and Functioning of the Police and the Law No. 360/2002 on the Statute of Policemen.

52 See subsequent Annual Reports of APADOR-Helsinki Committee at www.apador.org/en/index.htm, last visited 5.11.2006.

53 Such practices included excessive use of firearms by law enforcement officials, ill-treatment of detainees and of persons in preventive arrests, discrimination and violence against members of the Roma community. For more details, see for example: Amnesty International Report 2002; CCPR Report 1999; HRW World Report 2000.

54 For example, Bucharest police on July 27 2006 responded to a dispute between Maria and Lucian Tamaris, an elderly couple, and a neighbor, against an alleged property trespass. As soon as police arrived, they allegedly handcuffed the couple, told them to lie on the ground, and kicked them. The couple filed complaint against the police for abusive behavior. Subsequently, one of the officers involved was fired and five other police officers who took part at the incident were admonished for failing to observe appropriate police procedures [US Department of State (2006), *Romania. Country Reports on Human Rights Practices 2006*, Bureau of Democracy, Human Rights and Labor. Online. Available HTTP: http://www.state.gov/g/drl/rls/hrrpt/2006/78834.htm]

55 Apador-Helsinki Committee, Amnesty International, US State Department Human Rights Reports.

5 Turkey: Reforms for a consolidated democracy

Senem Aydın Düzgit and Ali Çarkoğlu

Introduction

The Turkish experience of democratization reforms goes back to nineteenth century Ottoman rule and hence provides a rich case in its historicity. However, the impact of external actors in the Turkish example has recently begun to be discussed primarily with respect to the country's relations with the EU and its attempts to fulfill the Copenhagen criteria in order to start accession negotiations for EU membership. Here our focus will be on the most recent wave of reforms during the 1991 to 2006 period. The prospect of EU accession, initiated at the Helsinki Summit of 1999, provides the most recent and crucial turning point in Turkey's democratic reform path. After the granting of candidacy at Helsinki, in order to fulfill the Copenhagen political and economic criteria necessary to begin accession negotiations, Turkey undertook various political reforms over a wide field encompassing most particularly human rights and freedoms, the judicial system, legislative and administrative capacity, corruption and strengthening of civilian control over the military. This chapter undertakes a critical assessment of these reforms, within the EUCLIDA theoretical framework.

Strengthening the protection of basic rights

Since late 2001 in particular, fundamental reforms in the area of basic human, civil and political rights have been undertaken in Turkey. After the Helsinki Summit of 1999, the European Commission published the first Accession Partnership document in March 2000, which was followed by the preparation of the Turkish 'National Program for the Adoption of the *Acquis*' by the Turkish authorities in March 2001.[1] These first signs of EU membership conditionality provided the initial trigger for change. Immediately following the approval of the National Program, political reform was initiated with 34 constitutional amendments in October 2001, a new Civil Code in January 2002 and three 'harmonization packages'[2] adopted in the follow-up to the Copenhagen Summit of 2002. The legislative changes introduced significant reforms, most particularly in the fields of human rights and the protection of minorities, freedom of expression and freedom of association. There was also significant legislative progress in the area of gender equality – via the new Civil Code (Law 4721/2001) and the Penal Code (Law 5237/2004) – realized through the combination of EU conditionality and domestic pressure for reform from national women's rights organizations – most notably the Women's Coalition.

These reforms were the first crucial responses to EU conditionality and culminated in the Copenhagen Summit of 2002, at which the EU decided to open negotiations with Turkey as and when it fulfilled the Copenhagen political criteria (Aydın and Keyman 2004). The summit decision reinforced the EU's commitments by providing Turkey with the prospect that full EU membership is indeed a real possibility (Keyman and Öniş 2004). Meanwhile, the EU has also decided to increase significantly the amount of financial assistance to Turkey (European Commission 2003a): Hence, the EU impact was not merely confined to pure conditionality, but extended to cover financial and technical aid. Pre-accession financial assistance would reach €250 million in 2004, €300 million in 2005 and €500 million in 2006 to help Turkey prepare to join the EU as quickly as possible. (European Commission 2003a; Chapter 3 in this volume). Given the size of the Turkish economy, which was about €300 billion at the end of 2005, such assistance may mean little. Despite its relative modesty in financial terms, however, the new pre-accession aid was important in signaling the shift in Turkey's status and EU commitment, raising the credibility of EU conditionality. Similarly, administrative and judicial capacity-building mechanisms, primarily through the twinning instrument, were now made available to Turkey. The strengthening of the credibility of conditionality was reflected in the adoption of four subsequent harmonization packages and two sets of constitutional amendments, leading up to the decision to open accession negotiations at the Brussels Summit of 2004.[3]

The political reform process, however, did not come to an abrupt end or face a serious reversal in the period following the decision to open accession negotiations. In fact, the 2005 Progress Report on Turkey highlighted the country's continuing efforts to fulfill the Copenhagen political criteria despite the slower pace of reform and the remaining problems with implementation. Important legislative reforms came into force in 2005, including the new Penal Code and the Code of Criminal Procedure among others. These are expected to lead to structural changes, particularly in the judiciary (European Commission 2005c). With respect to training in basic rights and freedoms, the Turkish authorities have pursued a number of programs targeting relevant personnel in the Ministry of Interior Affairs, Ministry of Justice, the gendarmerie and the police. These reforms have led to significant improvements, specifically in the areas of the fight against torture, freedom of expression, freedom of association minority rights and gender equality, albeit with remaining problems.

Fight against torture

Reports of torture incidents have significantly decreased in Turkey since 2002. As mentioned in the 2005 Progress Report on Turkey, both Bar Associations and Nongovernmental Organizations (NGOs) confirm that reports of torture and ill-treatment are diminishing in the country (see European Commission 2005c, 33). This is partly due to the advanced set of provisions in this area introduced via strict EU conditionality (see Chapter 3, this volume). The EU has also been active in strengthening institutional capacity on this front by active engagement in the training of forensic medicine experts and judges/public prosecutors through TAIEX (Technical Assistance Information Exchange Unit) seminars and the large-scale Twinning Project, in combination with the extensive training programs of the Ministry of Health in this area.[4] Hence the growth of knowledge resources and a certain degree of value diffusion were facilitated by the EU, which was the only international actor behind change on this front, with no other credible alternative. Similarly, this issue was one where adoption costs were not high for the governing party in question and thus did not necessitate a shift of cost-benefit balance to begin with. In our opinion, the Justice and Development Party (AKP) government seems to be genuinely committed to reform on this front, with a 'zero tolerance' policy towards torture demonstrated in the way in which the Human Rights Presidency under the office of the Prime Minister has been dealing with torture cases. In fact, we believe that a certain degree of societal rule internalization is also occurring as shown by the immediate exposure of torture cases in the media and the public reactions.

Despite considerable progress, it is too early to state that the issue is fully resolved in Turkey. There are still cases where effective investigations do not take place, creating 'impunity' for torturers. According to the August 2005 Amnesty International Report on Turkey, the problem here lies mostly with the public prosecutors, who ally with the security forces to issue decisions not to prosecute ('*takipsizlik kararlari*'), and judges that in some cases do not deliver sentences commensurate with the gravity of the crime. This goes to show that despite all the progress on paper, rule implementation can still be hampered due to insufficient internalization by potential veto players from within the system (Amnesty International 2005). Hence the remaining potential veto players here are some members of the judiciary, namely certain public prosecutors and judges.

Freedom of expression

Freedom of expression is one of the major areas of reform in Turkey where probably the most intense struggle between change agents and conservative elements is currently taking place. Legislative reform in this field, most particularly through the new Penal Code, began to be applied in practice.

According to Human Rights Watch, as of November 2005, there were no individuals serving prison sentences for the non-violent expression of their opinions (Human Rights Watch 2006a). Despite these positive developments and a considerable degree of rule adoption, there is still a constant emergence of new cases where individuals expressing non-violent opinions have been prosecuted and in some cases convicted under the new Penal Code.[5] These cases demonstrate that reform-resistant forces in Turkey are now working in a concerted and persistent fashion to block the reform process from within by utilizing the Turkish judicial system.[6] These Euroskeptic forces have found their main allies among some members of the Turkish judiciary. The defective articles of the new Penal Code, such as Article 301,[7] which are too broad and vaguely phrased, also help them in their resistance.

Part of the explanation behind the resistance of the judiciary can be found in institutional/procedural matters. Many public prosecutors feel compelled to bring such cases to court rather than declare them as non-meritorious, since they perceive that their careers may be at risk from judicial inspectors – functioning under the Ministry of Justice – who may believe they are not filing the necessary cases, which links into the issue of judicial independence.[8] In a similar vein, some constituencies within the judiciary may also be using this opportunity as an interlude into a new political career, betting on the probable rise of the anti-EU forces in the short to medium term.

Another important issue in this respect concerns the methodological difference between Turkish courts and the European Court of Human Rights (ECtHR) in determining whether an expression threatens public order. The ECtHR takes into account four different conditions in determining whether thoughts or opinions create a real danger to public order: the content of the relevant statement, the identity of the speaker, the context in which the statement is made and the form of the expression of the statement. Some of the decisions taken in the Turkish courts, however, still take into account only the content of the statement, resulting in contradictory decisions (Uygun 2004). The bulk of the explanation behind resistance lies in entrenched ideological legacies rooted in the so-called 'Sèvres Syndrome', named after the Sèvres Treaty that partitioned the Ottoman Empire among the European powers. This situation becomes particularly severe when the cases at hand concern the crucial ingredients of this fear-loaded legacy, such as the Armenian taboo and the Kurdish question (Çarkğlu and Kirişçi 2004).[9]

It is indeed the case that the costs for the governing party are not reduced to a sufficient level in the area of freedom of expression. The EU conditions have been relatively clear from the start and involved the reform of the penal code. Rule adoption was undertaken with a new Penal Code, with the reservation of Article 301, which the government is reluctant to reform, despite heavy pressure from the Union (Turkish Daily News 2007).[10] We believe that the government views its overhaul as not only too costly in the face of upcoming elections where the competition is characterized by nationalist issues, but also irreconcilable with the nationalist ideological leanings in crucial segments of its own party. Since it is the members of the judiciary who bring Article 301 cases to court and convict individuals on its basis, one can talk of little diffusion of democratic values among them. This may be harder to achieve in the Turkish case with a large and deeply established judicial system.

Freedom of association and the protection of minorities

The ideological baggage discussed above can also be discerned in resistance to reform attempts regarding freedom of association and the protection of minorities in Turkey. With respect to freedom of association, the New Law on Associations that came into force in November 2004 constituted a major step in expanding the freedoms accorded to civil society organizations by reducing the possibility of state interference and thus helped resolve many of the state restrictions that hampered civil society activity until recently (Law 5253/2004). The most problematic aspect of the right of association, however, is intimately linked to the debate on the protection of minorities in Turkey. Regarding this protection, progress has mostly been achieved on the discursive front. The issue has in fact for the first time penetrated into the public sphere as well as on the legislative/institutional front, where certain advances have been made with respect to the status of both non-Muslim and Muslim minorities, in particular the Kurdish minority.

The legal status of minorities in Turkey was established by the 1923 Treaty of Lausanne, which defined minorities on the basis of religion.[11] The main problems suffered by religious minorities in Turkey have been the lack of legal personality and the impossibility of acquiring or selling property. Despite the fact that the reform packages (specifically the third, fourth and sixth) have addressed the problem by allowing non-Muslim minorities to register the property they actually use as long as they can prove ownership, the regulation that was issued following the amendment required foundations to follow incredibly lengthy and cumbersome bureaucratic procedures, as well as creating the mechanisms for further bureaucratic intervention in the process. Moreover, it failed to bring about a just solution regarding the return of their already confiscated properties by the state. The new draft Law on Foundations prepared by the Directorate General for Foundations with the aim of easing these problems received many criticisms, primarily from the EU. While it expanded the grounds for claims to property, the new law failed to resolve the problems over confiscation, especially of property sold to third parties (Radikal 2005a).[12] The government took action to revise the draft law in January 2006, not only in response to EU criticism but also due to the daunting prospect of cases piling up at the ECtHR (Radikal 2006a).[13] However, as of June 2006 the draft report of the European Parliament on Turkey's progress towards accession clearly states that restrictions still remain as regards legal personality, the training of clergy, work permits, schools and internal management as well as issues pertaining to confiscated properties (European Parliament 2006, 6).

Hence in this sphere of reform, rule implementation especially has been very slow and insufficient, due mainly to the mindsets of the bureaucracy – particularly in the Directorate General for Foundations – that prepare the implementing regulations and deal with the activities of the associations on a daily basis. This is once again driven by a perception of non-Muslim minorities as a threat to 'national security' that needs to be strictly controlled. Such a conceptualization also lies at the heart of the ban on the training of non-Muslim clergy, which also remains untouched by the reform initiatives. This issue has figured regularly in the National Security Political Documents, apart from the most recent one adopted in October 2005 (Radikal 2005b).[14]

The progress in reform has also been mixed for the most numerous Muslim minority in Turkey, namely the Kurdish minority. The eventual capture of the Kurdish Workers' Party (PKK) leader, the emergence of EU conditionality and the growing attraction of Northern Iraq for Turkey's Kurds contributed in Turkey to the increasing perception of the Kurdish problem as a minority issue with socioeconomic and identity-related dimensions to it, rather than just a military matter. This led to gradual shifts in the official views on this front, leading to certain reforms directly intended to improve the lives of the Kurdish minority.

It is difficult to talk of 'rule transfer' from the EU in the case of the Kurdish minority issue, since the EU refrains from providing clear prescriptions in this field to candidate countries and applies a rather fuzzy type of conditionality in this sphere (Hughes and Sasse 2003). This ambiguity leaves the candidate states with wide options to pursue. In the Turkish context, since the Kurdish issue is linked to wider human rights matters, one can argue for a high degree of rule transfer and even some degree of rule internalization by the political elites in the executive in this respect, whereas reform exclusively oriented for the Kurdish minority (i.e. language rights) remains limited both in legal terms and in implementation. This is mainly due to the fact that the shift – at both elite and public levels – from the traditional interpretation of the Turkish nation to a redefined pluralist notion of political community, which requires a more inclusive concept of citizenship and the recognition of cultural and ethnic pluralism in the country, is proving to be a very painful process in Turkey (Kurban 2003).

This once again demonstrates the prevalence of the Sèvres Syndrome and the problems of past ideological legacy, which are major impediments to the internalization of the political reform process, not only regarding the protection of minorities, but also democratic reforms in all spheres and at all levels of decision-making in the country. The combination of the prevalence of this ideological legacy with increasing terrorist activity makes it very difficult to attain sustainable lower costs for the policy makers to undertake substantial reform in this field. This also casts doubts on the future trajectory of reform, since it makes it very vulnerable to the state of internal security in the country.

Judicial capacity and independence

The Turkish judicial system has historically been bound by three major problems, which have become subjects of EU conditionality to varying degrees: excessive workload hampering efficiency, insufficient independence and impartiality, and inconsistent interpretation of the law.

Excessive workload and efficiency issues

Over the last three years there have been certain important reform initiatives to address the problem of efficiency in the Turkish judiciary. As identified by the December 2004 Report of the European Commission for the Efficiency of Justice (CEPEJ) of the Council of Europe, public expenditure on the judiciary, in terms of the national budget or as a percentage of gross average salary, is low in Turkey compared with EU member countries (Council of Europe 2004). Recent attempts have aimed to increase spending on the judicial system in Turkey.[15] The EU has often emphasized the need for reform in this sphere, primarily through its progress reports. However, this issue has never attained fundamental importance in EU–Turkish relations. Hence the steps taken can be better conceptualized as a response to the reactions from the judiciary and other civil servants, who are also insufficiently remunerated. Improving economic conditions in the aftermath of the 2001 economic crisis were also helpful in this respect.[16]

The EU impact is more visible in other reforms aiming to increase efficiency in the Turkish justice system. In line with recommendations from the EU, 136 courthouses with an inadequate caseload were closed and 511 judges and prosecutors were transferred to other locations (European Commission 2004b, 26). The Ministry has also lifted the division of labor between Peace Courts and General Courts of First Instance in order to reduce the number of artificial suits. Alternative Dispute Resolution (ADR) mechanisms will now be introduced through the Law on General Administrative Procedures, to deal with minor disputes between individuals or between individuals and the administration. The Criminal Procedure Law has significantly simplified rules regarding jurisdiction to prevent artificial suits. The new Penal Code and the Criminal Procedure Code has introduced a system of plea bargaining. The Criminal Procedure Code now brings the right of courts to reject indictments brought on insufficient evidence, aiming to curb the number of unmeritorious cases brought by public prosecutors. The Ministry of Justice, in line with EU recommendations, has also made the necessary legal changes to create a judicial police to ensure more effective criminal investigations enabling public prosecutors to present complete files to courts and thus reducing the duration of trials and the delays (Bjornberg and Cranston 2005, 95–100). The Law on Judges and Public Prosecutors adopted in December 2005 provides for the recruitment of 4000 additional judges and public prosecutors, which will lead to an almost 50 percent increase in their number, significantly reducing the delays in the system.[17]

Similar steps have also been taken with respect to the improvement of information and communication technology. The National Judicial Network Project – which started in 2001 and was concluded by the end of 2006 – with a budget of 170 million Euros, aims to establish an information network between the courts and the other institutions of the Ministry of Justice, in order to speed up court proceedings and ensure uniformity (Bjornberg and Cranston 2005, 98). According to a judge in Anatolia, 'even the early stages of the National Judicial Network Project have led to a significant increase in efficiency of judicial services, although the amount of work remains constant, the workload seems to have decreased'.[18]

While the general efficiency problem in the Turkish judiciary has been a recurring theme in EU progress reports on Turkey, the specific steps outlined above were clearly articulated as recommendations in EU advisory reports to the Ministry of Justice (Bjornberg and Richmond, 2004; Bjornberg and Cranston, 2005). According to official reports on the Ministry of Justice, it is also clear that there were no significant veto players resisting steps on this front. In fact, these reforms were strongly backed by most members of the judiciary as well as the political elite, since they largely coincided with their interests in a well-functioning judiciary (Bjornberg and Cranston 2005, 94–100). Hence the way in which specific EU recommendations, such as the establishment of a judicial police and the introduction of ADR mechanisms, have been adopted demonstrates how EU conditionality with clear guidelines and without any veto players in the domestic sphere can lead to rule adoption. However, as for rule implementation, since the new measures for efficiency are very recent or are still being finalized, it remains difficult to make a definitive judgment. It is only with the measures introduced in the new Penal Code and the new Criminal Procedure Code that one has emerging evidence on this front and can see signs towards rule implementation. Although updated quantitative data is not yet available, there are accounts from various courts across the country that especially the new provisions on plea bargaining and the better preparation of indictments are already helping to decrease the number of cases filed at courts (Bjornberg and Cranston 2005, 47–8). Hence there are signs that the new measures are being well received and utilized by members of the judiciary, with no major problem regarding rule internalization, making implementation easier. However with respect to some of the other measures specified above, rule implementation may prove more difficult. Establishment of the judicial police is one of those measures that will need to be supplemented by significant capacity building to be effectively implemented.

Another measure requiring a considerable degree of institutional/administrative capacity, which is strongly supported by the EU, relates to the establishment of Regional Courts of Appeal in 2005. Aside from the previously mentioned reforms where the EU gave direction to reform through recommendations, the EU – through the twinning mechanism – is directly and financially involved in the establishment of the Regional Court of Appeals, which is intended to reduce partially the workload of the High Court of Appeals and help to make it concentrate on its main function, which is to 'ensure a unity of legal practice and to enlighten the interpretation of provisions of legal codes' (Bjornberg and Richmond 2004, 100).

Judicial independence

Articles 138 and 140 enshrine the principle of judicial independence in the Turkish constitution. In practice, however, its independence is undermined by several other constitutional provisions, which establish a link between the judiciary and the executive in the process of selecting, training, appointing, promoting, transferring and disciplining judges. Although the constitution provides for security of tenure, the career paths of judges and prosecutors (through appointments, transfers, promotions, reprimands and other mechanisms) are determined by the High Council of Judges and Prosecutors, which is chaired by the Minister of Justice and of which the under-secretary of the Ministry of Justice is also a member. Judges in Turkey are regularly evaluated by judicial inspectors, who are civil servants working within the Ministry of Justice. The Council is entirely dependent upon a personnel directorate and inspection board of the Ministry of Justice for its administrative tasks. Limits on independence are also observed at the point of entry into the judicial profession, where the Ministry of Justice is highly involved.

This issue is regularly brought up by members of the judiciary, civil society institutions and academics as well as external actors, particularly the EU via its Progress Reports and Advisory Visit Reports.[19] However, the Ministry of Justice, as the major veto player, remains very resistant to change on this front. Provisions impeding judicial independence were prepared after the 1980 military coup and reversed the 1961 constitution's order of the administration of judges by the judges themselves. They all seem to be upheld today without significant change. Maintenance of this status quo arises from a combination of two factors. First, there is the reluctance of the EU to insist on change on this front. Commission Progress Reports and Advisory Reports touch upon the issue, but it never gains prominence as a benchmark in any high-level statements or contacts. So far it has never been pressed as a formal condition tied to EU policy towards Turkey, such as the opening of accession negotiations.[20] This relatively weak conditionality is combined with the strength of the veto player, namely the executive. While judges and public prosecutors are generally in favor of reforms geared towards judicial independence, the executive seems to be the primary actor resisting reform on this front, due principally to the high costs it perceives to its interests (Bjornberg and Cranston 2005, 8–17).

Inconsistent interpretation of the law

Until recently, when Turkey became subject to EU conditionality, courts (in particular the High Courts, i.e. Court of Cassation) were very reluctant to expand fundamental freedoms in their judgments. This was particularly the case in the 1990s, when internal conflict was at its peak. As fundamental freedoms began to be introduced after the Helsinki Summit of 1999, the courts have started to apply these reforms, but rather slowly and inconsistently. Although criminal proceedings launched against individuals on the basis of infamous articles of the old Penal Code, such as Article 312 (incitement to class, ethnical, religious or racial hatred), Article 169 (actions facilitating the operation of terrorist organizations in any manner whatsoever) and Article 159 (insulting state institutions), were generally concluded with acquittals, following the relevant amendments in 2003 and 2004, there are still signs of the inconsistent use of articles of the new Penal Code adopted in 2005, particularly in cases concerning the freedom of expression. Hence the picture on this front remains mixed.

This is best demonstrated through the presentation of a crucially relevant case study, involving the use of Article 301 of the new Penal Code (see Note 7). This is the case brought against the famous Turkish novelist Orhan Pamuk (Radikal 2006b).[21] In an interview for a Swiss newspaper in February 2005, he was quoted as stating that '1 million Armenians and 30,000 Kurds have been killed in this country'.[22] A complaint was filed against him by a civil initiative of a group of lawyers called the 'Lawyers' Union' (*Hukukçular Birliği*), on the basis of the claim that the statement contravened Article 301 of the new Penal Code by 'insulting Turkishness'. The court decided in the end that the permission of the Ministry of Justice was required on the grounds that the old Penal Code was in favor of the defendant. It needs to be pointed out that the High Court of Cassation (*Yargitay*) played a crucial role in this decision since it ruled, in the period following the opening of the case against Pamuk, that cases opened prior to 1 June 2005 – before the new Penal Code – require permission from the Ministry of Justice and hence set a precedent for the Pamuk case. Upon the decision of the Ministry stating that it does not have the right to give permission for a trial, the court dropped the case in January 2006.[23]

These cases provide many insights into the current ideological state of the judiciary in Turkey, where the EU has an important, albeit limited impact. EU impact is most visible in the reformed laws in the new Penal Code, which were closely monitored by the Commission and were even set as clear benchmarks in the opening of accession negotiations, leading to formal rule adoption.[24] The Pamuk case also demonstrates that EU reactions may have an impact on final decisions concerning popular cases. The EU is also influential through its mechanisms of 'democratic socialization' when it comes to the ideological matters of the judiciary. Drawing upon EU recommendations, the responsibilities regarding in-service training have now been transferred from the Ministry to the Justice Academy, also responsible for in-service training, legally established in 2003. The quality of the curriculum in both pre-service and in-service training is being substantially improved, owing partly to EU efforts in this area. As well as Turkish law and legal procedure, both types of training now extensively cover the European Convention on Human Rights (ECHR) and EU law as well as foreign languages (French and English in particular). As part of an EU Commission-funded project, administered in cooperation with the Ministry of Justice, 225 judges and public prosecutors attended training seminars on the ECHR and the case law of ECtHR in order to be trained as human rights trainers. These 225 judges and public prosecutors subsequently conducted human rights training for all other judges and public prosecutors in Turkey. Moreover, again with the financial assistance of the EU, seminars were held throughout Turkey for judges and prosecutors on EU law, judicial cooperation, intellectual property rights, juvenile criminal justice and organized crime. Various judges and public prosecutors have been sent abroad for training on specific issues such as industrial and intellectual property rights and corruption. A new project has recently been initiated to train a number of judges and public prosecutors, forensic medicine experts and candidate judges and public prosecutors specifically on issues relating to torture and ill-treatment.[25]

Such attempts are clearly paying off in reforming the Turkish justice system, as seen in the stances of some judges and public prosecutors in the cases described above. The fact that judges and public prosecutors have been increasingly referring to ECtHR decisions in their cases, especially in the last two years, is also indicative of the positive change occurring in the judicial system.[26] However, as seen in the lower court decisions outlined above, examples of restricted jurisdiction are also occurring – albeit less frequently than before. Hence it is clear that there is currently a division within the judiciary itself (both among judges and public prosecutors), mainly on ideological lines, which goes to show that rule internalization among the members of the judiciary is a crucial variable, the lack of which is hampering the political reform process. The lower courts, in particular, are more intent on 'preserving the national interest' whereas the Higher Courts, while far from being perfect, are a few steps ahead in the shift of mentality. It is in fact the case that there are loopholes provided by the vague wording in some provisions of the new Penal Code, which were explained in the previous section on the basis of the cost-benefit calculations of the government in relation to prevalent ideological legacies. However, the most crucial reason behind such restricted jurisdiction lies in the way in which judges and public prosecutors internalize traditional state sensitivities and reflect these in their decisions, which will eventually form the basis for their career evaluations within the framework summarized above, where judicial independence remains questionable. The fear of separatism and partition of the country among different ethnic groups – the Sèvres Syndrome – seems to be strongly entrenched in Turkish judiciary. The Sèvres Syndrome underlines the arguments within an isolationist, nationalist framework with a focus on the necessity for 'independence' and makes it very difficult to attain value diffusion, despite the growth of knowledge resources among the members of the judiciary and their increasing EU-aided socialization efforts described above.

It is also important to note that heterogeneous and well-entrenched interest groups that cooperate well with the veto players continue to use their extensive links within the judicial system to create obstacles that polarize the reform debate and effectively slow it down. So far, as seen in the cases described above, most of their attempts have been resolved in favor of the reform initiative in the country. However, the underlying concern is that such eventually inconsequential cases opened against the intellectual elites in the country have provided a framework for self-censure and timidity on the part of the reformist forces. Especially going towards the presidential and general elections of 2007 these cases help to silence the pro-EU reformist rhetoric in favor of increasingly outspoken nationalist, xenophobic speakers of the Sèvres Syndrome unilaterally dominating the public agenda.

The first two sections presented above can help us argue that Turkey now displays the characteristics of a 'minimal' democracy having taken the necessary steps to be considered as a 'substantial' democracy. The existing gray zones in certain areas of basic rights, most particularly in the area of freedom of expression together with problems of institutional and administrative capacity, suggest that Turkey is struggling to improve its democratic standards. However, the characteristics of Turkish democracy, especially in the aftermath of the reform process initiated in the late 1990s and early 2000s, also go beyond the mere existence of free, fair, recurrent and competitive elections and a sufficiently viable institutional structure. The country has a vibrant civil society where conflicting opinions are voiced and heard,[27] a system in which basic rights and freedoms are largely being respected and an experienced bureaucracy able to implement policy despite the remaining difficulties with the pace and efficiency observed in this area, due to the 'entrenchment' of its bureaucratic strata.

The entire EU-related political and economic reforms have been undertaken within a very competitive party system long divided along ethnic, sectarian lines that typically did not allow the formation of a stable and non-fragmented Assembly. The most recent November 2002 elections could be seen as a peculiar exception that allowed only two major parties to gain representation, given the 10 percent nationwide vote threshold for gaining representation in the Turkish Grand National Assembly (TBMM). However, this 'forced stability' and low fragmentation in the Assembly resulted in the increased importance of intra-party divisions, especially in the AKP and the opposition outside the TBMM. The fact that the AKP has its roots in the anti-systemic pro-Islamist movement renders the opposition particularly sensitive on libertarian reforms that allow pro-Islamist groups to gain more access to the inner mechanisms of the secularist Turkish state. Thus, the election of a new president in May 2007, who controls important veto players and has power over appointments to key bureaucratic posts, gained salience in shaping the resistance to the AKP rule, which was almost automatically transformed into criticism of and resistance to EU reforms as well. With the approach of the election of the president, followed in a few months by the next general election, resistance to the reform movement seems to gain momentum rendering the AKP government more timid than ever in its willingness to continue with the reforms. Hence, interestingly enough, the fact that Turkey has a well-functioning party competition and electoral democracy with many diverse interest groups forms the very basis of sporadic anti-democratic reactions and problematic functioning of the country's system of protection of basic rights. As such, the resistance of the anti-EU groups, who find access within the political and administrative system for creating problem cases in proper protection of basic human rights and freedom of expression, has an electoral logic. Such seemingly elite decisions have larger mass bases as well. Interplay between the pro-reform and resistance forces is thus likely to continue until the end of the next general election campaign.

The ongoing cycles of progress and regression have become more volatile with the passing and implementation of reform packages and thus form perhaps the most credible evidence that Turkey has become a more democratic polity than ever. Reform and its implications are being debated and wrong paths are being taken, as well as the paths necessary for a fully functioning quality democracy. The question of consolidation of a well-functioning quality democracy, however, could only be answered after the next general election. Unless a clear winning position is obtained in that election by the pro-EU forces, consolidation may remain questionable.

Strengthening institutional and administrative capacity

Ever since the first competitive elections in 1950, albeit with interruptions by the military, an institutional memory has been built up in the Turkish parliamentary system. Following a decade of increasing authoritarian tendencies of the popularly elected Democratic Party (DP), in power during the 1950s, the first military regime brought a constitutional framework that opened the country to a competitive multi-party system and allowed for a liberal institutional setting. Nevertheless, the turbulent two decades that followed ended with a reactionary constitution imposed by the 1980 military regime.[28] Ever since, the civilian governments have been unable to liberalize the constraining institutional setting imposed by the 1980 regime.

The most recent reform packages were in a sense all aimed at this historical mission of freeing the Turkish constitution from the impositions of the 1980 regime in particular. In other words, the whole reform movement of the most recent few years is rooted in the civilian efforts to liberalize the constitutional framework during the last two decades. They thus draw on a considerable intellectual heritage not only of running a competitive multi-party electoral system but also one in which a long series of policy initiatives for reform and capacity building in public administration has taken place. In this specific sense the Turkish experience stands as a unique example in contrast to that of other countries involved in past EU expansions. Compared with Spain, Portugal and Greece, as well as all the Eastern European countries of the last round of EU expansion (see Morlino 1998 and Mattina 2004), Turkey has accumulated a considerably longer tradition of reforms which were all conducive to building a resistance capacity through well-established circles of interest groups in the bureaucracy and their collaborators in various sectors of the Turkish economy. Veto players in the Turkish case are considerably more diversified than their counterparts in other comparable settings. They are not only outside the electoral scene but also well integrated into the party system, which is constantly seeking coalitions that could win elections. They are part of sectarian coalitions as well as economic interests and ethnically based ideological groups. They are also deeply rooted in the economic sectors with considerable sums of capital they carry with them into this inherently risky political competition on the issue of EU-related reforms. Accordingly, when one looks at the military, or some segments of security or civilian bureaucracy, in Turkey one is also looking into their extensive networks of partners in private sector businesses of different sizes, in different sectarian organizations, in interest groups of different geographic and agricultural localities. Similar multi-dimensionality around crosscutting cleavages characterizes all the veto players as well as pro-reform groups. As such, the historical complexity of the Turkish reform movement constitutes a serious obstacle, as well as providing a considerable accumulation of experience in reform.

Ability to implement policy

On May 21, 2004 a new Law of Statistics was sent to the TBMM. To date, the Law has not been acted on since it still remains to be discussed and voted on by the Parliament. The collection of official statistics has been the official responsibility of the State Institute of Statistics (SIS). It is known that from time to time private and scientific collection of social data through surveys, for example, has been problematic. An odd and ambiguous wording in the law that instituted the SIS was interpreted as saying that all statistical data collection has to go through the SIS and has to have its approval.[29] Therefore private and scientific survey interviewing was restricted. The new law aims not only to provide a modern and unambiguous framework for data collection, storage and access but also to set up a Turkish Institute of Statistics to coordinate all such efforts in the public sphere.

In the meantime the SIS has speeded up its efforts to collect data on various aspects of Turkish social life that it has traditionally avoided handling. Such data is still slow in being disseminated to the public. Scientific purpose access is also very limited to the university and research community. Raw data is not stored in a way that would make it accessible to proper statistical analysis by all users. Usually it is the insiders who get access to such usefully coded and stored data. Census data is also known to be full of faults and access to it is restricted. In short, meaningful and dependable statistical data is still difficult for the public to access and is unreliable. These inconsistencies have been largely corrected in the trade and monetary Central Bank statistics.

However, the data on regional investment figures across provinces comes from different ministries in a largely contradictory fashion. Data concerning agriculture, culture and social life is relatively rare, unreliable and problematic for policymakers who want to make sensible use of it. In short, reform of the statistical base has been slow.

The IMF and the World Bank have been effective in pushing for better data collection and meaningful data storage, especially in the monetary sector.[30] The EU has allocated resources for the betterment of other statistical data collection and improvement of the statistical system in the country. Progress has again been slow, primarily due to insufficient bureaucratic capacity and insufficient funding. Data collection has been so multi-layered and uncoordinated that joining long-established branches of data collection agencies under a single coordinated umbrella has proved to be very difficult. Resistance in principle was not observed in this area.

Organization and quality of civil service

Civil service reform also has been on the agenda for decades in Turkey. There are elaborate-looking merit, performance and promotion evaluation schemes. However, all in all these are far from effective in de-politicizing the administration of the bureaucracy. The most notable change over the last few years is the institutionalization of a single bureaucracy entrance exam. We believe, however, that the merit evaluation schemes within the bureaucratic institutions are simply out of date and ineffective. Most importantly they depend on the final appreciation and discretion of the supervisors. There simply are no objective evaluation schemes beyond examination results that are binding for promotions, for example. Equally important in this chaotic environment is the fact that different institutions have different internal statutes for the regulation of the performance of their own personnel. Most notable among these are those in the Ministry of Foreign Affairs, the Ministry of Finance, the Central Bank and of course the military. Given the natural differences in the expected merit criteria for different institutional contexts, such differentiation is intuitively appealing. However, the differing extent of the impact of political patronage based intervention and the large variance in minimum merit expectations are undermining effective coordination and advance in the composition of public administration.

The Law on the Right to Obtain Information (ROI) which was passed by the parliament in October 2003 (Law 4982), provides an extensive list of opportunities for ordinary citizens to ask for information from different branches of the public administration and they are entitled to obtain these in due time. The main problem with the ROI Law is that there is very little capacity in many branches of the public institutions to provide whatever information is being sought from them. The supply side of this process will have to develop over time and will depend especially on the tenacity of civil society and private citizens to pursue sensitive information in the courts if necessary. Without organized demand for such information, this law will not be effective and cannot be developed to modern standards.[31]

The analysis above indicates the intricate ways in which the reforms towards strengthening the legislative and administrative capacity were shaped, primarily by internal political and bureaucratic forces. The role of the EU in this area had remained limited, due largely to an already well-established system with entrenched interest groups.

Combating corruption and increasing state accountability

The execution and regulation of elections is quite well organized in Turkey, where fair and free elections are not disputed. The issue of corruption, however, was salient in Turkish politics only a few years ago during the coalition government of DSP-MHP-ANAP (*Dmokratik Sol Parti* – Democratic Left Party/*Milliyetçi Hareket* Partisi – Nationalist Action Party/*Anavatan Partisi* – Motherland Party), which came to power after the general election in 1999. At that time combating corruption was seen as a prerequisite for economic reform that was aimed at removing unproductive segments in the economy that captured funds via corruption and therefore impeded economic growth. The breaking point came when a major lender to the state went bankrupt in the process of which the whole financial system started to feel the coming crisis. A few months after the collapse of this major bank came a political crisis that broke the camel's back. After a harsh exchange of words between the president and cabinet ministers at a regular National Security Council (*Milli Güvenlik Kurulu,* MGK) meeting, the then Prime Minister Būlent Ecevit publicly declared that there was a major crisis in the executive office between the government and the president. Interest rates soared to over 3000 percent overnight. The most serious economic crisis of the Republican period had begun.[32]

At that stage, there were corruption scandals every other day that exposed one or the other coalition partner in a big public tender, privatization project or similar context where public authorities and private sector met. Civil society, as reflected in the media, as well as in think tank activities – the most prominent one being the Turkish Economic and Social Studies Foundation (*Türkiye Ekonomik ve Sosyal Eüdler Vakfi,* TESEV) – were all using this opportunity to keep the issue on the agenda (Adaman, Carkoğlu 2002; and Şenatalar 2003).

The World Bank and, to a lesser extent, the IMF was also pushing for anti-corruption reform to show that loans obtained from the international funding agencies were being used properly and that the overall business environment in Turkey did not allow for corruption practices that provided favors for groups in competition with one another and thus creating inefficiencies in the process.[33] However, despite these pressures, virtually nothing was accomplished when the economic crisis required a new economic policy regime under the control of Kemal Derviş. The extraordinary circumstances that brought Derviş to head the Ministry of State in charge of the economy seem to have led him and his team to underplay the importance of corruption.

They focused on budgetary discipline and macro-economic balances and monetary policy aggregates, rather than going into the real economy and its relationship via corrupt networks with the state. It seems that the crisis administration at the time did not want to muddy the waters by investigating corruption scandals that might only disrupt business morale and break trust relationships between private and public sectors.

Within 18 months of Derviş arrival in Ankara an early election was on the agenda. Corruption did not surface as a major point of contention during the election campaign. When Abdullah Gül formed the first AKP government after the election, the *Emergency Action Plan* included some remarks about corruption. However, nothing substantial came out of it, primarily because the whole approach of the politicians and civil society players by then had been completely reshaped. The AKP came to power when the emergency economic policies had already been in effect for more than a year. The Iraqi crisis was approaching and uncertainty was continuing on the European front. So for the first few months the AKP hesitated to do anything substantial about the economy. Then came the unexpected no vote in the parliament concerning the American use of Turkish soil for military action in Iraq. As a consequence, Turkey was faced with a lukewarm, if not totally cold, welcome by the Americans and at best considerable uncertainty concerning its relations with the EU, as reported by newspapers at the time. Therefore the AKP's first choice was not to disturb the economy because, if it became necessary, the kind of help that might be forthcoming from the western capitals might be substantially smaller than that had been guaranteed in the previous crisis of 2001. Slowly but surely the AKP adopted 'wait and see' and 'don't muddy the waters' policies. It was evident that civil society representatives also hesitated to air any concerns about corruption cases. This quietness of the civil society players is also evidence of a lack of self-confidence and effective power on their part, facing an all-powerful single party government of the AKP in office following a series of coalition governments marred by infighting and indecisiveness for more than a decade (see Ozbudun 2007, 206–21).

Conflict of interest standards for public employees and international treaties

Over a long period a number of precautions have been taken to regulate conflict of interest in the public sector, especially concerning public sector employees and their conditions of work if they resign from their public office. For instance, under the terms of existing law all public employees declare a detailed list of their properties and are expected to update them regularly. However, it is not unusual to see a high-ranking state bureaucrat from the Treasury, the Central Bank, or some regulatory or investment ministry, resigning from their post only to immediately begin working for the private sector. Such experiences were very common, especially in the banking sector prior to the 2001 crisis. Despite long-established regulations against this, very little seems to have been achieved.

Over the past five years a number of laws have been passed by the parliament against corruption. Some have been international treaties. The World Bank and the IMF have actively sought most of these laws and the progress reports of the EU have also underlined their necessity.[34] In other words, the fight against corruption exemplifies a case where the EU and the international financial institutions complemented and strengthened one another's demands of the domestic players.

Right to information, protection of whistle-blowers and ombudsman

As noted above, a Right to Obtain Information (ROI) Law has been enacted. However, outside independent audit provision was vetoed by the president as part of the Basic Law of Public Administration on the basis that it was against the constitution. The ROI Law resulted primarily from pressure from the EU combined with domestic forces. However, it is too early to know if regular citizens are actually using the new law.

The issue of workers' protection when they are the whistle-blower in a corruption case has been little discussed in Turkey and no provision for such protection is presently available. Nor are there any anti-corruption watchdog agencies. TESEV once formed a civil initiative to prevent corruption but this was also short-lived. So far, there is no umbrella institution to coordinate anti-corruption policies. International cooperation is mostly approved under international treaties. However, it is not clear which of the range of institutions will take up the responsibility to be the counterpart in Turkey of these international agencies from other countries as well as international organizations.

The issue of an ombudsman has been brought to the public agenda several times. There seems little opposition to the idea, but there is also little, if any, agreement as to who should undertake this responsibility. It seems that the idea of an independent authority who is not responsible to anyone and is empowered by special legal forces is a notion foreign to the Turkish elites The AKP government passed legislation to establish an ombudsman in the Turkish public administration system but the president vetoed it on the grounds of being anti-constitutional. So, if the outcome of this debate is dependent on political culture alone, the surest expectation is that it will never happen.

All in all, the area of anti-corruption policy-making in Turkey has remained mostly isolated from any impact of the EU conditionality requirements. Although this area is covered critically in EU progress reports on Turkey, the influence of the IMF and World Bank demands during economic crises has been much more instrumental.[35]

Police reform and civilian control of security forces

The role of the military in the Turkish context deserves special attention, since it is very much linked to the issue of democratic governance and the rule of law in the country. From the founding years of the Republican regime onward the military has been a critical player in the political scene of modern Turkey. It directly intervened in 1960 and 1980 by a coup d'état, took over the executive powers and intruded significantly in legislative and judiciary functions for several years in each period. In 1971 it issued a memorandum, which came to be recognized as a 'coup by memorandum' (Hale 1994). Most recently in 1997 the demands by the military side of the National Security Council (MGK) led to a similar impact to that of the 1971 intervention and came to be referred to as the 'post-modern coup'.[36] As a result of all these interventions and regimes, the military gained important guarantees that enhanced its role in subsequent civilian regimes. This was accomplished through two main strategies. One was to incorporate into the constitution certain substantive values cherished by the military – i.e. the territorial and national integrity of the state and the modernizing reforms of Kemal Atatürk. The second was to create formal institutions dominated by the military with the duty of preserving such values, namely the MGK (Özbudun 2000, 105–24).

The role of the police in Turkish politics, when compared with that of the military, has been limited. At times, the civilian powers in office used the police to intimidate and oppress certain groups in the country. Once these were sympathizers and members of certain parties in opposition, at other times they included fractions of certain marginal ideological groups and civilians of an ethnic or sectarian background. Often, the targets for police oppression included members of groups where these interests overlapped. However, most if not all such incidents have been under the strict control of the civilian authorities, or have involved a small circle within the security network aiming to serve the interests of some civilian authority. During the chaotic years before the 1980 coup the police were divided along ideological lines, coalescing with larger right- or left-wing like-minded organizations. These were effectively eliminated by the 1980 military regime (see, among others, Cao and Burton 2006).

Military sector reform

In the last few years, there have indeed been serious attempts to realign civilian–military relations in Turkey. Against this background, Turkey chose to reform those areas specified clearly by the EU, such as the powers of the MGK, the presence of military representatives on public bodies, the transparency and control of the military budget. With the 2001 constitutional amendments, the sixth and seventh harmonization packages and the May 2004 constitutional amendments, a number of fundamental changes have been made to the duties, functioning and composition of the MGK, as well as to the conditions relating to the monitoring of military spending.[37]

The number of civilian members of the MGK was increased and the MGK secretariat has been transformed into a consultative body that is no longer able to conduct national security investigations on its own initiative. The seventh harmonization package and the May 2004 constitutional amendments brought state assets utilized by the military under the inspection of the Court of Auditors, with no reservations regarding 'secrecy clauses'.[38] With the new Public Finance Ruling and Controlling Law that came into force in December 2003, the long-criticized extra-budgetary funds were brought into the defense budget and more detailed information and documentation are now required with defense budget proposals (Law 5018/2003). Parliamentary control is further enhanced by changes in the method of budgeting, which now require performance reports to be submitted to the Turkish Grand National Assembly – Türkiye Büyük *Millet Meelisi*. The new law also paves the way to value-for-money inquiries by the TBMM.

Despite the fact that these new laws give the TGNA enhanced powers to review a now more transparent military budget, it still remains to be seen whether the lawmakers themselves will be willing to make use of their new rights (Heper 2005, 28). There is already some evidence that the legislature is now more forthcoming than before on questioning the military's bids for funds. Regarding the preparation of the 2005 budget, the Minister of Defense has stated that one-third of the proposed defense budget was reduced by parliamentary reviews, leading for the first time in a decade to a reduction in military spending to second rank behind education (*Hürriyet* 2004).[39] Despite the fact that military spending increased by 0.5 percent in the 2006 budget, education spending is higher than defense expenditure for the second successive year (European Commission 2005c, 13).

Thus, important steps have been taken on the way to attaining further civilianization of Turkish politics, due to a combination of EU conditionality and a favorable domestic climate. The EU's emphasis on aligning civil–military relations in Turkey with European standards for the fulfillment of the Copenhagen political criteria was an important driving force in these reforms. The issue has been brought up regularly and consistently in Progress Reports of the Commission.[40] However, change on this front did not occur due to purely exogenous pressure. In fact, the reforms were the outcome of the interconnection between the changing domestic climate and EU accession. The political costs of compliance were reduced to a considerable extent by the end of Kurdish separatist terrorism in the 1990s, weakening the previous opposition of the military establishment. At this juncture, we also want to underline the windows of opportunity that opened the way to the reform process in Turkey since 1999. The coming to power of the AKP as a single-party government for the first time since 1991 reduced the effectiveness of the use of the MGK as a strong arm of the military in balancing the civilian initiatives and maintaining its control and assertiveness upon the civilian government. A popular single-party government made it very difficult to raise a dissenting military voice on the political scene. Moreover, the security environment became increasingly hazardous with the occupation of Iraq by the allied forces under US leadership. The inability of the AKP government to support the use of Turkish soil by the invading US forces at the very beginning of the war in Iraq left the country uneasy about its strategic prerogatives.

It is not clear which side the military took on this decision. However, in its aftermath the AKP was willing to take responsibility for it, as it quickly became a popularly supported decision (Kardas 2006).

For the first time since the mid-1970s, Turkish and American security establishments were talking different languages and having second thoughts as to one another's real strategic intentions. Such uncertainty in the strategic arena left the Turkish military unable to use the sobering American card in support of its strategic objectives. The AKP government was experiencing a similar isolation in the international arena. They also felt that Turkey's alternatives in the international arena were seriously narrowed by the effective alienation of the US. The anchoring of the country into the EU framework was increasingly being seen as an option without an alternative. Obviously the dynamics of reform were shaped by the declining potency of a key veto player such as the military[41] and by the increasing awareness of the civilian forces that the alternative options were getting ever narrower.

It is also important to note that the reforms demanded by the EU in this field coincide to a large extent with the AKP's own agenda, having no veto players in the executive. Relations between the Islamic political parties and the military have never been smooth in Turkey. Decreasing the military's role in politics would certainly send a positive signal to its constituencies and enhance their legitimacy. Hence, rule internalization for the governmental elite is not a new issue here, since this is already part of their ideological leanings and a further guarantee of their political survival as a centrist party.

Nevertheless, it is still difficult to argue that civil–military relations in Turkey are fully aligned with the EU standards and that rule implementation is complete on this front. There are important issues still to be addressed, such as the limited role of the Ministry of Defense – hence, civilian input – in decision-making concerning security issues (which would itself require an immense amount of institutional capacity building). In addition to this, and even more importantly, statements of military officials on political matters, albeit to a lesser extent, are still communicated via public speeches and press briefings and can still have serious ramifications for the democratic rule of law in the country.

One reason behind this limited rule adoption and implementation can be found in the fuzziness of EU conditionality. Apart from specific issues addressed, such as the functioning of the MGK, civilian control over military spending and the removal of military representatives from civilian boards, the EU chooses to refer to vaguely identified 'informal mechanisms' that need to be overcome for full 'civilian control'.[42] This can be partially explained by the EU's general reluctance to offer a specific recipe in this area of reform, similar to its stance on reforms regarding minorities. However, the bulk of the explanation lies in the underlying societal reasons behind the omnipresent role of the military in Turkey. This mixed picture in military reform hinges to a large extent on the fact that the role of the military in the Turkish context still lies primarily in people's beliefs and expectations, continuously strengthened by the media and the education system.

As the country approached the presidential and the general elections in 2007, the military became increasingly willing to step out in protest at several EU officials' statements and the overall policy drive to establish complete civilian control over the military. This reached a peak after the last-minute nomination of Abdullah Çl as the AKP's candidate for the presidency. The main critique directed at the AKP and Prime Minister Erdogan in the run-up to the presidential elections was the way in which no consensual agreement mechanisms were sought with the opposition and civil society, with the aim of selecting a candidate accepted by a large segment of Turkish society. The fact that Çl himself was a major figure of the National Outlook movement from the days of the Welfare Party and that his election would introduce the headscarf to the top public office in Turkey, via his wife, aggravated the controversy mainly among the secular elite, including the military and certain segments of civil society. On the eve of the first round of votes held in the Turkish Grand Assembly on the election of the president, the military issued a statement on its official website, highlighting the threat to secularism and hinting at a possible intervention if deemed necessary (Office of the Chief of Staff, Turkish Armed Forces 2007). While this was interpreted by most commentators as yet another military memorandum issued to intervene in civilian politics, the statement needs to be situated in a wider framework for a better understanding of what it implies for Turkish internal politics, as well as for Turkey's relations with Europe. The statement has demonstrated once again that the military perceives itself as the guarantor of secularism as well as the territorial integrity of Turkey. However, the way in which the statement was issued (via an electronic website), combined with its highly rudimentary language, shows that it was significantly different from the military warnings of the past, which were delivered either through officially and publicly declared memoranda or through National Security Council meetings. One can interpret this as a restricted warning circumscribed by the fear of external reaction, primarily from the EU, and even an indirect tool to influence the Constitutional Court's decision on the constitutional validity of the presidential elections.[43] Furthermore, what was novel to the Turkish political scene was not just the indirect means and the ambiguity in the way in which it was claimed by the high command, but also the reaction of the governing party. The AKP responded that this was unacceptable in a democracy where the military would have to be subordinate to the government (Minister of Justice 2007). The military did not retaliate. This testifies once again that although civil-military relations are far from being normalized in Turkey, the shape in which they are evolving is not independent of the context provided by Turkey's relations with the EU. The fact that such an obvious defiance of civilian authority was largely supported by the media, as well as representatives of a large body of interest groups, university representatives and intellectuals, also provides further evidence of the heterogeneous character of civil society and its veto players that can easily find or create opportunities for cooperation against reform in the country.

Police reform[44]

We already noted the peculiar role of the police in the Turkish political system. Compared with the role played by the military, the police are historically under much stricter civilian control. Nevertheless, given the ethnic and sectarian cleavages in the country, the long-running deficiencies in the budgetary allocations for the development and maintenance of the administrative capacity in the police force, together with fast developing market economy within the changing global environment Turkey finds herself in, the role of the police has also changed. Domestically, fast urbanization, urban poverty and the consequent rise in urban petty crime have imposed significant pressures upon the police. Concomitantly, a changing international environment where Turkey undertook the role of overseeing a transit route towards the EU countries from its immediate neighborhood, as well as from remote corners of Africa and Central Asia, has increased these pressures even more. Such rising geographical salience is most suitably reflected in the justice and home affairs regulations that had to meet the EU standards both in letter and in implementation (Apap, Carrera and Kirişçi 2004).

The EU accession process has effectively forced the Turkish National Police (TNP) to review its structures, functioning and overall performance. Consequently, the reform process aimed at raising the standards of its organizational capacity, especially in terms of human resources. In so doing, we observe that the primary objective was to have the police carry out their function within the law, to which they themselves are subject. However, three main problem areas can still be diagnosed concerning police services and organization (see European Commission 2003c, 3).[45] One concerns the quality of police services to the public and respect for human rights in the discharge of police tasks, in particular the detention conditions of detainees. The second is pre-service and in-service training. The third is the personnel system including promotions and appointments.

Improving the quality of police services and enforcement of human rights laws

Over the last decade or so the TNP has undergone a continuous restructuring and reorganization to improve its service quality and law enforcement, especially in the area of human rights. For this purpose, many new departments and training facilities have been set up in addition to numerous legislative changes adopted with regard to procedures, operations and the responsibility areas of the police. These changes have primarily been the result of an intensive public debate within the framework of the EU accession process. As such there is no doubt that all of these reforms have at their root the guidance of the EU accession process, the *acquis* and the National Program. Although domestic constituencies have always existed in this regard, incessantly pressurizing the executive office for improved standards, the momentum behind the recent reforms has predominantly come from the EU process. However, given the guidance and incentives provided by the EU, the domestic actors have risen to the occasion and actively taken part in the reform process.

The administrative management of pre-trial detentions continues to be an area of concern, in particular with regard to the prevention of torture and mistreatment. From a legislative perspective, there have been significant improvements in this area. However, practical problems remain in the establishment of a set of standards for the protection of human rights for detainees in police facilities, for the accurate collection and protection of evidence from detained persons, witnesses, victims and crime scenes, and for the design of facilities for the detention of suspected persons.[46] In all these areas, EU-guided and funded projects are underway exemplifying the role of the accession process beyond rule adoption into capacity building.

Improvement of police services and practice critically depends on the working load and conditions of police officers. Typically the Turkish police work under very hard conditions. An average Turkish police officer works 72 hours per week, as compared with 37.5 hours for the average EU officer. A minimum 12-hour working day is the usual practice (European Commission 2003c, 4). It seems that there is also very little predictability in shift patterns. Sometimes on the orders of their superiors, officers may stay on duty for a whole day. There is no pay for overtime and salaries are in general low. Besides the difficulties in raising the service standards, such conditions also make it very difficult to deal with the issues of corruption. However, the financial difficulties of the employees are an acute problem for the whole public sector in Turkey, which will be resolved with increased productivity and better public sector finances. With regards to improvements in administrative productivity, research and planning gains importance and in this regard the EU framework seems to provide ample opportunities to the Turkish police.

Pre-service and in-service training

There are three main branches of the TNP training system. One includes the National Police Academy, which provides basic training to both ranked officers and constables. The Police Academy and the Training Department of the Headquarters provide in-service training. The Police Academy was reconstructed as the Police University by April 2001. Despite reorganization efforts, problems continue to exist in the content, methodology, faculty and the training material. A more serious problem is the fact that training policies are not supported by personnel policies. In quite a number of cases, trained personnel are not appointed in accordance with their areas of expertise. In-service training lacks qualified personnel and coherence in the curriculum content, and remains sporadic (European Commission 2003c, 5).

Apart from the Training Department, individual departments such as the Public Order Department, The Department for Anti-smuggling and Organized Crime, and the Anti-terrorism Department organize their own in-service training with resources available to them. Although these are carried out based on the yearly plan of their respective training departments, there is first of all a lack of coordination among these training programs. Secondly, not only do just a fraction of the officers receive adequate training, but also this training remains of low quality in many instances. Cooperation within the EU programs is effective in changing this picture but the sheer size of the existing needs of the police training system means that a stage has not yet been reached where significant changes are observable in the service delivery systems.

Personnel issues

Personnel evaluations and promotions are handled in a strictly hierarchical centralized fashion by the Department of Personnel of the TNP. According to the 'Regulation of Appointment and Transfer', each sworn member of staff has to serve in the eastern provinces of the country for two to four years. Ranked officers have to do this twice during their career. Even in the western provinces, officers have to be transferred after a certain period of time within the western region, resulting in a very high turnover rate. Each year approximately 40,000 personnel are transferred from one region to another (European Commission 2003c, 7).

There are eight ranks in the TNP ranking system. Currently, there is no effective screening for the selection of officers for promotion. There is a set minimum waiting period of three or four years for promotion to the next rank. Officers are promoted to the next higher rank almost automatically every three or four years without being subject to much of an objective assessment process (European Commission 2003b, 7). The lack of personnel planning, coupled with the lack of a screening process and the large number of officers waiting to be promoted, makes the police force vulnerable to external influences. Highly centralized promotion decisions are made without access to first-hand information on the candidates. All decisions are made based on records, which cannot be processed in a systematic objective fashion. Accordingly, all promotions and appointments are either seen as not based on merit or political (European Commission 2003c, 7).

As such, there is also little incentive on the part of the officers to invest in their own education and training, and their morale is also adversely affected. Unless an objective and rigorous evaluation and promotion system is put into place, implementation of the reform packages is bound to remain only partial and service delivery quality will remain sub-optimal. So far, EU-originated funds, training facilities and cooperation therein have helped towards significant improvements in the system. However, the acute problem of establishing a meritocratic public sector personnel regime applies to the police as well.

Through the momentous legal changes that we have underlined in different parts of this chapter, the legal framework within which the TNP functions has been greatly altered and reformed. The capacity-building investments and restructuring of the personnel management of the police organization also are steps in the right direction for the longer-term internalization and implementation of these changes. In all of these efforts the guidance of the EU in rule adoption has been very instrumental. Especially through twinning programs, a hands-on approach to capacity building and rule internalization is currently underway. It seems that, more than anywhere else in the Turkish administrative and bureaucratic system, the changes in the police have been most drastic and consequential for the layman. The fact that detention periods have been shortened and that incommunicado detentions have been abolished have significantly reduced the number and gravity of torture incidents in police stations.

On September 2005 Turkey signed the Optional Protocol to the UN Convention against torture and other Cruel, Inhuman or Degrading Treatment and Punishment (OPCAT), thereby fully committing itself to the highest standards in this area. Clearly, the OPCAT framework requires 'a system of regular visits undertaken by independent international as well as national bodies to places where people are deprived of their liberty, in order to prevent torture and other cruel, inhuman or degrading treatment or punishment' (OPCAT 2002, Art. 1).[47] A Human Rights Watch briefing paper in March 2006 reported that there have been independent police station visits carried out by provincial human rights boards at which civil society representatives were present.[48] However, such visits occur mostly in the western provinces and they are not publicly reported, which makes their effectiveness questionable. Often boards are apparently too shy to carry out visits unless there is an official complaint. Provincial governors are too closely identified with these boards, facilitating their activities in the short run but also endangering their longer-term independence. The real challenge in all of this remains the sustained and active participation of the civil society representatives in the provincial human rights boards, especially in the critical eastern and south-eastern provinces, where potential for violations of human rights and torture incidents is higher. The response to such a challenge is clearly dependent upon rule internalization on the part of both the police and civil society actors. Equally important is the building up of clear administrative capacity for the police as well as the civil society actors. The case of independent visits to police stations and the monitoring of police stations and gendarmeries provides a critical example, wherein one can observe genuine efforts not only to adopt rules of the highest standards, but also an effort on the part of local authorities as well as civil society to enhance these standards as fitting the country-specific needs of Turkey. As such, it exemplifies the reform process that EUCLIDA aims to capture.

Conclusion

We believe the Turkish case provides a good test to support EUCLIDA framework, by underlining six salient traits that are effective in shaping the Turkish reform context, as Table 5.1 also suggests. First, there is the importance of the historical window that opens opportunities to political entrepreneurs who use the reform process as a way of building their political careers. The rise of the AKP single-party government within a collapsed centrist political sphere and increasingly uncertain and fluid international environment, coming together with the rising potency of civil society players, helped open a historical window of opportunity for reform in the case of Turkey.

Second is the importance of competing or cover-up issues in the political context, which are in constant interaction in their impacts upon the ability, determination and stamina of the reformers and their collaborating change agents to push the reforms through the political agenda. In the Turkish case deep-rooted struggles around the issues of the Kurdish minority and the rising salience of Islamist movements in Turkish society serve as cover-up issues that ignite resistance to EU-related reforms. In particular, the military establishment as a veto player uses these issues as a way of pressurizing and criticizing the popularly elected government. These veto players, among whom the military and some circles of the judiciary play significant roles, effectively use these issues to build cooperative linkages with a wide variety of civilian actors to slow down the reforms. In the process, electoral incentives also foster alliances within the party system to derail the executive single-party government, to the advantage of their own parties. As a result the EU-related reforms fall victim to such tough party competition strategies.

Third, the impact of the external actor, that is, the EU in our case of EUCLIDA, is significantly complemented by other international institutions, such as the World Bank and the IMF. The EU has been most effective in strengthening basic rights, judicial reform and military/police reform in the country. The weakening of the presence of alternatives – most particularly the US – (military/civilian reform and basic rights), the relative tilt in cost-benefit calculations (all three areas) and the growth of knowledge resources (basic rights and judicial reform) have been particularly instrumental in bringing about change in these realms. In areas where there were clearer conditions attached (basic rights and judicial reform), progress has been more visible, with the exception of those cases where cost/benefit calculations and ideological resistance open to little value diffusion were at stake (i.e. judicial independence, minority rights and freedom of expression). The impact of other international actors in these areas was almost non-existent. The only other

Table 5.1 Summary of issues, actors and mechanisms of change

Key area	*Issue*	*Factors/Change agents*	*Mechanism/Problems*
Civil freedom and political rights	Death penalty	(+) Change agents: EU conditionality	Rule adoption complete. Rule implementation complete
	Fight against torture	(+) Change agents: domestic NGOs, civil society, government (+) International Actors: EU conditionality (–) Attitudinal problems with segments of Turkish judiciary (public prosecutors and judges)	Rule adoption works. Difficult rule implementation due to internalization problems
	Freedom of expression	(+) Change agents: domestic NGOs, civil society (+) International actors: EU conditionality, international NGOs (–) Problematic legislation (Article 301) (–) Cultural and attitudinal problems with segments of Turkish judiciary: Sèvres Syndrome (public prosecutors and judges)	Rule adoption incomplete. Rule implementation incomplete due to legislative loopholes and insufficient internalization
	Freedom of association and the protection of minorities	(+) Change agents: domestic NGOs, civil society (+) International actors: EU uncertain conditionality, international NGOs (–) Cultural and attitudinal problems: Sèvres Syndrome	Rule adoption incomplete. Rule implementation incomplete due to incomplete legislation and internalization problems
	Gender equality	(+) Change agents: domestic NGOs, civil society (in particular the Women's Coalition) (+) International actors: EU conditionality (–) Cultural and attitudinal problems	Rule adoption almost complete. Rule implementation incomplete due to problems with socialization and internalization

Continued

Table 5.1 Summary of issues, actors and mechanisms of change—cont'd

Key area	*Issue*	*Factors/Change agents*	*Mechanism/Problems*
Judiciary reform	Workload and efficiency	(+) EU conditionality, EU advisory reports to the Ministry of Justice, the twinning instrument (+) Improved economic conditions in the aftermath of the 2001 economic crisis. (–) Poor institutional capacity	Rule adoption works. Rule implementation is mixed depending on the sub-area in question. It is high with respect to technology building, general efficiency measures (plea bargaining, regional courts of appeal provisions on the preparation of better indictments) along with internalization, and lower in areas where institutional capacity needs to be strengthened (judicial police)
	Judicial independence	(–) Fuzzy EU conditionality (–) Major domestic veto player: Ministry of Justice (–) Ideological discrepancies between the present AKP government and the judicial establishment	No rule adoption
	Inconsistent interpretation of the law	(+) EU conditionality and assistance via intensive training (+) Change agents: NGOs, civil society, the judicial establishment (High Courts in particular) (–) Strong veto players: Certain segments of the judicial establishment, heterogeneous and well-entrenched interest groups with close links to the resistant forces in the judicial establishment (–) Cultural and attitudinal problems: Sèvres Syndrome	Rule adoption incomplete. Rule implementation incomplete with low levels of internalization
Institutional and administrative structures	Better quality legislation	(–) Low administrative capacity	Rule adoption slow and incomplete

	Ability to implement policy	(+) IMF, World Bank (+) EU conditionality (–) Low administrative capacity (–) Insufficient funding	Slow and difficult rule adoption. Slow and difficult rule implementation
	Formulation and allocation of budget	(+) IMF, World Bank (+) EU conditionality (+) Government (–) Ideological divisions on the interpretation of the constitution (primarily between the government and the presidency)	Rule adoption slow, difficult and incomplete
	Decentralization and strengthening of local authorities	(+) IMF, World (+) EU conditionality (+) Government, civil society (–) Ideological divisions on the interpretation of the constitution (primarily between the government and the presidency) (–) Lack of participatory culture at the level of the citizen	Rule adoption slow, difficult and incomplete. Rule implementation slow
	Civil service reform	(–) Low administrative capacity (–) Deeply entrenched mechanisms of patronage	Rule adoption incomplete. Rule implementation ineffective
Corruption	Conflict of interest standards for public employees and international treaties	(+) EU conditionality (+) IMF, World Bank (+) 2001 financial crisis: landmark case (–) Government and civil society: 'don't muddy the waters' policy	Rule adoption almost complete. Rule implementation slow and incomplete
	Free and fair elections	This has not been a problematic issue in the history of republican Turkey with the exception of the first elections in 1946.	Rule adoption complete. Rule implementation and rule internalization complete

Continued

Table 5.1 Summary of issues, actors and mechanisms of change—cont'd

Key area	*Issue*	*Factors/Change agents*	*Mechanism/Problems*
	Parliamentary control over wrongdoing in the public sector	(−) Low administrative capacity (−) Government	Rule adoption incomplete. Rule implementation very weak
	Right to information, protection of whistle-blowers and ombudsman	(+) EU conditionality, World Bank (−) Ideological discrepancy between the President and the government (specifically on the establishment of an Ombudsman) (−) Low administrative capacity (−) Low participatory political culture (specifically on the Right to Obtain Information)	Rule adoption complete on the Right to Obtain Information. Rule implementation slow and difficult due to low administrative capacity and insufficient participatory political culture. Rule adoption non-existent on the protection of whistle-blowers and the Ombudsman
Police reform and the civilian control of security forces	Military sector reform	(+) EU conditionality (+) Change agents: NGOs, civil society, government, military with its general pro-EU orientation (+) Weakening of PKK terrorism (+) Souring relations between USA and the Turkish military. (−) Fuzzy EU conditionality (indeterminacy of conditions) (−) Problems linked to cultural characteristics at the societal level (−) Certain segments of the media and civil society	Rule adoption advanced but incomplete. Rule implementation incomplete. Rule internalization low
	Police reform	(+) EU conditionality, EU assistance, the twinning instrument (+) NGOs, civil society, government (−) Low administrative capacity (−) Insufficient funds	Rule adoption almost complete. Rule implementation incomplete. Internalization rising fast, yet incomplete

international actors to play an important role in the reform process were the IMF and the World Bank, whose impact was confined to combating corruption and increasing state accountability together with improving institutional/administrative capacity. In these areas where the EU has played a markedly minor role, reforms were greatly facilitated by a fluid political and economic environment in the aftermath of the 2001 economic crisis in Turkey.

Fourth, at least in the Turkish case it seems that institutional administrative capacity constitutes a minor issue in the very short run and is not really a binding constraint upon the reform process in medium to long run. When there is a will there always seems to be a way.

Fifth, in a similar vein, rule internalization is mainly an issue of the longer term rather than the short run. There is also a great deal of difference in this respect between the reformers, implementers, and the mass public. However, as we have noted repeatedly above, the current lack of internalization and Euroskeptic tendencies among the masses are constantly being used by veto players. As such, mixed signals are being sent to the masses as to the worth of the reforms and further rule internalization, both at the elite and the mass level, is accordingly hindered. This obviously delays normalization through rule internalization.

Lastly, the political mobilization capacity of the political system with all its institutions and leaders provides a critical binding constraint on the ability of the whole system to prepare the ground for reform and to cope with the difficulties during the implementation phase. Here it must be admitted that at the elite level the division between the reformists and resisters has largely overlapped with the long-running divide between the centrist and peripheral forces in the country (Mardin 1973).[49] As long as the current division continues and one side does not dominate the other, the still developing nature of the Turkish democracy cannot transform itself into a full-scale quality democratic system.

Notes

1 See National Program for the Adoption of the Acquis Communautaire, Official Gazette Number 24352, 24 March 2001.

2 A term of reference for a draft law consisting of a collection of amendments to different laws designed to amend more than one code or law at a time, which was approved or rejected in a single voting session in the parliament.

3 Four comprehensive sets of democratic reforms entered into force in 2003, aiming at improving the most-criticized aspects of Turkish democracy, such as limits to freedom of speech and expression, freedom of association, torture and mistreatment along with the strong influence of the military on domestic politics. With the two democratization packages that entered into force in January 2003, the Political Parties Law was further liberalized, the fight against torture was strengthened, freedom of the press was further expanded, the procedures for setting up associations were eased and the restrictions that applied to the acquisition of property by non-Muslim community foundations were abolished. The retrial of cases on the basis of decisions taken by the European Court of Human Rights was also made possible, paving the way for the retrial of some former

Kurdish nationalists such as Leyla Zana. The sixth reform package that entered into force in mid-July 2003 became widely famous for the lifting of Article 8 of the Anti-Terror Law (thus further expanding the freedom of speech), as well as the limitation on use of the death penalty and the expansion of broadcasting rights in Kurdish. It was the last set of democratic reforms, however, which entered into force at the end of July 2003, that has probably attracted the most attention, owing to its emphasis on strengthening the civilian control of the military as well as additional measures it has introduced to strengthen the fight against torture and the exercise of fundamental freedoms. In May 2004, another set of amendments to the constitution was approved, some of which consisted of harmonizing the constitution with the previous democratization packages. More significant amendments regarding the further civilianization of Turkish politics, reform of the judiciary and freedom of the press were also passed by parliament. The subordination of domestic law to international law in the area of fundamental rights and liberties was now secured in the Turkish constitution. The constitutional package adopted in July 2004 resolved yet another long criticized issue by repealing the provision that had allowed the nomination of a member of the High Audio-Visual Board (RTÜK) by the Secretariat-General of the National Security Council. See Aydın and Keyman (2004, 16–17).

4 See http://www.abgs.gov.tr/index.php?p=40989&l=1 andhttp://www.abgs.gov.tr/index.php?p=203&l=1, last access: 14 December 2007.

5 See the section on judicial reform.

6 See our discussion of the Penal Code.

7 Article 301 regulates offences that involve 'insulting Turkishness, the Republic, the parliament and state institutions" and in fact constitutes a revised version of the infamous Article 159 of the old Penal Code by considering those statements that are not intended to 'insult' but 'criticize' outside its jurisdiction.

8 Based on an interview with Oktay Uygun, Istanbul, April 2005.

9 Poll after poll has provided evidence of different sorts as to how deep-rooted this Syndrome is among the Turkish masses. See Çarkoğlu & Kirişçi (2004).

10 Turkish Daily News, 23 November 2007, www.turkishdailynews.com.tr, last access: 14 December 2007.

11 The Treaty of Lausanne grants non-Muslim minorities (represented by approximately 25,000 Jews, 3,000 Greeks and 50,000 Armenians) substantial negative rights as well as positive ones, with obligations for the Turkish government to undertake measures for the enjoyment of those rights. Most significantly, the Treaty gives non-Muslim minorities the right to equal protection and nondiscrimination,the right to establish private schools and provide education in their own language, the conditional entitlement to receive government funding for instruction in their own languages at the primary level in public schools, the right to settle family law or private issues in accordance with their own customs and the right to exercise their religion freely. See Kurban (2003, 51–214).

12 See www.radikal.com.tr, last access: 14 December 2007.

13 See www.radikal.com.tr, last access: 14 December 2007.

14 See www.radikal.com.tr, last access: 14 December 2007.

15 In May 2004, the monthly salaries of all judges and public prosecutors were raised by between 100 and 250 euros. All civil servants also benefited from a further 15 percent rise in salaries in July 2004. The budget of the Ministry itself was increased by 16.5 percent in 2005 compared to 2004. See Official Gazette No 26222, 8 July 2006.

16 It is now almost a *sine qua non* that the presidents of the High Courts, in their inauguration speeches, draw attention to the financial inadequacies of the Turkish judicial system.

17 See Official Gazette No 5435, 22 December 2005.

18 See http://www.bidb.adalet.gov.tr/aliakin/uyap1512.htm, last access: 29 July 2005.

19 See all European Commission Progress Reports published since 1999. For advisory visit reports, see Bjornberg and Richmond (2004), Bjornberg and Cranston (2005).

20 See references in the previous footnote.

21 www.radikal.com.tr, last access: 14 December 2007.

22 Interview of Peer Teuwsen with Orhan Pamuk, *Das Magazin* (cultural supplement of *Tages Anzeiger*), 5 February 2005. The full text of the interview is accessible at http://tages - anzeiger.ch/dyn/news/kultur/560264.html, last accessed 30 November 2007

23 European Parliament Report of September 2006 notes the mixed picture in the area of freedom of expression featuring some positive developments as well. The acquittal of Professors Ibrahim Kaboglu and Baskin Oran, prosecuted under Articles 216 and 301 of the Penal Code, similar to the case of Orhan Pamuk, presents such a positive development. See European Parliament (2006).

24 When Turkey got a date – 3 October 2005 – for the opening of accession negotiations at the European Council Meeting held on 16-17 December 2004, the opening of negotiations was made conditional on the passage of six specific pieces of legislation, including the new penal code. The other remaining pieces of legislation that Turkey was obliged to adopt prior to the opening of negotiations were the law on associations, the law on intermediate courts of appeal, the code on criminal procedure, legislation to establish the judicial police and the law on execution of punishments. See European Council 2004b.

25 See http://www.abgm.adalet.gov.tr for the details of EU-funded projects in the area of justice in Turkey, accessed 16 May 2007.

26 Among such ground-breaking judgements, on June 2004, the Ninth Criminal Chamber of the High Court quashed the decision of No.1 Ankara State Security Court convicting four former Kurdish Democratic Party (DEP) deputies for membership of an illegal organization in accordance with Article 168 of the Turkish Penal Code. The decision of the Court was based in part upon the fair trial guarantees enshrined within Article 6 of the European Convention on Human Rights. Between January 2004 and November 2005, the courts have referred to the ECHR in 224 judgements. See European Commission 2005c, 17.

27 For the role of Turkish civil society in Turkey's democratisation trajectory, specifically relating to its EU accession process, see Diez, Agnantopoulos and Kaliber 2005, 1–15.

28 See Ahmad (1993, 129–30, 186–7), Özbudun (1988, 1995), Tanör (1996) on Turkish constitutions.

29 See the law on SIS Official Gazette # 11136 and 18435 for the June 1984 version http://www.mevzuat.adalet.gov.tr/html/338.html, Article 26, last access: 14 December 2007.

30 See, for example, the two reports of World Bank (2006) and IMF (2007).

31 Refer to TESEV's website for an extensive debate on the ROI and its practice in Turkey: http://www.tesev.org.tr/eng/events/democ_gov_right_info.php, last access: 14 December 2007.

32 See Önis (2003) and Van Rijckeghem and Üçer (2005) for a historical and analytical analyses of the economic crisis. See Van Rijckeghem and Üçer (2005) especially Chapter 6 on the details of the February 2001 crisis.

33 See Eder (2003, 2006) as well as the World Bank sources such as the following: World Bank News Release No:2002/284/ECA.(http://econ.worldbank.org/WBSITE/EXTERNAL/EXTDEC/EXTRESEARCH/EXTPROGRAMS/EXTTRADERESEARCH/0,,contentMDK:20042671~menuPK:162686~pagePK:210083~piPK:152538~theSitePK:544849,00.html). Also see the Turkey Country Brief which provides a depiction of Country Assistance Strategy for Turkey for 2001–03 that details the position of the Bank about anti-corruption strategy(http://lnweb18.worldbank.org/ECA/eca.nsf/Countries/Turkey/7E9A5E38A2F3946385256C3E0052C28E?OpenDocument).

34 This can be seen in IMF and World Bank Country Reports on Turkey between 1999–2006 and in European Commission Progress Reports published since 1999.

35 See, for example, IMF (2001) 'Turkey Letter of Intent and Memorandum (to IMF) on Economic Policies', 3 May 2001,http://imf.org/external/np/loi/2001/tur/02/index.htm#mep, last access: 14 December 2007 and World Bank (2003), 'Turkey: Poverty and Coping after Crises', Turkey Main Report No. 24185, 28 July.

36 The National Security Council Meeting held on 28 February 1997 submitted a report to Prime Minister Necmettin Erbakan of the pro-Islamic Welfare Party, characterizing Islamists as the number one security threat in Turkey. The report's recommendations included the extension of elementary education from five to eight years to tightening state control of Qur'anic schools. The report initiated what is commonly known as the 'February 2008 process' and the 'postmodern coup' that led to the end of the coalition government led by Erbakan and the Welfare Party's closure by the Constitutional Court on 18 January 1998. See Cizre Sakallioglu and Cinar (2003, 309–32).

37 The sixth Reform package was enacted on July 19, 2003 and the seventh package was enacted on August 7, 2003. See *Official Gazette (*2003a), and *Official Gazette (*2003b).

38 With an amendment to Article 160 of the Constitution, the Court of Auditors was given full mandate and the constitutional right to audit the accounts and transactions of all types of organisations including the state properties owned by the armed forces. It shall inspect the revenues and property of the armed forces, on behalf of the Turkish Grand National Assembly.

39 See www.hurriyet.com.tr, last access: 14 December 2007.

40 For the EU requirements to align civil–military relations mainly through making changes to the composition and functions of the MGK prior to the adoption of reforms in this field, see Regular Reports from 1999 until 2004. The 1999 Regular Report highlights that no improvement has been made with respect to curbing the military influence on the political decision making where through the National Security Council, the Military continues to have an important influence in many areas of political life'. The 2000 Regular Report states that 'civilian control over the military still needs to be improved .... Contrary to EU, NATO and OSCE standards, instead of being answerable to the Defence Minister, the Chief of General Staff is still accountable to the Prime Minister. It is also noted that the Council of Higher Education, which controls the activities of the institutions of higher education, as well as the Higher Education Supervisory Board, include one member selected by the Chief of General Staff'. The 2001 Regular Report notes progress in legislation, but highlights that this might not be enough since it remains to be seen whether this will lead to civilian control in practice This line of reasoning is continued in the 2002 Report where the changes do not appear to have modified the way in which the MGK operates in practice. The 2003 Report acknowledges progress that has been made, yet points to the existence of unspecified 'informal mechanisms' through which the military exercises influence. See European Commission (1999, 10); European Commission (2000, 14); European Commission (2001, 19); European Commission (2002a, 24); and European Commission (2003d 19).

41 In addition to its silence over intervention in Iraq, a more recent case where the military-security establishment chose to remain silent concerns the developments in Cyprus. Despite being attacked by some members of the opposition party and the conservative voices in the media for not adopting a stance on the issue, the military made it very clear that this was a political matter that would be handled by the governing parties in Turkey and Northern Cyprus. The fact that the military did not try to reverse these decisions underlines the process of change in the modalities of governance in the country. See Aydın and Keyman 2004.

42 Interview with a European Commission official, 9 May 2006.

43 On May 1 the Constitutional Court annulled the first round of parliamentary voting for the president, saying not enough members were present.

44 Parts of this section draw on the European Commission's Project Fiche TR 0301.01 Strengthening accountability of police(http://ec.europa.eu/enlargement/fiche_projet/document/TR%200301.01%20Strengthening%20accountability%20of%20police.pdf), accessed 16 May 2007.

45 See also TESEV's joint report with Geneva Center for Democratic Control of the Armed Forces (DCAF) which covers the issues on police as well: report on http://www.tesev.org.tr/eng/events/democ_hor.php.

46 See also on the whole topic the 2007 European Commission Report on Turkey (2007,11-24).

47 Optional Protocol to the Convention against Torture and other Cruel Inhuman or Degrading Treatment or Punishment (adopted December 18, 2002), Article 1.

48 On this see the report by Human Rights Watch (2006c), published on 6 March.

49 This divide mainly refers to the often conflictive and antagonistic relationship between the staunchly secular state elite of the Republican tradition, in line with the centrist Ottoman bureaucratic tradition and its legacy of the benevolent father state, and the rural populations and traditional cultural, religious and ethnic groups in Turkey.

6 Serbia

Borderline democracy?

Cristina Dallara

Introduction

The defeat of the Slobodan Milošević regime in October 2000 marked the official start of EU–Serbia political relations. During the 1990s, EU attention towards Serbia, and the other Balkan countries, was mainly focused on conflict containment through joint actions with other international actors. The isolation of the country, the economic crisis in the late 1990s and the military conflict with NATO contributed to a drastic reduction in public support for Milošević and his government. Meanwhile, the opposition parties were able to organize an effective electoral campaign, choosing Vojislav Koštunica of the Democratic Party of Serbia (DSS) as a suitable candidate to defeat Milošević. As a consequence, the Serbian Democratic Opposition (DOS)[1] coalition won the 2000 elections.

After transition to democracy in 2000 Serbia became part of the Stabilization and Association Process (SAP) and, in accordance with the Council of Feira (2000), acquired the status of *potential candidate* for EU membership. On the whole, however, EU–Serbia relations have been characterized by a turbulent fits-and-starts dynamic, with several substantial ups and downs.[2] In May 2006 the suspension of the Stabilization and Association Agreement (SAA) negotiation, due to the lack of collaboration with the International Criminal Tribunal for the former Yugoslavia (ICTY), is the best illustration of this discontinuous relationship. In the aftermath of the transition, EU conditionality towards Serbia was mainly directed to the solution of its troubled political relations with Montenegro.[3] Another key priority was collaboration with the ICTY. This immediately became one of the more controversial and critical aspects of the EU–Serbia relationship and proved to be the most difficult task for the Serbian political elite (Batt 2005, Vejvoda 2004). In 2001, the different attitudes of the parties towards this issue, especially towards the extradition of Milošević, caused the break up of the DOS coalition. Even after the transition to democracy and the opening up of the membership perspective, the strategic vision of integration into the EU has been perceived by substantial parts of the Serbian political elites as weak and insufficiently attractive, because of the high political fragmentation, complemented by practical difficulties related to the reforms requested by the EU. In reality EU conditionality continues to be perceived mainly as forced cooperation with the International Criminal Tribunal for the former Yugoslavia (Jovanovic 2006). This negative perception of the EU is particularly stressed by those parties that are publicly anti-EU and act as veto players inhibiting the adoption and implementation of the EU-driven reforms. Among the Serbian parties, the Radicals are currently the principal actor opposing EU integration, envisaging close relations with the old communist countries, namely Russia, as an alternative to integration into the western community (International Crisis Group 2006; The Economist 2006). Domestic politics has continued to be dominated by the state-building issue, in particular by relations with Montenegro[4] and by the final status of Kosovo. Nationalism, foreign policy and the territorial organization of the state are the main issues dominating Serbian political debate, and the different approach towards this kind of issue marks the main difference among the parties (Marceta 2004). The dominant political cleavage is not between left and right in socioeconomic terms, as almost all parties belong to the centre-right. The composition of the party system in Serbia still reflects the conflicting historical and cultural developments of the country.

The Serbian party system was formed during the communist breakdown and when the ethnic conflict in the former Yugoslavia was starting. The early 1990s were the scenario for the emergence of two big cleavages: on the one hand, the change in political system from a one-party to a multi-party system; on the other hand, the ethnic conflict between different ethnic groups. Serbian political parties emerged at this critical period. They embody exclusively the Serbian ethnic groups. Consequently, they ideally represent the interest of the 'Serbian nation' (Marceta 2004; Goati 2000; 2001).

An important legacy that the Serbian political regime bears from the 1990s is the lack of confidence in political parties. In fact, one of the most important features of Serbian political parties is their clientalist attitude. The idea that parties are used as instruments for satisfying personal interests is still widespread in Serbian society. What Serbian citizens learned during the Socialist regime is that 'the first condition for reaching personal goals is being a member of the ruling parties' and that 'the same rule is valid in the multi-party system' (Marceta 2004, 197).

The results of the general elections of January 2007 and subsequent developments provide further evidence for this situation. The Serbian Radical Party won the majority of the votes, with 28.7 percent (81 seats), followed by the Democratic Party (DS) of Tadić with 22.9 percent of votes (65 seats) and the Koštunica's Democratic Party of Serbia (DSS)-New Serbia 16.7 percent of votes (47 seats) (see CESID, election results 21 January 2007[5]). The government was formed in May 2007 after four months of troubled bargaining and difficult parliamentary debates. In the end, DSS-New Serbia, DS and G17+[6] have agreed to form a coalition government, keeping out the largest party in parliament, the nationalist Radicals. The coalition was agreed four days before a deadline for new polls expired (see BBC News, 11 May 2007).

The EU and the US have been putting strong pressures on DS to form a government with the DSS in order to keep out the radicals, but it is questionable if this coalition will prove to be a good choice to the Serbian democratic future (International Crisis Group 2007). The ideological differences between DS and DSS are increasing and Koštunica has proved to be much closer to the conservative and nationalistic position of the radicals than to that of Tadić's Democratic Party (Pešic 2007). The election of the radical leaders Nikolic as parliamentary speakers (with the support of Koštunica) and his declarations against the EU 'neocolonial' policy and against any form of independence for Kosovo, stressed again as the Serbian parties' attitude toward the EU and the integration in the West continues to be a matter of division and debate (The Economist 25 January 2007). The EU and the Western community can no longer count on the DS and G17 to press DSS toward a different foreign policy (International Crisis Group 2007; Nenadic 2006; FRIDE 2007).

As several prominent observers point out (Rettman 2006, Helsinki Committee for Human Rights 2007, Pešic 2007, Dallara and Marceta 2007, Nenadic 2006) the deepest cleavage in Serbian politics is provided by the distinction between the few pro-Western parties (DS, G17+ and LDP[7]) and the nationalist bloc; the latter suspicious of Western integration and resistant to EU-bound liberalization. Although the DSS of Koštunica is, in general, more moderate in its public discourse and formally in favor of EU integration, it is closer to the nationalist bloc for what concerns the key sensitive issues of the Serbian foreign policy. These issues are: resistance to the independence of Kosovo, opposition to the cooperation with the International Criminal Tribunal for the former Yugoslavia, and a highly skeptical attitude towards the prospect of EU integration. On these issues the nationalist bloc looks to an increasingly authoritarian, assertive, anti-Western Russia for political alliance and support in foreign policy matters. The recent declarations of President Putin about Kosovo independence support this conviction (Pešic 2007, Noutcheva 2007, The Economist 2007).

As a consequence, during the last few years, the results of democratic rule of law reforms have been difficult and partial at best. The aim of this chapter is to evaluate the nature of external influence and the degree to which external actors have been able to encourage rule of law reforms in Serbia, following the EUCLIDA analytical framework. The time frame of the analysis covers the period from the early 1990s to 2006. The chapter will assess how democratic rule of law reforms have been enacted analyzing both the EU requirements in each policy domain and the domestic actors' responses to them.

Civil freedoms and political rights

As a post-conflict society, Serbia continues to struggle in finding an adequate operational mechanism to guarantee the effective protection of human rights of all its citizens. The legacy of the Milošević ethnic cleansings of the 1990s and of the continued denial of civil and political rights, makes the establishment of the required legislative and institutional framework a more complex task. With the democratic changes in 2000, Serbian governments have become more active in this field and some progress, at least in formal rule adoption, was achieved after joining the Council of Europe in April 2003.

Protection of ethnic minorities

The first step towards the protection of minorities' rights was taken by the Zoran Djindjic led government, shortly after the Milošević defeat, by signing the Framework Convention on the Protection of National Minorities (2001), which was later ratified by the federal parliament. In February 2002, the Law on the Protection of Rights and Freedoms of National Minorities was then passed. A year later, with the adoption of the Constitutional Charter of the State Union of Serbia and Montenegro (2003), the Human and Minority Rights and Civil Liberties Charter (2003) also came into force. This document is now a part of the Constitutional Charter and lays down all the major provisions of the previous law (Council of Europe 2002a).

As the Helsinki Committee for Human Rights (HCHR) 2004 Report underlines, the adoption of this Charter opened the process of building a legislative framework for the protection of minority rights. However, this complex and delicate process has faced the challenges of unfinished constitutionalization, weak institutions and political fragmentation. After the adoption of the Charter, the federal parliament passed the Law on the Protection of Rights and Freedoms of National Minorities and the Serbian National Assembly adopted the Law on Local Self-Government (Helsinki Committee for Human Rights 2004). Both laws are significant, as they institutionalize the notion of minority rights (Forum for Ethnic Relations 2006).

In spite of the formal institutional framework, which was relatively developed and in line with international standards, in 2006 the NGO Human Rights Watch denounced several cases of minority rights violations, particularly in relation to the Hungarian minority in Vojvodina.[8] In October 2005, the European Parliament also adopted a resolution asserting that the rights of minorities were being violated in Vojvodina and denounced several cases of vandalism, verbal abuse, and physical attacks on ethnic Hungarians. The Serbian and the State Union governments responded with an increasing involvement of the ethnic minority leaders in the political institutions. The Serbian government agreed to improve ethnic relations in the province, including education and public awareness campaigns, and support for greater representation of minorities in the police and the judiciary (US Department of State 2005, Forum for Ethnic Relations 2006).

The most relevant step in the minority rights protection was achieved with the adoption of the new Constitution in 2006, as it contains detailed provisions for human and minority rights. However, the Council of Europe and the other international actors continue to express concerns about the monitoring of minority rights violations and about the work of the institutions in charge of such a task. Until June 2007, the human rights Ombudsman (or Protector of Citizens) was not appointed, although the relevant law was passed in 2005. After two years of failed attempts, in June 2007 the National Assembly reached agreement on the first Serbian Ombudsman, Saša Janković, previously a legal advisor to the OSCE (Organization for Security and Cooperation in Europe) Office for Democratic Institutions and Human Rights (ODIHR). The establishment of the institution of the ombudsman had been strongly requested by the international actors. The EU referred to the necessity of setting the Ombudsman office since its very first report on Serbia (see European Commission 2002b). In fact, in 2003 there was the request of a law on Ombudsman among the issues that needed attention; in 2004 such a law was indicated as a short term priority, and in 2005 Feasibility Report the lack of it was pointed out as a shortcoming. The same is true for the Council of Europe, which made the adoption of the Ombudsman office one of the post-accession obligations of the State Union of Serbia and Montenegro (Dallara and Marceta 2007).

The international actors have also assisted the drafting process, providing the technical and legal assistance (CoE, OSCE, EU and UNHCR),[9] and engaged in the advocacy and law adoption activities. The material resources were also made available to the Serbian government, as the international actors have immediately initiated programs of the institutional capacity building, EU thus dedicating one million of Euro for developing the office and OSCE signing the partnership agreement of support to the Office of the Citizens' Protector (Dallara and Marceta 2007). The OSCE was the international actor mainly engaged in the establishment of the Ombudsman office. OSCE assisted the Serbian government in the draft of the Ombudsman law, insisted on the government to find an agreement within the National Assembly on the Ombudsman person and finally signed a partnership agreement to support the office in the next years (OSCE 2006). This is mainly the result of the work of the OSCE Mission in Belgrade.[10]

Rule adoption was basically working in the field of ethnic minority protections, as international actors, such as the Council of Europe, exercised serious pressure on this issue. The inputs of international actors also contributed to support the work of local and international Nongovernmental Organizations (NGOs), improving the relationship between political elites and civil society organizations. National decision makers have understood that the work of NGOs is valuable in implementing the demands coming from the international community, as they are the only actors able to maintain direct contact with local ethnic communities. In this case, local and international NGOs could be seen as change agents that improve their position thanks to the support of international actors. According to the press agencies and to international observers, President Tadić was the one who exerted most pressure on Koštunica to introduce effective provisions for human rights in the 2006 Constitution.

Freedom of the media

Political control over the media was progressively increasing during the final years of the Milošević regime. Stronger attacks on the media were launched in 1998, when a new media law was passed as part of Milošević's increasingly desperate attempts to curtail opposition forces. The new law, the most restrictive in the history of Serbian journalism, enabled anyone who felt 'hurt' by a journalistic article to resort to a civil court against the author of the article, the editor, as well as the owner of the media source (Balkan Media and Policy Monitor 5: Media in Serbia).[11] In spite of these restrictive measures, the survival of some independent media was crucial in the decline of Milošević's popularity. Critical coverage of Milošević's wars, his economic policies, and his government's violent arrests and abuses of young protestors contributed to undermine his support within the population (McFaul 2005).

One of the first acts of the Djindjić government was the abrogation of the 1998 media law. However, even after Milošević's defeat, media independence continued to be out of step with the European standards. The laws on broadcasting and public information were approved in 2003 and created the Broadcasting Council, in charge of the implementation of the two laws. The Council was created only in late 2004 after lengthy bargaining among political parties for the appointment of its members. Until 2004, international actors monitoring media independence, such as the Organization for Security and Cooperation in Europe (OSCE) and the Council of Europe, had been expressing concerns about the administration of Radio Television Serbia (RTS), requiring its transformation into a genuine public service broadcaster, and about the regulation of frequencies allocation to different broadcasters (Freedom House 2005a). The legislation on public information was adopted in 2004, but monitoring the media independence in the area, the OSCE stated that improvements still needed to be made. Further concerns were expressed by some of the international observers (Freedom House, the OSCE and the Council of Europe) when the Serbian parliament amended the Broadcasting Law in a way that increased potential government control over the media (Freedom House 2006, OSCE 2006, Council of Europe 2006b). The amendment allowed government-appointed members of the Broadcasting Council to serve a six-year term while the NGOs and journalist members had only a four-year term (Freedom House 2006). In its 2006 Progress Report the EU expressed criticisms of the government attitude towards media regulation, citing in particular other amendments to the Broadcasting Law, passed by the government without proper consultation in July 2006 and increasing the discretionary power of the Broadcasting Council. On the whole, the EU still points to insufficient transparency and effective independence in decision-making concerning media regulation.

Thus, rule adoption was working as the fundamental legislation was finally passed under the pressure of international actors on this issue, but the quality of the passed legislation was poor. Council of Europe and OSCE monitoring was efficient, as well as their requirements about the content of the laws,[12] but in the end the legislation adopted only partially met these requirements. Furthermore, the international actors did not meet with national change agents committed to improve media independence. The communist legacy of political control over the media is still influencing the elite in power. In this way, one could speak of the communist legacy in the sense of learned behavior, and the legacy of the 'illusion of democracy' created during the period of Milošević (Marceta 2004).

Freedom of association and civil society

Civil society organizations began to develop during the final phase (1999–2000) of the Milošević regime, as in that period the widespread common goal among civil society was fighting Milošević. Djindjić was smart enough to perceive this feeling, understanding that civil society was indispensable in defeating Milošević. For this reason, all parties created NGO-type groups or think-tanks. OTPOR[13] and G17+ were the most active associations in 2001–02. G17 is now a political party, but it was created as a civil society organization. In that period, the only existing law on the right of association was that approved during the Milošević regime. Even if NGOs were important in defeating Milošević, politicians seemed not to care about the legislative status of these associations. At that time, there were 5,000 NGOs, but the majority of them were collapsing and disappearing over time. Civil society activists[14] claimed that since 2004 the relevance of civil society organizations was progressively decreasing. Active citizens, mainly from local NGOs, denounced in particular the extremely difficult conditions imposed by the government to take advantage of national funding.

Since 2004, both the Council of Europe and the EU,[15] have included the adoption of a proper law on associations among the priorities that Serbia has to address in order to fulfill the standards and obligations required. The Council of Europe, in particular, has frequently provided expertise on the drafting of such a law. During the second half of 2001, the Serbian Ministry of Justice and Local Self-Government prepared a draft law aiming at regulating the registration and activities of associations. Representatives of NGOs were consulted during the preparation of the draft and were also invited to participate in public discussions. In spite of this, the law has not been formally adopted. During 2005, the Koštunica government worked again on such a law, with the support of many international organizations (in particular the OSCE and the Helsinki Committee for Human Rights). However, the most significant result concerning freedom of association could be found in Article 55 of the new Constitution, which for the first time in Serbian history guarantees the 'freedom of political, union and any other form of association, as well as the right to stay out of any association'.

To conclude, it has to be underlined that on the whole the situation regarding civil freedoms and political rights has partly improved. In the national domain, the agents that mainly drove the adoption of such provision were, on the one hand, the Serbian President Tadić and, on the other hand, the national and international NGOs working in Serbia. The implementation of the constitutional provision is still ongoing. Certainly, NGOs' representatives will be crucial in making it effective (Freedom House 2007). One could argue that, in addition to the massive pressure of international organizations on this issue, such as the Council of Europe, one of the reasons for this improvement can be found in the peculiar 'nature' of this issue. First of all, compliance on this issue has a high impact on the international community and, at the same time, it is perceived by domestic actors as a legitimate requirement, as it does not undermine the sovereignty structure of the state. Moreover, from 2000, the Koštunica party, as the other DOS party, always put civil freedoms and political rights guarantees among the key priorities in their party program. Thus, on this issue, international actors' demands fit with the national political actors' strategies. This will be further developed in the concluding section.

Judicial independence and capacity

Immediately after Milošević's defeat, the first step taken by the *ad interim* Koštunica cabinet was to re-establish the old judicial system legislation and to cancel all those decisions made by Milošević that caused the collapse of the Serbian judiciary during the 1990s. The first significant stage of the judicial system reform seemed to have been reached in November 2001 with the approval of an important group of judicial system-related laws. They were: (1) Law on Judges; (2) Law on Public Prosecution; (3) Law on High Judicial Council; (4) Law on Courts Organization; (5) Law on Seats and Districts of Courts and Public Prosecutor's Offices.[16] This set of laws, however, was not proposed by the cabinet, but by a parliamentary group belonging to the DSS (Koštunica's party), which would shortly go over to the opposition. Hiber (2005) underlines that such laws were voted for by the DOS coalition parties in exchange for the vote of Koštunica's party for the Work Law approved during the same weeks. Overall, the five laws should have made some fairly relevant changes. The introduction of a new self-government body, which was meant to play an important role in the recruitment process, represented the most relevant of them. Until 2001, the judicial system's governmental functions were centralized in the hands of the Minister for Justice. Furthermore, Article 46 of the Law on Judges established that magistrates would be elected by the National Assembly on the basis of the proposal of the High Council of the Judiciary (HCJ). The same article established that the National Assembly should elect only the candidates proposed by the HCJ. In cases where some candidature was rejected by the assembly, the HCJ had the right to make new ones.

As early as July 2002, the DSS proposed a set of amendments to the five laws on the judicial system. The National Assembly adopted them at once. They aimed specifically at changing Article 46 of the Law on Judges, by establishing that the National Assembly could reject candidatures proposed by the HCJ and appoint some other candidates nominated by a special commission within the National Assembly. There was therefore an attempt to institute another body in charge of appointment proposals, directly connected to the National Assembly. At the beginning of 2003, the DSS proposed new amendments aimed at reaffirming the role of the National Assembly in the recruitment of magistrates, while the HCJ had not been created because of delays and general problems in achieving an agreement on the choice of members.

The approval of the five laws on the judicial system was especially supported by Djindjić, who saw in the reshaping of the judicial system and of its rules a symbolic change and a new start. During the first transition stage, Djindjić represented a prominent change agent by virtue of his genuine commitment to pro-democratic culture. From the beginning of his term he insisted on the importance of trial fairness and on the supremacy of the rule of law. However, on the basis of the discussion so far, it should be clear that any action to that effect was totally nullified by the parties' actual attitudes in relation to this issue. Party control over the nomination and dismissal of judges represented the crucial point of the discussion. The attempt to reaffirm the power of the National Assembly over the nomination of judges, to the disadvantage of the self-government body, represented a thread running through the different amendments. In this first phase of judicial reform, political parties could be seen as veto players that always tried to prevent changes, due to their anxiety over losing political control over the judiciary (Dallara 2006). The assassination of Zoran Djindjić in March 2003 worsened the situation. Huge cracks in the fragile Serbian democracy were revealed, when the role of the military and paramilitary forces, and their connection with organized crime, emerged with dramatic clarity. Immediately after Djindjić's assassination, a state of emergency was declared. This phase represented another period of stalemate for judicial reform. The EU and other international observers (ABA-Ceeli 2005; OSCE 2003; EU SAP Report 2004) openly criticized most of the actions taken during the 'state of emergency'.[17] In fact, taking advantage of that situation the executive made a number of strong decisions to reinforce its power over the judiciary and in some cases violated citizens' civil and political rights.

In the early months of 2004, the Koštunica government came into office and seemed to give new impetus to overcoming the stalemate created during the state of emergency. Meanwhile the EU set out the first European Partnership for Serbia and Montenegro, listing the short- and medium-term priorities that both countries would have to address in order to advance in the Stabilization and Association process. To comply with the priorities set out in the 2004 European Partnership, the Minister of Justice (Stojkovic) openly declared his determination to continue with the reform of the judicial system by following the path indicated by the EU experts.[18] A Special Commission for judicial reform was created in 2004. This aimed at drafting a coherent reform test, but it quickly became evident that this platform was merely one of the 'cosmetic innovations'. In April 2004, the government proposed some new amendments intended to update the Law on Judges on the basis of the different rulings delivered by the Constitutional Court in the previous years. These new amendments gave back to the HCJ the power to propose candidates for the nomination of magistrates and court presidents. But the government kept rejecting any nomination submitted by the HCJ until December 2004. Consequently the HCJ was virtually prevented from performing its functions (Dallara 2006).

A new start ... on paper: The 2006 judicial reform strategy

The relationship between the EU and Serbia accelerated in early 2005. In April 2005, the European Commission affirmed that on the basis of the Feasibility Study the region once called Serbia-Montenegro was ready to move forward with the Stabilization and Association process and that the negotiation for that agreement would begin in the autumn.[19] This opening of the EU pushed the government leaders to reaffirm their 'European belief' and to commit themselves to undertake reforms shortly. However, at least as far as the judicial system is concerned, no relevant progress was made in 2005 (Gajin *et al.* 2005). Some reports (ABA-Ceeli 2005; Human Rights Watch 2006b) claimed that the situation actually worsened. A particularly conflictual phase occurred in 2005, when many court presidents came to the end of their term of office. The National Assembly should have renewed them according to the HCJ proposals. Leaders of the government coalition opposed most of the candidates proposed by the HCJ and refused to appoint or promote them (Dallara 2006).

A definitive text for the Judicial Reform Strategy was presented by the government in April 2006 and approved shortly afterwards by the National Assembly. The government highlighted this event and affirmed that it was an essential step in the judicial reform process. However, once again the recruitment rules and the self-government functions represented crucial sticking points. In spite of the Reform Strategy approval (May 2006), few of the provisions it contains have been implemented. In addition, the new Constitution, approved by a national referendum at the end of October 2006, will bring substantial changes in relation to the judiciary. For the first time in Serbian history, the Constitution mentions the existence of a self-governing body for the judiciary that will be in charge of appointment and promotion procedures. However, no clear provisions for that body could be found in either the Reform Strategy or other laws (Council of Europe – Expert Comment – Opinions on the concept paper on National Judicial Reform Strategy', PCRED/DGI/EXP(2005) 33.)

Such a situation is the result of the interplay among different factors concerning both the domestic level and the EU leverage on Serbian judicial reform. Firstly, it could be pointed out that the EU support was not focused on the crucial problem of the Serbian judiciary, that is, its lack of independence. Analyzing the EU programs for judicial reform assistance many 'appealing matters' can be found, such as *Modernisation of Belgrade Courts, Refurbishment of Court Rooms, Introduction of Alternative Dispute Resolution*, but few efforts were made to target the crucial problem of the Serbian judiciary – the influence of the executive and the parties over the judicial system (CARDS Project Fiche 2.1.1 to Action Programme 2005 for Serbia/Justice and Home Affair). It is a broader problem, having to do with the credibility and determinacy (Schimmelfennig and Sedelmeier 2005a) of EU conditionality towards Serbia and towards the so-called 'potential candidate' countries in general (International Commission on the Balkans 2005). Looking at the priorities of the European Partnerships (2004, 2006), only broadly-framed conditions can be found, without clear requirements that give great freedom to the government to modify them according to their interest and standards. To give just one example, in the 2004 European Partnership the short-term priorities related to judicial reform are the following: 'Modernize and increase efficiency and independence of court system, in particular its commercial courts; ensure independence of war crime prosecutor. Prepare for the setting-up of administrative and appellate jurisdiction' (European Partnership with Serbia and Montenegro, 2004/520/EC). As these priorities show, the determinacy of the conditionality – meaning the specificity and the formality of the EU requirements – was too low to suggest a clear track of reform and consequently allowed the government the freedom to interpret them according to its own standards.

Concerning the national domain, one can first of all highlight the fact that only a few, weak domestic change agents can be found in the judicial reform sector. Within the judiciary, the only actor that could be seen as a change agent is the Judges Association. This association is the only collective actor that expresses a precise point of view on judicial reform and tries to be a interlocutor of the government (Judges Association of Serbia 2005). In contrast, the political parties can be seen as veto players that inhibit concrete changes in the judiciary. Political parties (both majority and opposition) acted as a sort of cohesive block, intended to inhibit the reform process, being afraid of the possible consequences of the reform. The judiciary is one of the key sectors where the so called 'state capture' takes place, that is, 'group or social strata [...] exercises decisive influence over state institutions and policies for its own interests against the public good' (Pešic 2007, 1). As Pešic (2007, 1 and 8) argues '[...] in Serbia, political parties are the main agents being used to appropriate state and public assets' as 'the executive branch (which again means party influence) has gained control over the parliament, the courts and public prosecution'. The key mechanism of this influence lies in the power of appointment that is yet in the hand of the parliament. On many occasions executive members managed to appoint 'their party loyals' to the top judiciary positions (Helsinki Committee for Human Rights 2007).

As Begović and Hiber (2006) suggest, one of the most explicit anti-reform alliances is between judges, fearing removal from office (either due to incompetence or lack of integrity) and consequently trying to avoid changes, and political parties trying to preserve effective control over the judicial system. This is to say that, within the judicial system, there is an imaginary thin line between two states of mind: that of those judges who are afraid of the political pressure over the judiciary, and the other of those judges who are not afraid and who see their career linked to the political will. The latter are so impressed by the power of the politicians that they just think that it is not the duty of judges to make any changes to reform the system. Thus, they passively accept the political will.[20] This is one of the most evident legacies of the past that Serbia has not overcome.

A few relevant laws were adopted during the 2001–06 period. Moreover, the government considered the laws approved, especially during 2006, as their biggest success in the judicial sector. However, the content of those laws was subsequently modified through legislative reforms and strategically adapted to the parties' interests. The result of this situation is what Noutcheva (2006, 11) defines a 'fake compliance', that is, 'a simulation of compliance to avoid the higher costs of manifest confrontation'. Such a simulation involves the adoption of legal norms partially in line with the EU requirements, which then reveal as a sort of camouflage intended to maintain the status quo. Enforcement of those laws remained totally sidelined (Helsinki Committee for Human Rights 2007). This is again a way by which parties inhibit actual changes, acting as veto players. Thus, in spite of the judicial strategy approval, a year later the government has not taken a single step towards translating into practice the principles contained in that strategy. As a consequence, the criteria to be adopted used to appointment and evaluation of judges are still ambiguous and unknown to the public opinion (Helsinki Committee for Human Rights 2007; Freedom House 2007). The assessment of the EU about this situation was expressed in its 2006 Progress Report. The Commission affirmed that 'the new Constitution presents some areas of concern, notably the lack of objective mechanisms free of political influence to appoint, promote and dismiss judges and prosecutors'. (6) In spite of this (and a few other areas of non-compliance) the EU decided to resume the SAA negotiation with the Serbian government in June 2007.

Institutional and administrative capacity

The overall functioning of the Serbian institutions has improved if compared with the 1990s, although concerns remain regarding the lack of transparency in government and parliament procedures. In this context, the constitutional framework adopted at the end of October 2006 could be seen as a step forward, contributing to strengthen some of the provisions regarding public administration adopted in the last years by ordinary laws, such as the introduction of the ombudsman, and the adoption of the civil service legislation. However, the adoption of the new Constitution brings concerns and criticisms from part of the international community, due to some key provisions regarding in particular the status of Kosovo, judicial independence and territorial decentralization.

Constitutional politics: from the 1990 Milošević Constitution to the 2006 constitution

The reform of the 1990 Serbian Constitution was one of the issues that the EU and the Council of Europe[21] always listed as a real priority for the democratization of the country. It became particularly crucial after the establishment of the state Union of Serbia and Montenegro as the Union Constitution, set out in 2003, explicitly required the reform of both countries' constitutions. In spite of this, until October 2006, although exactly six years had passed since the 2000 democratic revolution, the 1990 Milošević Constitution was still in force (Begović and Mijatovic 2005). It was an authoritarian Constitution in many respects and when Milošević decided to have it approved,[22] his aim was the legalization of his personal power. The 1990 Constitution foresaw a mixed presidential-parliamentary system with a strong and independent president and a subordinate parliamentary assembly (Vejvoda 2000).

During the electoral campaign of the late 1990s, the revision of the 1990 Constitution was one of the main promises of the DOS coalition, which considered the Constitution one of the most distinctive symbols of the Milošević regime. In spite of this, in the aftermath of the October 2000 revolution, every effort to reach agreement on a new Constitution was in vain. The two main DOS parties, the DSS (Koštunica's party) and the DS (Djindjić's party), disagreed on many aspects of a new Constitution; the DS and other larger parties of the coalition pushed for a modern Constitution with an emphasis on decentralization and liberal democratic values in the context of a civic state. On the the other hand, Koštunica wanted to increase centralization and to redefine Serbia as a civic state.[23]

In late 2003, when new parliamentary elections were called, Koštunica promised that, if the DSS won the elections, then a new Constitution would be passed immediately. The election result was rather different: although the DSS emerged as the primary party, the largest single party was the SRS with 32.8 percent of votes and 82 seats, while the Milošević Socialist Party (SPS) gained 8 percent (22 seats). This meant that the approval of these two parties would have been necessary to change the Constitution. The new government entered the political scenario as a minority government led by Koštunica's DSS with G17+, the Serbian Renewal Movement (SPO), and with the external support of the SPS (the former Milošević party).

Until 2006 the issue of a new Constitution remained in the background, emerging only occasionally. In spring 2006, the UN declaration on an upcoming final status solution on Kosovo and the EU's suspension of the Stabilization and Association Agreement brought with them the spectre of a serious political crisis. It became clear that if the Koštunica government wished to survive, it would need to find a solution to avoid losing Kosovo.[24]

During 2006 the Radical Party and the Socialists continued to press the government to defend Kosovo as Serbian territory and to find legislative and political ways to maintain power in that province. Moreover, in May 2006 the suspension of the SAA negotiation provoked negative reactions by one of the coalition parties, G17+ (the pro-European party, which considers EU integration its major goal), which threatened to resign from the government. In this troubled situation, Koštunica considered the approval of a new Constitution as the final opportunity to solve the political problems inside his coalition, as well as to prevent the government's fall (International Crisis Group 2006; Nenadic 2006; The Belgrade Times 19 October 2006). After the summer, it became clear that G17+ would find a way to stay in power, although the government showed no sign of strengthening cooperation with the ICTY, in order to restart the SAA negotiation with the EU. The first real government signal of a move toward a new Constitution was given in the middle of September 2006, with the approval of a special budget (€7.3 million) for a constitutional referendum. Some days later, Koštunica announced that a draft Constitution would be approved by the parliament by 30 September, just before the final deadline set by G17+ (International Crisis Group 2006).

The main concern related to this rapid ending of the constitutional reform process was the absence of public debate and consultations on the Constitution's content (The Belgrade Times 2006). Some Serbian online journals (i.e. Blic and B92[25]) and some international monitoring agencies (e.g. the International Crisis Group, the Helsinki Committee for Human Rights and Freedom House). underlined that, apart from the total absence of public debate due to the speed of the decision, many senior politicians were not included in the preparation of the draft and the vast majority of the parliament members had never seen the text. Thus, the draft of the Constitution was the result of an enforced political bargain between the DS, the DSS, the SRS and the SPS. In return for DS support for the constitutional draft, the President of Serbia, Tadić (the DS leader) received some guarantees on human and minority rights and some changes regarding the definition of property rights. Moreover, Koštunica promised Tadić a call for new elections by the end of the year. On 30 September, the parliament approved the draft Constitution in an emergency session and scheduled a national referendum for 28–29 October. The referendum campaign, financed directly by the government,[26] was massive but lacking in public debate about the constitutional contents (ReliefWeb 2006). A weak opposition calling for a referendum boycott, made up of the League of Social-Democrats of Vojvodina, the Liberal Democratic party of Jovanovic and the SDU alliance, with the support of some NGOs,[27] was allocated only a few places in the public debate.[28]

The referendum ended with 51.6 percent in favor of the Constitution on a turnout of 53 percent.[29] Some international press agencies and monitors, such as the International Crisis Group, CESID, Global Voice, and Osservatorio sui Balcani,[30] complained of procedural and technical problems, especially regarding the fulfillment of the minimum required turnout. In spite of this, the international community was absolutely silent before and after the referendum.

Also the majority of the NGOs operating in Serbia did not make any objection to the referendum. This was obviously a strategic decision. It is possible to hypothesize that the international community saw in uncritical support of the referendum a way to obtain new elections by the end of the year and to facilitate the entry into office of a new government guided by the pro-European party, the DS, led by the current President of Serbia, Tadić. However, in the 2006 Progress Report the EU pointed out, in a few words, that the Constitution adoption had taken place without adequate public consultation and that the text presented some areas of concern (European Commission 2006, 6).

Currently, the only concrete result is a new Constitution that proclaims Serbia 'a state of Serbian people and all citizens who live in it' (Article 1) and Kosovo and Metohija as Serbian territories. At the same time there are obviously some good aspects to the new Constitution, such as the provisions for human and minority rights, the abolition of the Socialist category of owned property and the simplification of the constitutional amendment procedure, but there are also other provisions that can only slow down the democratization process of the country.

The government used the silence of the international community to its own advantage, interpreting it as a form of support for its action, in order to gain credibility and to contrast the minor opposition to the Constitution's adoption.[31] No change agents can be found in the domain of constitutional reform. In fact, the opposition was completely overridden by the massive pro-referendum campaign and by the lack of attention of the national media, which formed a cohesive block of referendum supporters. At this stage, the major losers in this political bargain seem to be President Tadić, his DS party, and the G17+ party, which supported the Constitution believing in Koštunica's promises of a quick resumption of talks with the EU. In a nutshell, the rule adoption path worked formally, as a new Constitution was eventually adopted, but it is again another form of 'fake compliance' (Noutcheva 2006, 11), as a number of the provisions inside the Constitution do not meet EU standards.[32] As already mentioned, in the 2006 Progress Report the EU stressed that the Constitution presents areas of concern not only on appointment, promotion and dismissal of judges and prosecutors, but also on 'the political parties' control over parliamentary mandates; the scope of territorial decentralisation; and the ambiguous relationship between domestic law and international law' (p. 6). In spite of this the EU decided to go ahead with negotiations with Serbia, and these were resumed in June 2007.

Public administration reform and civil service legislation

After the fall of Milošević, the reform of public administration began rather late in comparison to the interventions in the economy. In fact, the Djindjić government concentrated its efforts mainly on economic issues, pursuing administrative reforms only in a confused way. By contrast, after 2004 the Koštunica government adopted a more coherent approach towards public administration reform, pressed by the EU and other international actors. As a consequence, the government approved the official Public Administration Strategy in October 2004, together with the related Action Plan. The text of the Strategy was drafted with the assistance of many international donors, especially the OECD with its SIGMA Project (a joint initiative of the EU and the OECD to support governance and management), the EAR (European Agency for Reconstruction), the World Bank and the UNDP. Formally, the Strategy fulfills the majority of the international standards fixed for the functioning of public administration, but as highlighted by the EAR in its monitoring reports, the effectiveness of the administrative reforms continues to be low, with poor results. During 2005, some steps towards the implementation of the Strategy were achieved. The human resources management service was set up in December 2005 and it is now partially operative. The Ministry of Public Administration has started transferring human resources to this service, which is also implementing a training program for civil servants. The new Law on the Civil Service came into force in July 2006, with a number of other related laws. Particularly important was the Law on Salaries of Civil Servants, designed to restructure the payment system. Inadequate salaries remain in fact one of the main concerns for the performance of public administration. In the 2006 Progress Report the EU observed that

> Overall, there has been further progress in setting the legal framework for the civil service which is now in line with general European standards ... The relevant institutional setup – including the representatives of ministries, agencies and non-governmental organisations – has proven to be well established and effective (p. 8).

Other international monitors, such as Freedom House (2007) and Council of Europe[33] in their last reports also observed that the administrative capacity of Serbia has improved in the last two years.

In 2005, the Law on Ombudsman was also adopted, as it was listed among the Accession Partnership priorities. At the local level, a specific law provides that local government can establish an ombudsman to protect citizens' individual and collective rights. In spite of this, the 2006 EU Progress Report underlines that by November 2006 no ombudsman had been appointed by the parliament. In the last two years, public administration reform, and especially the policies aimed at strengthening institutional capacity have become increasingly linked to the European integration process. The EC intentionally created a functional link between public administration reform and European Integration. Thus, the responsibilities for the administrative reforms were gradually moved from the 'old Ministries' to the new institutions created in the European integration sector.

The European integration institutional framework

In spite of the problems regarding constitutional policy and public administration reform, the policies related to the creation of an adequate European integration institutional framework have been particularly successful, especially in the last two years. The reason for this success can be found in the work done by the Serbian European Integration Office (SEIO) in collaboration with the EC in its Brussels and Belgrade offices. SEIO was established in March 2004 by the Government to meet the EU requirements and to give a clear sign of its determination to step up the preparations for European Union integration. This was in fact one of the priorities listed in the 2003 European Partnership for Serbia. SEIO is the institution that deals with the day-to-day management of the pre-accession process and with communication with the EC. Starting from 2004, SEIO has performed all the activities related to the Strategy for association and accession to the EU and, until May 2006, to cooperation with the State Union and Montenegro institutions. The main targets of the office's activity are both the EU and the Serbian government and its ministries. A key role within SEIO is played by the EU Law Harmonization Department, which is the coordinator of the entire European integration process. The Department has two main dimensions of activity. The first one is linked to the reviewing of all governmental procedures, laws and acts, to make them compatible with EU legislation. The second domain of activity is the negotiation process with the EC offices. The Department is supposed to produce all the documents about the SAA negotiation. The functionaries are also directly involved in the negotiation working group and have direct contacts with the EC functionaries in Brussels (SEIO 2005).

According to the EU Progress Report, the work done by SEIO in the last two years received a positive evaluation. In fact, the EU underlines that the relevant institutional setup for the European integration process has proven to be well established and effective. The SEIO functionaries admit that the EC's assistance in building an adequate EU integration institutional framework was particularly effective and helpful. One concrete example of this assistance is the PLAC (Policy and Legal Advice Centre). The PLAC is in charge of supporting the Serbian and Montenegro governments in undertaking the European integration process. The PLAC was formally established in Belgrade in February 2005.[34] The Centre deploys EU and national resources according to a three-fold objective requiring expertise in the fields of EU integration, WTO accession and structural reforms. Operationally, the Centre is made up of three teams combining EU and national experts. Although the second contract formally expired in April 2007, two experts for each pillar are still working in Serbia. As far as the EU integration pillar is concerned, although the negotiation for the SAA agreement was stopped, there remains one local expert and one Slovenian expert currently working on legislation harmonization. The collaboration of Slovenian experts was particularly appreciated by the functionaries of SEIO and by other civil servants working on European integration issues. Slovenia is perceived to be a country very close to Serbia, both for historical and linguistic reasons. Moreover, it recently joined the EU; thus, Serbian politicians hope that the Slovenians will give them guidance on the right way to conclude the SAA agreement.[35]

To sum up, major developments concerning the empowerment of administrative capacity were achieved only in the last two to three years. Overall, the process of rule adoption was improved in the last two years, as the international actors' action was appropriately targeted and credible in supporting the SEIO action, which could be regarded as a domestic change agent. This cooperation between SEIO and the European Union allowed the implementation of projects, e.g. PLAC, which were efficient in improving the adoption of relevant EU-driven law. Rule implementation is relatively developed as regards the European integration framework.

Reforms to combat corruption, illegality and abuse of power

Unlike the problems affecting the Serbian judiciary, from a formal legal standpoint the Serbian anti-corruption legislation is relatively developed and in line with European standards. Serbia has taken many important steps, largely thanks to intensive cooperation on different programs with the Council of Europe and European Commission. However, the main problems in this field still relate to the public perception of corruption as a constant element of public life, compounded by a selective justice (Fatić 2004).

Anti-corruption legislation

From an official, legal standpoint, provisions on corruption are set out in the Criminal Law of the Republic of Serbia and in the new Criminal Code, which came into force in January 2006. The 2002 and 2003 reforms of the Serbian Criminal Code represented the first significant stage in the fight against corruption. They were the result of two years' efforts by the Serbian Ministry of Justice and the Management Centre (an NGO based in Belgrade specializing in policy design). The result was a law (Criminal Law), with an entire chapter (Chapter 21A) devoted to Criminal Offences of Corruption. The assassination of Djindjić in 2003 triggered the most extensive anti-organized crime operation in the history of Serbia, highlighting how organized crime was connected with systematic corruption in the security services and in some public administration sectors (Fatić 2004).

The anti-corruption legislative framework was then improved after 2003, when Serbia joined the Council of Europe and the Group of States Against Corruption (GRECO). Serbia became part of the Council of Europe Criminal Law Convention on Corruption and of the UN Convention against Corruption. Serbia is now considered compliant with most of the Conventions' requirements.[36] At the end of 2004, in order to comply with the GRECO requirements, the government finalized a National Anti-Corruption Strategy.

That Strategy was approved in May 2005 and finally implemented at the end of 2005. The process that led to the Anti-Corruption Strategy highlights the crucial role played by international organizations in influencing Serbian anti-corruption legislation. Such a process points out the role of international organizations in drafting Serbian anti-corruption legislation. As a matter of fact a working group for preparing the draft of the strategy was created to prepare the draft of the strategy in the context of the Council of Europe PACO project[37]. PACO is the Council of Europe program created to fight corruption and organized crime in Southern Europe and the project is implemented together with the SPAI, that is the Stability Pact Anti-Corruption Activity. The working group was composed by government members, national legal experts, donors representatives and, most importantly, by members of Serbian NGOs working on corruption, such as Transparency Serbia and Clean Hands Serbia.[38]

Participation within GRECO and in other international programs, clearly functioned as an anchoring mechanism in terms of anti-corruption legislation. The most relevant laws in the anti-corruption field have been drafted within these programs. This confirms the relevance of international actors, such as Council of Europe and OSCE, in making the governments of Balkans countries at least formally compliant with European anti-corruption standards. The relative success in anti-corruption rule adoption is, thus, explained by specific, concrete action of the international actors, in this case the Council of Europe and OSCE programs, complemented by the presence of local NGOs and think-tanks working on corruption issues.[39] In addition, corruption was one of the main issues of the anti-Milošević campaign and for that reasons a few local groups and associations continued to be active in this field also after 2000. This confirms that when a concrete action of the international actors meet domestic change agents rule adoption is much easier. Concerns remain regarding the effective implementation of those laws.

In a prominent analysis of the corruption in Serbia, Pešic (2007) argues, the Koštunica government went on by having approved a number of anti-corruption laws, which contributed to a trend towards improvements of the situation, mirrored by Serbia's rating on the Transparency International score.[40] In spite of this, adequate institutional reforms have not been established and the implementation of some laws was postponed or had no relevant consequence. In this perspective reforms of the state institution seems to have merely been a matter of rhetoric (Pešic 2007).

The anti-corruption council and the special court on organized crime

Until 2001 no anti-corruption agencies or special bodies were to be found among Serbian institutions. The Anti-Corruption Council[41] was in fact created by the Djindjić government in 2001. The idea was to establish an 'independent' advisory body with the aim of providing support for the government in establishing and implementing anti-corruption policies.

Members of the Council were chosen among respectable people from civil society, academia and media (Anti-Corruption Council 2004). At the moment of its creation, it was considered a good example of transparency and efficiency in the fight against corruption.[42] Problems emerged when corruption scandals also involved some of the Council members. Moreover, concerns were raised about the fact that the Council was wholly financed by the government. The Council aims to be independent – at least it claims independence – and still expects funding from the government, but the related expenditures were not included in the budget (Begović and Hiber 2006).

Although the idea was to establish the Council as a consultative body, it has been involved in much wider activities of investigation of corruption cases, making public statements on specific cases (actual or alleged) of abuse of public office, i.e. taking over the authority of the judiciary (both prosecution and courts). Furthermore, from the very beginning, the Council's operations were caught up in scandals. Allegations regarding the integrity of the former president of the Council (not related to his activities in the Council, but to his academic career) led to his resignation and to the resignation of most members of the Council (Begović and Hiber 2006). As a consequence, the Council lost public credibility and proved to be counterproductive in its anti-corruption efforts.

Another interesting example, concerning the creation and functioning of anti-corruption institutions, is the Special Court on Organized Crime within the Belgrade District Court. The Special Court was established in July 2003, in the aftermath of the Djindjić assassination (together with the Special Court on War Crimes), pursuant to the Law on Organization and Competencies of Government Authorities in Suppression of Organized Crime (2002). From a formal, legal standpoint this court would have had jurisdiction over offences involving criminal conspiracies, such as money laundering, human trafficking, and extortion, as well as illicit trade in arms, ammunition and explosive substances. Technically, the Special Court is simply a chamber of the Belgrade District Court. Many concerns were raised about the actual independence of this institution and about its efficacy in fighting organized crime. In 2003, the Special Court was immediately charged with the Djindjić assassination case, subsequently with the assassination of Stambolic and then with the attempted assassination of Draskovic.[43] The Special Court also dealt with some cases of drug trafficking. International monitoring (OSCE 2003, Freedom House 2005b) evaluated as fair and correct the trials related to these few cases. However, they only represent a small number of cases in three years of activity.

Also some judges of the Judges Association of Serbia (JAS)[44] expressed their doubts about the effectiveness of this court; they pointed out that the first ambiguity lies in the fact that the judges and the prosecutors are appointed only for two years, from all judges in office in Serbian courts. There are no clear and professional criteria for the appointment of these 'special judges', who are often not adequately skilled to deal with organized crime matters.

Moreover, the frequent turnover, due to the limited appointment term of two years, prevents the conclusion of in-depth investigations.

The example of the Special Court is to some extent similar to that of Anti-Corruption. Rule adoption was fairly easy and driven mainly by domestic actors (Fatić 2004). Problems arose over institutional capacity to implement the law, since there were no specialized magistrates to rule on the 'special issues'. Thus, the efficacy of those courts is very low. Therefore, rule implementation was filtered and halted by the lack of adequate institutional and administrative capacity.

Police reform and civilian control of the security forces

The reform of the armed forces and the effective control of civilian government were rather difficult, given the legacy of the wars during the 1990s and the strong interest groups organized around the military. The police have been involved in organized crime operations, including the assassination of Prime Minister Djindjić. This can be seen as a legacy of the paramilitary troops of the 1990s. Public opinion is still divided on this issue. A substantial part of the population still considers those belonging to some military and police sectors to be national heroes who should not be controlled, because of the role they played during those wars. International actors are very active in this area, although local experts claimed that the main goal of the international community is to make the Serbian military controllable, but not necessarily by domestic democratic institutions (Begović and Hiber 2006).

Armed forces reform

With the democratic change of 2000, the first concrete problem that the DOS coalition had to face was how to prevent the intervention of the Yugoslavian Army during that phase of change. The DOS decided to negotiate with the leadership of both the military and the police forces persuading them not to intervene in defense of Milošević (Simić 2005). Although successful, this decision was very telling and the majority of the commentators agree that it deeply influenced the developments of the transition (Edmunds 2005; International Helsinki Federation for Human Rights 2002). Koštunica used the negotiation to build his personal support within the Yugoslavian army and Djindjić did the same with the Serbian police. Others (Simić 2005) suggest that the non-intervention during the October revolution was obtained with the promise of a soft approach towards military and police reform, especially concerning personnel change.

The security sector reform should have been decided and implemented after the DOS coalition came to power. However, apparently they did not prepare a plan for such a reform. It seems that the DOS leaders did not realize that the reform of this sector would have been a precondition for a successful reform of all the social institutions (Simić 2005). Such a possible process of radical security sector reform was replaced with individual compromises made by DOS leaders with prominent military and police generals. The end result was the strengthening of these centers of power. Considering that they should be grateful to the police and to the commanders of the special units for not provoking violent incidents during the 2000 street demonstrations, the DOS leaders plainly assumed that these forces could be involved in a patronage relationship, continuing the arrangements of the Milošević regime (Hadžić 2003)

From 2000 to 2002, the army and security sector reform was largely in a situation of stalemate. Koštunica, at that time President of Serbia, appeared reluctant to push through reforms, above all concerning the dismissal of the high-level leadership. Pressure from the international community, namely NATO and the Council of Europe, to dismiss the leadership appointed by Milošević, in particular the controversial Chief of Staff General Pavković, gradually increased, so that Koštunica moved in this direction in June 2002 (Edmunds 2005). A Law on Security Service of the Former Republic of Yugoslavia (FRY)[45] was adopted in 2002. This established that the military security service, military intelligence and the documentation service were to be put under the control of the Federal Assembly and the Federal Government. Short after the creation of the State Union, its new Constitution seemed to provide the basis for completing the legislative framework for reform. However, the final text of the State Union Constitution did not provide the necessary normative framework for the army and security sector reform, or for the full realization of democratic civil control over the armed forces (Simić 2005).

At that time Tadić (DS) was appointed Minister of Defense but until 2004 further reforms were stopped because of the state of emergency declared after the Djindjić murder. The only positive achievement was the introduction of the Civil Service at federal level, in late 2003. During 2004 the National Assembly at federal level also failed twice to adopt a National Defense Strategy because of continual disagreements between the Serbian and Montenegrin leaders. The Strategy was finally adopted in November 2004. At the national level, the Law on the State Security Agency (BIA) was adopted and enforced in 2002 and it provided legal grounds for parliamentary control of the secret police. A General Inspectorate was established after a change of government, following accusations of alleged mass violation of human rights by the police, after the assassination of Djindjić in spring 2003 (Hadžić 2003). Moreover, a number of scandals involving senior military personnel severely weakened the public reputation of the military during 2004–05 (Begović and Hiber 2006). The new Serbian Constitution, in its Title 6 on 'The army of Serbia', finally deals with the regulation of the national armed forces. These provisions represent an improvement on the previous Constitution, although it is still too vague and its implementation depends on an ordinary law that has not been drafted.

In a nutshell, the major events that brought about the change were those linked to the ousting of Milošević from power and the consequent dismantling of his security apparatus. Public opinion is not very interested in these issues. Thus, the political incentives for additional reform in the area remain rather weak. There are, however, some NGOs active in this field: the Center for Civil–Military Relations, the Atlantic Council of Serbia and Montenegro, and the School for the Security Sector organized by G17. Nevertheless, the impact of NGOs on defense matters has remained low because the military remains suspicious of the involvement of these external actors in its matters (Edmunds 2005). The EU and the Council of Europe activity remains limited in this field. They set armed forces reform as one of the country's priorities, but they were not able to influence the whole reform process. Looking at the EU and the Council of Europe reports it also seems that the monitoring activity on this issue is less rigorous, compared with other policy issues. Rule adoption continues to be slow and difficult, and rule implementation is still unfeasible.

Police reform

Immediately after the democratic change in 2000, the provisional government faced a serious crisis in South Serbia, where the armed insurgency of the Albanians induced the government to adopt a 'Programme for the Peaceful Resolution to the Crisis'. One of the main provisions of the program was the creation of a Multi-Ethnic Police Element (MEPE) with the aim of recruiting Albanian people into the police. The crisis was overcome with the cooperation and crucial assistance of the international community, in the interest of peace and stability in the region as a whole (Simić 2005).

The international community has been massively involved in the police reform since its first steps. The OSCE and the Council of Europe, as official partners of the Ministry of the Interior, were the main actors driving changes and innovations in this sector. Both the OSCE and the Council of Europe produced important reports and assessments that constituted the basic documents for the reform development.[46] Overall, in 2001–02 the police reform process was characterized by good cooperation between national and international actors and by good results in terms of modernization. This favorable cycle was interrupted by the Djindjić murder (Bakic and Gajic 2006). Violations of criminal justice procedures (prolonged detainment without indictment, interrogation without legal representatives, lack of provision of legal advice, etc.) took place during the 2003 state of emergency. Later, as regards abuse of power by security agencies, both internal and external, legal and institutional measures became much more efficient than in the 1990s, when there were no measures at all. In recent years (2003–07), there have still been a substantial number of investigations into prosecution abuses (Bakic and Gajic 2006).

With the Koštunica government, the need for comprehensive police reform came back onto the agenda, due also to pressure from the EU and the Council of Europe. Both the EU and Council of Europe included the adoption of a Law on Police and a Law on Police Education into the priorities that the country had to abide by to comply with criteria established by the two organizations.[47] Hence, the Law on Police was finally adopted in November 2005 after a long preparation process. However, the Council of Europe pointed out that the legislation does not seem to reflect experts' opinion provided by the Council itself, with several shortcomings remaining. The Council of Europe also reported that in 2005 the number of police officers from communities of national minorities was still too small (Council of Europe SG/Inf 2006.01). The situation slightly improved in 2006, when the Law on Police came into force (Council of Europe, SG/Inf 2006 15 final).

Conclusions: A cross-sectional analysis

Table 6.1 summarizes various factors that influence the process of rule adoption, rule implementation and rule internalization of democratic rule of law reforms in Serbia. Before considering the critical factors that characterized the case study, following the EUCLIDA model, it seems useful to analyze, 'cycles' and 'layers'[48] through which anchoring of democratic rule of law standards develops. In the Serbian case one could identify at least three cycles with different directions of democratic rule of law reform. The first phase started at the end of the 1990s and ended in the first half of 2001. It was characterized by the progressive collapse of the Milošević regime, the democratic change of 2000 and the consequent 'reformist euphoria' and the country's inclusion in the SAP. As some experts suggest, the first half of 2001 represented a sort of 'honeymoon' for Serbian politics:[49] the span of time from the 2000 election to mid-2001 was the only period of strategic thinking in terms of rule of law reforms because within the DOS coalition there was relative political stability. The issues that became the subject of the reform immediately after the democratic instauration in October 2000 were those where the EU recommendations were most successfully met (Marceta 2004).

The situation changed in June 2001 with the arrest of Milošević and with the collapse of the coalition. In this second cycle the issue of cooperation with the ICTY became one of the key priorities of EU conditionality. The forced cooperation with the ICTY was in fact immediately perceived as an attempt to undermine state sovereignty. Consequently nationalistic feelings quickly regained the consensus. During this phase the problems of democratic rule of law worsened with the Djindjić assassination and the state of emergency. All the reform processes were halted and some of the results previously achieved, in terms of democratic rule of law improvement, were even overridden by many civil and political rights violations. Thus, this second cycle can be seen as moving in the opposite direction to that of democratic rule of law reform. Finally, the third cycle started in 2004 with the Koštunica government and it is still ongoing. The period from 2004 to 2005 can be still considered as an extended pause to the democratic rule of law reforms: on the one hand, the

Table 6.1 Summary of issues, actors and mechanisms of change

Key area	*Issue*	*Factors*	*Mechanism/Problems*
Civil freedoms and political rights	Protection of ethnic minoritie's	(+) EU conditionality: medium (+) International actor pressure: mainly Council of Europe (+) Change agents: President Tadić and NGOs (+) No Veto players	Rule adoption: works. Institutional and administrative capacity development: works. Rule implementation at early stage
	Freedom of the media	(+) EU conditionality: medium (+) International actors pressures: mainly Council of Europe (–) No change agents (–) Communist legacy (political control over the media)	Rule adoption: works. Institutional and administrative capacity development: poor. Rule implementation slow and difficult
	Freedom of association	(+) EU conditionality: medium (+) International actors pressure: mainly Council of Europe (–) Change agents: President Tadić and NGOs (+) No veto players	Rule adoption: works. Institutional and administrative capacity development: poor. Rule implementation at early stage
Judicial independence and capacity	Reform of the judiciary in line with democratic standards	(–) EU conditionality: weak (–) International actors pressure: weak (–) Change agents: Few and weak (only the Judges Association) (–) Veto players: strong (incumbent parties in the National Assembly and conservative members of the judiciary.) (–) Institutional and administrative capacity (IAC): very poor	Rule adoption: slow and difficult. Institutional and administrative capacity development: poor. No Rule Implementation. No Rule Internalization
Institutional and administrative capacity	Constitutional reform	(–) EU conditionality: Weak (–) International actors pressure: Weak (–) Change Agents: Few (some parties in the opposition) (–) Veto players: strong (Radical Party and other incumbent parties) (–) Institutional and administrative capacity: poor	Rule adoption: partial. Institutional and administrative capacity development: poor. Rule implementation: at early stage. No Rule internalization
	Public administration reform and civil servant legislation	(+) EU conditionality: strong (+) International actors pressure: UNDP, OECD/SIGMA, EAR, World Bank (+) Change Agents: some functionaries and local research centres (+) No veto players (+) Institutional and administrative capacity: quite developed	Rule adoption: works (especially starting from 2003). Institutional and administrative capacity development: improving. Rule implementation: at early stage. Rule Internalization: Poor

	The European integration institutional framework	(+) EU conditionality: strong (+) Change Agents: Implementation agencies and local research centers (+) No veto players (+) Institutional and administrative capacity: quite developed	Rule adoption: works. Institutional administrative capacity developments: work. Rule implementation: works. Rule internalization: poor
Reforms to combat corruption, illegality and abuse of power	Anti-corruption legislation	(+) EU conditionality: strong (+) International actors pressure: mainly Council of Europe with GRECO. (+) Change agents: Djindjić government, international and local NGOs (+) No veto players (−) Bureaucratic inertia	Rule adoption: works. Rule implementation: improving (especially starting from 2003). Institutional and administrative capacity developments: work. No rule internalization
	Anti-corruption council and special court on organized crime	(−) EU conditionality: weak (−) International actors pressure: weak (−) No change agents (−) Veto players: Minister of Justice, incumbent parties, parties in the National Assembly (−) Bureaucratic inertia	Rule adoption: works. No rule implementation. No institutional and administrative capacity developments. No rule internalization
Police reform and civilian control over military	Armed forces reform	(+) EU conditionality: medium (+) International actors pressure: Council of Europe (−) Few Domestic Change agents (−) Veto players: groups within the armed forces (−) Institutional and administrative capacity: poor	Rule adoption: slow and difficult. Rule Implementation: slow and difficult. Institutional and administrative capacity developments: poor. No rule internalization
	Police reform	(+) EU conditionality: medium (+) International actors: OSCE and Council of Europe (+) Change agents: Djindjic (until 2003) (−) Veto players: groups within the Police (−) Institutional and administrative capacity: poor	Rule adoption: works. Rule implementation: partial institutional and administrative capacity developments: improving. No rule internalization

nationalistic anti-EU parties (especially the Radical Party) were progressively increasing their power and, on the other hand, the EU attitude towards Serbia was ambiguous. From 2005 some selective progress can be identified on five democratic rule of law dimensions (World Bank 2005). However, these few selective improvements were limited to rule adoption or, rather, to façade rule adoption.

The description of the three cycles allows us to identify some critical factors that seem to explain the poor results in term of democratic rule of law reform: first of all, the presence of a cohesive anti-EU bloc within the Serbian party system; secondly, the nationalism/sovereignty issue; thirdly, the presence of a 'symbolic' alternative (Russia), and finally the EU's vagueness and ambiguity toward Serbia. As for the first point, in Serbia, unlike the majority of Eastern European and Balkan countries, one can find a real political conflict over accession to the EU. It is the only country with active anti-EU political parties. Thus, the electorally strongest Serbian political party, the SRS, has a strongly anti-European position and continues to question the credibility of a European future for Serbia, the legitimacy of the conditionality as well as the norms promoted by EU (Marceta 2004). The Radical Party's electoral success increased especially after 2001, shortly after the EU started to focus its conditionality on ICTY cooperation and on the status of Kosovo. Radical leaders use the Milošević arguments against the western community that bombed Serbia and contributed to its defeat in the 1990s wars. Those anti-EU elites usually play the role of veto players in the process of rule adoption and rule implementation. But even Koštunica and his party (DSS), have a 'conditional' orientation to cooperation with ICTY: it could be acceptable, but only if it does not undermine the legitimacy of the Serbian state and does not require any yielding of sovereignty. The high share for the Radical Party, 28.5 percent of the vote, in the most recent parliamentary elections (January 2007), is a telling indication of how those ideas still influence Serbian society. In light of this, it is not surprising that the only democratic rule of law dimensions where some progress was achieved are those not dealing with the matter of sovereignty. This is the case of administrative and institutional capacity, the general framework for the anti-corruption policy, the police reform and to some extent political freedoms and civil rights.

In opposing the EU and its conditionality policy, the Radical Party, the Socialists and some of the DSS elite propose to look to Russia, which they – especially the Radicals – perceive as a partner who can be close to Serbia and its nationalist aspirations. Although Russia cannot be considered as an alternative to EU membership, it continues to be perceived as a friendly-oriented country also, by virtue of the Christian Orthodox religion shared by the two countries. For this reason, on the issue of the final status of Kosovo, diplomatic and political relations between Serbia and Russia have recently improved. Sectors of the Serbian political elite still believe that Russia could support Serbia in affirming its position within the international community concerning a final decision on Kosovo. Putin's declarations about the final status of Kosovo contributes to strengthening this feeling. As Noutcheva (2007) argues, Putin sees Kosovo as a potential precedent case that could be applied to other secessionist entities in the Post-Soviet area. For this reason Russia made clear that in the UN Security Council it will stop any decision that has not been accepted by Belgrade's authorities (Peel 2007). The influence of Russia as a 'potential alternative' is obviously more perceptible in relation to those issues related to sovereignty matters, and in particular on the Kosovo issue.

Finally, the EU's vagueness was mentioned as one of the critical factors in explaining democratic rule of law reforms. Until 2005 the EU attitude towards Serbia was undoubtedly ambiguous. The prospect of EU membership was too remote and the attitude of Brussels officials toward Serbia was extremely rigorous. With the start of the SAA negotiation, the EU's promises gained more credibility with a subsequent improvement in compliance with EU requirements. However, on the whole, the attitude of the EU towards Serbia was unclear, at times tolerating Serbian non-compliance and at other times severely punishing it. This situation has a negative impact on the determination of political actors and public perception on the meaningfulness of the EU integration process. Such EU policies weakened change agents and pro-EU civil society and, in the meantime, increased the power of veto players. Moreover, even the low determinacy of the EU requirements contributed to inhibit rule adoption, as in the case of judicial reform and of constitutional politics.

In conclusion, in terms of the three 'layers' of EUCLIDA, rule adoption was overall relatively easier than rule implementation and rule internalization, as in the other countries considered in this book. Poor rule implementation and extremely weak rule internalization were caused both by the presence of veto players (nationalist political parties and anti-EU elite) and by an inadequate institutional and administrative capacity, especially in the judiciary and in the anti-corruption field. To be more precise, rule adoption was 'selective' and in some cases took the form of fake compliance (Noutcheva 2006). Rule adoption worked only in relation to those priorities that did not imply an 'intrusion' into the sovereignty of the country or that were considered 'fitting' or appropriate by the governing elite. As Noutcheva (2006) argues, the existence of sovereignty-linked conditions makes the domestic community very divided and in some cases brings about serious opposition to EU demands. On this point we agree with Noutcheva (2007, 11) who emphasizes that in order to understand the dynamics of EU influence in the Balkans one has to bear in mind 'the perceptions of the political elites in these countries of the motivation behind the EU's policy and the related impact on compliance decision'. In Serbia, the legitimacy of the EU conditions is openly questioned by political players. Moreover, as Noutcheva (2007, 12) suggests 'in the Western Balkans the question of whether the EU is genuinely concerned about spreading its norms or is merely serving its own security interests has been more prominent in the political thinking on the receiving end of

EU conditionality'. For this reason compliance characterized by conditions tied to sovereignty has been largely fake compliance.

Concerning the five democratic rule of law dimensions, it has been noted that rule adoption was partially effective in the case of civil freedoms and human rights, as membership of the Council of Europe combined with the presence of NGOs working on the territory brought some successful results. Formal protection of ethnic minorities, as well as the predisposition of a legal framework for the right of association, fit well with the 'legalist' approach of Koštunica, who gave the impression of a moderate leader not keen to support reforms that would bring heavy costs on his constituencies. A similar analysis can be made for the administrative and institutional capacity reforms, the anti-corruption reforms and the police reform. The reform of the public administration and the bureaucracy modernization were in fact the issues on which Koštunica based his electoral campaign. Moreover, not only do such issues not imply interference in the country's sovereignty, but also formal results could be easily achieved without high adaptation costs. Public administration reform and civil servant legislation were in fact only formally adopted, accepting the EU requirements on paper, but their implementation is still lacking. Rule adoption on anti-corruption legislation partly improved after Council of Europe membership, but only few dispositions were really implemented and effective. Corruption is pursued only at low level, but few changes occurred in terms of parties' clientelism and financial corruption. Thus, the case study confirms that the legitimacy and appropriateness of the EU demands is crucial in determining the outcome of reform. This is particularly true in the case of the Balkan potential candidate countries where the prospect of EU membership is undoubtedly uncertain.

The case of media freedom and judicial reform is different. On these issues there is a particular factor that plays a key role in undermining them: the strong role of the parties within the political system. In the context of the patronage and corruption that are widespread among Serbian political parties, truly free media and judiciary are almost impossible, as genuine independence of these sectors would deeply undermine the basis of elite power. To understand the point better, it can be recalled how there is a substantial difference between an issue such as the ethnic minority rights and that of media independence or judiciary independence. Protecting minority rights is an issue that cuts across the party system: one can distinguish between 'nationalistic' and 'civic' approaches to ethnic minorities, and this distinction is also present within public opinion (horizontal conflict). But issues of media freedom or judiciary independence impinge upon a different potential division, that between elite and public opinion (vertical conflict) (Marceta 2004).

Finally, the examples of SEIO and of the PLAC program are clearly an exception, due to a combination of factors: high determinacy of the EU demands regarding the work of the SEIO institution, the concrete and precise aid disposed throughout the twinning project with Slovenia, the high visibility of the institution at the international level and, finally, the pro-reform and adequately skilled functionaries working in the institution. In this respect, the mechanisms of rule adoption and rule implementation followed closely the EUCLIDA model. This supports the conclusion that, on the whole, EU conditionality is more effective when the EU relies on other international agents, in particular the Council of Europe and the OSCE. As a matter of fact, in the case of Serbia the EU has been making reference to the programs and to the principles of these organizations as a way of reinforcing the leverage of its conditionality. In addition, the EU does that as the programs implemented by the Council of Europe, OSCE, and in some fields also by OECD, seem to be fairly working in promoting the adoption of rules and norms for a few reasons: first, these other organizations are perceived by both political elites and public as more objective and constructive in their relations with Serbia, as compared with the EU;[50] second, they are proposing technical assistance programs, working pragmatically within the national institutions; finally, OSCE in particular has a very active mission located in Belgrade that was able to find the right channels to enable talks with both the political elites and the local NGOs.

Seven years after the fall of Milošević, Serbia is still at the crossroads of its democratic development and the country is clearly looking for political stability to complete the unfinished transition. After the approval of the new Constitution and the parliamentary elections of January 2007, the EU decided to reopen the Stabilization and Association negotiation (June 2007) even if Serbia continues to fall short of meeting EU requirements, particularly in the collaboration with the ICTY. On this point Chris Patten (former European Commissioner for external relations) has publicly denounced that 'dropping conditionality for Serbia will tell the rest of the Balkan countries that rules and standards don't matter and will surrender what little leverage the EU has over Belgrade.'[51] The final decision on Kosovo status and the consequent reaction of Serbia will reveal whether the country will finally be on the road to Europe or not.

Notes

1 Eighteen parties composed the DOS (Serbian Democratic Opposition) coalition. The DS (Democratic Party of Serbia) led by Djindjić and the DSS (Social Democratic Party of Serbia) led by Koštunica were the larger parties. On 6 October 2000 Koštunica, during his first official speech, stated he was willing to create an *ad interim* government. This lasted until December, when official elections took place and Djindjić was nominated Prime Minister of a majority government, in which all the parties of the democratic coalition participated.

2 See Baracani's chapter in this book.

3 In 2002 the Montenegrin secessionist drives caused the break up of the Federal Republic of Yugoslavia (FRY). In 2003, a massive diplomatic intervention organized by the EU led to the creation of the State Union of Serbia and Montenegro.

4 The referendum held in May 2006 established the definitive split between the two countries.

5 See Election results, Parliamentary Election January 2007, Final estimate on CESID (Center for Free Election and Democracy) web-site: http://www.cesid.org/eng/rezultati/sr_jan_2007/index.jsp. Last accessed 29 October 2007.

6 G17 Plus is a liberal conservative Serbian party. Its core consisted of a group of 17 experts (economists, historians, and political scientists) originally constituted as an NGO in 1997. The organization officially became a political party in 2002, led initially by Miroljub Labus (for further details see http://www.g17plus.org.yu, last accessed 29 October 2007).
7 Liberal Democratic Party of Jovanovic that is the only party open in favour to Kosovo independence.
8 See Human Rights Watch, 'Dangerous Indifference: Violence against Minorities in Serbia'(http://hrw.org/english/docs/2006/01/18/serbia12242.htm). Last accessed 19 November 2007.
9 The UN Refugees Agency (http://www.unhcr.org/cgi-bin/texis/vtx/home). Last accessed 19 November 2007.
10 Based on an e-mail interview from the deputy director of the Rule of Law and Human Rights Department of the OSCE Mission to Serbia (17 October 2007).
11 Balkan Media and Policy Monitor 5. News and analysis digest special issue. Media in Serbia, Vol. 5, November 1998. (http://www.nettime.org/Lists-Archives/nettime-l-9812/msg00002.html). Last accessed 19 Novembre 2007.
12 Council of Europe, Information Documents – SG/Inf(2006)15final.(https://wcd.coe.int/com.instranet.InstraServlet?Command=com.instranet.CmdBlobGet&DocId=1042806&SecMode=1&Admin=0&Usage=4&InstranetImage=132552). Last accessed 19 November 2007.
13 OTPOR (in English: *Resistance!*) was a pro-democracy youth movement in Serbia, born within the University of Belgrade, which has been widely credited for leading the successful struggle to overthrow Milošević in 2000. It was formed in 1998. After NATO airstrikes, OTPOR started a political campaign against Milošević and became one of the defining symbols of the anti-Milošević struggle and his subsequent overthrow (for further details see http://www.unesco.org/courier/2001_03/uk/droits.htm). Last accessed 17 October 2007.
14 Derived from interviews with members of Optor (see Note 13), with members of the Center for Non-Violent Resistance and with a journalist of BLIC, 25 October 2006, Belgrade.
15 See European Commission Proposal for a Council Decision on the principles, priorities and conditions contained in the European Partnership with Serbia and Montenegro including Kosovo as defined by the United Nations Security Council Resolution 1244 of 10 June 1999, adopted by the Council on 14 June 2004 – Western Balkans – GAER Council Conclusions (2004/520/EC).
16 All published in the Official Gazette of the Republic of Serbia, No. 63/2001.
17 Several articles in daily newspapers and basically all the humanitarian agencies' reports highlighted that during the state of emergency, the Serbian government explicitly violated citizens' human rights. There were many arrests, mistreatments of detainees, and irregular detentions by the police were denounced. In the days following the murder of Djindjić a particularly serious case was registered: the parliament dismissed 35 judges without receiving permission from the Superior Court, which was formally necessary (OSCE 2003; FIDH 2004; EU SAP Report 2004; ABA-Ceeli 2005).
18 See Carter, T. (2005), 'Playing by the rule of law', in *ABA Journal Report*, ABA Journal, October 2005 issue (http://www.abanet.org/journal/redesign/10fserb.html), last accessed 19 November 2007.
19 See Note 2.
20 Derived from interviews with Serbian judges within the JAS (Judicial Association of Serbia), 24 October 2006, Belgrade.
21 See Note. 15.
22 In June 1990 the regime held a referendum on whether first to have free elections or to have a new constitution drafted by the outgoing Serbian Assembly. The latter was supported by 97 percent of the voters, allowing Milošević to tailor the new constitution to his own needs (Vejvoda 1998).

23 The 1990 Constitution, in one of its more modern and democratic parts, defines Serbia as a civic state made up of all citizens and/or residents. Unfortunately, this remained only a statement as Milošević always considered Serbia as a nation of exclusively Serbian people.

24 For a detailed reconstruction of this final phase see International Crisis Group Europe Briefing, No. 44, 8 November 2006, '*Serbia's New Constitution Democracy Going backwards*' (http://www.crisisgroup.org/library/documents/europe/balkans/b44_serbias_new_constitution___democracy_going_backwards.pdf) and Nenadic D. '*La Serbia verso una nuova Costituzione*' Osservatorio sui Balcani, 30 October 2006 (http://www.osservatoriobalcani.org/article/articleview/6343/1/49/). Last accessed 19 November 2007.

25 Blic (http://www.blic.co.yu/); B92 (http://www.b92.net/indexs.phtml). Last accessed 19 November 2007.

26 International Crisis Group (2006) and ReliefWeb (2006) denounce that during the week before the referendum, the government directly distributed funds to the parties of the coalition, without public scrutiny, violating the law on campaign financing.

27 The International Crisis Group Report (Note 24) cites Helsinki Committee for Human Rights, Youth Initiative for Human Rights, the Lawyer Committee for Human Rights and the Women in Black.

28 As confirmed during the interviews with members of OPTOR (see Note 13), 25 October 2006, with members of the Center for Non-Violent Resistance, 25 October 2006, with members of the Forum for Ethnic Relations, 25 October 2006, with a journalist of BLIC (25 October 2006) and with judges from the JAS, 24 October 2006, held by the author in Belgrade.

29 See Center for Free Election and Democracy (CESID), Referendum for confirmation of proposition of Constitution of the Republic of Serbia (http://www.cesid.org/eng/rezultati/sr_okt_2006/index.jsp) last accessed 19 November 2007.

30 International Crisis Group (see footnote 24); CESID (http://www.cesid.org/eng/onama/index.jsp); Global Voice (http://www.globalvoicesonline.org/2006/11/02/serbia-referendum-fraud-and-other-issues/); Osservatorio sui Balcani (http://www.osservatoriobalcani.org/article/articleview/6343/1/49/). Last accessed 19 November 2007.

31 Derived from interviews with members of Optor (see footnote 13), with members of the Center for Non-Violent Resistance and with a journalist of BLIC, 25 October 2006, Belgrade.

32 The Council of Europe 'Information Documents' [SG/Inf(2006)15 final – 18 December 2006] (see Note 12), 'Constitutional provisions of interest' p. 7.

33 Council of Europe, Serbia and Montenegro: Compliance with obligations and commitments and implementation of the post-accession co-operation programme, Document presented by the Secretary General. SG/Inf (2007) 05 final. (http://www.coe.org.yu/uploads/news/eng/council-of-europe/serbia-2nd-report-update-on-developments-november-2006-june-2007/monitoring-report-nov-2006---june-2007.doc?PHPSESSID=af5f60cdd414eb426b9485a46a04407d) Last accessed 19 November 2007.

34 The PLAC project started in 2001 under another name: SCEPP. The first contract expired in 2002 but it was then extended until 2004. In 2005, a new project began and it was then renamed PLAC. For further information see: http://www.plac-yu.org, last accessed 19 November 2007.

35 Derived from interview with Head of the EU Law Harmonization Department within the Serbian European Integration Office, 25 October 2006, Belgrade.

36 See GRECO, Second evaluation round report (2003–2006)(http://www.coe.int/t/dg1/greco/evaluations/round2/GrecoEval1-2(2005)1rev_Serbia_FR.pdf). Last accessed 19 November 2007.

37 Following the adoption of the Stability Pact in June 1999, the Council of Europe undertook to prepare a specific Programme against corruption and organised crime in South-Eastern Europe – PACO – which was launched in December 1999. The PACO Programme builds upon and complements other activities of the Council of Europe, that is other technical cooperation projects, standard setting activities (such as conventions) and monitoring mechanisms (GRECO for corruption and MONEYVAL for money laundering).

38 For further details see Transparency Serbia (www.transparentnost.org.yu/) and Clean Hands Serbia (www.beta.co.yu/korupcija/eng/). Last accessed 19 November 2007.

39 PACO Working Group for drafting the text of the national strategy for combating corruption. December 2004, Belgrade (http://www.transparentnost.org.yu/dokumenti/prilozi/National_Anticorruption_Strategy_Draft.pdf).Last accessed 19 November 2007.

40 Pesic underlines that 'the most recent publication of the TI Corruption Perception Index (CPI) for 2006 shows that Serbia has slightly improved its position, rising from a 97–103 ranking to a 90–92 ranking..' (p.3).

41 See http://www.antikorupcija-savet.sr.gov.yu. Last accessed 19 November 2007.

42 Derived from the interview with President of Centre for Liberal Democratic Studies. 24 October 2006, Belgrade.

43 Minister of Foreign Affairs of Serbia and Montenegro Union; after the independence of Montenegro, Minister of Foreign Affairs of Serbia. The attempted assassination of Draskovic took place during the rule of Milošević, when Draskovic was one of the most popular leaders in opposition.

44 Derived from interviews with the President and some members of the Judicial Association of Serbia (JAS). 24 October 2006, Belgrade.

45 In 1991, after the break up of the Socialist Federal Republic of Yugoslavia (SFRY), Serbia and Montenegro were unified in the Federal Republic of Yugoslavia (FRY).

46 In particular: 'A study on policing in the FRY' by Richard Monk (Monk Report) on behalf of the OSCE (http://www.osce.org/documents/spmu/2001/07/17633_en.pdf, last accessed 19 November 2007) and the 'Council of Europe and OSCE Final Joint Report on Police Accountability in Serbia' (http://polis.osce.org/library/results?ga%5B%5D=&d=&ta%5B%5D=1467&ca%5B%5D=RPT). Last accessed 19 November 2007.

47 See Council Decision of 30 January 2006 on the principles, priorities and conditions contained in the European Partnership with Serbia and Montenegro including Kosovo as defined by the United Nations Security Council Resolution 1244 of 10 June 1999 and repealing Decision 2004/520/EC.

48 See the Introduction to this book.

49 From the interviews with the President of the Center for Liberal Democratic Studies, 24 October 2006, Belgrade.

50 This opinion comes out of the interviews that the author made in Belgrade to members of OPTOR (see Note 13) 25 October 2006, members of the Center for Non-Violent Resistance 25 October 2006, members of the Forum for Ethnic Relations 25 October 2006, a journalist of BLIC (25 October 2006) and the President of the Center for Liberal Democratic Studies, 24 October 2006.

51 See Patten C. (2007) 'Serbia and the EU: Mladic First, Then Talks', *EU Observer*, 11 October. (http://www.crisisgroup.org/home/index.cfm?id=5119&l=1). Last accessed 19 November 2007.

7 Ukraine

The quest for democratization between Europe and Russia

Roman Petrov and Oleksander Serdyuk

Introduction

The European Union (EU) enlargement not only shaped the modern political and economic appearance of the expanded Europe, but also tested the democratic legitimacy of the integration machinery, since it assumed the importation of the vast European democratic heritage into candidate countries. Gradually, results of this endeavor were reflected in member states and candidate countries and in 'non-applicant' countries, such as Ukraine, which associate themselves with the enlarged Europe and have thereby embarked upon the drift away from the old legacy of Socialism.

Among the countries which are studied in this book, Ukraine is distinguished by the strongest communist legacy, a dubious honor. The Ukrainian Soviet Socialist Republic was one of the most important political, military and industrial bastions of the USSR. In fact, Ukraine had for many years enjoyed a dominant political position in Moscow among other Soviet republics. Two General Secretaries of the Soviet Communist Party came from Ukraine. The process of democratization in Ukraine started shortly after gaining independence in 1991, and was supported by the newly emerging political elite, which mainly included former leaders of the Ukrainian Party (Kravchuk) and recognized leaders of the National Movement (Rukh). As a priority, Ukraine set a political objective of integration into international political and economic structures and, consequently, the achievement of membership of the Council of Europe and the EU. Once the Council of Europe and the EU established criteria for achieving that goal, substantive attempts were launched to prove the conformity of Ukraine's political and legal systems in the spheres of democracy and human rights. However, the efforts of change agents in the country have met strenuous resistance from veto players, who defended their privileged political and economic positions at the expense of democratic reforms and the rule of law. The fact that the EU never endorsed the possibility of Ukraine becoming a full member state further undermined the chances of change agents gathering sufficient strength to promote deep liberalization changes in Ukrainian society. The EU policy of strict conditionality without any prospect of membership hampered rule adoption and rule implementation of Western democratic values in Ukraine. At the same time veto players in Ukraine could credibly advocate alternatives to EU integration, particularly closer alignment with a resurgent Russia.

The objective of this chapter is to analyze democratic rule of law reforms in Ukraine in the five sectors, and to evaluate whether and to what degree, if at all, external actors – and especially the EU – has managed to affect rule of law reforms in Ukraine, using the EUCLIDA analytical framework. We will scrutinize the positive and negative role of international actors in the process of rule adoption, rule implementation, and rule internalization of democratic rule of law. Attention will be paid to specific features of the Ukrainian political and legal environment which imply certain specifications in the implementation of democratic rule of law standards in Ukraine. It is argued that the major specification is the historical and ethnic split of the Ukrainian nation, which led to never-ending conflict between change agents and veto players on the main issues of democratic rule of law reforms in Ukraine. The time frame of our analysis embraces the period from Ukrainian independence in 1991 to the post-Orange Revolution era in 2004–06. The remainder of the introduction will present a general overview of the Ukrainian political scene since 1991 with a focus on the main political actors who form change agents and veto players' camps. The other sections of the chapter will discuss the democratic rule of law implementation in Ukraine in line with the EUCLIDA model (see Chapter 2, in this volume).

Modern independent Ukraine inherited many political, economic and ethnic problems from the former USSR. From the early days of its history until today Ukraine has been sharply divided by diverging political and ethnic influences. Such divergence implies political and economic imbalances, which have constantly to be kept in right equilibrium to maintain the political stability and peaceful coexistence of Ukraine's multinational society.

From the early days of independence deep geographical divisions between the west and the east of Ukraine have become apparent. Such divisions have been engendered by Ukraine's complex history. Representatives of various Russian-speaking national minorities populate the industrial east of Ukraine. The Autonomous Republic of Crimea maintains strong political and cultural ties with the Russian Federation (until 1963 Crimea was part of the Russian Federation). The western areas of Ukraine experienced strong political and cultural influences from Poland and the former Austrian-Hungarian Empire in the nineteenth and early twentieth centuries. Consequently, the political life of modern Ukraine reflects a historical kaleidoscope of pro-west and pro-east preferences and traditions of multinational Ukraine.

From the early 1990s the Communist Party gained popular support in the industrial Russian-speaking east of Ukraine (gaining 20 percent of the popular vote in the 1994 parliamentary elections and 25 percent in 1998). The pro-nationalistic party 'Rukh' received a significant share of the electorate in the rural Ukrainian-speaking west (5 percent of the 1994 parliamentary election votes and 10 percent of those in 1998). To some degree, the 2002 parliamentary elections highlighted the depth of this geographical split, by bringing a wider range of political parties into the Verkhovna Rada. Change agents grouped around the pro-European 'Our Ukraine' Party (which won 30 percent of seats), headed by former Prime Minister Viktor Yuschenko and the Yulia Tymoshenko Bloc – 'BUT' (5 percent of seats). Veto players managed to create a political coalition around the pro-Russian president party 'For United Ukraine' (25 percent of seats), Communist Party (15 percent), and Social Democratic Party (5 percent).[1] Such a strong representation of non-liberals inhibited the long awaited acceleration of the rule adoption and implementation/internalization of internationally recognized democratic values in Ukraine. The veto players' coalition supported President Kuchma's 'multivector foreign policy' directed at closer integration both with the EU and with former Soviet republics. The EU and other international actors applied the policy of conditionality towards Ukraine, and, therefore, constantly questioned the credibility of the Ukrainian government by emphasizing its poor record in human rights protection and in the fight against corruption. The still unsolved killing of the opposition journalist Georgiy Gongadze demonstrated the low standards of human rights protection in Ukraine.

However, the kaleidoscope of the ruling elites in Ukrainian society has drastically changed since the Orange Revolution in December 2004. On the one hand, this revolution raised popular concern not only about such issues as the fight against corruption and economic recovery, but also about more widespread and effective endorsement of European liberal political values and alignment with EU rules in particular. On the other hand, the Orange Revolution has considerably shaken the fragile balance between the constantly diverging west and east of Ukraine.

From the outset, the newly elected President Victor Yuschenko and his government, headed by Prime Minister Yulia Tymoshenko, endeavored to eliminate the influence of veto players by making more than 17,000 new appointments within the executive, security agencies and civil services of people who claimed support for the pro-western policy of the Ukrainian government. Soon after the victory of the Orange Revolution the coalition of veto players in the Verkhovna Rada collapsed. Many of the former coalition members fled to the change agents' blocs 'Our Ukraine' and 'BUT'. Major security positions were distributed between political leaders who took active part in the Revolution and openly declared their pro-western views. People with a strong pro-Western orientation filled the civil service as well. However, newly appointed pro-western top executives rarely managed to employ competent civil servants to replace experienced members of the old administration who retired or were dismissed. As a result, the efficiency of the executive branch of power immediately declined in the aftermath of the Orange Revolution. The position of the government was considerably strengthened by the signing of the EU–Ukraine Action Plan on 21 February 2005 in Brussels. The Plan was presented to the Ukrainian public as a step forward in relations between the EU and Ukraine, and as an expression of the EU's support for democratic and market reforms in the post-Orange Revolution Ukraine.

However, the Action Plan was not welcomed by all political parties in Ukraine. The fact that it did not provide any prospect of Ukraine's membership of the EU was loudly criticized by some veto players.[2] Furthermore, President Yuschenko and the Orange Revolution government strongly advocated the need for Ukraine to join NATO as a prerequisite for full EU membership. However, these initiatives have not been welcomed, especially in the pro-Russian east of Ukraine. As a result the issue of NATO membership decreased support for further integration of Ukraine into the EU and deepened the split in the country between the west and the east.[3]

The Orange Revolution also affected the balance of external influence on processes in Ukraine. The 2006 parliamentary elections sharpened the ever-present conflict between pro- and anti-Western elites in Ukraine. These elections reflected new problems in Ukrainian society. Continuing standstill in economic growth and a worsening of political and economic relations with Russia, against the background of a rather lukewarm reception by the EU to Ukrainian integration initiatives, led to dissatisfaction among the Ukrainian public with the Orange Revolution change agents.[4] Pro-Western circles became more and more convinced that the EU is leaving Ukraine all alone with Russia, at a time when the latter is becoming increasingly authoritarian domestically, and possessive of the former territories of the USSR, Russia has been trying to increase its influence over Ukraine, by using first of all the 'gas factor' and making political and business elites doubt the necessity of pro-European orientation.

The 2006 parliamentary elections opened old wounds and divided Ukraine geographically, as had happened in the aftermath of Ukrainian independence. As a result of these elections veto players gained a significant share of seats in the Verkhovna Rada (the Party of Regions gained 32 percent of seats and the unreconstructed Communist Party 3 percent). Change agents grouped around the 'democratic coalition', which comprised 'BUT' (26 percent), 'Our Ukraine' (16 percent) and the Socialist Party (5 percent). However, due to internal disagreements and power ambitions, change agents missed the opportunity to form the majority coalition for three months after the elections. This situation led to political and economic instability in the country and threatened the second parliamentary elections. As a result, the 'democratic coalition' collapsed in July 2006 after the Socialist Party jointed the illiberal camp and initiated the building of the 'anti-crisis coalition' with the Party of Regions and the Communist Party in summer 2006.

The change in the political balance in the Verkhovna Rada and the adoption of new laws, which transferred considerable powers from the President of Ukraine to the Prime Minister with the so-called 'Constitutional reform' led to a serious constitutional crisis in April 2007. On 2 April 2007 President V. Yuschenko disbanded the Verkhovna Rada and called new parliamentary elections. After the prolonged political standoff and the risk of nationwide disturbances, the leaders of the opposing political camps decided to prevent any possibility of further escalation of the conflict and agreed to conduct new parliamentary elections in September 2007.[5] The outcome of these elections served to further emphasize the depth of the political cleavage between national elites, which was not only maintained, but also deepened by the ineffectiveness of political institutions and the absence of traditions of parliamentarianism and democratic politics. In spite of having a relative majority in the Verkhovna Rada (45.2 percent, but, with a majority of only two seats), pro-Western parties ('BUT' and 'Nasha Ukraina') were still unable to form an effective Parliamentary coalition. In fact, their action has been constantly blocked by the Party of Regions, which is trying to preserve its influence in the country by manipulating the constitutional procedures. After the elections it also became evident that the narrow-minded policies supported by a few politicians and political forces cannot be kept back by any restraining institutional mechanism. This forms the systematic drawback of the model of parliamentary republic which they tried to carry out in Ukraine with the Constitutional reform. In such a situation of conflict, the actual influence of external actors decreases significantly, and previous reforms that set up the basis for developing of democratic standards are called into question.[6]

Protection of civil freedoms and political rights

One can argue that protection of civil freedoms and political rights was always guaranteed by the constitutions of the USSR and Soviet Ukraine. In these documents the scope of civil freedoms and political rights was specified and proclaimed as an attribute of real democracy. However, the declarative character of these provisions and the lack of correspondence with the realities of public life were perceived with displeasure by a significant part of Ukrainian society. In the time of political repressions before Gorbachov's perestroika, the issue of human rights acquired a particularly important value. In the opinion of political dissidents the civil freedoms and political rights proclaimed in the constitutions of the USSR and Soviet Ukraine were engendered from western democratic standards of the supremacy of human rights. Public criticism of the fictitiousness of human rights declared, and the impossibility of their practical realization in the conditions of the Soviet regime, was one of the reasons for popular dislike of the Soviet regime, which collapsed in 1991.

Newly independent Ukraine initiated a political dialogue with the Council of Europe in 1992. Change agents, who included pro-Western political elites (mainly opposition political parties), with a clearly defined agenda for democratic political system based on international standards, advocated the idea of Ukraine moving beyond general political declarations on democratic choice and the priority of human rights and launching concrete steps to ensure practical implementation of these values. The position of the Council of Europe became a determining external factor in these processes in Ukraine. In 1995, after joining the Council of Europe, Ukraine took up obligations which provided real tools for protection for civil freedoms and political rights in the country.[7] In 1998 Ukraine agreed to political conditionality set by the EU under the framework of the EU–Ukraine Partnership and Cooperation Agreement (PCA). This agreement provided that the attainment of economic objectives (free trade area between Ukraine and the EU) was dependent on the success of economic and political reforms in Ukraine. Henceforth, the Council of Europe and the EU played the leading role among international actors in the course of monitoring the protection of civil rights and political freedoms by various Ukrainian regimes.[8]

At various stages, the history of these relationships was rather dramatic. International organizations, such as the Council of Europe, the EU, and the OCSE, constantly criticized Ukraine for non-observance of its human rights obligations. This criticism encouraged and directed the activity of domestic change agents (human rights NGOs, independent mass media, political opposition, etc.). It can be emphasized that during that period Russia was not an alternative model, which would contrast the influence of European standards, since the Yeltsin administration was also more dependent on the West and at least partially oriented towards liberalizing market and political reforms.

Ukraine pursued the democratic anchoring to Western standards through the ratification of fundamental conventions of the Council of Europe in the field of civil rights and political freedoms. However, this process was not smooth. Before the Orange Revolution the Verkhovna Rada ratified only 20 out of the 30 basic human rights conventions expected from Council of Europe members. The refusal to even formally endorse the remaining commitments can only be reasonably explained as a deliberate restraining of reform processes, chosen by the government and parliamentary majority at a time when anti-liberal elements in the Kuchma regime were powerful enough to block the submission of appropriate draft laws for ratification or even consideration.[9]

This situation caused constant anxiety in the Council of Europe. The resolution of the Parliamentary Assembly of Council of Europe (PACE) No. 1466 and the Recommendation of PACE No. 1722 of October, 5, 2005 noted that the new Ukrainian government had made progress in reducing the number of non-observance of human rights obligations, but it continued to delay the ratification of several important conventions in the field of the protection of human rights and was not carrying out the actions needed to resolve some questions in the area of practical realization of those already ratified.

Responding to evolving external pressure from international actors, President Yuschenko issued an Action Plan on the acceleration of the ratification process of the basic Council of Europe conventions in January 2006. The Plan envisaged the following measures: (a) the signature and ratification of Council of Europe Treaties in relation to the fight against corruption, human rights protection, and the strengthening of democratic institutions; (b) alignment of Ukrainian legislation to European democratic and human rights standards; and (c) effective implementation of European democratic and human rights standards by Ukraine (Edict of the President of Ukraine 39/2006).

However, the continuing political crisis in Ukraine hampered any real progress towards the realization of this plan. Below we try to focus on major gains and mishaps in setting democratic rule of law standards in the area of civil freedoms and political rights in Ukraine.

The new contents

Ukraine's adoption of European standards of civil and political rights required not only formal rule adoption (for example, ratification of the Council of Europe conventions), but also essential efforts to ensure rule implementation and rule internalization. Hitherto, Ukrainian legislation did not recognize human rights concepts, such as the right to freedom and integrity of individuals; prohibition of torture and inhuman treatment; and the right to privacy. Moreover, from the very beginning, Ukraine faced a conflict between US and European models regarding the interpretation of the contents of civil and political rights. This was particularly evident in the fact that in the early 1990s change agents, such as third sector, oppositional politicians, journalists, mostly familiarized themselves with the US experience of democracy (thanks to various educational and information campaigns), and the idea that the USA was the best example of democracy for Ukraine was very popular. The US model promoted its legal and constitutional heritage as one of the prime sources of reference for universal civil and political rights standards to be applied in Ukraine. In addition, the US model put considerable emphasis on the role of the judiciary, consequently to the case law of the US courts, as a source of law making, which was not compatible with the civil law traditions existing in Ukraine (McFaul 2007).

On the other hand, the European model advocated the experience of specific European countries (France, Germany and the UK) and the European regional organizations (the Council of Europe and the EU) as a prime source of reference for civil and political rights for Ukraine. This situation caused certain difficulties for the new generation of Ukrainian judges, lawyers and politicians in applying US and European legal traditions in their everyday work. Ukrainian judges have been encouraged to apply the case law of the European Convention on Human Rights (ECHR) in their decisions. Therefore, in the end, the European model has prevailed due to the dominance of the Council of Europe and the EU vis-à-vis other international actors in Ukraine. The 'first wave of reforms' focused on the alignment of the Ukrainian Civil Code, Civil and Criminal Procedure Codes, information legislation, election laws, and the legislation on associations of citizens with best European standards. The reform of Ukrainian legislation took place in line with European standards. However, this influence was not uniform in every field. In some cases new Ukrainian legislation was inspired by relevant European legislation (Council of Europe, EU), while in other cases the Ukrainian legislation was influenced by Russian legal standards. For example, draft laws on peaceful assemblies submitted to the Verkhovna Rada in 1997–2004 were strongly influenced by comparable Russian laws. Even Ukrainian human rights NGO's were influenced by their Russian, rather than American or European counterparts. Indeed, the process of legal and institutional change in Ukraine in the last decade in particular has been a multilevel process, influenced by both liberal and illiberal external actors.

Moreover, even where formal rule adoption of Council of Europe and EU standards did take place, the Kuchma regime largely ensured that formal rule adoption was not followed by effective rule implementation. In fact, some of the new laws had provisions which did not improve, but worsened, standards of civil and political rights in Ukraine. For example, the new Civil Code of Ukraine contained regulations about unreliable information, which substantially interfered with the activity of the mass media and the implementation of the right to freedom of expression. The new Criminal Procedure Code, similarly, contained numerous drawbacks, which made possible arbitrariness and other infringements in law enforcement. Existence of these legal obstacles was used by the political opposition, and most actively on the eve of Orange Revolution as a proof of unwillingness of the Kuchma's regime to carry out the actual implementation of European standards into the Ukrainian political and legal systems. Hitherto, the most prominent international actors (the Council of Europe and the EU) still remain concerned about effective rule implementation of rule of law standards in the area of civil and political rights, even after the Orange Revolution. International actors expressed their concern over the lack of decisive steps by the ruling political elite in Ukraine to reform the judicial system and the key democratic institutions, and that there was a delay in the ratification of human rights agreements and the arrangement of the national legislation and practice in accordance with them (Council of Europe 1466/2005).

An additional serious challenge to the process of the 'Europeanization' of Ukraine became the strengthening of the model of 'sovereign' or 'managed' democracy in Putin's Russia, which is characterized by a significant constrain of freedoms and related growth of authoritarianism. This model, which became a clear, open alternative to the European one, inspired Ukrainian veto players and hampered the strengthening of human rights protection at the expense of unhindered executive power.

Abolition of the death penalty: the long search for a decision

The fundamental right to life functioned as the 'litmus test' for Ukraine's place in international democratic society. This problem was on the periphery of the political legal discourse during the first years of Ukrainian independence, remaining a problem of moral, rather than legal value. For the first time the issue of the abolition of the death penalty became a subject of discussion during negotiations on Ukrainian membership of the Council of Europe. Abolition of the death penalty was recognized as one of the primary obligations, which Ukraine had assumed after joining the Council of Europe. Ukraine's delay in abolishing the death penalty led to a considerable increase in pressure from international actors (mainly again the Council of Europe) on the Ukrainian political regime. International organizations, by means of numerous programs of technical assistance and grants, encouraged change agents (pro-western political elites, which comprised opposition political parties and pro-western intellectuals) to accelerate the abolition of the death penalty through public opinion and educational programs. The Council of Europe issued resolutions criticizing the delay in the abolition of the death penalty in Ukraine. Pro-Western members of the Verkhovna Rada of Ukraine (the 'European choice' bloc) decided to apply to the Constitutional Court of Ukraine with a request to recognize the death penalty as unconstitutional. After long deliberations the Constitutional Court of Ukraine decided to support this request. This decision led to the eventual ratification by the Verkhovna Rada of Protocol No. 6 (on interdiction of the death penalty) of the ECHR in April 2000. Among the post-socialist member states of the Council of Europe, Ukraine was the country where the abolition of the death penalty took longest. The decision to abolish the death penalty has happened due to the constant pressure of external agents (Council of Europe, EU). The political establishment in Ukraine was not ready to achieve this objective without an external pressure. In conclusion, one may argue that the influence of external actors on politics in Ukraine does not fully correspond to the Checkel's 'socialization' process (see Checkel 2005). Instead, it was a more complex and multilevel process which reflected competing influences of external agents in the east and west of Ukraine.

Freedom of expression and democracy 'watchdogs'

Independent mass media and freedom of expression have a special value in the European model of democracy. The ECHR has recognized the mass media as a 'watchdog of democracy'. Unfortunately, freedom of expression became a key problem in relations between international actors (the Council of Europe and the EU, and – to a lesser extent – the USA) and the Ukrainian government during the authoritarian regime of President Kuchma. Starting from the mid-1990s the government directly or indirectly (through several oligarchic families close to President Kuchma) monitored the majority of key national mass-media groups: censorship existed in different forms, legal guarantees of independence of the mass media were essentially limited, and the state did not carry out any investigations of the murders of journalists. The practice of the destruction of the independent mass media by the judiciary became common. For instance, in 1999 alone 2,258 judicial claims against the mass media and journalists were considered by Ukrainian courts (Misyo and Petrova 2000). The opposition journalists Georgiy Gongadze and Ygor Alexandrov were murdered. It became obvious that freedom of expression in Ukraine was impossible without considerable reforms.

International actors' strategy to improve standards of freedom of expression used political and legislative tools. The Council of Europe and the EU issued political statements urging Ukraine to improve standards of freedom of expression in line with best western standards. Practically all PACE Resolutions established a deterioration of freedom of expression in Ukraine and demanded a response from the Ukrainian government. Moreover, the Council of Europe assisted the Verkhovna Rada in examining draft laws on the subject of compliance with European standards. In addition to these measures international actors provided considerable technical assistance in monitoring the situation over freedom of expression. This technical assistance resulted in the establishment of independent centers on human rights research, networking activities, and training. As a result of international actors' pressure, several important judgments, based on precedents of the ECHR, were issued in Ukraine, and this actually allowed a neutralization of the judicial mechanisms of influence on the mass media, and essentially increased the level of legal protection of Ukrainian journalists. For example, only 514 claims against the mass media, totaling US$150,000, were submitted to courts in Ukraine in 2004. One should note that the quantity of claims against mass media decreased several times in the preceding years.[10]

The Orange Revolution became a turning point, giving hope for further radical changes to improve freedom of expression. However, these hopes had to meet political realities. Members of the new 'Orange' government gained a notorious reputation for being involved in actions aimed at limiting freedom of expression. In October 2005, PACE noted that freedom of expression reforms in Ukraine are rather slow and that the level of freedom of expression does not comply with recognized international and European standards (Council of Europe 1466/2005).

The ECHR: a new engine for protecting human rights

Since joining the Council of Europe as a member in 1995 the European Court of Human Rights (ECtHR) has enjoyed a significant influence on the development of the system of protection of human rights in Ukraine. Obviously, the ECtHR has been one of the most active external change agents for the past ten years (even if its judgments did not concern Ukraine). In the *Sovtransauto-holding v Ukraine* judgment in 2002, the ECtHR established the existence of serious violations of human rights in the Ukrainian legal system (absence of guarantees on protection of the right to property, and risks of intervention of the executive power in the activity of courts). In further judgments the ECtHR raised other important issues, which required serious legal reforms in Ukraine (Zhukovska 2004, 7–12). As a result of influence exercised by international actors such as mainly by the Council of Europe, the Ukrainian courts became more inclined to refer in their judgments to decisions of the European Convention on Human Rights (ECHR). This was especially notable in cases involving journalists and mass media as defendants at the suit of public bodies or civil servants. The ECHR's commentary on the meaning of Article 10 of the European Convention on Human Rights became the basis of the approach of Ukrainian courts in such cases, which played a principal role in the strengthening of freedom of speech.

In conclusion, we highlight the fact that in the area of civil rights and political freedoms international actors, such as the Council of Europe, the EU, the Organization for Security and Cooperation in Europe (OSCE) and Western democratic governments, especially the two most active governments, i.e. those of the USA and the UK, successfully achieved good standards in rule adoption of law. This goal was achieved through the anchoring to fundamental conventions on human rights and the provision of technical assistance to the Ukrainian judiciary. As a result, the new generation of change agents within the Ukrainian judiciary was formed: a part of the judicial corps, which successfully perceived the values of the European standards and started their implementation in the consideration of court cases and significantly influenced the rule adoption of civil rights and political freedoms. However, progress in rule implementation and rule internalization still is to be achieved.

Judicial independence and capacity

The need for a fundamental reform of the Ukrainian judiciary system has never been questioned. This is because both international actors (the Council of Europe, the EU, the OSCE, and some established Western democracies such as the USA and the UK) and change agents (pro-Western political elites, and members of political opposition) considered the Soviet model of the judiciary as a major impediment to the democratic rule of law and rule implementation, and rule internalization of democratic values in Ukraine.

From the 'Soviet court' to ... ?

The foundations of judiciary reform in Ukraine were laid in the Concept of Judiciary Reform approved by the Decree of Verkhovna Rada of Ukraine in 1992 (Decree of Verkhova Rada of Ukraine 2296/1992). The Concept of Judiciary Reform called for the adoption of a number of framework laws on the reform of the judiciary system and legal proceedings in the course of the next two years, which 'had to bring to life democratic ideas of justice developed by world practice and science' and to 'ensure the correspondence of the judiciary legislation to international agreements ratified by Ukraine'. Unfortunately, the goals of the Concept of Judiciary Reform were more ideological in their nature than legal. As a result, its implementation did not go further than enhancement of the independence of judges (judicial self-government) and the creation of the system of specialized economic courts.

In fact, the Soviet-type judiciary was not significantly influenced by these cosmetic changes. Thus, the foundations of judicial procedures remained constant, as did the legal conscience of judges, and the whole system of law-enforcement agencies in Ukraine. Nevertheless, pro-Western political forces in Ukraine asserted the necessity of radical changes in society, though the directions of reforms were not precisely clear. The new political elites felt a sharp deficiency of constructive ideas concerning the reform of the judiciary. However, this gap started to fill in rather quickly. A number of Western programs (governmental and non-governmental) targeted the diffusion of democratic values, the promotion of the best practices of Western democracies with the aim of creating an efficiently functioning judiciary system in Ukraine. Two basic centers of Western influence (the USA and Europe) have emerged. In practice, the geographical origin of such influences was not so important. However, these two different centers of influence entailed certain legal complications and contradictions for the evolving Ukrainian judicial system. The issue of diverse legal influences came to the top of the Ukrainian legal reform agenda when the Ukrainian government began negotiations to join the Council of Europe in 1992. At this time intensive internal discussion about the optimal model of court procedure and the judiciary system in Ukraine was launched. It was the first time that Ukrainian decision-makers had faced the rule adoption problem. Henceforth, change agents, such as political forces of pro-western orientation and, although partially, a few members of magistracy, contemplated which democratic examples are most suitable for Ukraine. The 'third sector' in Ukraine was too weak yet to take full part in the discussion on these issues. The development of the new Constitution stimulated a search for the most appropriate models of justice, which could guide Ukraine to establish a modern and democratic judiciary. As a whole, the lack of institutionalization of international actors in Ukrainian society and the vagueness of democratic values led to a failure of those change agents to promote Western democratic values in the Ukrainian judiciary at the time of adopting the new Constitution in 1996. Traditional judicial conservatism, hardened by the traditions of the Soviet court, prevented Ukrainian judges from appreciating these ideas and applying them in their practice.

Legitimacy of the political regime of President Kuchma at the price of small judiciary reform

The adoption of the Constitution of Ukraine in 1996 gave additional impetus to the reform of the judiciary. In November 1995 Ukraine obtained membership of the Council of Europe, which was accompanied by Ukraine's assumption of essential duties in the field of judiciary reform, in line with the Council of Europe standards. On the EU side similar requirements were specified in the EU–Ukraine Action Plan on Justice and Home Affairs (see *Official Journal* 2003). The Council of Europe Convention on Fundamental Rights and Freedoms, ratified by Ukraine in 1997, articulated the concrete scope of democratic freedoms and rule of law standards to be implemented by the Ukrainian government (for example, in a context of 'a right to a fair trial'). However, for the time being, these standards remain insufficiently enforced in Ukraine. Even pro-Western change agents in the judiciary are insufficiently familiar with the scope of fundamental democratic standards and the means of their interpretation by the ECHR.

In 1990s, the judicial reform in Ukraine was strongly influenced by Russia, where a parallel reform was enjoying a relative success. For the change agents, who were the supporters of the reform, the Russian 'positive' experience was an additional argument in favor of the necessity to adapt best European judicial standards, taking into account the post-Soviet realities in Ukraine and in Russia, dominated by corruption and lengthy court procedures.

Subsequently, in the late 1990s Ukraine witnessed the emergence of an authoritative political regime associated with the former President Kuchma ('Kuchmism'). This situation constituted a main challenge to the judiciary reform at the time, characterized by the struggle of the executive power for total control over the judiciary system. Besides, one began to see the formation of powerful financial and industrial clans (oligarchic structures), which endeavored to control the judiciary in order to ensure smooth distribution and redistribution of state property to private hands. In particular, it caused the preservation of an independent system of economic courts in Ukraine, which have been influenced by mighty oligarchic clans and presidential power.

In such circumstances the problem of judiciary reform became a key issue in the conflict between the Verkhovna Rada and the President.[11] President Kuchma vetoed and publicly criticized many draft laws on judicial reform, which were based on best standards of democratic court procedure and provided for the enhancement of court independence from the influence of executive power. Pro-presidential circles within the Verkhovna Rada prepared alternative draft laws containing mechanisms of direct or indirect influence of the executive power (already precisely personified by the presidential vertical of power) on the Ukrainian judiciary system.

At this time, international actors, such as the EU and the Council of Europe, consistently demanded the proper performance of membership duties by Ukraine through the adoption of democratic standards. Numerous programs of assistance to the Ukrainian government and civil society institutions in conducting the judiciary reform were realized jointly with international donors. As a result of consistent external support and pressure from the Council of Europe and the EU, the position of domestic change agents was strengthened. In this period the composition of change agents was rather mixed. Apart from a section of the judicial corps (primarily in national supreme courts), it included the representatives of the political elites (both in the Parliament and Presidential environment), who supported the pro-western orientation on the issues of reforming the legal system. However, this similarity in the positions of change agents was to a great extent not stable but pragmatic. The majority of domestic change agents openly joined the political opposition and various civil society institutions (representatives of the 'third sector', opposition journalists, and to a lesser degree, scholars and representatives of the public bureaucracy and judiciary). External assistance from international organizations (Council of Europe, EU, OSCE) and Western democratic governments (USA, UK, Canada, Germany, the Netherlands) through the provision of financial and technical assistance with informational and educational programs, expert assistance, internships at the international organizations brought about successful rule internalization of democratic values among domestic change agents and enabled their association with the 'European democratic community'.

Further strengthening of the presidential power in Ukraine gave rise to serious concern among international actors. European organizations, such as the Council of Europe, the EU, and the OSCE, became most active and openly criticized the Ukrainian political regime. The US position was similar and was mostly realized by means of 'implicit' political recommendations. On the eve of the presidential elections in 1999, the Parliamentary Assembly of Council of Europe (PACE) expressed 'deep concern' over Ukraine's slow implementation of duties it had assumed as a member of the Council of Europe (Council of Europe 1179/1999a; Council of Europe 1194/1999b; Council of Europe 1239/2001a; Council of Europe 1244/2001b). European experts pointed out that since the adoption of the Constitution in 1996, the Ukrainian authorities 'took no measures in the implementation of the judiciary reform'. As a last measure the Parliamentary Assembly of the Council of Europe warned Ukraine about the possibility of 'suspension of membership' (Council of Europe 1513/2001c).

In response to the external pressure of western governments (USA, UK and other western European governments) and international organizations (Council of Europe, EU, OSCE) the Verkhovna Rada adopted in June 2001 a set of ten laws – with the addition of a significant Law on Judicial Organization one year later – which were informally entitled 'small judiciary reform'. These laws inserted a few democratic novelties in the judiciary system in Ukraine: a uniform system of general jurisdiction courts headed by the Supreme Court of Ukraine; a new procedure of assignment and election of judges; the Supreme Council of Justice responsible for supervision of judges; more democratic system of appeal and cessation of judgments; better judicial control on legality of detention and arrest of persons, and on limitation of correspondence privacy, telephone conversations, cable and other communications (see Ogorodnik 2004). A direct link between these changes and the position of Council of Europe, which consistently supported the necessity of the judicial reform, can be easily seen. However, the main explanatory factor is still the will of the ruling political elite in Ukraine to preserve the (constitutional) legitimacy of the recent political regime, because the five-year term set by Constitution of Ukraine for the changes in the judicial system, was almost over.

On the whole, regardless of the motives of the political elites, these actions marked the beginning of the formation of institutional and administrative preconditions for a democratic judiciary in Ukraine. In addition, as mentioned above, the 'small judiciary reform' was made because the consistent pressure from external actors. Thus, ultimately, the adoption of a rather cut-down variant of this reform with its discrepancies, inconsistencies and disregard of some important European standards, was a decision, which the ruling elite was forced to make, not only because of the pressure from the Council of Europe, but to avoid formal 'unconstitutionality' of the regime before international actors and the international community.

'In the end, the judiciary system needs to be reformed!'

Although the 'small judiciary reform' laid down the main institutional foundations of democratic judiciary in Ukraine, it was conducted in a rather incomplete way, both institutionally and procedurally. One could say that the general social efficiency of the judiciary system remained low. Moreover, it could neither function as a high-level democratic institution, nor avoid conversion into a functional appendix of the ruling political elite. Disapproval of the existing situation in the Ukrainian judiciary became the dominant topic of political debate between the ruling elite and political opposition. It became clear that the adoption of rule of law standards has not led to the elimination of 'Soviet judiciary' standards in Ukraine. The Council of Europe, the EU, and a few western democratic governments realized that utmost efforts has to be made to accelerate an effective rule implementation and rule internalization of Western democratic standards inside the Ukrainian judiciary. International actors had to reassess the means of influence on the Ukrainian judiciary and to combine technical assistance with direct and indirect political pressure on members of the judiciary.[12]

As a result of international actors' influence, two wings of domestic change agents were formed. The first is the 'reformatory' wing, which consistently asserted the necessity of reforming the entire judiciary system in line with European standards of court procedure. Representatives of this wing championed the adoption of common European legal values, active social interactions with international actors in the framework of scientific exchange programs, trainings, conferences, and seminars. They advocated the enforcement of European legal standards and values through the application by Ukrainian courts of ECHR case law (according to some estimates, between 2002 and 2004 almost 1,000 judgments were issued taking into account judgments of the ECHR) (Zhukovska 2004, 18). In the final years of the Kuchma regime, the Supreme Court of Ukraine enjoyed more independence and freedom. This could be due to the fact that the Supreme Court maintains close international connections with the supreme courts of European democratic countries.

The second is the conservative wing, which was not in the majority but was able to hamper reformatory initiatives within the Ukrainian judiciary. Backed by the support of the conservative wing the Kuchma regime managed to subordinate the judiciary to its own interests on the eve of the Orange Revolution. This took place via the procedures of appointment of judges and the organization and financing of the judiciary system. However, due to the influence of international actors, standards of democratic court procedure and common European legal values have penetrated deep into the minds of Supreme Court judges, which led to their taking an active position in protecting democratic values during the Revolution. It showed itself in decisions taken by the Supreme Court of Ukraine during the 2004 presidential election campaign, especially in the decision of the third and final round of elections, when the grounds for it were not only a doctrinal interpretation of the corresponding Ukrainian law on elections, but also the explicit application of fundamental law of democratic principles.

In the aftermath of the Orange Revolution the new government did not take immediate actions to accelerate the reform of the judiciary system, which was explained as 'lack of understanding of the problem by the new government'. Society became discontented by the fact that political practice separated itself from the rhetoric of the Revolution period. Furthermore, in line with the best traditions of the old government the pressure upon judges continued, the practice of selection of judges among 'acquaintances' remained unchanged, and higher public officials made incorrect comments and estimations of certain court decisions. Eventually, such practice undermined public trust in the new government. On 5 October 2005, the Parliamentary Assembly of the Council of Europe urged the Ukrainian government 'to continue the reform of the judiciary in order to ensure its independence and effectiveness' (Council of Europe 1466/2005). As a result of growing external and internal pressure, President Yushchenko entrusted the National Commission on strengthening democracy and the supremacy of law with preparing the Judiciary Reform Concept in November 2005. This Commission comprised representatives not only of the Ukrainian government and non-governmental institutions, but also of international organizations (the OSCE, the Council of Europe, the European Commission and others). During the campaign for the parliamentary elections in March 2006 and also the anticipated elections in September 2007, President Yushchenko confirmed that the task of initiating the judiciary reform in Ukraine constitutes one of the top priorities for his party 'Nasha Ukraina' and democratic forces in general. However, there was and there is no single understanding of specific directions of the judicial reform among democratic leaders and parties, which undedermines the perspectives of success.

In conclusion, we can highlight two approaches to judicial reform in Ukraine during the Kuchma regime. The first approach focused on the need to continue cooperation with European institutions in the field of judicial reform on the basis of pro-Western democratic standards. The second approach prioritized the need to strengthen 'administrative and controlling mechanisms in the judiciary' in order to gain control over the judiciary system from the executive. The 2001 Judiciary Reform Concept represented a compromise between these two approaches. On the one hand, there was the formal rule adoption of Western democratic standards. On the other hand, veto players within the government managed to maintain 'controlled courts' at their disposal. Thus, it became more advantageous to preserve the current situation than to accelerate rule implementation and rule internalization of rule of law standards by the judiciary in Ukraine. However, the changed political situation after the Orange Revolution led to the revision of the format of the judicial reform in Ukraine. In March 2006 the new Concept on Judiciary Reform was drafted. This 'Concept' targets the establishment of fair trial in Ukraine in accordance with best European standards. On the whole, the content of the new Concept corresponds to established values of the democratic court procedure, though the possibility of effective rule implementation and rule internalization of this Concept is under question. Within a few days of the issuing of the Concept, the Council of Judges of Ukraine requested President Yushchenko to suspend this process, because the consequence of its introduction could be the 'destruction of the entire judiciary system'. The issue was the conflict over specific institutional and administrative models of implementation of the Concept. In our opinion, ways to resolve this conflict will be defined not only by the relations between internal institutions and political forces, but also by the reaction of the Council of Europe and the EU. In early 2006, several programs of technical assistance to Ukraine, which were financed mainly by the European Commission and USAID, were initiated to reform the judiciary system,. These programs had two goals: (1) to create material pre-conditions for the reform (technical equipment of the courts, renovation of the premises, etc.), and; (2) to form public support for values of the reform. This had to provide not only formal democratic rule adoption, but also its real implementation in Ukrainian society. However, the contemporary political situation in the country became an obstacle to these reforms. Parliamentary elections in 2006 brought to power veto players led by the Party of Regions, As a result, progressive draft laws on judicial reform prepared by the President's secretariat were not adopted by the Verkhovna Rada, due to the lack of ideological and legal incentives, and the desire for counteraction by the Presidential power and political forces, united around the Prime Minister. Delay in realizing judicial reform in Ukraine resulted in the inability of the judiciary to resolve the constitutional crisis in April 2007. The Ukrainian judiciary was frequently used by either side of the Ukrainian political elite in the course of their political struggle. The Constitutional Court of Ukraine was pressed by all political powers to produce a decision on the constitutionality of the Edict of the President of Ukraine to disband the Verkhovna Rada in their favor (Edict of the President of Ukraine 264/2007a). Furthermore, in the course of exercising this pressure President Yuschenko dismissed two judges of the Constitutional Court of Ukraine without legal reason. In response to this situation the Parliamentary Assembly of the Council of Europe

> deplore[d] the fact that the judicial system of Ukraine has been systematically misused by other branches of power and that top officials do not execute the courts' decisions, which is a sign of erosion of this crucial democratic institution. Independent and impartial judiciary is a precondition for the existence of a democratic society governed by the rule of law. Therefore, there is an urgent necessity for the Ukrainian political elite to carry out a comprehensive judicial reform, including through amendments to the Constitution.[13]

To conclude these two sections, reforms in the area of civil freedoms and political rights, as well as improvement of the judicial independence, give us grounds to argue that Ukraine has achieved a successful transition from authoritarian regime to hybrid regime. Suppression of freedom of expression and democracy underpinned by the declarative character of democratic and rule of law reforms during the period of Kuchmism entailed the emergence of the authoritarian regime in the pre-Orange Revolution era between 1991 and 2005. The decline of democratic standards in Ukraine was illustrated by the rigging of the first round of presidential elections in November 2004 and by the murders of opposition journalists. Popular disappointment combined with increasing pressure on the part of international actors and change agents caused a nationwide uprising, which led to the non-violent Orange Revolution and the triumph of Viktor Yuschenko in January 2005. Democratic reforms in the post-Revolution period resulted in the adoption of fundamental western democratic and rule of law standards by Ukrainian society. The independence of the mass media was strengthened, and the Ukrainian judiciary underwent reforms aimed at its independence, transparency and impartiality. In general, after the Revolution Ukraine was transformed into a more pluralistic and democratic society. The constitutional reform, which resulted from the Revolution, moved Ukraine from a presidential republic closer to a parliamentary republic. The political opposition obtained more confidence in expressing its own views and protecting its own rights. However, democratic reforms have not been completed to the point to consider Ukraine as a democracy. The Ukrainian political elite has not been able to ensure the full independence of the judiciary. The judiciary in Ukraine has been used to protect and promote political interests and objectives of both change agents and veto players. As a result, the judiciary in Ukraine has not been able to play a significant role in resolving the constitutional and political crises in 2007. In the end, the perspectives of reforming the Ukrainian judicial system remain undetermined because there is no unity in the understanding of objectives and actions within the change agents themselves.

Reforms aimed at increasing institutional and administrative capacity

Insufficient attention on the part of international actors (the EU) to the institutional and administrative capacity reforms led to a delay in democratic transition in Ukraine. In particular, this concerns the increase in the institutional and administrative capacity of legislative and executive powers. Before the Orange Revolution the legislative and executive became closely interrelated branches of power that served the interests of strong oligarch lobby groups. The legislative power gained a notorious reputation of being a nontransparent and closed institution where MPs serve their business interests. The executive became known for its corruption and nepotism. Turbulent changes in the civil service in the aftermath of the Revolution led to an immediate flow of qualified professionals from their positions. These people have been replaced by new individuals who claimed loyalty to the new 'Orange' government but who, in many cases, lacked impartiality and sufficient experience in public administration. As a result, the government faced a difficult dilemma – either to bring back the professionals to the civil service, disregarding their party preferences, or to improve the training of existing civil servants in line with best European standards. So far the government has tried to pursue both paths. The newly launched constitutional reform has been designed to accelerate these processes through: (1) improving the drafting, discussing and passing laws; and (2) administrative and public service reform.

Improving drafting, discussing and passing laws in Ukraine

The process of preparing and adopting draft laws in Ukraine resembles the legislative pipeline procedures in other European countries. However, there are drawbacks which seriously reduce the transparency of the entire legislative process. Veto players, that is, representatives of the bureaucratic elite and strong financial and industrial groups, created these drawbacks in order to keep the legislative process in Ukraine as non-transparent and non-objective as possible, in order to lobby for their political and business interests. The new political configurations of the Verkhovna Rada do not provide for final solution to these problems, because the interest of the dominant parliamentary forces in the 'manual regulation' of the legislative process is growing.

Every draft law has to be scrutinized by the parliamentary committees of the Verkhovna Rada. However, decisions adopted by parliamentary committees on the legality of draft laws have the status of recommendations. This means that they are not binding for MPs, who can easily disregard recommendations proposed and act by means of consensus. This situation significantly strengthens the role of veto players, who can easily ignore the decisions of parliamentary committees in favor of own political interests. Especially, this situation inhibits the effective implementation of international democratic standards, such as the EU and Council of Europe *acquis*.

The possibility of public discussion of draft laws to be adopted by the Verkhovna Rada illustrates the bureaucratic inertia and strong influence of veto players (bureaucrats, politicians who lobby for the interests of powerful oligarch groups). Public discussion of draft laws is envisaged by Article 9 of the Law of Ukraine 'On Basis of the State Regulatory Policy in the Sphere of Business Activity' (1160/2003). This law allows everyone to present comments on a bill proposed for public discussion. Moreover the rules of Article 9 oblige the parties to take into account proposed comments while preparing a final draft law. However, only a limited number of bills can fall within these categories, which are 'regulatory acts in the sphere of business activity'. Thus, bills or other acts, which do not belong to the category of regulatory ones, are not being opened for wide public discussion.

On 3 January 2006 the constitutional amendments adopted in December 2004 came into force and significantly changed the political system in Ukraine. These changes gave more power to the Verkhovna Rada with regard to the appointment of the executive, and control over its activity. Besides, it is believed that the make-up of the parliamentary majority will render the process of preparation and law adoption more controlled and predictable. However, this can be accompanied by the limitation of the opposition's opportunity to influence the situation in the drafting of laws.

Administrative and public service reforms

The administrative reform that commenced in 1998 envisaged the application of measures aimed at increasing the effectiveness of state executive authorities in Ukraine. It was initiated by the Edict of the President of Ukraine 'On Measures for Implementing the Concept of the Administrative Reform in Ukraine' (Edict of the President of Ukraine 817/1998). The concept itself was developed by the State Commission on Administrative Reform in Ukraine – a special advisory body that functioned under the President of Ukraine's office. This body closely cooperated with international actors, that is, more precisely the Council of Europe, the EU, and the OCSE, in order to conduct the administrative reform in line with best international and European practices. The reform pursued the following objectives: effective organization of executive power at central and local levels of administration; formation of a modern system of local self-government in line with European standards; protection of human rights and freedoms by the executive and local government; creation of a modern system of training and retraining of public employees; and the establishing of the efficient administrative system in Ukraine.

Since the Orange Revolution the objectives of the administrative reform have been revised and complemented with new objectives, such as transparency of public authorities, decentralization of governance, reform of law enforcement bodies, minimization of controlling functions of public bodies and increase of local self-government resources through territorial and budgetary reforms (Edict of the President of Ukraine 39/2006). The administrative reform was formally launched on 1 January 2007. The Council of Europe, the EU, representatives of western democratic governments and domestic change agents, such as pro-western political parties and pro-western political elites, hope that the administrative reform will enable decentralization of state regional administrations and, consequently, increase regional administrations' revenues through liberalization of tax legislation and adoption of the new Budget Code of Ukraine.

The first law on public service in Ukraine was adopted in 1993. This established the general framework for the organization and functioning of public service in Ukraine. However, this law, which has been amended several times, hardly allows the formation of a system of public service in line with European standards. European experts emphasized the following substantive drawbacks: vagueness of the scope of the legislation on public service, service; lack of clear regulation of administrative procedures; lack of clear and transparent rules for state employees' salaries (the main problem in this case being that the existing legislation considers a state employee's *rate* of salary as an insignificant part of their salary whereas at the same time all other parts of state employees' incomes are at the discretion of their manager and the award depends on subjective factors). Consequently, there is a lack of standards to assess the results of bureaucratic activity. Acknowledging the weaknesses of the law on public service, change agents initiated rule adoption and approximation of Ukrainian legislation on public service to European and international standards. Over several years, with the assistance of European consultative and expert programs, the government developed a new draft law on public service that was to be completed in detailed form and adjusted to European standards by the 'Code of Ethical Standards of Behaviour of Persons Authorized to Implement State Functions'. For this purpose, issues of the improvement of the quality of public service and enhancement of the procedure for appeals by individuals against public employees' actions were put at the top of the administrative reform agenda.

Constitutional crisis (April 2007): a new call for institutional and administrative reform

On 2 April 2007 the almost year-long confrontation between the minority 'Orange' coalition ('Nasha Ukraine', 'BUT') and the so called 'anti-crisis' majority coalition ('Party of Regions', Socialist Party, Communist Party) culminated in an open constitutional crisis, when President Yuschenko issued an Edict to disband the Verkhovna Rada of Ukraine and to call new parliamentary elections in May 2007 (Edict of the President of Ukraine 264/2007a). The major motivation for this radical step on the part of the President of Ukraine was to terminate the 'unconstitutional' transfer of MPs – members of the 'Orange' coalition – to the 'anti-crisis' coalition. However, the constitutional crisis provoked further instability in Ukraine and the division of Ukrainian people into the west and the east. The Verkhovna Rada did not recognize the legality of the Edict of the President and asked the Constitutional Court of Ukraine to consider whether the Edict complied with the Constitution of Ukraine.

In an atmosphere of escalating nationwide political crisis the Constitutional Court of Ukraine was expected to deliver a decision which had to be recognized by both parties to the conflict. For the second time since the Revolution, all members of the political elite in Ukraine expressed their readiness to accept the decision of the judiciary and not to continue the confrontation. However, due to the decision, expected by many experts, of the Constitutional Court in favor of the Verkhovna Rada, President Yuschenko exercised serious pressure on the judges of the Constitutional Court by dismissing two of them without legally justified reasoning. Further, President Yuschenko repealed the 'expected to be unconstitutional' Edict from 2 April 2007, issued a new Edict on 26 April 2007 and called for a new postponement of the date of the parliamentary elections (Edict of the President of Ukraine 335/2007b). This decision ended all hopes of settling the conflict by legal means and risked further escalation of the political battle.

Finally, after exhausting all legal and institutional means to settle the conflict and following active political mediation by the EU High Representative for the Common Foreign and Security Policy, Javier Solana, leaders of the opposing camps (President Yuschenko and Prime Minister Yanukovich) reached a shaky compromise at a private meeting on 4 May 2007 and agreed to hold new parliamentary elections in July 2007.

Several weeks later, after intensive consultations with representatives of all political parties, President Yuschenko set a new date for the parliamentary elections of September 30th 2007. The constitutional crisis in April 2007 displayed several failures of the Ukrainian political elite. First, there was the inability of both change agents and veto players to solve continuing political confrontation by legal and institutional means. Second, there was the need to develop democratically functioning and respected institutional and administrative capacity of the legislative and executive in Ukraine in order to avoid further confrontations. Keen competition between the political forces, their irresponsibility and the fight for posts and authorities were the direct causes of the crisis. However, this explanation is not complete, since it had deep institutional roots as well. According to Council of Europe Parliamentary Assembly Resolution 1549, they were caused as a result of the incomplete constitutional reform of 2004, which came into effect at the beginning of 2006. From the very beginning European institutions paid attention to the fact that its provisions did not correspond to European democratic standards (such assessments were presented in detail in the conclusion of the Venetian Commission in 2004). A full proportional electoral system does not guarantee the representation of the interests of the whole people of Ukraine and may lead to a distortion of people's will. On the level of branches of powers the lack of an effective system of restraints and counterbalances gives grounds to political forces to feel their supremacy, in terms of the law as well. Even the principles of Constitutional Court formation are such as to make it dependent on political forces and individuals. The constitutional reform of 2004 took place as an internal process only. No external factors had influence over it and its logic was defined by the interests of the political elite only, which regarded it as a means of achieving their specific aims in the power struggle.

Finally, we would argue that enhancement of the institutional and administrative capacity (improving its transparency, observation of democratic and human rights standards) of the legislative and executive in Ukraine was not on the priority list of international actors, that is, of the Council of Europe, the EU, the OCSE, and western democratic governments. As a result, domestic change agents did not manage to create modern and efficiently functioning institutional and administrative capacity in Ukraine, which caused the sharp constitution confrontation in April 2007. Declared reforms have been limited by rule adoption, but omitted effective rule implementation and rule internalization. One can argue that for a long time after gaining independence Ukraine remained a hybrid regime with elements of autocratic and democratic government. However, the democratic reforms in the aftermath of the Orange Revolution significantly raised democratic standards in Ukrainian society and pushed forward democracy in the whole governmental machinery. Thus, contemporary Ukraine approached the level of a country with solid minimal democracy. International actors, such as the Council of Europe, EU, and OCSE, acknowledged the results of democratic parliamentary elections in Ukraine in March 2006 and praised Ukraine's results in ensuring freedom of speech and media. However, serious work should be done to enhance democratic standards not only in Kiev and other big regional centers, but also in smaller regions so as to promote standards of democracy and good governance in Ukraine as a whole.

Reforms to combat corruption, illegality and abuse of power

The existence of corruption in Soviet society was publicly admitted during Gorbachyov's perestroika at the end of the 1980s. It was acknowledged that corruption is not an exception or atypical phenomenon in the conduct of officials, but a more systematic phenomenon, caused by serious problems in society. Therefore, after achieving independence Ukraine embarked upon overcoming the institutional causes of corruption. Romantic illusions about the possibility of eliminating this phenomenon by means of a 'democratic choice' vanished rather quickly. Since the early 1990s, the Ukrainian government and political elites, that is, the leading political parties and representatives of business, endeavored to search for a pattern for an efficient anticorruption policy, optimum legislative tools and law-enforcement mechanisms. The first mention of corruption in Ukrainian legislation appeared on 16 December 1993 in the Law of Ukraine 'On Public Service' (Law of Ukraine 3723/1993). This law stated that a public official cannot 'commit actions, which can be considered as a way of exploiting an official position in mercenary motives in his/her own interests, and also actions, which according to the current legislation are considered as corruption' (Law ofUkraine 3723/1993, part. 2, para. 5). Nevertheless, the provisions of this law became rather declarative since Ukrainian legislation neither defined the concept 'corruption', nor the actions that should be referred to as corruption or abuse of power. It happened because at that time neither members of the executive nor members of the legislature were aware about best Western practices to combat corruption, illegality and abuse of power.

In this situation the best European experiences and corresponding political legal standards did not help domestic change agents very much, for two reasons. The first is that the formation of the Ukrainian pattern to fight corruption and abuse of power coincided with the process of formation of the relevant European standards. Only in 1999 did the Council of Europe draft and adopt two fundamental anti-corruption conventions (Criminal and Civil).[14] The second reason is the absence of sustainable political will in Ukraine to apply best European and international standards to combat corruption and abuse of power. In the end, the Ukrainian government pursued imitation of anti-corruption activities in order to maintain positive cooperation with international institutions.

Anti-corruption legislation: hopes and disappointments

Ukrainian anti-corruption legislation displays the complexity and discrepancy of the political and legal reforms in the 1990s. At this time corruption gradually became an inherent part of life in Ukraine. Neither the state nor civil society could find solutions and potential to tackle this problem. For the state it was the 'fight against its own shadow', and civil society was in the process of post-totalitarian social transformations and was rather weak at that time.

The starting point for the development of the anticorruption legislation in Ukraine was the adoption of Laws of Ukraine 'On Fight Against Corruption' (Law of Ukraine 356/1995a) and 'On Amendments and Additions to Some Legislative Acts of Ukraine in View of Adoption of Law of Ukraine 'On Fight Against Corruption' in 1995 (Law of Ukraine 358/1995b). These laws are in line with general tendencies in the European post-socialist countries, where similar laws were also adopted in the same period. The Council of Europe agencies took an active part in drafting Ukrainian laws against corruption, granting consulting assistance, and examining the relevant projects. The Russian experience, where the initial conditions for the anti-corruption reform were almost identical to Ukraine, had the most evident influence on the drafting of Ukrainian anti-corruption legislation.

Ukrainian laws to combat corruption are rather repressive because they provide a uniform method of fighting corruption – bringing administrative (disciplinary) action against persons committing corruption offences. The prevention of corruption is limited to establishment of interdictions (limitations) concerning the actions of public officials and other persons authorized to fulfill functions of the state. The adoption of anticorruption laws became the subject of prolonged political disputes within the Ukrainian political elite at that time. In the end veto players managed to lobby for legal drafts of a rather repressive nature, rather than drafts of a precautionary nature. Such an approach was the reflection of an inclination to follow a repressive way of solving these problems, in line with the traditions of the Soviet criminal justice. It was this approach that was supported by the members of law-enforcement bodies imposing it on the political elites in the Verkhovna Rada. The absence of a clearly formulated alternative (in this period, in particular, the formation of general European anti-corruption standards was only just beginning), and also the interest of the presidential power to take some steps that would not pose a threat to the existing relationship, but would constitute some response to the needs of society, created the basis for the choice of the simplified repressive model.

As a result, the fight against corruption in Ukraine moved towards formalism. The government issued new laws and measures to combat corruption, but in practice the level of corruption did not change (Buromenskiy and Serdyk 2004a, 4–15). In other words, it became limited to reporting to law-enforcement agencies and bringing charges against representatives of the lowest rank of the state apparatus, such as secretaries of rural councils, for committing minor corruption offences. Very soon the imperfection of the anticorruption laws became obvious to many people, both in law-enforcement bodies and in Ukrainian society. Change agents initiated the drafting of almost 20 new anti-corruption laws in close cooperation with the Council of Europe and other international agencies. These draft laws did not fundamentally change the general approach to corruption control and related only to specific problems, which were, nevertheless, quite important. For example, there were proposals to extend the range of subject liability for corruption activity, to implement a mechanism of financial accountability of civil servants (avowal of receipts and expenditures). In this period the position of change agents was neither clearly formed, nor were they strictly identified. The initiators of the draft laws were members of the Verkhovna Rada and their content was fragmentary. It should be noted that in some cases even proposals to weaken anti-corruption measures were adopted. However, these drafts were given a lukewarm reception by the veto players, who claimed that the new anticorruption laws looked exotic and did not correspond to Ukrainian realities. For example, experts in the field of criminal law rather actively denied any possibility of establishing criminal responsibility of legal persons for corrupt actions in Ukraine.

The issuing of the Council of Europe Criminal and Civil Conventions on corruption in 1999 accelerated the necessity to align Ukrainian anti-corruption legislation with best European practice. However, the veto players (political and business elites supporting the regime of President Kuchma) preferred immediate cosmetic changes rather than radical reconsideration of Ukrainian legislation. They could never accept the general approach to these Conventions, because it threatened the existence of the whole system of corruption relations, which were already formed on the basis of political institutions in Ukraine. That is why the political elites, united around the presidential power, became major veto players.

The Orange Revolution inspired further acceleration of anti-corruption law-drafting initiatives in Ukraine. Representatives of European organizations initiated political consultations with the new government on the improvement of Ukrainian anti-corruption legislation. Western donors launched new large-scale projects with this in mind in 2006. However, the new political elites, which supported President Yuschenko, did not support these initiatives, thereby acknowledging the conflict between further anti-corruption reforms and their political and business interests. Actually their position coincided with the attitude of veto players towards the tasks of reforming the anti-corruption legislation in Ukraine. Indeed, one of the first slogans of the Orange Revolution, the separation of business from government, could hardly be implemented, since key figures in the movement endeavored to improve their business through the new government. Notorious corruption scandals in autumn 2005, arising from the process of re-privatization and redistribution of state property, hampered anti-corruption activities and led to complicated results of parliamentary elections in March 2006 and the sudden ruin of the

'Orange' coalition in July 2006. The beginning of this crisis is attributed to public charges preferred by one of the coalition leaders, Alexander Zinchenko, against politicians from President Yushchenko's inner circle (O. Tretyakov, P. Poroshenko and others) when he pointed out their use of state positions to strengthen their private business, contrary to the public interest, using administrative pressure, corrupt lobbying and also favoritism.

These circumstances, the inefficient working of the Verkhovna Rada and the absence of the Constitutional Court raised serious doubts over the feasibility of adopting a new generation of anticorruption laws that could serve as a basis for the new strategy of fighting against corruption in 2006. However, the situation changed radically when the agreement between the President and political forces united around the Party of Regions was attained in August 2006. The Universal of National Unity was signed by representatives of all the ruling political parties in Ukraine (with the exception of the Communist Party) and provided support for the presidential package of anti-corruption laws. This package, attached to the Universal of National Unity, included the following legislative acts: ratification by the Verkhovna Rada of UN Anti-corruption Conventions, as well as Council of Europe Civil and Criminal Law Conventions on corruption; adoption of draft laws that aligned Ukrainian anti-corruption legislation with best international standards, i.e. a new framework law 'On Corruption Prevention Principles', the law on 'Amendments and Additions for Criminal Legislation and Legislation on Administrative Responsibility' and a landmark draft law for Ukraine on liability of legal persons for corrupt actions.

This package was submitted to the Verkhovna Rada in September 2006. However, it was not formalized due to the failure to form a united parliamentary coalition between pro-Russian political parties (the Party of Regions, the Socialist Party, and the Communist Party) and presidential forces (Party 'Nasha Ukraina' and 'BUT'). As a result, the parliamentary majority, which was formed on the basis of the Party of Regions, started to hamper the adoption of anticorruption laws. During the entire period when they were in power, veto players did not make any attempts in reforming the Ukrainian anti-corruption legislation.

GRECO membership as major factor in enhancing effectiveness of anti-corruption activities

In January 2006 the Ukrainian government and the Verkhovna Rada took major steps to reinvigorate the anti-corruption program through democratic anchoring. In particular, Ukraine ratified the Council of Europe Civil Law Convention on Corruption (ETS 173) and joined the Group of Countries Against Corruption (GRECO) in 2006. This meant that Ukraine fell under the GRECO control mechanism, which allows better implementation of European anti-corruption standards. However, the decision to join GRECO did not meet with universal approval in Ukraine. There were continuous discussions between members of the political elite concerning probable consequences for Ukraine, because real implementation of GRECO standards demanded radical changes to the entire Ukrainian legal system.

At the end of 2006 Ukraine was scheduled to go through the procedure of the monitoring of the progress of the national anti-corruption program. Obviously, for this purpose the Ukrainian government was endeavoring to accelerate the implementation of the anti-corruption program. Such steps were envisaged in the framework of the political agreement between President Yuschenko and the ruling political elite. Besides the above-mentioned package of anti-corruption drafts, President Yuschenko approved by decree the National Program of Fight against Corruption 'On the Way to Integrity' in September 2006. However, practical implementation of this decree was blocked by the Party of Regions as a response to the failure of the negotiations to create the united parliamentary majority. This led to the dismissal of the anti-corruption laws package by the Verkhovna Rada. This situation demonstrates the weakness of the internal preconditions for the real implementation of European anti-corruption legal standards in Ukraine (lack of clear position of change agents, public awareness, perception of value bases, etc.). At the end of October 2007 the official position of GRECO was published: it affirmed that Ukraine was behind in the actual implementation of the European anti-corruption standards. The reason of this was the continuing divergence within the Ukrainian political elite in understanding how to combat corruption in Ukraine and what kind of European experience is better to adopt and implement.

Police reform and civilian control of the security forces

The senior officers in the Ukrainian police and security services were raised and trained in the USSR. Therefore, the newly born Ukrainian police and security forces have inherited problems that were common in the vanished Soviet police system: low effectiveness; centralization and militarization; absence of civil control over law-enforcement; and non-correspondence of Ukrainian criminal legislation to international and European standards. However, the Ukrainian government decided to pursue gradual police reform, in line with best European standards and practice, in order to meet the criteria of membership of the Council of Europe. The EU and the Council of Europe encouraged a certain degree of policy reassessment and democratic anchoring within the activities of the police and enhancement of civil control over police and security. Hitherto, problems in rule internalization and embedding of democratic rule of law remain at the top of the police reform and civil control agenda. However, the progress achieved in these areas continues to be quite modest. This is because police reform and civil control never became top priorities in the EU–Ukraine relations and have been given secondary attention from international actors, including the EU and the Council of Europe.

Issues of the reform of justice, police and good governance are not covered by the EU–Ukraine PCA – the basic legal document in force, which regulates bilateral EU–Ukraine relations. Instead, attention to these issues has been limited to a few non-binding EU documents, such as the EU–Ukraine relations agenda in the EU–Ukraine Justice and Internal Affairs Action Plan 2001, the European Council Common Strategy on Ukraine 1999, and the EU–Ukraine Action Plan 2005. However, none of these documents provides serious impetus and comprehensive framework for substantial reform of the Ukrainian police and the enhancement of civil control over police and security. The 1999 European Council Common Strategy on Ukraine states that the EU supports Ukraine in all its efforts aimed at 'properly functioning independent judiciary, a professional police force, the development of a meritocratic, well-trained public administration at national, regional and local levels are all key elements in the effective implementation of government decisions' (Article 10 of the European Council Common Strategy on Ukraine 331/1999). The EU–Ukraine Action Plan envisages training of the police in the prevention of ill-treatment and torture.[15] The EU–Ukraine Justice and Internal Affairs Action Plan 2001 foresees exchanges of information and police cooperation between the Ukrainian police and police forces of the EU member states, as well as prevention of crimes, and training of Ukrainian police officers to the level of the EU. However, these documents scarcely tackle issues of low effectiveness, centralization and militarization, absence of civil control over law-enforcement, and non-correspondence of Ukrainian criminal legislation with international and European standards.

Problems of effectiveness and civil control

The number of police and security force has grown immensely since Ukrainian independence in 1991 but they have not proved to be more effective. Since 1991 their number has increased seventeen-fold. As a result, the contemporary Ukrainian police and security force is bigger than the Ukrainian army. This means that there is one policeman per 120 citizens of Ukraine. At the same time, this increase in numbers has not brought with it an increase in Ukrainian police effectiveness in fighting constantly growing crime, especially organized crime.

The issue of civil control over police forces in Ukraine remained unresolved. In accordance with Ukrainian legislation none of the law-enforcement agencies can avoid civil control. Provisions of the Law of Ukraine 'On Democratic Civil Control over Military Units and State Law-Enforcement Organs' set a mechanism, which extends civil control to absolutely all the law-enforcement agencies (Law of Ukraine 975/2003a). Nevertheless, although the control system envisaged by Ukrainian law is comprehensive, the issue of the civil control effectiveness has hardly been improved. High profile criminal cases (the murder of opposition journalists Gongadze and Alexandrov) remain unsolved. The investigation process is insufficiently transparent to give the public appropriate information about the case.

Training of police officers and other law-enforcement agencies

One of the reasons for the low effectiveness of democratic reforms in the Ukrainian police and security force is the inadequate system of training of future police and security officers. Firstly, the system is based on Soviet military traditions, which did not teach to best European democratic practices. Secondly, the training of future and present police officers is carried out by military police academies and does not promote independent training (reform of curricula in line with European standards and participation of students in exchange programs abroad).

Specific educational establishments organized within the relevant law-enforcement agencies have a certain degree of initiative and independence. However, EU financial and technical assistance provide very little help for curriculum development in police and security educational establishments in Ukraine. As a result, there has been very little impact on the police academies in implementing new curricula on democratic rule of law. This system of education does not create change agents, such as pro-Western senior officers and decision-makers among future police and security officers.

Conclusions

Table 7.1 displays the various factors that inhibit the process of rule adoption, rule implementation, and rule internalization of democratic rule of law standards in Ukraine. To conclude, we have set out a number of specific characteristics that lead us to believe that Ukraine enjoys a specific path in adopting western democratic rule of law standards. These distinguish Ukraine from other countries – the subjects of case studies in this book. The first characteristic is the geographical split of the country caused by numerous historical, ethnic and cultural disparities between the west and the east of Ukraine. This has far-reaching political consequences on the attempts by change agents to promote democratic rule of law reforms in Ukraine. It is because the west of Ukraine traditionally supports political parties with a clear pro-European orientation, while the east backs political circles which advocate reinvigoration of regional, political and economic integration in the post-USSR area under the leadership of the Russian Federation. That is why pro-western political parties usually play the role of change agents and pro-eastern political elite usually act as veto players in the process of rule adoption and rule implementation of western democratic rule of law standards in Ukraine.

The second characteristic is the vagueness of the EU external policy towards Ukraine. The EU pretends to play a leading role among international actors in exporting democratic rule of law values to third countries. Ukraine is no exception. Throughout the last decade the EU has skilfully applied the policy of conditionality in order to accelerate democratic reforms in Ukraine. However, while 'welcoming European aspirations' the EU never promised Ukraine the prospect of EU membership, justifying this policy by the need to absorb twelve new members and to solve a turbulent internal constitutional crisis. Such an approach led to the weakening of domestic change agents vis-à-vis strong veto players. It could be argued that the European Neighbourhood Policy (ENP), devised as a substitute for full membership of

Table 7.1 Summary of issues, actors and mechanisms of change

Key areas	*Issues*	*Factors*	*Mechanisms/Problems*
Civil freedom and political rights	Strengthening civil and political rights by adopting European standards	(+) Council of Europe and EU strict conditionality (+) Change agents: opposition in legislature, civil , society NGOs, President of Ukraine after the 2004 'Orange Revolution' (–) strong veto players: legislature and executive, President Kuchma, members of the judiciary	RA works. Diverse and contradictory influence of IA (US and European). Poor knowledge of change agents about the Councilof Europe and EU democratic standards. Poor IAC development. Poor rule internalization
	Abolition of the death penalty and strengthening of freedom of expression	(+) Council of Europe and EU strict conditionality (+) Change agents: opposition in legislature, civil society, NGOs, President of Ukraine after the 2004 'Orange Revolution' (–) strong veto players: legislature and executive, President Kuchma, members of the judiciary	RA works. Poor IAC development. Poor rule internalization
Judiciary reform	Judges' independence	(+) Council of Europe and EU (+) Change agents: (–) strong veto players: legislature and executive, President Kuchma, members of the judiciary	RA works. Poor IAC development. Poor rule internalization
	The 'small reform'	(+) Council of Europe and EU strict conditionality (+) Change agents: opposition in legislature, civil society, NGOs, President of Ukraine after the 2004 'Orange Revolution' (–) strong veto players: legislature and executive, President Kuchma, members of the judiciary (–) Reduced IAC	RA works. Poor knowledge of change agents (judges) about the Court judgments. Poor IAC development. Poor rule internalization
Institutional and	Improving	(+) EU conditionality	Slow and difficult RA.

administrative structures	drafting, discussing and passing laws	(–) Reduced administrative capacity of the Parliament (–) Veto players: parties in the Verkhovna Rada (–) Bureaucratic inertia	Non-binding decisions of parliamentary committees. Strong resistance of veto players (local bureaucrats, MPs, representatives of economic oligarch groups). Poor IAC development
	Administrative and public service reform	(+) EU conditionality (+) Change agents: opposition parties to President Kuchma regime, NGOs (–) Veto players: executive, parties in the Verkhovna Rada (–) Bureaucratic inertia	Slow RA. Poor IAC development. Poor rule implementation and rule internalization
Corruption	Adopting anti-corruption legislation	(+) Council of Europe and EU pressure (+) Change agents: opposition parties to President Kuchma regime, NGOs (–) Veto players: executive, parties in the Verkhovna Rada (–) Bureaucratic inertia	Formation of national anti-corruption legislation coincided with formation of European anti-corruption standards. Formal RA but slow and difficult. Poor IAC development. Poor rule implementation and rule internalization
	Establishing effective IAC to combat corruption	(+) Change agents: opposition parties to President Kuchma regime, NGOs (–) Strong veto players: executive, parties in the Verkhovna Rada (–) Bureaucratic inertia	No National Strategy to combat corruption. National Anti-corruption Coordinating Committee cannot issue binding decisions. Slow and difficult RA. Poor IAC development
	Democratic anchoring through GRECO membership	(+) Change agents: Ministry of Justice, 'Orange' coalition political parties, NGOs (–) Veto players: executive, parties in the Verkhovna Rada (–) Bureaucratic inertia	Formal RA but slow and difficult. Poor IAC development. Poor rule implementation and rule internalization

Continued

Table 7.1 Summary of issues, actors and mechanisms of change—cont'd

Key areas	*Issues*	*Factors*	*Mechanisms/Problems*
Police reform	Effectiveness and civil control	(+) Council of Europe and EU conditionality (+) Change agents: 'Orange' coalition political parties, NGOs (−) Veto players: executive, parties in the Verkhovna Rada, groups within the police; (−) Reduced IAC	Very little RA. Poor IAC development. Poor rule implementation and rule internalization
	Training of police officers	(+) Change agents: members of the police with western training, NGOs (−) Veto players: conservative members of the police (−) Reduced IAC	Poor RA. Poor rule implementation and rule internalization

the EU, brought modest results to both the EU and Ukraine. On the one hand, the ENP did not undermine the influence of the Russian Federation over Ukraine. On the other hand, ENP conditionality, without the prospect of full membership of the EU, did not justify the deterioration of Ukraine's relations with the Russian Federation, which led to painful conflicts over gas, meat and sugar between the two countries.

The third characteristic is the strong political and economic influence of Russia on the Ukrainian political elites. The densely populated Russian-speaking eastern regions of Ukraine enjoy historically close cultural and economic links with the Russian Federation. Most of the Ukrainian steel and machinery industry is experiencing considerable difficulties in accessing the highly competitive and protective European and US markets. Instead, they find valuable alternatives in the east. Pro-EU and pro-NATO aspirations in Ukraine might question the strength of Russian political and economic leverages in Ukraine. That is why the Russian Federation is keen to maintain its influence through powerful veto players (the anti-crisis political coalition and representatives of business) in Ukraine. The EU's adherence to the policy of conditionality without adequate economic 'carrots', on the one hand, and the relative openness of the Russian internal market to Ukrainian products, combined with soaring dependency on Russian energy sources, on the other hand, ensure the continuation of significant Russian political and economic influence in Ukraine in the near future.

Finally, we consider how the entire model of EUCLIDA has worked for Ukraine. In general, rule adoption proved to be very difficult for Ukraine. Strong veto players used their utmost influence to prevent rule adoption of democratic rule of law standards in order to maintain control over the judiciary and police force. Unfortunately, veto players managed to preserve their control over the judiciary and police in the time of Kuchmism and in the post-Orange Revolution period. In addition, rule adoption of democratic rule of law standards process was hampered by the contradictory and diverse influence of international actors. In particular, in the mid-1990s European and US international actors promoted their different standards in the area of the judiciary almost simultaneously, thereby causing problems in rule implementation and rule internalization of rule of law for Ukrainian change agents. A slow and difficult rule adoption took place in the fields of the reform of institutional and administrative capacity, combating corruption and police reform. The problems of adopting appropriate rules in combating corruption can be explained by the fact that the reform of Ukrainian anti-corruption legislation coincided with formation of European anti-corruption standards. Membership of the Council of Europe, combined with consistent EU conditionality towards Ukraine, led to successful rule adoption in the area of civil freedoms and human rights. After heated political debates, the death penalty was abolished and freedom of expression was enhanced.

The processes of rule implementation and rule internalization of democratic rule of law standards were not achieved at the desired level. In most cases, veto players (bureaucrats, extremist political parties, and the political elite supported by strong industrial and financial capital) torpedoed any progress of rule adoption. Moreover, poor rule implementation and rule internalization were caused by objective factors, such as the inadequate knowledge of members of Ukrainian judiciary about practice of the ECHR and the EU *acquis*. Unfortunately, international actors have not been effective in filling in educational gaps in the preparation of change agents within the Ukrainian judiciary and police force. There were also serious setbacks in institutional and administrative capacity. Change agents were hardly in a position to promote democratic rule of law standards, since key agencies set up as flagships of democratic rule of law reforms had no competence to issue binding decisions.

For the last decade the EU has advocated intensive anchoring of western democratic values in Ukraine. However, rule adoption of these values has not brought efficient rule implementation and internalization. One of the reasons is the fact that, hitherto, European integration has not become a widely accepted objective of political and economic reforms in Ukrainian society. For the time being Ukrainian political elites are unlikely to pursue further rapprochement with the EU at the expense of deteriorating relations with Russia. The Russian government has skillfully used Ukraine's dependence on energy supplies from Russia. As a result of the new Russian energy policy towards Ukraine, ordinary Ukrainians have experienced a sharp increase in their energy bills. On the other hand, the Ukrainian public realizes that other alternatives, such as closer integration with Russian and other CIS member states, could bring cheaper energy supplies and better access to less competitive eastern markets. Yet, by 2007 the ENP objectives had not become widely accepted as an appropriate alternative to CIS integration. As a result, there is no national consensus on the future of the pro-European policy in Ukraine.[16] Nonetheless, the process of democratic rule of law implementation has achieved considerable progress in Ukraine, due to constant pressure from change agents and international actors. Fundamental democratic values have become a mandatory part of the programme of all the political parties in Ukraine. Change agents ('BUT' and the 'Our Ukraine Party') and veto players (the anti-crisis coalition headed by the Party of Regions) unequivocally endorse the pro-European foreign policy of Ukraine and need to continue implementation of common European democratic values. This leads us to conclude that the process of democratic rule of law implementation in Ukraine has indeed been developing along the lines suggested in the EUCLIDA model.

Notes

1 Relevant information about the results of parliamentary elections in Ukraine could be found at the web site of the Central Electoral Commission of Ukraine <http://www.cvk.gov.ua> (last access: November 14, 2007).

2 For instance, immediately after signing the EU-Ukraine Action Plan the leader of the Communist Party of Ukraine, Symonenko, accused the EU of seeing Ukraine as an

unequal partner. Instead, he urged Ukraine to accelerate economic integration with former USSR republics. See www.liga.kiev.ua (last access: November 14, 2007).

3 According to independent surveys 44 percent of Ukrainians support improving relations with Russia, 30 percent of Ukrainians support improving relations with the EU. Support for Ukraine's membership of NATO was expressed only 17.2 percent of Ukrainians. In the east of Ukraine 67.6 percent of those asked do not support Ukraine's membership of NATO. www.liga.kiev.ua (last access: November 14, 2007).

4 According to independent surveys, signing the EU–Ukraine Action Plan did not increase public support for Ukraine joining the EU. From May 2005 till now only 44 percent of Ukrainians support Ukraine joining the EU www.liga.kiev.ua (last access: 22 October 2007).

5 See below for details of the Ukrainian constitutional crisis of 2007.

6 Information from the web site of the Central Electoral Commission of Ukraine <http://www.cvk.gov.ua> (last access: November 14, 2007).

7 See the Conclusions of the Parliamentary Assembly of the Council of Europe (Council of Europe 1995).

8 On this see the document on the Compatibility of Ukrainian Law and Practice with the Requirements of the European Conventions on Human Rights, Strasbourg, 2001 (HRCAD 2001, 4)

9 European institutions were very concerned about the delay in the ratification of the key conventions, among them: Protocol No. 12 and No 14 for European Convention on Human Rights, European Social Charter, European Convention on Citizenship, European Convention on Trans-boundary Television, European Convention on Legal Status of Migrant Workers. Available at http://conventions.coe.int/Treaty/Commun/ListeTraites.asp?CM=8&CL= ENG (last access: November 14, 2007).

10 See Human Rights in Ukraine, No. 34 (2004, 4–11).

11 For details see the discussion on draft laws at the web site of the Verhovna Rada of Ukraine <http://www.rada.gov.ua> (last access: November 14, 2007).

12 See the Resolution of the Parliamentary Assembly of Council of Europe on 'Implementation of its Duties and Obligations by Ukraine on Acceding Council of Europe' (Council of Europe 2003a).

13 On this our source is the provisional edition of the Resolution of the Parliamentary Assembly of Council of Europe 'Functioning of democratic institutions in Ukraine' (see Council of Europe 2007a).

14 See on this the Council of Europe Criminal Law Convention on Corruption on 1/07/2002 (Council of Europe 2002c) and Council of Europe Civil Law Convention on Corruption on 1/11/2003 (Council of Europe 2003b).

15 On this see article 2.1 (8) of the EU-Ukraine Action Plan. Recommendation No. 1/2005 of the EU–Ukraine Cooperation Council of 21/02/2005 on the implementation of the EU/Ukraine Action Plan. 14 The Centre of Economic and Political Studies, named after Razumkov <http://www.uceps.org/eng/show/335> (last access: November 14, 2007), conducted a survey on the eve of parliamentary elections in Ukraine in March 2006. Results showed that 42.2 percent of respondents were in favor of prioritizing relations with the Russian Federation over relations with the EU. Only 25.4 percent of respondents prioritized developing relations with the EU. At the same time 61.4 percent of respondents were against joining NATO and 40.7 percent wanted Ukraine to obtain full membership of the EU.

16 The Centre of Economic and Political Studies, named after Razumkov <http://www.uceps.org/eng/show/335> (last access: November 14, 2007), conducted a survey on the eve of parliamentary elections in Ukraine in March 2006. Results showed that 42.2% of respondents were in favor of prioritizing relations with the Russian Federation over relations with the EU. Only 25.4% of respondents prioritized developing relations with the EU. At the same time 61.4% of respondents were against joining NATO and 40.7% wanted Ukraine to obtain full membership of the EU.

8 Scope, depth and limits of external influence

Conclusions

Leonardo Morlino and Amichai Magen

> Institutional change rarely satisfies the prior intentions of those who initiated it ... Change cannot be controlled precisely ... there are frequently multiple, not necessarily consistent, intentions ... intentions are often ambiguousinitial ... intent can be lost.
>
> (March and Olsen 1989, 65–66)

Introduction

Defenders of the liberal international order (Ikenberry 2006; Ikenberry and Slaughter 2007) and those who seek to support the spread and consolidation of liberal democracy around the globe are today, as perhaps never before, confronted by fundamental questions regarding the nature, extent and limitations of external influence on domestic democratic development (Burnell 2005). In the first chapter we addressed those questions. For clarity's sake let us recall them again. Do Western international actors, including the EU, play a significant role in encouraging processes of institutional, legal and normative change in transitional states? If so, when and how do external incentives, financial and technical aid, supported by conditionality, international democratic socialization, diplomacy or sheer democratic example, influence national decision-makers to pursue alignment with a given externally driven model of law, practices and beliefs? What combination of domestic structural factors and agency-driven considerations, on the one hand, and external influence mechanisms, on the other, are most likely to result in convergence with European rules and practices? Does EU influence, where it exists, generate genuine implementation and internalization of reforms ('real change'), or does it only solicit shallow, formal compliance, i.e. rule adoption alone? Does EU influence, where it exists, follow the pathway of direct intergovernmental bargaining, or does it act indirectly, surreptitiously, through persuasion of epistemic communities and other non-state elites who then promote a pro-EU alignment policy internally?

The way we conceptualize and pursue these questions is important, not merely for the purpose of plugging gaping holes in comparative politics, democratization, international relations and international legal studies, but for the many thousands of policy-makers and practitioners – in national development and security agencies, multilateral institutions at the regional and global levels, as well as non-state organizations and networks – who are struggling with these very issues, with high stakes for the future of the international system (Fukuyama and McFaul 2007; Ikenberry and Slaughter 2007).

In this volume we have sought to contend with this daunting conundrum by sequentially: conceptualizing the key components of the puzzle and then proceeding to propose an integrated analytical framework containing the key variables necessary to capture the dynamics of external influence on domestic democratic development. The resulting EUCLIDA model, therefore, provides an integrated set of propositions against which the empirical findings of this research can be applied and tested. More specifically, we have approached the puzzle using the questions: whether and how a prominent international actor has influenced processes of change in a given area of substantive dimensions of democratic rule of law in countries struggling to achieve the transition from hybrid regime to fuller, higher quality democracy? To address these questions we have sought to trace evidence of external influence, as well as the interaction between domestic and external factors, in four case study countries and across five components of the democratic rule of law: (1) protection of civil freedoms and political rights; (2) independent judiciary and a modern justice system; (3) institutional and administrative capacity to formulate, implement and enforce the law; (4) effective fight against corruption, illegality and abuse of power by state agencies; and (5) security forces that are respectful of citizens' rights and are under civilian control. The five dimensions, accordingly, were analyzed through a set of indicators of changes in democratic rule of law.[1] Table 8.1 presents the different specific topics we analyzed in greater depth.

Conceptually, we have approached the puzzle armed with a number of key notions. First, we unequivocally endorse the view that even under conditions of the strongest forms of external intervention, processes of democratization are in reality an essentially domestic drama, in that they fundamentally concern the manner in which a given demos is governed – a demos which properly exists only at the national-state and sub-national (hence domestic) levels. In the arena of democratization, in other words, the domestic and the external are distinct, even though the modes of interaction between the two levels may sometimes defy neat separation (see Chapter 1).

Second, we articulated a typology by which there exist different methods of possible external influence on democratic development – control, conditionality, socialization and the more passive, diffuse, democratic example – and suggested that these varying methods may operate utilizing different logics of influence (drawing on rationalist and norm-based theories of human conduct), and may affect different domestic constituencies, both governmental and societal (see Chapter 2).

Table 8.1 The most relevant empirical sub-dimensions of rule of law, per country

Dimensions	*Countries*			
	Romania	*Turkey*	*Serbia*	*Ukraine*
Civil/political rights	Death penalty Arrests Hungarian minorities Roma minorities International adoptions	Death penalty Freedom of expression Fight against torture Freedom of association and protection of ethnic minority Gender equality	Death penalty Protection of ethnic minority Freedom of media Freedom of association	Death penalty Adopting European standards of civil and political rights Freedom of expression Prevention of torture
Judiciary/justice system	Technology in courts Increased salaries Independence of judiciary	Workload and efficiency Judicial independence Inconsistent interpretation of law	Reform of judiciary Judicial independence from executive	Enhancement of judges' independence Preservation of specialized economic courts The 'small' reform
Institutional/ administrative structures	Rule by decree Civil service reform	Better quality legislation Capacity to implement policies Formulation and allocation of budget Decentralization Civil service reform	Constitutional reform Public administration reform European integration Institutional framework	Improvement of drafting, discussing and passing laws Public administration reform

Combat of corruption, illegality and abuse of power by state agencies	Asset declarations Sunshine laws National anti-corruption department	Free and fair elections Parliamentary control on wrongdoing in public sector Protection of whistleblowers Ombudsman	Adopting anticorruption legislation, also vis-à-vis public administration Effect of GRECO membership Anti-corruption Council and special court on organized crime Conflict of interest legislation	Adopting anticorruption legislation Establishing effective IAC to combat corruption Effect of GRECO membership
Civilian control of army, police and security forces	Demilitarization Sanctions on abuses	Reform of military sector police reform	Armed forces reform police reform	Demilitarization Attempt at higher effectiveness of civil control Training of police officers

Third, in an attempt to overcome the prevailing tendency among lawyers and the few comparativists and international relations scholars who have so far engaged with the topic, we posit that there are in reality different types or depths of change we should be conscious to observe in the domestic system as the result of external influence; that these types may be conceptualized as constituting three main layers of impact – formal rule adoption, rule implementation and rule internalization; that each of these changes involves different internal processes, and that the sustainability or reversibility of change depends to a considerable degree on which layer of impact is attained.

Fourth, we highlighted the need to open up the black box of external–internal interaction in democratization processes by proposing which actors, conditions and modes of interaction may explain each of our three layers of change, as well as positing an integrated framework that may help explain the relationship among all three. In doing so, we were conscious that we may find ourselves under attack on charges that the EUCLIDA model neglects one or more important variables, that it oversimplifies fiendishly complex processes of change, or any other reasonable allegations of conceptual and methodological crimes and misdemeanors. In reply we would offer only this: in outlining EUCLIDA as a model we have responded to the desperate need to unpack the proverbial black box within which external–internal interactions in democratization processes have largely taken place; to propose a model so that it can be the subject of debate; and, more immediately, to offer a concrete model against which our four case studies can be tested. It is only through such trial and error, we believe, that existing theoretical expectations can be checked, rejected, refined, and ultimately improved.

Fifth, we have been mindful of the temporal dimension and the need to build into our analyses clearer expectations regarding sequencing and durations of change through the notions of 'cycles', or phases of change, in which the true significance of a given shift (the passage of legislation which the existing government has no intention of fully implementing, the signing of a treaty, or even the emergence of public discourse on a given topic) is manifested only later, sometimes in unexpected ways.

Finally, differently from the 'spiral model' of human rights change, aimed at establishing causal mechanisms in the process of change within that domain with specific attention to the dominant actors and the dominant mode of social interaction (see Risse 1999, 537–9; Risse and Sikkink 1999, 1–38), EUCLIDA was developed to offer an integrated framework drawing on both interest- and norm-based theories of external influence on domestic change. Moreover, the topics covered concern the five components of the rule of law mentioned above and empirically analyzed in the country chapters. In a nutshell, EUCLIDA serves different purposes in largely different domains. As we also will see in these conclusions, the model of 'membership conditionality' (Schimmelfennig 2005a; Schimmelfennig and Sedelmeier, 2004; 2005a) has also been very useful both in the development of EUCLIDA and in singling out variables and the empirical mechanism of conditionality detected in the empirical research. That model, however, is more effective for rule adoption rather than rule implementation and internalization. Moreover, in our complementing in pragmatic way (see Chapter 2 and Fearon and Wendt 2005) the rationalist approach and the constructivist one as well as the agency dominated literature on comparative democratizations, the net gain of tracing empirically the 'chain of anchoring' should stand out in these conclusions (see below).

At this point we can summarize the essential findings across the different dimensions of the democratic rule of law in Table 8.2. More descriptively and analytically, let us turn to highlight and examine the most salient findings.

Conditionality works for rule adoption! Sometimes ...

Our findings support the assertion articulated by a number of recent studies (Kelley 2004b; Schimmelfennig and Sedelmeier 2005a; Vachudova 2005) that the credible promise of large material and symbolic benefits – particularly the 'golden carrot' of full EU membership, as Romania displays – is generally effective in persuading national governments formally to adopt rules and institutions they would otherwise resist. Conversely, where determinate, credible, positive EU conditionality has been absent or weak – as is generally the case in Serbia and Ukraine – and where only lesser material incentives are on offer, such as financial aid without market access and institutional links, the achievement of formal compliance with externally mandated rules has proven generally more difficult and less complete.

Examples of the two halves of this basic dynamic abound throughout our case studies, lending empirical credence to the external incentives, rationalist bargaining-based theory of external influence methodology (Schimmelfennig and Sedelmeier 2005a). For instance, where the EU did not place pressure for reform of the Romanian civil service in the early to mid-1990s, practically no progress on legislation in the field was achieved, despite the fact that later on[2] the topic was flagged as an area of concern in the Commission reports. In a bid to improve Romania's shaky stance vis-à-vis the EU and NATO, a draft law was prepared in the aftermath of the first post-Communist coalition government in 1997, but was consistently obstructed in the legislature until its sudden passage by the same parliament on 8 December 1999 – days ahead of the Helsinki European Council, which was to decide whether or not to open accession negotiations. The 2006 revisions to anti-corruption laws, long lobbied for by the Council of Europe and the Commission, were similarly enacted barely two months prior to the Commission's scheduled verdict on whether to invoke the delay clause that would have pushed back Romanian accession by a year, from 2007 to 2008.

In the sensitive area of civil freedoms and political rights in Turkey, an analogous pattern emerges. It was only following the December 1999 decision of the Helsinki summit to grant Turkey candidate status and the publication of the first Accession Partnership reform program in March 2000,

Table 8.2 Conditionality, rule adoption, implementation and internalization: sectors and results (2005–06)*

Sectors	*Country*	*Conditionality*			*RA*			*RImp*			*RInt***		
		Str.	*We.*	*Ab*	*Com*	*FInc*	*LInc*	*Com*	*FInc*	*LInc*	*Com*	*FInc*	*LInc*
Civil freedom and	Romania			X	X			X					
political rights:	Turkey	X			X			X					
death penalty	Serbia			X****	X			X					
	Ukraine	X			X				X				X
Civil freedom and	Romania	X				X			X				X
political rights:	Turkey	X				X			X				X
minority rights	Serbia	X			X				X				
	Ukraine***	-	-			X			X				X
Civil freedom and	Romania		X		X				X				X
political rights:	Turkey	X				X			X				X
freedom of press,	Serbia	X			X					X			
speech and association.	Ukraine	X****			X				X				X
Independence of	Romania	X				X			X			X	
judiciary	Turkey		X				X			X			X
	Serbia		X				X			X			X
	Ukraine	X			X				X				X
Justice System:	Romania	X			X				X				X
modernization and	Turkey		X		X				X				
growth of effectiveness	Serbia		X			X			X				X
	Ukraine	X			X					X			X
Constitutional reform	Romania	X			X				X			X	
	Turkey	X				X			X				
	Serbia		X		X				X				X
	Ukraine	X				X				X			

Civil service reform	Romania	X			X				X			X	
	Turkey			X		X				X			
	Serbia	X				X			X				X
	Ukraine	X				X				X			X
Anti-corruption policies	Romania	X				X			X				X
	Turkey			X		X				X			X
	Serbia	X				X			X				X
	Ukraine	X				X				X			X
Improving AC to combat corruption	Romania	X			X				X			X	
	Turkey				X				X				
	Serbia			X		X				X			X
	Ukraine			X			X			X			
Civil control of Army	Romania			X	X			X			X		
	Turkey		X			X			X			X	
	Serbia	X				X			X			X	
	Ukraine	X					X			X			X
Police reform	Romania	X			X				X			X	
	Turkey	X				X			X			X	
	Serbia			X****	X			X					
	Ukraine	X				X			X			X	

Notes: * Conditionality: Str= strong; We = weak; Ab = absent; RA = rule adoption; Rimp = rule implementation; RInt = rule internalization; Com =complete; FInc = fairly incomplete; LInc = largely incomplete.

** On some issues it was not possible to assess internalization because either it was not relevant or data were insufficient for a fair, accurate analysis.

*** This issue has low salience in Ukraine.

**** On this there was a major role for the Council of Europe.

that no less than 34 constitutional amendments were pursued by the Turkish government (with the overwhelming blessing of the legislature) in October 2001; reforms that were followed by a series of 'EU harmonization packages' adopted in the immediate aftermath of the December 2002 Copenhagen European summit, which set December 2004 as a target date for the opening of accession talks, subject to compliance with EU rules.

Another important effect of the conditionality method of influence, and one that has so far attracted less systematic attention (see Jacoby 2005; Jones 1999) relates to its constraining, as opposed to enabling, role. In evaluating the impact of democratic conditionality, in other words, we ought to be ready to detect instances where the threat of external sanctions (either through the imposition of punitive measures or the withholding of a benefit that would otherwise have been provided) limits the range of policy options – producing a 'bounded rationality' effect (Jones 1999) – which is perceived by domestic decision-makers as being realistically available to them. The Turkish military's hesitant warning that it might intervene over the perceived threat to the secularity of the state caused by the nomination of Abdullah Gül to the presidency by the Islamist Justice and Development Party (*Adalet ve Kalkinma Partisi* – AKP) in April 2007, serves as a case in point, with the military's response seen as circumscribed by fear of international opprobrium, notably by the EU.

In contrast to the two membership-track case study countries, we found generally weak rule adoption in Serbia, and even more so, in Ukraine – suggesting again the existence of a robust correlation between both the size and credibility of EU rewards and the relatively insufficient power of alternative sources of external influence, notably US aid, the Council of Europe and the OSCE, to achieve large scale adoption of formal reforms. The allocation of financial aid, in particular, proved to be a poor predictor of formal rule adoption. As Tables 3.2, 3.3 and 3.18 clearly demonstrate, although since 2000 Serbia has been by far the largest recipient of financial assistance among the four countries (and the second largest recipient in rule of law sectors specifically), even with regards to formal rule adoption alone, levels of aid appear to be a poor predictor of positive external influence. Indeed, contrary to the assertions of a recent impact assessment of USAID funding (see Finkel, Perez-Linan, and Seligson 2006), we find little correlation between levels of financial assistance and progress in rule of law development, suggesting that financial aid may well be a relatively fringe factor in the totality of external influence mechanisms.

Just as importantly, perhaps, the granting of 'potential candidate' status to Serbia appears to have only moderately empowered change agents in the country; insufficiently at any rate to solicit the higher rates of formal rule adoption identified in Romania and Turkey. In the field of fundamental freedoms, for instance, EU, Council of Europe and OSCE pressure on Serbia, from 2003 onwards, to reform its media and broadcast laws, produced the adoption of legislation that was only partially in line with prescribed standards. Similarly, despite the fact that both the Council of Europe and the EU have made the adoption of new legislation on associations a priority for Serbia, with technical expertise and financial support provided by the Council of Europe for this specific purpose, the Kostunica government has for years failed to legislate in this area,[3] and a similar pattern is evident in other policy areas, including the reform of the judiciary and civil service. Moreover, unlike the Turkish case, the risk of international sanctions did not appear to delimit effectively the range of policy options perceived to be available to the Serbian government at a moment of crisis. Following the assassination of Prime Minister Zoran Djindjić in Belgrade in March 2003, rather, the state of emergency declared by the government was in practice used to justify widespread score settling with political rivals and a host of extra-constitutional actions, including the firing of 35 judges by the legislature, without the legally mandated requirement that the Supreme Court consider and approve such a move.

On the whole, until 2005 the EU attitude towards Serbia was ambiguous. The prospect of EU membership was too remote and the attitude of Brussels officials toward Serbia was inconsistent: at times tolerating Serbian non-compliance and at other times severely punishing it through strict implementation of conditionality. As a consequence, there was a basic lack of credibility that made political actors and people more and more sceptic on the possibility and meaningfulness of the EU integration process. When negotiation on the Stabilization and Association Agreement started (2005), that was five years later than the initial granting of the status of 'potential candidate', the EU's promises gained more credibility with a partial improvement of compliance. But this actually took place in the domains where European requests fitted into the political designs of the incumbent leaders (see chapter on Serbia). Thus, the end result was an unstable, provisional one, and it could even be reversed as stressed by the negative consequences of 2007 elections,[4] characterized by the success of the anti-European Radical Party (28.6 percent and 81 seats) and several months of non government.[5] Here, ultimately, the role of party elites and their electorate, closely bound up by the sovereignty claims on Kosovo with the Russian support, largely accounts for those negative results.

The lack of a membership horizon and weak incentives offered to Ukraine under the Partnership and Cooperation Agreement (PCA) framework were, similarly, correlated with weak rule adoption and a negative example supporting the principles of rationalist-bargaining models of external influence. Throughout the period of study what sparse evidence of formal rule adoption there is – notably the Judiciary Reform Concept of 2001, and the 2006 ratification of the Council of Europe's criminal and civil law conventions on corruption – appears to have been driven by Ukraine's membership of the Council, rather than the result of EU conditionality. Indeed, out of the four case study countries examined, Ukraine is undoubtedly the one where EU influence has been weakest. It remains to be seen whether the ratcheting up of incentives promised in the framework of the European Neighborhood Policy (ENP) would produce any concurrent shifts in EU influence (Magen 2006).

Two years into the ENP, it appears, however, that the lack of a membership perspective, coupled with ill-defined alternatives of sufficient allure or credibility, is matched by generally disappointing reform outcomes in targeted states, even at the level of formal rule adoption.

Rationalist theories of external methods of influence are supported by our findings regarding dynamics of change and resistance to change in low and high cost areas of policy. Where costs of adaptation for potential veto players were low or negative, i.e. where such actors perceived a net gain from change, a quick cost-benefit analysis appears to have been made, and reforms easily endorsed. A case in point is the raising of judicial and court staff salaries in Romania and Turkey. Where the perception of the need for reform existed prior to the advent of EU conditionality, and where no significant veto players coalesce to prevent reforms, similarly, we find evidence that mild conditionality or even the mere presence of specific externally supplied recommendations for reform, can be sufficient to galvanize internal reform constituencies, particularly where institutional capacity is strong. Concrete examples of this dynamic are found in Turkey's reorganization of courts and introduction of case management modernization with Council of Europe and EU guidance in 2004.[6] Indeed, observation of this area of Turkish justice system reform suggests an impressive degree of positive 'under the radar' change, which can be readily missed against the background of more controversial, 'high politics' issues – such as freedom of expression and Kurdish rights. In 'low politics' policy areas, normative pressure alone (Kelley 2004a; 2004b), coupled with the absence of overt political sensitivity, Ministry of Justice bureaucrats and court administrators have been able to coalesce around Council of Europe and EU promoted standards and drive rule adoption and implementation in seemingly technocratic, efficiency enhancing areas.[7] More interesting, of course, are the hard topics where, for a variety of reasons, internal costs of adaptation are high and powerful elites are strongly resistant to the direction or degree of change sought by external actors. Several findings emerge from our analysis in this context.

Although the specific issues of contention varied somewhat from one country to another, all 'high cost' subject areas in the four case study countries shared important underlying characteristics. In Romania, Serbia and Ukraine it was the tasks of ending political control of the judiciary, reforming the civil service, and fighting public sector corruption, which encountered the greatest resistance to change. In addition, the establishment of effective civilian control over a myriad of security forces represented an extremely difficult area of reform in Serbia. For Turkey, in contrast, Kurdish minority rights and freedom of expression – notably the use of Article 301 of the Penal Code to punish 'insults to Turkishness' – proved the most contentious topics.[8]

What united all areas of special resistance to change can be summarized in the two notions of 'legacy' and 'executive control'. In all three post-Communist countries the persistence of elites, formal institutions, socioeconomic networks and political culture constructed under the previous, non-democratic regimes, translated into the most stubborn, reform recalcitrant veto players. In Romania and Serbia, legacies were generally temporal in nature (with old elites controlling key positions in post-transition state institutions), whereas in Ukraine an additional spatial legacy hampered change, with the country divided geographically into regions generally EU-oriented, and others firmly controlled by Russia-oriented elites. Where no such legacies existed, as in Turkey, areas of contention were different. Indeed, both of Turkey's topics of greatest resistance to change are attributable to the 'Sèvres Syndrome' – a legacy of the Kemalist world view.[9] Moreover, legacy barriers to change were notably severe where predatory elites of the old regime remained essentially intact – as in the case of Serbian security forces, and to a lesser degree in the Romanian civil service – or where a symbolically charged collective memory was popularly perceived to be reflected in a contemporary threat – as in the instance of Turkish fears over Kurdish separatist ambitions.

Persuading national executives to abandon or otherwise reduce their stranglehold over other branches of government emerged as a second prominent pattern. Whereas the goals of modernizing courts and improving the efficiency of case management encountered little opposition from national governments, the strengthening of judicial independence through removal of executive control of appointments, promotions or the finality of judgments, met with potent resistance across all four case study countries. In Romania, Serbia and Ukraine, moreover, legislatures were found routinely to obstruct legislation and institutional development that threatened vested interests, notably in the areas of the judiciary system and the fight against corruption.

More crucial than the variable cost of adaptation, however, has been found to be the related, and in some respects a priori, factor of the nature of domestic decision-makers themselves. The degree to which the EU has been able to affect rule adoption in targeted countries, more specifically, relates closely to the constellation of political parties in the country, and at the more micro level the presence or absence of 'change agents', which can sometimes be small groups or even individuals opportunely positioned within state institutions.

Regarding political party constellations, our findings support Schimmelfennig's expectations that the effects of EU membership incentives on compliance with liberal-democratic norms will depend in large part on the party constellation of the target country (Schimmelfennig 2005). Therefore, in countries with mixed party constellations – where no elite consensus on liberal democracy exists but where liberal parties or coalitions have been able to gain electoral power, often alongside superficially constructed communist, nationalist or populist parties – we should expect to see the most powerful EU incentives, at least, achieve effective influence, albeit at a more protracted rate and with 'fits and starts' patterns of change, as compared to countries with a liberal party constellation (such as the Czech Republic, Hungary, and Poland). In contrast, countries with illiberal party constellations – ones dominated by communist, nationalist parties reliant on anti-liberal ideologies or authoritarian practices of power retention – would be expected to be non-responsive to EU membership incentives.[10] The interplay between external incentives (their objective and subjective attractiveness, credibility and immediacy), on the one hand, and the constitution and conduct of domestic party constellation, on the other hand, remains a subject in need of more detailed inquiry. Nonetheless, our findings shed further light on the topic.

Our findings extend essentially the same logic beyond enlargement cases *per se*, to Serbia and Ukraine, suggesting that the essential dynamic holds even where the prospect of EU membership is shaky, though not entirely absent; EU leverage may still empower those we call change agents, i.e. elite reformists, operating within a mixed party constellation. In Serbia therefore (as in Romania) we observe that the replacement of illiberal party constellations with mixed party ones, under both the Djindjić and Koštunica governments, resulted in the predicted pattern of response to external incentives. In fact, two such patterns can be detected. Formal rule adoption (as well as internalization and implementation) proved quicker and smoother than under more illiberal party rule. Furthermore, areas of policy in which little or no progress could be made under an illiberal party constellation – notably civil service and police reform, and the adoption of rules improving judicial independence and attacking corruption – achieved breakthroughs, at least in terms of formal rule adoption. The relative weakening of veto players[11] and relative empowerment of change agents specifically in the executive and legislative spheres, in other words, not only increases the pace of rule adoption, but also opens up new possibilities for progress in areas deemed too costly for adaptation under the old regime. Conversely, as the frustrating experience of Serbian constitutional reform efforts in the period 2000–06 starkly demonstrates – with weak liberal forces contending with powerful anti-reformist veto players able to win substantial support in the ballot box – despite strong external pressure, basic changes to the Milošević era anti-democratic Constitution have proven slow and limited.

Significantly, the same dynamic appears to hold in the case of Ukraine, although here the picture is somewhat murkier, on account of the short duration since the Orange Revolution and the chaotic struggle for power between competing liberal and illiberal elites unfolding in the country since December 2004. With these reservations in mind, however, it appears that both the pace and boldness of rule adoption have increased slightly since the replacement of the Kuchma regime, as the January 2006 decision by the Yuschenko government and Verkhovna Rada to anchor Ukraine to the Council of Europe GRECO anti-corruption monitoring system attests. It remains to be seen whether the new Action Plan for Ukraine, in the framework of the ENP, leads to faster, smoother alignment of Ukrainian legislation and policies with those of the European bloc, and, if so, under what domestic party conditions.

A possible challenge to the liberal/mixed/illiberal hypothesis in explaining the propensity of liberal external actors to influence domestic reform dynamics successfully is posed by the experience of Turkey. Commentators are ambivalent about how to classify the moderately Islamist AKP, which gained a near-absolute majority in the Grand National Assembly in November 2002, better results in the local elections of 2004, and an even greater success in the general elections of July 2007. This party has pursued faster and costlier domestic reforms than were imagined possible under the more secular and classically liberal coalition government led by the Democratic Left Party (*Demokratik Sol Parti* – DSP) since 1999 (Çarkoğlu 2002; see also Özbudun 2007). What the Turkish experience seems to reveal instead – and what emerges as a consistent theme in our findings – relates to the degree of stability of the ruling government, rather than its composition *per se*.

Thus, with the singular exception of the crisis that involved the pro-European integration G17+ party credibly threatening to bring down the Serbian government over a lack of Constitutional reform, we find that political volatility (whether caused by a fractured coalition or state of national emergency) significantly hampers the pace and scope of rule adoption. The clearest case in point here is found in the experience of Ukraine from the aftermath of the Orange Revolution onwards, where despite the popular election of a pro-European bloc headed by Victor Yuschenko and Yulia Tymoshenko, incessant intra-coalition squabbles and prolonged constitutional crises have largely paralyzed even formal reform. Unlike the conditions that may precipitate democratic transition in the first place, in other words, the development of rule of law conditions, pushing hybrid regimes in the direction of liberal democracy, are best served by conditions of macro-political stability, rather than a sense of crisis. It is where a reformist single-party government or, to a lesser but still sufficient degree, liberal or mixed constellation party coalition, meet the credible incentives of a powerful external liberal actor, that the pace and scope of rule adoption in rule of law reforms proceeds best.

At a more specific level, we find evidence suggesting that meaningful progress in rule adoption (as well as implementation) can be attained in some sectors when external stimuli are matched by the presence of 'change agents' within a given arena of ministerial or bureaucratic power. Hence, in Turkey, for instance, the prescription of justice system efficiency reforms, coupled with the provision of financial and technical assistance, has spurred court administrators and Ministry of Justice officials to adopt significant modernization reforms. More interestingly perhaps, despite powerful veto player opposition, a former human rights lawyer, Monica Macovei, managed to leverage the threat of Romania's exclusion from accession, as well as civil society support, to push through substantial legislative changes in the composition and control of the country's judiciary, in her capacity as newly appointed Minister of Justice in 2004–05.

This analysis, however, still does not reply to the subsequent, obvious key questions. They are: where do the liberal-democratic parties or mixed coalitions come from and where does stabilization originate? Liberal parties or, in our terminology, change agents do not come out of the blue; likewise, a process of a party system or electoral stabilization is not without its own roots. But before dealing with these questions, other considerations have to be added. First of all, the experience of all four countries confirms that highly legalized, detailed external rules are more likely to be adopted by domestic decision-makers than less legalized or vaguer standards (Abbott *et al.* 2000; Goldstein *et al.* 2000). Although we should not discount the possibility of selection bias (i.e. that compliance with highly specific rules is more easily detectable than are broader, looser norms), the superiority of more determinate reform demands made by external actors runs as a consistent theme in our findings. We see this across a range of thematic issues, from the abolition of the death penalty in Turkey[12] and Ukraine, to the ban on inter-country adoptions in Romania, to the specific changes required by the EU of Turkey in the area of civilian control of the military (such as the powers of the National Security Council, the presence of military representatives on public bodies, and the transparency of the military budget). The ban on the lucrative business of providing orphaned children for inter-country adoption, passed into Romanian law in 2004, is a case in point. EU pressure on Romania to halt the supply of orphaned children for adoption worked, despite contrary pressure from the USA and, more curiously, from a number of EU member states, including France, Italy, and Spain.

Of course, highly determinate rules are by no means a panacea that guarantees success of rule adoption, as is starkly shown by the still unreformed Article 301 to the Turkish Penal Code, which the EU has long demanded be reformed. Yet such rules strengthen external influence by at once bolstering conditionality and providing a concrete roadmap, which change agents or domestic reformists can rally around and domestic governments find harder to eschew. In contrast to a generally weak picture of rule adoption in Serbia, therefore, the presence of the relatively comprehensive, detailed and institutionalized rules against corruption embodied in the Council of Europe's civil and criminal law treaties and GRECO peer monitoring mechanisms, appear to have significantly contributed to the speed and substance of the anticorruption legal framework in the country, especially from 2003 through 2005.

Conversely, where specifically framed international rules are absent, where the EU has applied less specifically framed conditions – as has been the case with standards on the judiciary in the 2004 European Partnership set by the EU for Serbia (see Chapter 6) – or where the core of change sought lies not in specific legal rules, but in changes to the spirit of the law and normative modes of conduct, positive developments are far fewer, or at least far more difficult to detect. Thus, on the whole we find greater progress in rule adoption in the areas of civil and political rights and technical reforms to the administration of justice, than the more diffuse, normative independence of the judiciary, institutional and administrative capacity, and civilian control of security forces. An operative conclusion that can be drawn from these findings pertains to the need for a broader range of detailed regional and international rules on key issues of democratic quality and good governance, similar to the Council of Europe's two treaties on corruption and GRECO monitoring mechanism.[13]

Moreover, when credibility is considered, its importance to the EU's ability to pressure targeted countries into rule adoption – in terms of capabilities, costs and consistency of reward or sanctions – has been conceptualized elsewhere (Schimmelfennig and Sedelmeier 2004, 661; 2005b, 13), requiring no lengthy discussion here. Suffice to say that our findings support the hypothesis that the external influence on rule adoption increases with the credibility of conditional promises and threats. This is clearly manifested in the changes in Romania's conduct, where relatively weak EU credibility (in the sense that throughout the 1999–2004 period Romanian elites generally assumed their accession would go through regardless of full commitment to reforms) were partially replaced by the insertion of the suspension clause into the 2004 Treaty of Accession. This suggests a degree of 'wasted leverage' in EU–Romania relations through most of the last decade. In contrast, popular and elite perceptions in both Europe and Turkey, regarding the reluctance of a number of member states to accept Turkish membership have paradoxically added a degree of seriousness to EU insistence on Turkish reforms. Yet the maintenance of credibility through the stretching out of conditionality in the Turkish case may well prove a delicate balancing act, with signs that EU enlargement fatigue, rising cultural bias against the inclusion of a populous, predominantly Moslem country, as well as French President Nicolas Sarkozy's blunt opposition to Turkey's membership, may already be undermining the pace of and commitment to reforms.

A further dimension of the credibility factor, and one less commonly recognized, is illustrated in the conduct of Turkish prosecutors and judges when confronted with the decision whether to bring forward and convict on charges relating to freedom of expression, under Article 301 of the Penal Code. Betting on the rise of anti-EU forces over the short to medium term, and fearing professional retribution when such elements do come to power, prosecutors and judges opt to defy the spirit of EU-mandated, liberalizing requirements. Hence the perception of a lack of credibility in the long-term prospects of accession is undermining conformity with externally driven norms at the level of the prosecution and lower judiciary.

An example of EU conditionality acting indirectly came in Romania in 2000, when the EU cajoled the newly elected Social Democratic Party (PSD) majority party into abandoning the option of including two extreme nationalist parties in the planned coalition – easing the inclusion of the Hungarian minority party (Democratic Alliance of Hungarians in Romania – UDMR) instead – by signaling that the alternative route would undermine accession prospects. On several occasions, particularly in Romania and Turkey, civil society organizations have been able to coalesce around externally proposed models for change, or even bypass their national governments by urging Brussels to include criticism and concrete reform demands in annual monitoring reports.

Another important aspect relating to formal rule adoption, which deserves special mention, is the phenomenon of establishment of new institutions in the domestic sphere in response to external demands. Two species of the phenomenon emerge from our four case study countries. In the two countries targeted for transformation via pre-accession, EU requirements that candidates develop regulatory and administrative capacities in preparation for membership have led to the creation of new specialized agencies either within or alongside existing ministerial structures. In Romania, for instance, the National Agency for Civil Servants (ANFP) was established as part of the 1999 Civil Servants Statute, but quickly marginalized through understaffing and non-cooperation on the part of the established bureaucracy. Similarly, under intense EU pressure, a National Anti-corruption Prosecutor's Office (PNA) was created in September 2002, subsequently to become a battleground on which successive reformist and obstructionist governments sought, respectively, to expand or restrict investigative capacity and powers of prosecution. A further example of this species of rule adoption can be found in the 2003 establishment of a new Justice Academy in Turkey – a measure recommended by the Commission and designed to bolster in-service training for judges and public prosecutors, notably in EU law and the European Convention on Human Rights.

Examples of a more overt form of imposition of institutions (Owen 2002), where external actors appear to seek the establishment of new institutions in targeted countries as a means of bypassing, rather than supplementing national ones, is found in Serbia and, to a lesser degree, Ukraine. Indeed, in Serbia, where state ministries in the post-Milošević era continue to be plagued with poor administrative capacity and endemic corruption, the 2003 European Partnership document made the establishment of a Serbian European Integration Office (SEIO) a specific priority, as the EU did for all the countries involved in the enlargement. SEIO, which was established in March 2004 in cooperation with the Commission (in Brussels and the Belgrade Commission office) performs as a sort of implant within the Serbian state, driving the day-to-day management of the Stabilization and Association Process, progressive harmonization of Serbian legislation with the *acquis communautaire*, and coordination with Serbian ministries. A different model of institutional adoption, but one which, like SEIO in Serbia, blurs the distinction between domestic and foreign institutions can be found in the Ukrainian formulation of the November 2005 Judiciary Reform Concept. Here, in response to mounting external pressure that Ukraine 'continue the reform of the judiciary in order to ensure its independence and effectiveness', President Yuschenko entrusted the task of formulating the proposed reform to a National Commission comprising OSCE, Council of Europe and Commission officials, as well as Ukrainian government representatives. These examples demonstrate the difficulty of drawing sharp lines of distinction not merely between purely external modes of influence and domestic decision-making in the area of rule adoption, but equally between conditionality and control.

The establishment of new institutions in the domestic sphere at the behest of the EU represents a form of external influence amounting virtually to a form of direct imposition. We observe two distinct forms of such institutional transplants. On the one hand, the specialized anti-corruption agency created in Romania, for example, constitutes a permanent professional agent introduced into the domestic system as part and parcel of legislative reform, in an area judged by external actors to require a high degree of technical specialization and ongoing monitoring and implementation. In this sense the insertion of a new institution can be seen as an integral part of alignment with modern regulatory practices. In contrast, SEIO constitutes a very different kind of externally driven domestic institutional development; one motivated by the EU's need for a competent domestic partner, coupled no doubt by a deep sense of frustration with the functioning of the established government machinery. In this context, the specialized agency created is intended not for the purpose of implementing a substantive policy area (anti-corruption, trade or competition), but as a surrogate decision-making institution, able to pool administrative capacity into a single functioning institution from generally weak state ministries for the primary purpose of acting as a liaison institution vis-à-vis the external actor.

In both cases the externally mandated establishment of new institutions creates at least new opportunities for domestic change agents. In the former, with the establishment of a new specialized agency, at a minimum a new policy discourse is created. Where the government does not completely obstruct the action of the new institution – allocating staff, funding and allowing a degree of political clout – opportunities for implementation and internalization greatly increase, at least within the substantive area of policy for which the new institution is responsible. Indeed, coupled with strong, credible conditionality and continued external monitoring, the insertion of specialized professional agencies into the domestic system may prove to be the most potent promoter of progressive rule adoption, implementation and internalization. On the other hand, institutions such as SEIO, although they also provide a forum for the development of domestic knowledge and change agent constituencies, run the risk of further disempowering existing state institutions and increasing local dependency on external actor capacities. However, here, a sort of socialization mechanism has a greater and better effect than the contracts and twinnings we mentioned in Chapter 3, but was disregarded in the empirical analysis of the countries as irrelevant for the actual development of the rule of law.

But mind the gap…

Thus, were we to limit our inquiry into the ability of the EU to affect the adoption of legislation and the establishment of formal institutions, our conclusions would be partial and possibly misleading. Such an inquiry would rightly leave open the question (at least for non-lawyers) of how 'real' is the change? Are rules adopted implemented? Do the norms and standards to which national governments subscribe taken seriously, even internalized and believed in by ruling elites? As the summary of our findings on these questions in Table 8.2 plainly demonstrates, in all four case study countries, and across practically every dimension tested, there exist substantial gaps between the formal commitments adopted by targeted states, and the reality of implementation and internalization found to have taken place.[14]

Although in our codebook and then in the fieldwork we paid special attention to the assessment of the implementation of various laws on the issues we were considering in greater depth (see Table 8.1), we accept a bias in the possible amplification of the gap, due to the inherent methodological difficulties of coding implementation (in the end we have to trust the evaluation of the interviewees, complemented by the expertise of the researchers) and, even more so, of assessing internalization (when is civilian control of the military sufficiently internalized?). However, even if we account for such an amplification, the pattern that emerges is stark. It provides both empirical support to Hathaway's suspicion of a yawning gap between a country's formal international obligations, on the one hand, and degrees of normative attachment to and implementation of those commitments, on the other (Hathaway 2002), as well as added impetus for policy-oriented research into the means of narrowing the gap (Chayes and Chayes 1995).

On the whole, even if we consider only the last periods of our research (2005–06), complete or fairly complete rule adoption has been achieved only in relation to the death penalty and the modernization of the justice system, while minority rights, independence of judiciary and civil service reform are still problematic. When implementation is assessed (see Table 8.2), the death penalty is the only sector where implementation has been fairly easily carried out, with the exception of Ukraine. The worst sectors in this respect are independence of the judiciary, civil service reform and policies to improve administrative capacity and to combat corruption. The comparisons among rule adoption and rule implementation show that the worst sectors in the first layer are also usually the worst in the second, but at the same time there are policies, such as anticorruption ones, especially those at bureaucratic level, where the gap is even more marked. That is, it is impossible to declare openly that those policies are actually refused or that refusal appears clearly at the moment of implementation. Internalization is the last, most difficult step, and in some cases it was also very difficult, if not impossible, to assess it adequately in the different sectors; it was out of public view.

Accordingly, we also find considerable evidence of deliberate 'emptying of content' – the practice of national governments, or veto players within government and the bureaucracy, proceeding to dilute the effects or otherwise subverting the intended goals of legal reforms following rule adoption – particularly in Romania, Serbia and Ukraine – though, interestingly, relatively less so in Turkey.[15] A telling case in point is the passage of the National Agency for Integrity (ANI) law submitted to the Romanian Chamber of Deputies as part of the country's specific commitments to the EU in the immediate post-accession period in 2007. Rather than reject the rule outright, which the four parties that opposed the law had the votes to do, amendments were introduced into the law at the last moment, which effectively obliterated the planned independent status of the ANI and took the sting out of its ability to carry out asset declaration investigations of public officials, including parliamentarians. Similarly in Serbia and Ukraine, coalition governments seeking to weather a coalition crisis, alleviate international pressure or gain a short-term reward, rushed to endorse a high visibility law or institution, and then proceeded quietly to subvert or dilute its implementation. In some instances a measure of formal rule adoption designed to improve the functioning of the justice system was subsequently utilized to undermine key rule of law principles. Thus, the establishment of specialized economic courts in Ukraine in 1992 was hijacked by predatory elites in an effort to enable them to gain and hold on to privatized state assets.

Not surprisingly, perhaps, such 'subversive compliance', as well as the more benign instances of 'fake compliance', tend to occur in the nexus between strong international pressure and areas of high adaptation costs for ruling elites – in our cases, notably the independence of the judiciary and measures to fight political corruption. In such circumstances, the domestic elite wishing to avoid the high costs of outright rejection of externally mandated reforms, accepts rule adoption and then proceeds to avoid the high costs of implementation by diluting the rules adopted or otherwise hampering implementation. Theoretically, the pattern lends credence to rational-choice explanations of agency conduct, displaying the workings of a 'logic of consequence', rather than a logic of 'appropriateness' (March and Olsen 1998) in domestic decision-making, while in operational terms it highlights the need for careful monitoring and other follow-up enforcement and implementation assistance mechanisms, particularly where domestic costs of adaptation are high (Chayes and Chayes 1995).

Existing substantial gaps between formal rule adoption, on the one hand, and implementation and internalization of rules and norms, on the other hand, do not suggest that we find no evidence of the latter. What emerges from a comparative reading of the cases (see Chapters 4–7) suggests that in those countries where transition to democracy took place a decade ago or more, and with which the EU has engaged using pre-accession strategies for a similar length of time, we find evidence of not insubstantial implementation of reforms, and to a lesser (but still significant degree) signs of habituation, perhaps even identity type of internalization.[16] So, for instance, the Romanian police force stands out as an institution that has experienced a significant shift in culture, as reflected in recent polling data, in which 50 percent of respondents expressed the view that police reform was heading in a positive direction – a higher ranking than those accorded by the public to the judiciary, healthcare and educational systems. In Turkey, similarly, instances of torture in police detention and prisons have dropped dramatically since 2002 (aided at least in part by strict EU conditionality, funding for training of forensic investigators and a large-scale twinning program for police, medical professionals, judges and prosecutors); courts have begun to apply reforms in the areas of fundamental freedoms, albeit only partially, and have undergone significant modernization; and there is credible evidence to suggest a genuine weakening of the military's control of civilian government, at least in the period 2002–06.

When internalization is considered, in all four case study countries, but particularly in Turkey and Romania, these rather weak effects are at least partially mitigated by the evidence of 'discourse diffusion' – characterized by recurrent liberal concepts and themes (the value of freedom of expression, the equity of minority rights, policing as a protective service to the citizenry rather than an instrument of state repression, the prevention and avoidance of corruption and so forth). In Turkey, especially, an intense public debate has emerged over the last several years over some of the most sensitive issues supporting liberal-democratic consolidation in the country – notably the treatment of Moslem and non-Moslem minorities, gender equality and the role of the military in public life – with both official and civil society actors using the language of European integration and supranational European norms (notably the European Convention on Human Rights) to justify and promote reforms.

In contrast, we find fewer indications of genuine implementation or induction into liberal norms in Ukraine, and even less so in Serbia. One area where financial and technical aid appears to have contributed to civil and political freedoms in Ukraine is that of freedom of the media, where in 2004 only 514 claims against journalists were submitted to the courts, compared to 2,258 such claims submitted in 1999. On the whole, however, the gaps between the limited rule adoption achieved in Ukraine and Serbia, and effective implementation appear to be larger than for Turkey in particular, but also Romania.

What accounts for these patterns? Under what conditions do we find more extensive, deeper forms of compliance involving genuine implementation and internalization? While the conceptual and methodological challenges of providing reliable answers to these questions are considerable, particularly on account of the psychological element involved in evaluating internalization, several important considerations can be proposed in this context.

As Table 8.2 demonstrates, the relationship among rule adoption, implementation and internalization is a weak one. That is, in spite of a stronger conditionality in terms of determinacy and credibility there is an incomplete or largely incomplete rule adoption and consequently poor implementation, and even poorer internalization.[17] For Romania, this is the case with minority rights, independence of judiciary, civil service reform, and anticorruption policies; for Turkey, with minority rights, independence of judiciary, constitutional reform, and police reform; for Serbia, with civil service reform and civil control of the army present the weakest links; finally, for Ukraine, with constitutional reform, civil control of the army and police reform.

As can be seen in Table 8.3, the sectors were conditionality has the weakest effect are characterized by the presence of relatively weaker change agents who are challenged by powerful veto players and can only be undermined by the protracted action of the external actor, such as the EU. Thus, for Romania

Table 8.3 Conditionality, change agents and veto players: sectors and results (2006)

Sectors	Country	Conditionality*			Change Agents		Veto Players	
		St	We	Ab	Yes	No	Yes	No
Civil freedom and political rights: death penalty.	Romania			X	Civil society immediately after 1989			X
	Turkey	X			Large acceptance			X
	Serbia			X	Large acceptance			
	Ukraine	X			Opposition in legislature, civil society, NGOs and President of Ukraine after 2004 Orange Revolution		Legislature and executive, President Kuchma and members of judiciary	
Civil freedom and political rights: minority rights.	Romania	X			For Hungarian minority and Hungarian ethnic party		Communist successor party plus communist legacy (Background cultural attitudes)	
	Turkey	X			Domestic NGOs and civil society		Background cultural attitudes: Sevres Syndrome	
	Serbia	X			President Tadić and NGOs		No explicit veto players, but active ultranationalist party	
	Ukraine	X			Low salience	X		X
Civil freedom and political rights: freedom of press, speech and association.	Romania		X		Domestic NGOs Catalyst crisis: the Pantea case		(Background cultural attitudes, complemented by poor quality of legislation)	
	Turkey			X	Domestic NGOs and civil society Note: problematic legislation (Article 301)		Background cultural attitudes in sectors of Turkish judiciary: Sevres Syndrome (public prosecutors and judges)	
	Serbia	X			President Tadic and NGOs		(Cultural legacy of communist years)	X

Continued

Table 8.3 Conditionality, change agents and veto players: sectors and results (2006)—cont'd

Sectors	*Country*	*Conditionality**			*Change Agents*		*Veto Players*	
		St	*We*	*Ab*	*Yes*	*No*	*Yes*	*No*
	Ukraine	X			Opposition in legislature, civil society, NGOs and President of Ukraine after 2004 Orange Revolution		Legislature and executive, President Kuchma and members of judiciary	
Independence of judiciary	Romania	X			Minister of Justice, civil society, President of Romania and government		Conservative Superior Council of Magistracy, Constitutional Court and successor Communist Party SDP	
	Turkey		X			X	Ministry of Justice Ideological discrepancies between present AKP government and judicial establishment	
	Serbia		X		Few and weak change agents, esp. Judges Association		Strong veto players: incumbent parties in Serbian National Assembly	
	Ukraine	X			Opposition in legislature, civil society, NGOs and President of Ukraine after 2004 Orange Revolution		Strong veto players: members of legislature and executive, President Kuchma and members of judiciary	
Justice System: modernization and growth of effectiveness	Romania	X			(Favors traditional veto players)		Bureaucratic inertia	
	Turkey		X		(Improved economic conditions in aftermath of 2001 economic crisis)		(Poor institutional capacity)	X

	Serbia		X		Few and weak change agents: Judges Association.		Strong veto players: incumbent parties in Serbian National Assembly and conservative members of judiciary.
	Ukraine	X			Opposition in legislature, civil society, NGOs and President of Ukraine after 2004 Orange Revolution		Strong veto players: members of legislature and executive, President Kuchma and members of judiciary
Constitutional reform	Romania	X				X	Reduced administrative capacity of parliament (some inherent contradiction between different EU-set objectives)
	Turkey	X			Government and civil society		Ideological divisions on interpretation of constitution (primarily between government and presidency) (-) Participatory culture at citizen level
	Serbia		X		Few change agents: some opposition parties		No veto players but, strong influence of incumbent parties and Prime Minister Koštunica
	Ukraine	X				X	Parties in Verkhovna Rada
Civil service reform	Romania	X			NGOs		Parties in government Bureaucratic inertia
	Turkey			X		X	Deeply entrenched mechanisms of patronage Low administrative capacity

Continued

Table 8.3 Conditionality, change agents and veto players: sectors and results (2006)—cont'd

Sectors	*Country*	*Conditionality**			*Change Agents*		*Veto Players*	
		St	*We*	*Ab*	*Yes.*	*No*	*Yes*	*No*
	Serbia	X			Few change agents: PA functionaries with western training and local research centers			X
	Ukraine	X			Opposition parties during President Kuchma regime and NGOs		Executive and parties in Verkhovna Rada (Bureaucratic inertia)	
Anticorruption policies	Romania	X			Minister of Justice, NGOs, government and liberal MPs		MPs cross-cutting political parties (Bureaucratic inertia)	
	Turkey			X		X	Government (Low administrative capacity)	
	Serbia	X			Djindjić government, international and local NGOs		Weak veto players: Socialist Party, Radical Party and some incumbent parties (Bureaucratic inertia)	
	Ukraine	X			Opposition parties during President Kuchma regime and NGOs		Executive and parties in Verkhovna Rada (Bureaucratic inertia)	
Improving AC to combat corruption	Romania	X			Minister of Justice and NGOs		Constitutional court and Communist successor party	
	Turkey					X		X
	Serbia		X			X	Minister of Justice, incumbent parties and parties in National Assembly (Bureaucratic inertia)	

	Ukraine			X	Opposition parties during President Kuchma regime and NGOs		Strong veto players: executive and parties in Verkhovna Rada (Bureaucratic inertia)	
Civil control of army	Romania			X		X		X
	Turkey		X		NGOs, civil society, government and military with its general pro-EU orientation (Weakening of PKK terrorism, souring relations between USA and Turkish military.)		Certain segments of media (societal widespread attitudes)	
	Serbia	X			Few domestic change agents		Strong groups within armed forces (reduced administrative capacity)	
	Ukraine	X			Orange coalition political parties and NGOs		Executive, parties in Verkhovna Rada and groups within army (Reduced IAC)	
Police reform	Romania	X			NGOs		Strong groups within police	
	Turkey	X			NGOs, civil society and government		(Low administrative capacity and insufficient funds)	
	Serbia			X	Djindjić (until 2003)		Groups within police	
	Ukraine	X			Orange coalition political parties and NGOs		Executive, parties in Verkhovna Rada and groups within police (Reduced IAC)	

Note: *See Table 8.2.

we find in the sectors just mentioned: Hungarian ethnic party versus the Communist successor party strengthened by the rooted cultural attitudes of the old communist legacy; the Minister of Justice and the cabinet versus the Conservative Superior Council of Magistracy and the Constitutional Court; the unopposed incumbent parties complemented by bureaucratic inertia; again, the Minister of Justice and the cabinet versus a number of MPs from different parties. For Turkey, domestic NGOs differentiated by widespread cultural attitudes, additionally strengthened by the Sèvres Syndrome; an unopposed Ministry of Justice in a context where there is an ideological division between the incumbent AKP (see above) and the judicial establishment; the government supported by civil society versus the conflicts between cabinet and presidency; cabinet supported by civil society, but blocked by a weakly effective bureaucracy. For Serbia, the weakness of change agents and the strength of groups within the armed forces is enough to explain the weak links. Finally, for Ukraine the contrast between the Orange coalition, as change agent, and other parties in parliament and groups inside the army and the police accounts for those weak links.

An additional litmus test can be carried out. From Tables 8.2 and 8.3, combining the qualitative analyses for the four countries, we can detect that conditionality is more effective, that is, the links between the impulse coming from the EU and the outcome are stronger, when either there are no veto players or they are weak or very weak, or, alternatively, when the topic is relatively minor in the country in the presence of change agents. Thus, for example, the first hypothesis applies in the case of minority rights in Serbia and the second in Ukraine; on freedom of press, speech, and association, in Serbia no veto players are manifest; on modernization of the justice system, in Turkey the first hypothesis applies, while in Serbia it is the second that explains the stronger influence and results; on civil control of the army, in Romania the first hypothesis applies.

This analysis helps us to make a first set of concluding remarks. The first one concerns the importance of institutional and administrative capacity for effective implementation. Unlike rule adoption, which entails governmental consideration and an official act of decision whether to accept, amend or reject a formalized idea, rule implementation requires the exercise of governmental command, often involving the coordination, instruction, mobilization and monitoring of large bureaucratic organizations. Even where few barriers to formal rule adoption exist and a genuine normative commitment to change on the part of all critical stakeholders prevails, implementation may be blocked or, at least severely hampered, by either bureaucratic inertia or sheer lack of institutional and administrative capacity on the part of agencies charged with implementation. Among the factors that may explain the relatively smaller gap between formal rule adoption, on the one hand, and implementation, on the other in Turkey, is the stronger institutional and administrative capacity of the Turkish state. In contrast, poorer implementation in Romania and Serbia, especially, seems at least partially attributable to weaker implementation capability. Where reformists detect that the effective implementation of formal legal and institutional changes is blocked by factors other than governmental veto player subversion, therefore, careful analysis should be undertaken of possible means to reduce bureaucratic inertia and strengthen the capacity of implementing agencies. At the same time, we should expect in advance that rule of law reforms requiring substantial mobilization of human and other resources – such as civil service modernization and the implementation of new anticorruption measures – would encounter greater bureaucratic difficulties, require heavy investment in resources, monitoring and lesson drawing, and take longer to implement than clear legal prohibitions (such as the abolition of the death penalty and the removal from the law books of criminal provisions used to sanction journalists). However, we should emphasize that in its action the EU has been laying particular stress on the need for civil service reform to improve administrative capacity, as can be seen in Tables 8.3 and 3.12, although the results have been fairly modest.

Second, more so even than in formal rule adoption, the a priori presence of domestic agents committed and powerful enough relative to veto players to affect change is a robust indicator of the chances of successful implementation and internalization. Change agents may not be able to implement all the formal commitments undertaken by the targeted country (i.e. we would expect a gap to exist between formal adoption and implementation even where powerful change agents do exist), but without their presence the gap between formal adoption and implementation will be larger, the propensity for fake compliance will be higher, and internalization will be practically nonexistent. The composition of party constellations, in particular, is a key factor shaping the implementation of reforms, as state bureaucracies, let alone civil society organizations and mass elements, are practically unable to implement rule of law reforms without the active support of governmental actors.

The divergent experiences of the Hungarian and Roma minorities in Romania serve as an illuminating example. Despite considerable normative pressure from Hungary, the OSCE and the Council of Europe, in the early to mid-1990s, the endorsement of minority rights norms was consistently resisted by the Romanian Social Democrat Party (PDSR) government. It was only after new elections, the subsequent change to a mixed-party constellation government in 1996, and the entry of the Hungarian minority political party UDMR into the coalition itself, that substantial policy, as well as legislative progress, was made in the treatment of Hungarians by the state. In contrast, where vocal, persistent external pressure to improve the lot of the Roma minority was met by poorly organized domestic constituencies, lacking effective political representation, change was slower and very limited. Whereas UDMR was able to pursue linkage politics to win advances for its minority constituency, in the absence of a politically organized Roma change agent (in particular a political party able to wield coalition votes) progress on Roma rights was significantly hampered. At the same time, the Romanian case suggests that a degree of 'spillover' in the field of minority rights did take place over the past 15 years. The voluble discourse over the issue, UDMR's presence in government, as well as the maintaining of the issue on intergovernmental and NGO agendas by persistent external pressure, have resulted in greater societal awareness and commitment of state resources to the integration of minorities, and not merely to the Hungarian sector.

A third, related theme pertains to the ability of veto players to block implementation. The experience of our case study countries demonstrates the fact that veto players populate different sites of power, at different levels of government, in different countries, highlighting the need for reformists, both domestic and external, to identify pockets of veto player concentration in the planning and execution of attempted reforms. In Romania and Serbia, for example, the most powerful veto players have tended to be in the legislature and senior civil service (with, in addition, the security forces acting as powerful retardants to the implementation of rule of law reforms in Serbia). In contrast, the AKP's overwhelming dominance of the Turkish legislature since 2002 has meant that governmental veto players have been relatively weaker, with parts of the judiciary and public prosecution service surfacing as centres of opposition to liberalizing reforms. Indeed, the role of the Turkish judiciary is instructive in this context, since it represents an example of a split institution, with the top echelons displaying greater openness to democratic rule of law developments (even a degree of internalization attested to by an increased use of EU law discourse in the pronouncements of the upper courts), while the lower courts and prosecutors adopted anti-EU rhetoric and assumed a more nationalist stance.[18]

At the same time, as in the area of rule adoption, we find some evidence of 'internal diffusion' of norms with cross-issue spillover taking place within a given country. In Turkey, for example, the strengthening of general civil freedoms and human rights legislation, coupled with the proliferation of civil society organizations and intense public discourse on these subjects since 1999, has also facilitated the promotion of Kurdish minority rights, as the dissonance between the two realms of rights became more visibly jarring. This would suggest that the promotion of broad systemic reforms, rather than narrow sectoral ones, could well produce positive externalities and unexpected synergies across different issue areas.

The fourth aspect to stress is how the different sectors of rule of law are interrelated. The most obvious set of considerations are those that stress the salience of an independent judiciary for the effective implementation of civil and political rights, for the policies against corruption or even the civil control of the police, once the related rules have been adopted. But an important additional point can be made explicit, by giving a closer look at Table 8.3 and keeping in mind the different analyses on the four countries, it becomes clear that change agents and veto players are often the same in the different sectors of rule of law. More precisely, the same change agents and veto players are found in different sectors and at the same time there are specific groups who are most directly affected by the change in the different sectors. Thus, among the recurrent actors involved, we find in Romania, on the one hand, domestic NGOs, parties, and government and, on the other hand, the Communist successor party and other incumbent parties, and bureaucracy. In Turkey there are domestic NGOs, government versus opposition parties, sectors of the judiciary, and patronage mechanisms. In Serbia, there are domestic NGOs, some opposition parties versus incumbent parties; in Ukraine, NGOs, the Orange Revolution parties or, previously, opposition parties versus components of the judiciary, members of parliament, members of the cabinet, complemented by bureaucratic inertia. An additional consequence of this is the presence of mutual influence among sectors. That is, progress in one sector can imply progress in another.

Moreover, veto players are sometimes not explicit and what prevents democratic change by giving a common background to governmental and non-governmental actors in the various countries is the persistence of widespread cultural attitudes. The Turkish case is very telling on this: what in the end prevents this country from changing are those attitudes manifest in the Sèvres Syndrome, in gender bias and in the other attitudes mentioned in the chapter on this country (see Chapter 5). Of course, those attitudes can eventually change, as has happened in other countries and at various points in time, but the process takes time. This line of reasoning brings us to the last brick of our theoretical building.

Times of change

Finally, what can we say about the temporal dimension of change – cycles of change – and the issue of sequencing? These are questions which are increasingly occupying scholars of democratic development (Carothers 2007). A substantial correlation emerged in the timing between periods where EU membership conditionality is at its most credible and phases of rapid rule adoption, and to a lesser degree implementation, in targeted countries. In Romania the confluence of the two occurred most strongly in the interim between the announcement of the suspension clause and the decision whether or not to invoke the clause and suspend the country's accession for a year. Similarly in Turkey, the period of greatest rule adoption activity took place during times when domestic elites were persuaded that the EU meant business, that is, in the immediate aftermath of the Helsinki European Council in 1999, but even more so in the period between the December 2002 Copenhagen summit and the 2004 decision to open accession negotiations with Ankara.

In Romania in particular, moreover, we see instances where initial 'lip service' reforms formally adopted by governments unable or, more often, unwilling to implement them, were utilized as bases or inspiration for more detailed, involved reforms several years later, by successor governments that were more liberal in their party constellations. Thus, for instance, the 1999 law on civil service reform, which was adopted only under intense EU pressure in the run up to the Helsinki European Council summit that year, and which failed to address a range of problems – including transparent recruitment mechanisms, poor wages for civil servants and lack of transparent rules for promotion – became the subject of civil society criticism and renewed EU pressure four years later, leading to the law's partial revision under the PSD government in 2003, and then further revisions that finally brought Romanian legislation into alignment with EU standards in 2006. Similarly, the weak 1996 legislation concerning asset declarations passed, but never implemented under the fractured Romanian Democratic Convention (CDR) coalition, strengthened on paper under intense EU pressure in 2003 and again in 2004, was seized upon in 2005 by a reformist Minister of Justice in an attempt to strengthen substantially legal mechanisms on asset declarations.[19] Although Romania was a laggard in this respect too, compared with those central and eastern European countries that acceded in May 2004, these examples illustrate the generation of a 'virtuous cycle' dynamic observed in other candidate states, with external pressure and reformist governments able to achieve a cyclical momentum of rule adoption and implementation, followed by another round of more demanding reforms.

A similar, though perhaps weaker, dynamic is present in Turkey, yet virtually absent in Serbia and Ukraine, suggesting that the 'virtuous cycle', where it exists, has so far been limited to pre-accession cases. At the same time, we do find evidence for a somewhat different version of sequential change in both enlargement and non-enlargement countries, one where discursive and activist constituencies emerge following rule adoption, coalescing around new topics or institutions. Although these groups are rarely able to achieve short-term implementation of reforms, they are occasionally able to keep the specific issue (freedom of expression, corruption, judicial independence, police reform and so forth) on the agenda, and leverage the earlier acceptance of the principles in legislation to further reforms when a relevant policy window emerges. Interestingly, instances of rule adoption which are then frustrated by lack of implementation or the perceived duplicity of the government that formally committed to them, may act as a galvanizing factor for domestic reformists. As the number of formal commitments to reform the 'Soviet judiciary' mounted in Ukraine during the 1990s, for instance, the gap between the Kutchma government's reform rhetoric, and the reality of its inaction attracted growing opprobrium from Ukrainian opposition groups, contributing to the drive for judicial reform in the immediate aftermath of the Orange Revolution.

When the time factor is added, our 'building' is completed and we can finally summarize the main elements of our empirical analysis and stress how it also enriched our EUCLIDA model. In different ways and to a different extent there has been a process of anchoring in all four cases. When the mist of membership is cleared, in Romania as well as in the other countries where this perspective was more distant, if present, the key mechanism of conditionality remains relevant for the beginning of the process. Conditionality brings rule adoption, but rule implementation to a much lower degree, and only when some reform of the civil service has been successful.

To understand better such an external–internal nexus, our research brought to light the salience of the emergence of opportunities created by external actors and perceived by domestic elites, and in a few cases transmitted to citizens. Such an open, and in some cases collective, perception is easier when there is a determinate and credible conditionality. Analytically, we could make a distinction between the understanding on the part of a leader or group that there is an opportunity to exploit and the translation of the opportunity into a successful change. So the end result of the entire game is in the complex, multifaceted relationships between change agents and veto players, where the public plays an indirect role that can become a determining one at the time of elections. However, in the four countries and within the several issues we explored, there were evidently situations characterized by a variable geometry. That is, there are strongly value-motivated reformist elites who challenge powerful veto players, even paying the costs of losing, or more pragmatically interest-oriented elites who decide to engage in change actions only when they think they are playing safe and success is very probable. In all four cases there are both kinds of actors in different combinations. Thus, following the EUCLIDA model the shift of cost-benefit balance is mainly the result of the creation of opportunities, followed by different calculus done by diversified actors, but in this the creation of opportunities is the crucial point in bringing about that shift and the related origin of larger liberal parties or change agents as well as some kind of contingent stabilization. Of course, a stronger, steady stabilization is the result of other important processes that may develop later on within the process of democratic consolidation.[20]

In this vein a negative position that affirms the failure of conditionality is not supported by our empirical research. Conditionality may be weak and at the end may even fail, but when all critiques are considered and even partially recognized as legitimate,[21] the mechanism of opportunity creation is still there and at its core is conditionality, not with its legal aspects, but with its actual effects. Moreover, while in the long run socialization can be an effective mechanism for bringing about change in democratic rule of law, actually, such a mechanism is virtually impossible to detect empirically in the short run, that is, within the limits of research such as ours. Thus, in the end we have only two actual possibilities: an effective socialization-like mechanism, which is characterized by the imposition of an office with the specific goal of inducing adaptation and change, and the conditionality mechanism. But the first mechanism is stronger when there is an accession path, as in Romania and Serbia, but it is more difficult to set up, as in Ukraine and Turkey, and even if established, would run into problems of sovereignty (see above on this). Hence, empirically, conditionality remains the main mechanism of influence. Of course, it can be greatly strengthened by more sophisticated monitoring practices. Moreover, in the process of anchoring, it is important to understand the necessity of continuity of action by the EU, even complemented by the Council of Europe and by other donors, as we have seen in our cases.

In conclusion, in a nutshell we found in our empirical research that the external/internal nexus is characterized by *a chain of anchoring* where, if successful, there are the following steps:

- continuous conditionality actions
- creation of opportunities
- perception of opportunities by different elites, and citizens
- weakening of veto players
- shift in cost-benefit balance
- rule adoption
- more substantive transformations
- rule implementation and related monitoring
- eventually, rule internalization when also structural or deeply rooted cultural factors (such as the presence of alternatives in Ukraine, the nationalism of Serbia and key widespread cultural attitudes in Turkey) are changed or reassessed differently.

Are there lessons to be drawn?

On the basis of such a chain of anchoring and the related experience of the research a number of lessons can be drawn. In a concise way, they include the following:

1. Anchoring takes time, or more explicitly, creating some form of democratic rule of law is often an ambitious goal that takes time and a large amount of external stimuli and resources.
2. The entire strategy of democracy promotion has to have two core complementary goals: strengthening change actors and weakening veto players.
3. These goals can be better achieved if there is a coordination of external actors, particularly of the EU and the USA, otherwise the negative consequences that took place in Ukraine (see Chapter 7) are unavoidable.
4. If there are structural reasons that give strong support to veto players, such as serious ethnic cleavages and the presence of alternative political models, a more moderate and modest strategy of promoting rule of law to stop the worst practices of suppression and, if possible, a combined action for modernization and protection of basic rights seem more appropriate.
5. As conditionality mainly brings rule adoption, the next steps such as implementation and internalization imply continuous action by the external actors.
6. In that action, continuous monitoring and flexibility at the same time are key, relevant aspects; a strictly legal approach may sound 'right' and 'clever', but can actually misconstrue the situation, with negative consequences in terms of rule of law, that is, achieving the opposite result.

7. No 'one strategy fits all'. On the contrary, there are different strategies according to the different combinations of external conditionality and the different domestic elites and citizens.
8. A close knowledge of each case is a prerequisite to develop a precisely tailored set of external actions toward that case. For this purpose EUCLIDA, which proved to be a useful integrated framework in our research, can also help us to analyze the case we are interested in. To use a metaphor EUCLIDA helps to make better X-rays or, if we prefer, a better total body CAT scan.

And more precisely:

9. The five dimensions of the rule of law we exploring can be specified as we did (see Table 8.1), and our research suggests that they are the most effective and relevant ones. Consequently, paying attention to those dimensions and more specific issues is important.
10. Those dimensions are partially or closely related. Consequently, every strategy has to take into account all five dimensions that can weaken or strengthen each other.

In sum, we are well aware that the recommendations above can only be applicable to some countries, and not to others. That is, first of all, they are applicable to hybrid regimes with groups, organizations, leaders, and movements that can be or become change agents. In all other cases of stable authoritarianisms, it would be a waste of resources and time. And we are not sure that in those cases there is actually an effective strategy of any kind.

A final point about this research. One of the main reasons for conducting it has been the belief of the editors that a wrong way to promote democracy is to promote façade democracies, where what there is behind the façade – for example, with regard to the rule of law – is ignored and only the strictly formal aspects are considered. In this case, in fact, the impact is inevitably one that delegitimizes this sort of regime as an unacceptable western product that does not solve the actual problems of the people.

Notes

1 The codebook developed by the first author is available upon request.

2 Since 1997.

3 Freedom of association was explicitly mentioned for the first time in the 2006 Constitutional Charter, mainly as a result of pressure by Tadić (see also Chapter 6 in this volume).

4 That took place when this research was already concluded.

5 Finally, a three party coalition cabinet with Democratic Party. Democratic Party of Serbia and New Serbia and G17+ Plus was formed in May 2007 after three months of negotiations, characterized by political scandals and clashes among those parties that upset the population. The Radical Party was finally left out, although it had gained the plurality of votes. But Kostunica introduced some of the Radical Party claims in his programme, namely the preservation of Kosovo and Metohija

6 These findings are in line with Judith Kelley's conclusions (Kelley 2004a; 2004b).

7 As Daniel Drezner (2007) demonstrates, the risk of losing sight of 'under the radar' changes in democratic developments exists in other regions of the world as well.

8 Other 'high cost' areas were the Cypriot issue for Turkey, Kosovo's secession and the cooperation with the International Criminal Court for ex-Jugoslavia for Serbia, although strictly speaking Cyprus and Kosovo are not aspects of democratic rule of law.

9 In Chapter 5, it is recalled that the Sèvres Treaty partitioned the Ottoman Empire among the European powers.

10 According to Schimmelfennig, in liberal party constellations EU incentives would not only be effective, but the change achieved would also be 'quick and smooth' (Schimmelfennig 2005b, 838). Writing in 2004–05, Schimmelfennig placed Romania in the mixed-party category, and Serbia-Montenegro and Ukraine in the illiberal party category.

11 Here, of course, we only consider those veto players who are against democratic rule of law reforms.

12 Although we know that it was a low cost reform, as that penalty has not been carried out since 1984 and there is low public support for retaining the death penalty.

13 For a detailed discussion of this topic, examining the different degrees of compliance with laws at the national, European and international levels, see Zurn and Joerges (2005).

14 As already discussed in Chapter 2. See there also for the bibliographical references.

15 In this country, however, there was an example of this kind that is worth recalling. As requested by the EU, in 2004 the courts for State Security were repealed. However, other criminal courts were created which, according to the association of lawyers and the association for human rights, are working in the same way as the previous courts, but under a different name. For example, the president of the association for human rights in Diyarbakir made this comment, adding that the president of the previous court had been also appointed as president of the new court in that same town. Apparently, according to the association of lawyers in Istanbul, the appointment of the same judges was a recurring pattern. This however, might be due to a lack of experienced personnel, as well as the intention of the government to maintain the status quo. What is more important is the claim that the decisions taken by the new organization follow those of the old one.

16 On the difference between different types of internalization, see Checkel (2005).

17 See in Table 8.2 the cases where there is at the same time strong conditionality and incomplete rule adoption, that is, cases of inconsistency.

18 As Ali Çarkoğlu stressed in a private communication, in order to understand the actual autonomy of the judiciary, what is critical is that the judiciary looks at the party competition and veto players' signals and acts accordingly. When the EU reformers are perceived to be weak and likely to lose the next election, then the actors in the judiciary tend to play into the hands of the opposition hoping to exploit political and professional career objectives when they come to power.

19 A law was finally passed recently in an improved version, but it remains to be seen when the agency will be created and how effective it will actually be.

20 This topic will not be analyzed here. See, among others, Morlino (1998) and Diamond (1999).

21 The main criticisms by Kochenov (2007) are: 'low threshold for meeting the Copenhagen criterion of democracy and the rule of law, making the acknowledgement that a country meets the Criterion largely meaningless';

- 'complete lack of clarity about the standards that the candidate Countries were expected to comply with, making pre-accession democracy and rule of law assessment extremely difficult, if at all possible';
- 'poor analysis quality provided by the Commission, including random choice of issues, unreliable conclusions, numerous contradictions and a curious approach to democracy and the rule of law. No serious assessment provided';
- 'lack of clarity about benchmarks to determine compliance. Consequently, no distinction was often made between genuine reforms and legislative window-dressing';
- 'unjustified differentiated treatment of the candidate countries at all stages of pre-accession process';
- 'complete lack of connection between the Commission's pre-accession monitoring and the candidate countries' progress towards accession'.

Bibliographical references

Literature

Abbott, K.W., Keohane, R.O., Moravcsik, A., Slaughter, A.M. and Snidel, D. (2000) 'The Concept of Legalization', *International Organization* 54, 3: 401–19.

Adaman, F., Çarkoğlu, A. and Şenatalar, B. (2002) 'Household View on the Causes of Corruption in Turkey and Suggested Preventive Measures', translation of the earlier TESEV report, Istanbul: TESEV publications.

Adaman, F., Çarkoğlu, A. and Şenatalar, B. (2003) 'İş Dünyasi Gözünden Türkiye'de Yolsuzluğun Nedenleri ve Önlenmesine İlişkin Öneriler' (Causes and Policies against Corruption in Turkey from the Perspective of Business Community), Turkish, Istanbul: TESEV publications.

Adler, E. and Crawford, B. (2004) 'Normative Power: The European Practice of Region Building and the Case of the Euro-Mediterranean Partnership', Paper 040400, Institute of European Studies, University of California Berkeley.

Ahmad, F. (1993) *The Making of Modern Turkey*, London: Routledge.

Almond, G. (1950) *The American Prople and Foreign Policy*, Harcourt Brace.

Almond, G. (1989) 'The International–National Connection', *British Journal of Political Science* 19, 2: 237–59.

Andreescu, G. (2001) 'Romania in the Council of Europe: Individual Rights, Discrimination and Special Measures', *Papeles del Este* 1, 1. Online. Available HTTP:<http://www.ucm.es/BUCM/cee/papeles/01/010201.htm> (accessed 31 October 2006).

Apap, J., Carrera, S. and Kirişçi, K. (2004) 'Turkey in the EU Area of Freedom, Security and Justice', EU–Turkey Working Paper Series 3, Brussels: Centre for European Policy Studies.

Ardnt, C. and Oman, C. (2006) *Uses and Abuses of Governance Indicators*, OECD Development Center Studies.

Arikan, H. (2003) *Turkey and the EU – An Awkward Candidate for EU membership?*, Aldershot: Ashgate Publishing.

Aydin, S. and Keyman, E.F. (2004) 'European Integration and the Transformation of Turkish Democracy', EU–Turkey Working Paper Series 2, Brussels: Centre for European Policy Studies.

Bakic B. and Gajic N. (2006) 'Police reform in Serbia: Five years later'. Conflict Studies Research Centre – Balkans Series 06/21. Online. Available HTTP: <https://www.defac.ac.uk/colleges/csrc/documentlistings/balkan/06(21)BB.pdf> (accessed 13 July 2007).

Baracani, E. (2007) 'Pre-accession and Neighbourhood: The European Union's democratic conditionality in Turkey and Morocco', in A. Jünemann and M. Knodt (eds.) *European External Democracy Promotion. Externe Democratieförderung durch die Europäische Union,* Baden-Baden: Nomos Verlag, 335–48.

Batt, J. (2005) *'The Question of Serbia'*, Chaillot Paper 81, Institute for Security Studies, Paris.

Begović, B. and Hiber, D. (2006) *EU Democratic Rule of Law Promotion: The Case of Serbia*, Center on Democracy, Development, and the Rule of Law, Working Paper. Online. Available HTTP:http://iisb.stanford.edu/pubs/21245/EU_Rule_of_Law_promotion-Serbia.pdf> (accessed 10 July 2007).

Begović, B. and Mijatović, B. (2005) 'Serbia four year of transition', CLDS publication, Online. Available HTTP:<http://www.clds.org.yu/pdfe/4_years_of_transition_in_Serbia.pdf> (accessed 10 July 2007): 263–81.

Berins Collier, R. (1999), *Paths Towards Democracy: the Working Class and Elites in Western Europe and South America*, Cambridge: Cambridge University Press.

Bermeo, N. (1990), 'Rethinking Regime Change', *Comparative Politics* 22, 3: 359-77.

Björnberg, K. and Cranston, R. (2005) 'The Functioning of the Judicial System in the Republic of Turkey: Report of an Advisory Visit', Brussels: European Commission.

Björnberg, K. and Richmond, P. (2004) 'The Functioning of the Judicial System in the Republic of Turkey: Report of an Advisory Visit', Brussels: European Commission.

Blake, C. and Klemm, N. (2006) 'Reconsidering the Effectiveness of International Economic Sanctions: An Examination of Selection Bias', *International Politics* 43, 1: 133–49.

Boerzel, T.A. and Risse, T. (2004) 'Que Size Fits All! EU Policies for the promotion of Human Rights, Democracy and the Rule of Law' Workshop of CDDRL, Stanford University, 4–5 October.

Boix, C. and Stokes, S. (2003), 'Endogenous Democratization', *World Politics* 55, 4: 517–49.

Bratton, M. and Chang, E. (2006) 'State Building and Democratization in Sub-Saharan Africa', *Comparative Political Studies* 39, 9: 1059–83.

Brooker, P. (2000) Non-Democratic Regimes: Theory, Government and Politics, New York: St. Martin's Press.

Brownlee, J. (2007) *Authoritarianism in an Age of Democratization,* Cambridge: Cambridge University Press.

Bunce, V. (1998) 'Regional Differences in Democratization: The East Versus the South', *Post-Soviet Affairs* 14, 3: 187–211.

Bunce, V. (2003), 'Rethinking Democratization: Lessons from the Postcommunist Experience', *World Politics* 55, 2:167–92.

Bunescu, I. (2007) 'EU Eastern Enlargement 'Conditionality' of Minority Protection as a Political Opportunity for Romanian Roma', *In-Spire*, June. Online. Available HTTP: http://www.in-spire.org/articles/ib02062007_Romanian_Roma.pdf> (accessed 1 July 2007).

Burnell, P. (2005) 'Political Strategies of External Support for Democratization', *Foreign Policy Analysis* 1, 3: 361–84.

Burnell, P. and Calvert, P. (2005) 'Promoting Democracy Abroad', *Democratization* 12, 4: 433–38.

Buromenskiy, M. and Serdyk, A. (2004a) *Corruption in Ukraine. Analysis of the Nature and Causes of Problem*, Kiev: IAHR, 4–15.

Buromenskiy, M. and Serdyk, A. (2004b) *European Conventions on Human Rights. Main Provisions, Practice, Ukrainian context*. Kiev: VIPOL, 760 (in Ukrainian).

Busch, M. and Milner, H.V. (1994) 'The future of the international trading system: International firms, regionalism and domestic politics', in R. Stubbs and G. Underhill (eds.) *Political Economy and the Changing Global Order*, New York: St. mastin's press.

Cao, L. and Burton, V.S. Jr, (2006) 'Spanning the continents: assessing the Turkish public confidence in the police', *Policing: An International Journal of Police Strategies & Management*, 29, 3: 451–63.

Cardoso, F. and Faletto, E. (1979) *Dependency and Development in Latin America,* Berkeley: University of California Press.

Çarkoğlu, A. (2002) 'Turkey's November 2002 Elections: A New Beginning?', *Middle East Review of International Affairs* 6, 4: 30–41.

Çarkoğlu, A. and Kirişçi, K. (2004) 'The View from Turkey: Perceptions of Greeks and Greek–Turkish Rapprochement by the Turkish Public', *Special Issue on Greek-Turkish Relations of Turkish Studies* 5, 1: 117–54.

Carothers, T. (1996) *Assessing Democracy Assistance: the Case of Romania*, Washington, DC: Carnegie Endowment for International Peace.

Carothers, T. (1997) 'The Observers Observed: The Rise of Election Monitoring', *Journal of Democracy* 8, 3: 17–31.

Carothers, T. (1999) *Aiding Democracy Abroad: The Learning Curve*, Washington, DC: Carnegie Endowment for International Peace.

Carothers, T. (2002) 'The End of the Transition Paradigm', *Journal of Democracy* 13, 1: 5–21.

Carothers, T. (2004) *Critical Mission: Essays on Democracy Promotion*, Washington, DC: Carnegie Endowment for International Peace.

Carothers, T. (ed.) (2006) *Promoting the Rule-of-Law Abroad: In Search of Knowledge*, Washington, DC: Carnegie Endowment for International Peace.

Carothers, T. (2007) 'The "Sequencing" Fallacy', *Journal of Democracy* 18, 1: 12–27.

Carter, T. (2005) 'Playing by the Rule of Law', *ABA Journal Report*, ABA Journal, October. Online. Available HTTP:<http://www.abanet.org/journal/redesign/10fserb.html> (accessed November 2007).

Chayes, A. and Handler Chayes, A. (1995) *The New Sovereignty: Compliance with International Regulatory Agreements*, Cambridge: Harvard University Press.

Checkel, J. (2001) 'Why Comply? Social Learning and European identity Change', *International Organization* 55, 3: 553–88.

Checkel, J. (2002) 'Persuasion in International Institutions', ARENA Working Papers, No. 0077, Oslo.

Checkel, J. (2005) 'International Institutions and Socialization in Europe', *International Organization* 59, 4: 801–26.

Chesterman, S. (2001) *Just War or Just Peace? Humanitarian Intervention and International Law*, Oxford: Oxford University Press.

Chesterman, S. (2004a) *You, the People: The United Nations, Transitional Administration, and State-Building*, Oxford: Oxford University Press.

Chesterman, S. (2004b) 'Building democracy through benevolent autocracy: Consultation and accountability in UN transitional administrations, in E. Newmann and R. Rich (eds.) *The UN Role in Promoting Democracy: Between Ideals and Reality*, Tokyo: United Nations University Press, 86–112.

Christiansen, T., Petito, F. and Torna, B. (2000) 'Fuzzy Politics Around Fuzzy Borders: The European Union's Near Abroad', *Cooperation and Conflict* 35, 4: 389–410.

Chudovsky, V. (2002) 'The Limits of Realism: Ukrainian Policy towards the CIS', in D.P. Moroney, T. Kuzio, and M. Molchanov, (eds.) *Ukrainian Foreign and Security Policy*, Praeger: Westport, 11–36.

Cizre Sakallioglu, Ü. and Cinar, M. (2003) 'Turkey 2002: Kemalism, Islamism and Politics in the Light of the February 2008 Process', *South Atlantic Quarterly* 102, 2/3: 309–32.

Collier, D. and Adcock, R. (1999) 'Democracy and Dichotomies: A Pragmatic Approach to Choices about Concepts', *Annual Review of Political Science*, 2: 537–65.

Collier, D. and Levitsky, S. (1997) 'Democracy with Adjectives, Conceptual Innovation in Comparative Research', *World Politics*, 49, 3: 430–51.

Collier, P. (1997) 'The Failure of Conditionality', in C. Gwin and J. Nelson (eds.) *Perspectives on Aid and Development*, Overseas Development Council, 51–78.

Collier, P. and Dollar, D. (2004) 'Development Effectiveness: what have we learnt?', *The Economic Journal* 114, June: 244–71.

Cox, M., Ikenbetty, J.G. and Inoguchi, T. (2000) *American Democracy Promotion: Impuses, Strategies and Impacts*, Oxford: Oxford University Press.

Cox, M., Ikenberry, J.G. and Inoguchi, T. (eds.) (2000) *American Democracy Promotion: Impulses, Strategies and Impacts*, Oxford: Oxford University Press.

Craig, P. (1997) 'Formal and Substantive Conceptions of the Rule-of-Law: An Analytical Framework', *Public Law*, 467-487.

Crawford, G. (2003) 'Promoting Democracy form without–learning from within (Parts I and II), *Democratization* 10, 1–2: 77–98 and 1–20.

Dahl, R.A. (1950) Congress and Foreign Policy, NK: W.M. Norton.

Dahl, R. (1971) *Polyarchy: Participation and Opposition*, New Haven: Yale University Press.

Dallara, C. (2006) 'L'Unione Europea e la promozione della rule of law in Romania, Serbia e Ucraina' [EU rule of law promotion in Romania, Serbia and Ukraine], unpublished PhD Thesis, University of Florence.

Dallara, C. and Marceta, I. (2007) 'Country report: Serbia'. Paper presented at the conference *Improving the Quality of Democracy in Central and Eastern Europe Through EU*. European University Institute, Florence. 30 November–1 December.

Darden, K. (2001) 'Blackmail as Tool of State Domination', *East European Constitutional Review*, 10: 40–45.

Del Sarto, R.A. and Schumacher, T. (2005) 'From EMP to ENP: What's at Stake with the ENP towards the Southern Mediterranean', *European Foreign Affairs Review* 10, 1: 17–38.

Dervis, K. (2006) 'Governance and Development', *Journal of Democracy* 17, 4: 153–9.

Diamond, L.J. (1999), *Developing Democracy: Toward Consolidation*, Baltimore: The Johns Hopkins University Press.

Diamond, L.J. (2000) 'Is Pakistan the (Reverse) Wave of the Future?', *Journal of Democracy* 11, 3: 91–106.

Diamond, L.J. (2002) 'Elections Without Democracy: Thinking About Hybrid Regimes', *Journal of Democracy* 13, 2: 21–35.

Diamond, L.J. (2005) 'The State of Democratization in the Beginning of the 21st Century', *Whitehead Journal of Diplomacy and International Relations* 6, 1: 13–18.

Diamond, L.J. and Morlino, L. (eds.) (2005) *Assessing the Quality of Democracy*, Baltimore: The Johns Hopkins University Press.

Dicey, A.V. (1908; 7th edn 2000) *Introduction to the Study of the Law of the Constitution*, Adamant Media Corporation.

Diez, T., Agnantopoulos, A. and Kaliber, A. (2005) 'File: Turkey, Europeanisation and Civil Society: Introduction', *South European Society and Politics* 10, 1: 1–15.

Dimitrova, A. (2002) 'Enlargement, Institution-Building and the EU's Administrative Capacity Requirement', *West European Politics* 25, 4: 171–90.

Dimitrova, A. and Pridham, G. (2004) 'International Actors and Democracy Promotion in Central and Eastern Europe: The Integration Model and its Limits', *Democratization* 11, 5: 91–112.

Dolowitz, D. and Marsh, D. (2000) 'Learning From Abroad: The Role of Policy Transfer in Contemporary Policy-Making', *Governance* 13, 1: 5–23.

Dorronsoro, G. (2004) 'The EU and Turkey. Between geopolitics and social engineering', in R. Dannreuther (ed.) *European Union Foreign and Security Policies*, London: Routledge, 48–61.

Drezner, D. (2003) 'The Hidden Hand of Economic Coercion', *International Organization* 57, 3: 643–59.

— (2007) 'The New World Order', *Foreign Affairs* 86, 2: 34–46.

Drury, C.A., Krieckhaus, J. and Lusztig, M. (2006) 'Corruption, Democracy and Economic Growth', *International Political Science Review* 27, 2: 121–36.

Dworkin, R. (1985) *A Matter of Principle*, Cambridge: Harvard University Press.

Eder, M. (2003) 'Implementing the economic criteria of EU membership: How difficult is it for Turkey?' *Turkish Studies* 4, 1: 219–45.

— (2006) 'EUniquesness of Turkey: Will it make to the EU?', in Naglaa El Ehwany (ed.) *Regional Integration and Economic Reforms*, Cairo: Center for European Studies and Kondrad Adenauer Stiftung, 108–29.

Edmunds, T. (2005) 'Civil-military relations in Serbia-Montenegro: An Army in Search of a State', *European Security* 14, 1: 115–35.

Ekiert, G. and Hanson, S. (eds.) (2003) *Capitalism and Democracy in Central and Eastern Europe: Assessing the Legacy of Communist Rule,* Cambridge: Cambridge University Press.

Elster, J., Offe, C. and Preuss, U.K. (1998) *Institutional Design in Post-Communist Societies: Rebuilding the Ship at Sea*, Cambridge: Cambridge University Press.

Emerson, M. (2004) 'ENP: Strategy or Placebo?', CEPS Working Document Number 215.

Endicott, T.A.O (1999) 'The impossibility of the Rule-of-Law', *Oxford Journal of Legal Studies* 19, 1: 1–18.

Epstein, D.L., Bates, R., Goldstone, J., Kristensen, I. and O'Halloran, S. (2006), 'Democratic Transition', *American Journal of Political Science* 50, 3: 551–69.

Fallener, G. (2000) 'How Persuasive are Euro-Politics? Effects of EU membership on a New Member State', *Journal of Common Market Studies* 40, 3: 953–73.

Fatić, A. (2004) 'Anti-corruption and Anti-organized Crime Policy in Serbia: Regional Implications', *Southeast European and Black Sea Studies* 4, 2: 315–24.

Fearon, J. and Laitin, D. (2004) 'Neotrusteeship and the Problem of Weak States', *International Security* 28, 4: 5–43.

Fearon, J. and Wendt, A. (2005), 'Rationalism vs. Constructivism: A Sceptical View', in W. Carlsnaes, T. Risse, and B.A. Simmons, (eds.) *Handbook of International Relations*, London: Sage Publications, 52–72.

Fierro, E. (2003) *The EU's Approach to Human Rights Conditionality in Practice*, The Hague: Martinus Nijhoff Publishers.

Finer, S.E. (1970) *Comparative Government*, Harmondsworth: Penguin.

Finkel, S., Perez-Linan, A. and Seligson, M.A. (2007) 'Effects of U.S. Foreign Assistance on Democracy Building: Results of a Cross-National Quantitative Study', World Politics 59, 3: 404–439.

Finnemore, M. (1996a) *National Interests and International Society,* Ithaca, NY: Cornell University Press.

Finnemore, M. (1996b) 'Norms, Culture, and World Politics: Insights from Sociology's Institutionalism', *International Organization* 50, 2: 325–47.

Finnemore, M. Sikkiuk, K. (1998) 'International Norm Dynamics and Political Change', *Inernatioal Organization* 52, 4: 887–917.

Fish, S. (1999), 'Postcommunist Subversion: Social Science and Democratization in East Europe and Eurasia', *Slavic Review* 58, 4: 794–823.

Foglesong, T. and Solomon, P.Jr. (2001) *Crime, Criminal Justice, and Crimonology in Post-Soviet Ukraine,* National Institute of Justice, 113.

Forsythe, D. (1992) 'Democracy, War and Covert Action', *Journal of Peace Research* 29, 4: 385–95.

Fox, G.H. and Roth, B.R. (eds.) (2000) *Democratic Governance and International Law*, Cambridge: Cambridge University Press.

FRIDE-Fundación para las Relaciones Internacionales y el Diálogo Exterior (2007) 'Serbia's Elections and the Challenges Ahead', Democracy Backgrounders. Online. Available HTTP:<http://www.fride.org/eng/File/ViewLinkFile.aspx?FileId=1287>(accessed 24 May 2007).

Fukuyama, F. and McFaul, M. (2007) 'Should Democracy Be Promoted or Demoted?', The Stanley Foundation. Online. Available HTTP:<http://www.stanleyfoundation.org/publications/other/FukuyMcFaul07.pdf> (accessed 12 July 2007).

Gajin, S., Roknic, A., Nikolic Soloman, D., Jovanovska, S. (2005) 'Politics Sways Serbia's judges', IWPR Balkan Crisis Report 562. Online. Available HTTP: <http://www.iwpr.net/?apc_state=hbgibcr2005&l=en&s=f&o=242054> (accessed 13 July 2007).

Gallagher, T. (2005) *Theft of a nation: Romania since Communism*, London: C. Hurst.

Geddes, B. (1999) 'What Do We Know About Democratization after Twenty Years?', *Annual Review of Political Science*, 2: 115-144.

George, A. L: and Andrew Bennett (2005), *Case Studies and Theory Development in the Social Sciences,* Cambridge: MIT Press.

Gershman, C. (2005) 'Democracy as a Policy Goal and Universal Value', *Whitehead Journal of Diplomacy and International Relations* 6, 1: 19–38.

Goati, V. (2000) *Parties of Serbia and Montenegro in political struggles from 1999 to 2000*, Bar: Conteco.

Goati, V. (2001) 'The Federal Republic of Yugoslavia at the historical crossroads', in H. Riegler (ed.), *Transformation Process in the Yugoslavia Successor States: between Marginalization and Europe Integration*, Austraian Institute for International Affairs, Baden-Baden: Nomos Verlagsgesellschaft, 65–83.

Goldstein, J., Kahler, M., Keohane, R.O. and Slaughter, A.M. (2000) 'Introduction: Legalization and World Politics', *International Organization* 54, 3: 385–99.

Goldstein, M. (2000) 'IMF Structural Conditionality:How Much is too Much?' Institute for International Economics, Working Paper No. 01–04. Available at http://ssrn.com/abstract=300885.

Gourevitch, P. (1978) 'The Second Image Reversed; The International Sources of Domestic Politics', *International Organization* 32, 4:881–912.

Grabbe, H. (1999) 'A Partnership for Accession? The Implications of EU Conditionality for the Central and East European Applicants', EUI Working Paper RSCAS 99/12.

Grabbe, H. (2002) 'European Union Conditionality and the Acquis Communautaire', *International Political Science Review* 23, 3: 249–68.

Grabbe, H. (2003) 'Europeanisation Goes East: Power and Uncertainty in the EU Accession Process', in K. Featherstone and C. Radaelli (eds.) *The Politics of Europeanisation*, Oxford: Oxford University Press, 303–30.

Grabbe, H. (2006) *The EU Transformative Power: Europeanization through Conditionality in Central and Eastern Europe*, Basingstoke: Palgrave Macmillan.

Greif, A. (2005) 'Commitment, Coercion and Markets: The Nature and Dynamics of Institutions Supporting Exchange', in C. Menard & M. Shirley (eds.) *Handbook on New Institutional Economics,* Dordrecht: Springer, 727–88.

Greif, A. (2006) *Institutions and the Path to the Modern Economy: Lessons from Medieval Trade,* Cambridge: Cambridge University Press.

Grigorescu, A. (2003) 'International Organizations and Government Transparency: Linking the International and Domestic Realms', *International Studies Quarterly* 47, 4: 643–67.

Grote, R. (1999) 'Rule of Law, État de Droit and Rechtsstaat', in *Proceedings Fifth World Congress of the International Association of Constitutional Law*, Online. Available HTTP:<http://www.eur.nl/frg/iacl/papers/grote.html> (accessed 9 July 2007).

Grugel, J. (1999) 'Conclusion: Toward an Understanding of Transnational and Non-State Actors in Global Democratization, in J. Grugel (ed.) *Democracy Without Borders: Transnationalization and Conditionality in New Democracies,* London: Routledge, 157–63.

Grugel, J. (2004) 'New Regionalism and Modes of Governance – Comparing US and EU Strategies in Latin America', *European Journal of International Relations* 10, 4: 603–26.

Haas, E.B. (1964) *Beyond the Nation State*, Stanford: Stanford University Press.

Hadžić M. (2003), 'Reform of the Security Sector'. Occasional paper No. 7, Centre for Civil-Military Relations, Belgrade. Online. Available HTTP: http://www.ccmrbg.org/cms/view.php?id=1854> (accessed November 2007).

Hale, W. (1994) *Turkish Politics and the Military*, London: Routledge.

Halperin, M. and Lomasney, K. (1998) 'Guaranteeing Democracy: A Review of the Record', *Journal of Democracy* 9, 2: 134–47.

Hart, R. (2000) 'Democracy and the Successful Use of Economic Sanctions', *Political Research Quarterly*, 53, 2: 267–84.

Hathaway, O. (2002) 'Do Human Rights Treaties Make a Difference?', *Yale Law Journal* 111, 8: 1935–2042.

Hathaway, O. (2005) 'Between Power and Principle: An Integrated Theory of International Law', *University of Michigan Law Review*, 72: 469–536.

Haughton, T. (2007) 'When does the EU make a Difference? Conditionality and the Accession Process in Central and Eastern Europe', *Political studies Review*, 5, 2: 233–46.

Haveman, H. A. (1993) 'Follow the Leader: Minetic Isomorphism and Entry into New markets', *Administrative Science Quarterly* 38, 4: 593–627.

Havrylyshyn B. (2001) 'Ukraine between East and West, North and South: Geopolitical Options and Constraints', in L. Hoffman, and F. Mollers, (eds.) *Ukraine on the Road to Europe*, Heidelberg-New York: Physica-Verlag, 11–20.

Hayek, F.A. (1944) *The Road to Serfdom*, Chicago: University of Chicago Press.

Hellman, J.S. (1998) 'Winners Take All: The Politics of Partial Reform in Post-communist Transitions', *World Politics* 50, 2: 203–34.

Henderson, K. (ed) (1999) *Back to Europe: Central and Eastern Europe and the EU*, London: Routledge.

Hendrickson, D. (1994) 'The Democratist Crusade: Intervention, Economic Sanctions, and Engagement', *World Policy Journal* 11, 4: 18–30.

Heper, M. (2005) 'The European Union, the Turkish Military and Democracy' *South European Society and Politics* 10, 1: 33–44.

Hiber, D. (2005) 'The reform of the judiciary and the judicial legislation', in B. Begovic and B. Mijatovic, *Serbia four year of transition*, CLDS publication, Online. Available HTTP:<http://www.clds.org.yu/pdfe/4_years_of_transition_in_Serbia.pdf> (accessed 10 July 2007).

Hillion, C. (2000) 'Institutional Aspects of the Partnership Between the European Union and the Newly Independent States of the Former Soviet Union: Case Studies of Russia and Ukraine', *Common Market Law Review* 37, 5: 1173–1210.

Hilpold, P. (2002) 'EU Development Cooperation at a Crossroad: The Cotonou Agreement of 23 June 2000 and the Principle of Good Governance', *European Foreign Affairs Review* 7, 1: 5372.

Horng, D.C. (2003) 'The Human Rights Clause in the European Union's External Trade and Development Agreements', *European Law Journal* 9, 5: 677–701.

Horwitz, M. (1977) 'The Rule-of-Law: An Unqualified Human Good?', *Yale Law Journal* 86, 3: 561–6.

Hufbauer, G.C., Schott, J.J. and Elliott, K.A. (1990) *Economic Sanctions Reconsidered,* Institute for International Economics, Washington DC.

Hughes, J. and Sasse, G. (2003) 'Monitoring the Monitors: EU Enlargement Policy and Minority Protection in the CEECs', *Journal on Ethnopolitics and Minority Issues in Europe*, 1: 1–38.

Huntington, S. (1991) *The Third Wave: Democratization in the Late Twentieth Century*, Norman and London: University of Oklahoma Press.

Hutchinson, A. and Monahan, P. (1987), *The Rule-of-Law: Ideal and Ideology*, Toronto: Carswell Legal Pubns.

Hysa, Y. (2004) 'Kosovo: A Permanent International Protectorate?' in E. Newmann and R. Rich (eds.) *The UN Role in Promoting Democracy: Between Ideals and Reality,* Tokyo: United Nations University Press, 282–301.

Ikenberry, G.J. (2000a) 'America's Liberal grand strategy: democracy and national security in the post-war era', in M. Cox, G.J. Ikenberry and T. Inoguchi (eds.) *American Democracy Promotion: Impulses. Strategies and Impacts*, Oxford: Oxford University Press, 103–26.

Ikenberry, G.J. (2000b) *Liberal Order and Impetial Ambition*, Cambridge: Policy Press.

Ikenberry, G.J. and Kupchan, C. (1990) 'Socialization and Hegemonic Power', *International Organization* 44, 3: 283–315.

Ikenberry, G.J. and Slaughter, A.M. (2007) 'Forging a World of Liberty Under Law: U.S. National Security in the 21st Century'. The Princeton Project Papers. The Woodrow Wilson School of Public and International Affairs. Princeton University. Online. Available HTTP: <http://www.wws.princeton.edu/ppns/report/FinalReport.pdf> (accessed 12 July 2007).

Ionita, S. (2006) 'Povestea unui Manager de Proiect [The Story of a Project Manager]', Romanian Academic Society SAR Policy Brief, 23.

International Crisis Group (2006) 'Serbia's New Constitution Democracy Going backwards', Europe Briefing 44, 8 November 2006. Online. Available HTTP:<http://www.crisisgroup.org/home/index.cfm?id=4494&l=1> (accessed 10 July 2007).

International Crisis Group (2007) *'Serbia's new government: Turning form Europe'*, Europe Briefing 46, 31 May 2007. Online. Available HTTP:<http://www.crisisgroup.org/library/documents/europe/balkans/b46_serbias_new_government__turning_from_europe.pdf> (accessed November 2007).

Jackson Preece, J. (1998) 'National Minorities Rights Enforcement in Europe: A Difficult Balancing Act', *The International Journal of Peace Studies* 3, 2. Online. Available HTTP: <http://www.gmu.edu/academic/ijps/vol3_2/Preece.htm> (accessed 13 October 2006).

Jacoby, W. (2004) *The Enlargement of the European Union and NATO: Ordering From the Menu in Central Europe,* Cambridge: Cambridge University Press.

Jacoby, W. and Cernoch, P. (2002) 'The Pirotal EU Role in the Creation of Czech Regional Policy', in Linden, R.H. (eds.) *Norms and Nannies: The Impact of International Organizations on the Central and Eastern European States,* Boulder, CO: Rowman & Littlefield Publishers, 317–40.

Jensen, E.G. (2003) 'The Rule-of-law and Judicial Reform: The Political Economy of Diverse Institutional Patterns and Reformers' Responses', in E.G. Jensen and T.C. Heller (eds.), *Beyond Common Knowledge: Empirical Approaches to the Rule-of-Law,* Stanford, CA: Stanford University Press, 345–8.

Jensen, E.G. and Heller, T.C. (eds.) (2003) *Beyond Common Knowledge: Empirical Approaches to the Rule-of-Law*, Stanford, CA: Stanford University Press.

Johnson, S., McMillan, J. and Woodruff C. (2000) 'Entrepreneurs and the Ordering of Institutional Reform: Poland, Slovakia, Romania, Russia and Ukraine Compared', *Economics in Transition* 8, 1: 1–36.

Johnston, A.I. (2001) 'Treating International Institutions as Social Environments', *International Studies Quarterly* 45, 4: 487–515.

Jomo K.S. and Fine, B. (eds.) (2006) *The New Development Economics: After the Washington Consensus Neo Liberal Thinking,* London: Zed Books.

Jones, B.D. (1999) 'Bounded Rationality', *Annual Review of Political Science*, 2: 369–404.

Jovanovic, J. (2006) *'EU rule of law promotion in Serbia'*, unpublished working document. Belgrade.

Kahler, M. (1992) 'External Influence, Conditionality and the Politics of Adjustment', in S. Haggard and R. Kaufman (eds.) *The Politics of Economic Adjustment*, Princeton: Princeton University Press, 89–138.

Kaplan, A. (1964) *The conduct of inquiry: Methodology for behavioral science*, San Francisco, CA: Chandler.

Kardas, S. (2006) 'Turkey and the Iraqi Crisis: JDP between Identity and Interest' in M. Hakan Yavuz (ed.) *The Emergence of a New Turkey: Democracy and the AK Party*, Salt Lake City: The University of Utah Press.

Karl, T.L. (1995) 'The Hybrid Regimes of Central America', *Journal of Democracy* 6, 3: 72–87.

Katzenstein, P.J. (1985) *Small States and World Markets,* Ithaca, NY: Cornell University Press.

Katzenstein, P.J. and Iankova, E.A. (2003) 'European Enlargement and Institutional Hypocrisy', in T. Boerzel and R.A. Cichovski (eds.) *The State of the Union: Law, Politics and Society*, Oxford: Oxford University Press, 269–90.

Katzenstein, P.J., and Okawara, N. (2002) 'Japan, Asian-Pacific Security, and the Case for Analytical Eclecticism', *International Security* 26, 3: 153–85.

Kaufmann, D., Kraay, A. and Mastruzzi M. (2006) 'Governance Matters V: Governance Indicators for 1996–05', World Bank Policy Research Working Paper 4012.

Keck, M. and Sikkink, K. (1999) 'Transnational Advocacy Networks in International and Regional Politics', *International Social Science Journal* 51, 159: 89–101.

Kelley, J.G. (2004a) *Ethnic Politics in Europe: the power of norms and incentives*, Princeton: Princeton University Press.

Kelley, J.G. (2004b) 'International Actors on the Domestic Scene: Membership Conditionality and Socialization by International Institutions', *International Organization* 58, 3: 425–57.

Keohane, R. (1984) *After Hegemony: Cooperation and Discord in the World Political Economy*, Princeton University Press.

Keohane, R.O. and Martin, L.L. (1995) 'The Promise of Institutionalist Theory', *International Security* 20, 1: 39–51.

Keyman, E.F. and Öniş, Z. (2004) 'Helsinki, Copenhagen and Beyond: Challenges to the New Europe and the Turkish State', in M. Uğur and N. Canefe (eds.), *Turkey and European Integration: Accession Prospects and Issues*, London: Routledge, 163–93.

Kitschelt, H. (2000) 'Linkages Between Citizens and Politicians in Democratic Polities', *Comparative Political Studies* 33, 6/7: 845–79.

Kleinfeld, R. (2006) 'Competing Definitions of the Rule-of-Law', T. Carothers (ed.) *Promoting the Rule-of-Law Abroad: in Search of Knowledge*, Washington, DC: Carnegie Endowment for International Peace, 31–73.

Kochenov, D. (2007) *The Failure of Conditionality. Pre-accession Conditionality in the Fields of Democracy and the Rule of Law: A Legal Appraisal of EU Enlargement*, PhD Thesis, University of Groningen.

Kopstein, J. and Reilly, D.A. (2000) 'Geographic Diffusion and the Transformation of the Postcommunist World', *World Politics* 53, 1: 1–37.

Krasner, S.D. (1976) 'State Power and the Structure of International Trade', *World Politics* 28, 3: 317–47.

Kubicek, J.P. (ed.) (2003) *The European Union and Democratization*, London: Routledge.

Kurban, D. (2003) 'Confronting Equality: The Need for Constitutional Protection of Minorities in Turkey's Path to the European Union, *Columbia Human Rights Law Review*, 151, 35: 151–214.

Kuzio, T. (2003) 'EU and Ukraine: a turning point in 2004?', Institute for Security Studies, Occasional Paper 47.

Lankina, T.V. and Getachew, L. (2006) 'A Geographic Incremental Theory of Democratization: Territory, Aid, and Democracy in Postcommunist Regions', *World Politics* 58, 4: 536–82.

Lavenex, S. (2004) 'EU external governance in "wider Europe"', *Journal of European Public Policy* 11, 4: 657–60.

Levitsky, S. and Way, L.A. (2002) 'The Rise of Competitive Authoritarianism', *Journal of Democracy* 13, 2: 51–65.

Levitsky, S. and Way, L.A. (2005) 'International Linkage and Democratization', *Journal of Democracy* 16, 3: 20–34.

Lewis A. (2001) *The EU and Ukraine: Neighbours, Friends, Partners?*, London: Federal Trust, 320.

Linden, R.H. (2000) 'Putting on Their Sunday Best: Romania, Hungary and the Puzzle of Peace', *International Studies Quarterly* 44, 1: 121–45.

Linden, R.H. (ed.) (2002) *Norms and Nannies: The Impact of International Organizations on the Central and Eastern European States*, Boulder, CO: Rowman & Littlefield Publishers.

Linz, J.J. (2000) *Totaliarian and Authoritarian Regimes*, Boulder, CO: Lynne Rienner Publishers.

Linz, J. and Stepan, A. (1996) *Problems of Democratic Transition and Consolidation: Southern Europe, South America, and Post-Communist Europe,* Baltimore: The Johns Hopkins University Press.

McAuslan, P. (1997) 'Law, Governance and the Development of the Market', in J. Faundez (ed.) *Good Government and Law: Legal and Institutional Reform in Developing Countries*, London: Palgrave Macmillan, 33–56.

McCormick, J. (1999) 'Supranational Challenges to the Rule-of-Law', in D. Dyzenhaus (ed.) *Recrafting the Rule-of-Law: the limits of legal order,* Oxford: Hart Publishing, 267–82.

McFaul, M. (2002), 'The Fourth Wave of Democracy and Dictatorship: Noncooperative Transitions in the Postcommunist World', *World Politics* 54, 2: 212–44.

McFaul, M. (2004) 'Democracy Promotion as a World Value', *The Washington Quarterly* 28, 1: 147–63.

McFaul, M. (2005) 'Transition from postcommunism', *Journal of Democracy* 16, 3: 5–19.

McFaul, M. (2007) 'Ukraine Imports Democracy: External Influence on the Orange Revolution', *International Security* 32, 2: 45–83.

Magen, A. (2004) EU Democracy and Rule of Law Promotion: The Enlargement Strategy and its Progeny', *Center on Democracy, Development and the Rule of Law Working Paper Number 27*.

Magen, A. (2006) 'The Shadow of Enlargement: Can the European Neighbourhood Policy Achieve Compliance?', *Colombia Journal of European Law,* 12: 383–427.

Magen, A. (2007) 'Rules and Engagement', unpublished manuscript on file with author.

Marceta, I. (2004) 'Serbian political parties and their programs', unpublished Master Thesis, ISIG Gorizia, Italy.

March, J.G. and Olsen, J.P. (1998) 'The International Dynamics of International Political Orders', *International Organization* 52, 4: 943–69.

Mardin, Ş. (1973) 'Center–Periphery Relations: A Key to Turkish Politics', *Daedalus*, 103: 7–34.

Maresceau, M. (ed.) (1997) Enlarging the European Union: *Relationship between the EU and Central and Eastern Europe*, London and New York: Longman.

Marinov, N. (2004) 'Do Sanctions Help Democracy? The US and the EU's Record 1977–2004', CDDRL Working Paper Number 28.

Mattina, L. (ed.) (2004) *La sfida dell'allargamento*. L'Unione Europea e la democratizzazione dell'Europa centro-orientale, Bologna: Il Mulino.

Mayhew, A. (ed.) (1998) Recreating Europe: The EU's Policy Towards Central and Eastern Europe, Cambridge: Cambridge University Press.

Merkel, W. and Croissant, A. (2004) 'Conclusion: Good and Defective Democracies', *Democratization* 11, 5: 199–213.

Merlingen, M. and Ostrauskaitė, R. (2005) 'The OSCE: the Somewhat Different Socializing Agency', in T. Flockhart (ed.) *Socializing Democratic Norms. The Role of International Organisations for the Construction of Europe*, New York: Palgrave, 127–46.

Meyer, J.W., Boli, J., Thomas, G.M., and Ramirez, F.O. (1997a) 'World Society and the Nation-State', *The American Journal of Sociology* 103, 1: 144–81.

Meyer, J.W., Franck, D.J., Hironaka, A., Schofer, E. and Brandon Tuma, N. (1997b) 'The Structuring of a World Environmental Regime, 1870–1990', *International Organization* 51, 4: 623–51.

Misyo, M. and Petrova, N. (2000) 'Ukrainian Legislation and Mass Media Protection', *Svoboda vuslovlyuvan ta Privatnist,* 1: 3–47.

Molchanov, M., (2002) 'National Identity and Foreign Policy Orientation in Ukraine' in D.P. Moroney, T. Kuzio, and M. Molchanov, (eds.) *Ukrainian Foreign and Security Policy*, Praeger: Westport, 227–62.

Monk, R. (2001) 'A study on policing in the Federal Republic of Yugoslavia' on behalf of the OSCE. Available HTTP: http://www.osce.org/documents/spmu /2001/07/17633_en.pdf (last access: November 2007).

Moore, B. (1966) *Social Origins of Dictatorship and Democracy: Lord and Peasant in the Making of the Modern World*, Boston: Beacon Press.

Moraru, A. and Iorga, E. (2004) *Romanian Civil Service Barometer*, Institute for Public Policy (IPP), Bucharest.

Moravcsik, A. (1993) 'Introduction: Integrating International and Domestic Theories of International Bargaining', in P. Evans, H. Jacobson and R. Putnam (eds.) *Double-edged Diplomacy: International Bargaining and Domestic Politics*, Berkeley: University of California Press, 3–42.

Morlino, L. (1998) *Democracy Between Consolidation and Crisis. Parties, Groups and Citizens in Southern Europe*, Oxford, Oxford University Press.

Morlino, L. (2003) *Democrazie e democratizzazioni*, Bologna: il Mulino.

Morlino, L. (2004) 'What is a 'Good' Democracy?', *Democratization* 11, 5: 10–32.

Mosley, P., Hudson, J. and Verschoor, A. (2004) 'Aid, Poverty Reduction and the 'New Conditionality'', *The Economic Journal* 114, 496: 217-243.

Müftüler Bac, M. (2005) 'Turkey's Political Reforms and the Impact of the European Union', *South European Society & Politics* 10, 1: 17–31.

Munck, G.L. and Verkuilen, J. (2002) 'Conceptualizing and Measuring Democracy: Evaluating Alternative Indices', *Comparative Political Studies* 35, 1: 5–9.

Mungiu-Pippidi, A. (1997) 'Crime and corruption after communism. Breaking free at last: Tales of corruption from the post-communist Balkans', *East European Constitutional Review* 6, 4: 85–90.

Mungiu-Pippidi, A. (2006) 'Europeanization without Decommunization: A Case of Elite Conversion', CDDRL Working Paper 64. Online. Available HTTP: http://cddrl.stanford.edu/publicaions/europeanization_without_decommunization_a_case_of_elite_conversion/ (accessed 9 July 2007).

Murphy, S. (1999) 'Democratic Legitimacy and the Recognition of States and Governments', *International and Comparative Law Quarterly* 48, 3: 545–81.

Nenadić, D. (2006) 'La Serbia verso una nuova Costituzione', Osservatorio sui Balcani, October 30. Online. Available HTTP:<http://www.osservatoriobalcani.org/article/articleview/6343/1/49/> (accessed November 2007).

Neuman, E. and Rich, R. (2004) (eds.) *The UN Role in Promoting Democracy: Between Ideals and Reality*, United Nations University Press.

Neumann, F. (1986) The Rule-of-Law: political theory and the legal system in modern society, Dover: Berg Pub Ltd.

Nonet, P. and Selznick, P. (1978) *Law and Society in Transition: Toward Responsive Law*, New York: Octagon Books.

Noutcheva, G. (2006) 'EU Conditionality, State Sovereignty and the Compliance Patterns of Balkan States', paper prepared for the 3rd Pan-European Conference on EU Politics, European Consortium for Political Research, Bilgi University, Istanbul 21–23 September 2006.

Noutcheva, G. (2007) 'Fake, Partial and Imposed Compliance: The Limits of the EU's Normative Power in the Western Balkan'. CEPS Working Documents. Online. Available HTTP:<http://shop.ceps.eu/BookDetail.php?item_id=1527> (accessed November 2007).

Noutcheva, G. and Huysseune, M. (2004) 'Chapter 3. Serbia and Montenegro', *Journal on Ethnopolitics and Minority Issues in Europe,* Special Focus 1. Online. Available HTTP:<http://www.ecmi.de/jemie/download/1-2004Chapter3.pdf> (accessed 13 July 2007).

Ogorodnik, A. (ed.) (2004) *Judicial Reform in Ukraine,* Kiev: Chernivci.

O'Donnell, G. (1994) 'Delegative Democracy', *Journal of Democracy*, 5, 1: 55–69.

O'Donnell, G. (1998) 'Polyarchies and the (Un)Rule-of-Law in Latin America', in J. Mendez, G. O'Donnell, and P.S. Pinheiro (eds.), *The Rule-of-Law and the Underprivileged in Latin America*, Notre Dame: University of Notre Dame Press, 303–38.

O'Donnell, G. (2005) 'Why the Rule-of-Law Matters', in L.J. Diamond and L. Morlino (eds.), *Assessing the Quality of Democracy*, Baltimore: Johns Hopkins University Press, 3–17.

O'Donnell, G. Schmitter, P.C. and Whitehead, L. (1986) *Transitions from Authoritarian Rule*, Baltimore: Johns Hopkins University Press.

Öniş, Z. (2003) 'Domestic Politics versus Global Dynamics: Towards a Political Economy of the 2000 and 2001 Financial Crises in Turkey', *Turkish Studies* 4, 2: 1–30.

Ott, A. and Inglis K. (eds.) (2002) Handbook on European Enlargement: A Commentary on the Enlargement Process, Hague: T.M.C. Asser Press.

Ottaway, M. (2003) *Democracy Challenged: the Rise of Semi-Authoritarianism*, Washington, DC: Carnegie Endowment for International Peace.

Owen, J.M. (2002) 'The Foreign Imposition of Domestic Institutions', *International Organization* 56, 2: 375–409.

Özbudun, E. (1988) 'Development of Democratic Government in Turkey: Crises, Interruptions and Reequilibrations', in L. Damond, J. Linz and S.M. Lipset (eds.) *Democracy in Developing Countries*, Boulder Colorado: Lynne Rienner Publishers.

Özbudun, E. (1995) *Türk Anayasa Hukuku* (Turkish Constitutional Law), Ankara: Yetkin Basim Yayim ve Dağitim, (in Turkish).

Özbudun, E. (2000) *Contemporary Turkish Politics: Challenges to Democratic Consolidation*, Boulder Colorado: Lynne Rienner Publishers.

Özbudun, E. (2007) 'From Political Islam to Conservative Democracy: The case of the Justice and Development Party in Turkey', in A. Bosco and L. Morlino (eds.), *Party Change in Southern Europe*, London: Routledge, 206–21.

Parvulescu, S. (2004) '2004 Romanian Elections: Test Case for a True Romanian Democracy', *Romanian Journal of Political Science* IV, 2.

Patten, C. (2007) 'Serbia and the EU: Mladic First, Then Talks', *EU Observer*, 11 October. Online. Available HTTP:<http://www.crisisgroup.org/home/index.cfm?id=5119&l=1> (accessed November 2007).

Peceny, M. (1999) *Democracy at the Point of Bayonets,* University Park: Pennsylvania State University Press.

Peel, Q. (2007) 'Serbian Election Highlights the West's Fears about Russia', *Financial Times*, 19 January. Online. HTTP:<http://www.ft.com/cms/s/0/b2485a3e-a7ec-11db-b448-0000779e2340.html?nclick_check=1> (accessed November 2007).

Peerenboom, R. (2002) 'Let One Hundred Flowers Bloom, One Hundred Schools Contend: Debating the Rule-of-Law in China', *Michigan Journal of International Law* 23, 3: 471-544.

Pehe, J. (2004) Consolidating Free Government in the New EU, *Journal of Democracy* 15, 1: 36-47.

Pešić, V. (2006) 'State capture and Widespread Corruption in Serbia', CEPS Working Documents. Online:<http://shop.ceps.eu/BookDetail.php?item_id=1478> (accessed November 2007).

Pešić, V. (2007) 'State Capture and Widespread Corruption in Serbia' CEPS Working Documents. No. 262. March 2007 Online: http://shop.ceps.eu/Book Detail.php?item_id=1478> (accessed November 2007).

Petrov, R. (2002) 'The Balkans and the NIS' in A. Ott and K. Inglis (eds.), *Handbook on European Enlargement,* the Hague: T.M.C. Asser Press, 177-191.

Petrov, R. (2003) 'Recent Developments in the Adaptation of Ukrainian Legislation to EU Law', *European Foreign Affairs Review* 8, 1: 125-142.

Pevehouse, J.C. (2002), 'Democracy from the Outside-In? International Organizations and Democratization', *International Organization* 56, 3: 515-549.

Pevehouse, J.C. (2005) *Democracy from Above? Regional Organizations and Democratization,* Cambridge: Cambridge University Press.

Phinnemore, D. (2003) 'Stabilization and Association Agreements: Europe Agreements for the Western Balkans?', *European Foreign Affairs Review* 8, 1: 77–103.

Piccone, T. (2004) 'International Mechanisms for Protecting Democracy', Democracy Coalition Project Paper. Online. Available HTTP:<http://www.demcoalition.org/pdf/Protecting_Democracy_Piccone.pdf> (accessed 9 July 2007).

Potnam, R.D. (1988) 'Diplomacy and Domestic Politics: The Logic of Two-Level Games', *International Organization* 42, 3:427–60.

Pridham, G. (1991) 'International Influences and Democratic Transition: Problems of Theory and Practice in Linkage Politics', in G. Pridham (ed.), *Encouraging Democracy: The International Context of Regime Transition in Southern Europe,* New York: St. Martin's Press, 1–29.

Pridham, G. (1994) 'The International Dimension of Democratisation: Theory, Practice and Inter-regional Comparisons', in G. Pridham, E-Herring and G. Stanford (eds.) *Building Democracy? The International Dimension of Democratization in Eastern Europe,* New York: St. Martin's Press.

Pridham, G. (2005) *Designing Democracy: EU Enlargement and Regime Change in Post-Communist Europe,* New York: Palgrave Macmillan.

Pridham, G. (2006) 'Political Elites, Political Will and Political Capacity in the Further Enlargement of the European Union: Romania in Comparative Perspective – the Views from Brussels and Bucharest', paper for the Fourth International Workshop Strategic Elites and EU Enlargement: Reactions by, and the Prospects for, East European States Currently Left Out, Kiev, Ukraine: October 2006.

Pridham, G. (2007a) 'The Effects of the EU's Democratic Conditionality: the Case of Romania during Accession', *Journal of Communist Studies and Transition Politics* 21, 1: 33–47.

Pridham, G. (2007b) 'The Scope and Limitations of Political Conditionality: Romania's Accession to the European Union', *Comparative European Politics,* 5, 4: 347–76.

Przeworski, A., M. Alvarez, J.A. Cheibub, and F. Limongi (1996), 'What Makes Democracies Endure?', *Journal of Democracy* 7, 1: 39–55.

Przeworski, A., M. Alvarez, J.A. Cheibub, and F. Limongi (2000), *Democracy and Development: Political Institutions and Well-Being in the World, 1950–1990,* Cambridge: Cambridge University Press.

Radelet, S. (2003) 'Will the Millennium Challenge Account Be Different?', *The Washington Quarterly* 26, 2: 171–87.

Radin, M.J. (1989) 'Reconsidering the Rule-of-Law', *Boston University Law Review* 69, 4: 781–819.

Raik, K. (2004) 'EU Accession of Central and Eastern European Countries: Democracy and Integration as Conflicting Logics', *East European Politics and Societies* 18, 4: 567–94.

Ramirez, F., Drori, G., Meyer, J. and Schofer, E. (2003) *Science in the Modern World Polity: Institutionalization and Globalization,* Stanford: Stanford University Press.

Recchia, S. (2007) 'Beyond International Trusteeship: EU peacebuilding in Bosnia Herzegovina', Institute for Security Studies, Occasional Paper Number 66.

Reisman, M. (1995) 'Humanitarian Intervention and Fledgling Democracies', *Fordham International Law Journal* 18, 3: 794–805.

Rettman, A. (2006) 'Serb radicalism threat puzzles EU', *EU Observer*, 11 December. Online. Available HTTP:<http://listserv.buffalo.edu/cgibin/wa?A2=ind0612&L=justwatch-l&D=1&P=34021> (accessed November 2007).

Risse, T. (1999) 'International Norms and Domestic Change: Arguing and Communicative Behavior in the Human Rights Area', *Politics and Society* 27, 4: 529–59.

Risse, T. and Ropp, S.C. (1999) 'International Human Rights Norms and Domestic Change: Conclusions', in T. Risse, S.C. Ropp, and K. Sikkink, (eds.) *The Power of Human Rights: International Norms and Domestic Change,* Cambridge: Cambridge University Press, 234–78.

Risse, T. and Sikkink, K. (1999) 'The Socialization of International Human Rights Norms into domestic practices: Introduction', in T. Risse, S.C. Ropp, and K. Sikkink, (eds.) *The Power of human Rights: International Norms and Domestic Change*, Cambridge: Cambridge University Press, 1–38.

Risse, T., Ropp, S.C. and Sikkink, K. (eds.) (1999) *The Power of Human Rights: International Norms and Domestic Change,* Cambridge: Cambridge University Press.

Romanian Academic Society (2003a) 'Sluggish Progress on Governance Reform', Policy Warning Report, October.

Romanian Academic Society (2003b) 'Low State Capacity Hinders Romania's European Accession', Policy Warning Report, May.

Romanian Academic Society (2005) 'The Political Scene is Marred by Confusion', Policy Warning Report, September.

Romanian Academic Society (2006) 'Annual Report and Forecast. Romania in 2006', Policy Warning Report, March.

Rose, R. (1991) 'What is Lesson-Drawing?', *Journal of Public Policy* 11, 1: 3–28.

Rose, R. (1993) *Lesson-Drawing in Public Policy: A Guide to Learning across Time and Space,* Chatham, NJ: Chatham House Publishers.

Roth, B. (2000) 'The illegality of "pro-democratic" invasion pacts', in G. Fox and B. Roth (eds.) *Democratic Governance and International Law,* Cambridge: Cambridge University Press, 328–42.

Rowen, H. (1995), 'The Tide Underneath the "Third Wave"', *Journal of Democracy* 6, 1: 52–64.

Rupnik, J. (2000) 'Eastern Europe: The International Context', *Journal of Democracy* 11, 2: 115–29.

Russett, B. and Oneal, J. (2001) *Triangulating Peace: Democracy, Interdependence, and International Organization*, New York and London: W.W. Norton & Company.

Rustow, D. (1970) *Transition to Democracy: Toward a Dynamic Model*, *Comparative Politics* 2, 3: 337–63.

Sadurski, W., Czarnota, A. and Krygier M. (2006) (eds.) *Spreading Democracy and the Rule-of-Law? The Impact of EU Enlargement on the Rule-of-Law, Democracy and Constitutionalism in Post-Communist Legal Orders*, Dordrecht: Springer.

Santa Cruz, A. (2005) 'Constitutional Structures, Sovereignty, and the Emergence of Norms: The Case of International Elections Monitoring', *International Organization* 59, 3: 663–93.

Schedler, A. (ed.) (2006) *Electoral Authoritarianism: The Dynamics of Unfree Competition*, Boulder: Lynne Rienner Publishers.

Scheuerman, W. (1994) 'The Rule-of-Law and the Welfare State: Towards a New Synthesis', *Politics and Society* 22, 2: 195–213.

Schimmelfennig, F. (2005a) 'Strategic Calculation and International Socialization: Membership Incentives, Party Constellations, and Sustained Compliance in Central and Eastern Europe", *International Organization* 59, 4: 827–60.

Schimmelfennig, F. (2005b), 'The EU: Promoting Liberal-Democracy Through Membership Conditionality', in T. Flockhart (ed.) *Socializing Democratic Norms. The Role of International Organisations for the Construction of Europe*, New York: Palgrave, 106–25.

Schimmelfennig, F. and Scholtz, H. (2007), 'EU Democracy Promotion in the European Neighbourhood: Political Conditionality Economic Development and Transnational Exchange', Zurich: National Centre of Competence in Research, working paper no. 9.

Schimmelfennig, F. and Sedelmeier, U. (2004) 'Governance by conditionality: EU rule transfer to the candidate countries of Central and eastern Europe', *Journal of European Public Policy* 11, 4: 661–79.

Schimmelfennig, F. and Sedelmeier, U. (eds.) (2005a) *The Europeanization of Central and Eastern Europe*, Ithaca, NY: Cornell University Press.

Schimmelfennig, F. and Sedelmeier, U. (2005b) 'Introduction: Conceptualizing the Europeanization of Central and Eastern Europe', in F. Schimmelfennig and U. Sedelmeier (eds.) *The Europeanization of Central and Eastern Europe*, Ithaca, NY: Cornell University Press, 1–28.

Schimmelfennig, F. and Wagner, W. (2004) 'Preface: External governance in the European Union', *Journal of European Public Policy* 11, 4: 657-660.

Schimmelfennig, F., Engert, S. and Knobel, H. (2003) 'Costs, Commitment and Compliance: The impact of EU democratic conditionality on Latvia, Slovakia, and Turkey', *Journal of Common Market Studies* 41, 3: 495–6.

Schmid, D. (2004) 'The Use of Conditionality in Support of Political, Economic and Social Rights: Unveiling the EMP's True Hierarchy of Objectives?', *Mediterranean Politics* 9, 3: 396–421.

Schmitter, P. (1995) 'The International Context of Contemporary Democratization', in G. Pridham (ed.) *Transitions to Democracy: Comparative Perspectives from Southern Europe, Latin America and Eastern Europe*, Aldershot: Dartmouth Press, 499–532.

Schmitter, P.C. and Karl, T. (1993) 'What Democracy is ... and is not' in L. Diamond and M.F. Plattner (eds.), *The Global Resurgence of Democracy*, Baltimore: Johns Hopkins University Press, 39–52.

Schraeder, P. (1992) 'Paramilitary Intervention', in P. Schraeder (ed.) *Intervention into the 1990s: U.S. Foreign Policy in the Third World*, Boulder, CO Lynne Rienner Publishers, 131–52.

Schraeder, P. (2003) 'The State of the Art in International Democracy Promotion: Results of a Joint European-North American Research Network', *Democratization* 10, 2: 21–44.

Selznick, P. (1999) 'Legal Cultures and the Rule-of-Law', in M. Krygier and A. Czarnota (eds.) *The Rule-of-Law After Communism: Problems and Prospects in East-Central Europe*, Aldershot: Ashgate/Dartmouth, 21–38.

Sen, A. (1999) 'Democracy as a Universal Value', *Journal of Democracy* 10, 3: 3–17.

Shagabutdinova, E. and Berejikian, J. (2007) 'Deploying Sanctions while Protecting Human Rights: Are Humanitarian "Smart" Sanctions Effective?', *Journal of Human Rights* 6, 1: 59–74.

Shihata, I. (1991) 'The World Bank and "Governance" Issues in its Borrowing Members', in I. Shihata *The World Bank in a Changing World: Selected Essays*, Dordrecht: Martinus Nijhoff, 53–96.

Shihata, I. (2000) 'Issues of Governance in Borrowing Members – The Extent of their Relevance under the Bank's Articles of Agreement', in I. Shihata, *The World Bank Legal papers*, Herndon: Brill, 268.

Shklar, J. (1987) 'Political Theory and the Rule of Law', in A. Hutchinson and P. Monahan (eds.) *The Rule of Law: Ideal or Ideology*, Toronto: Carswell Legal Pubns, 1–6.

Simić, D. (2005) 'The Evolution of Civil-Military Relations in FRY/the State Union of Serbia and Montenegro' in P.H. Fluri, G.E. Gustenau, and P.I. Pantev (eds.), *The Evolution of Civil-Military Relation in South East Europe: Continuing Democratic Reform and Adapting to the Needs of Fighting Terrorism*, Heidelberg: Physica-Verlag, 197–211.

Simmons, B., Dobbin, F. and Garrett, G. (2006) 'Introduction: The International Diffusion of Liberalism', *International Organization* 60, 4: 781–810.

Skrede Gleditsch, K. and Ward, M. (2006) 'Diffusion and the International Context of Democratization', *International Organization* 60, 4: 911–33.

Slaughter, A.M. (2004) *A New World Order*, Princeton: Princeton University Press.

Slaughter, A.M., Tulumello, A.S. and Wood, S. (1998) 'International Law and International Relations Theory: A New Generation of Interdisciplinary Scholarship', *American Journal of International Law* 92, 3: 367–97.

Smith, A. (1995) 'The Success and Use of Economic Sanctions', *International Interaction*, 21, 3: 229–45.

Smith, K. (2001), Western Actors and the Promotion of Democracy, in J. Zielonka and A. Pravda (eds.) *Democratic Consolidation in Eastern Europe: International and Transnational Factors,* Oxford: Oxford University Press, 31–57.

Smith, K. (2003a) *European Union Foreign policy in a Changing World*, Cambridge: Polity Press.

Smith, K. (2003b) 'The Evolution and Application of EU Membership Conditionality', in M. Cremona (ed.) *The Enlargement of the European Union*, Oxford: Oxford University Press, 105–39.

Smith, T. (1994) *America's Mission: The United States and the Worldwide Struggle for Democracy in the Twentieth Century*, Princeton: Princeton University Press.

Soederberg, S. (2004) 'American empire and 'excluded states': the Millennium Challenge Account and the shift to pre-emptive development', *Third World Quarterly* 25, 2: 279–302.

Sozen, S. and Shaw, I. (2003) 'Turkey and the European Union: Modernizing a Traditional State', *Social Policy and Administration* 37, 2: 108–20.

Stromseth, J., Wippmann, D. and Brooks, R. (2006) *Can Might Make Rights? Building the Rule of Law after Military Interventions*, Cambridge: Cambridge University Press.

Svensson, J. (2000) 'When is Foreign Aid Policy Credible? Aid Dependence and Conditionality', *Journal of Development Economics* 61, 1: 61–84.

Sypnowich, C. (1999) 'Utopia and the Rule-of-Law', in D. Dyzenhause (ed.) *Recrafting the Rule-of-Law: the limits of legal order*, Oxford: Hart Publishing, 178-195.

Szymanski, M. and Smith, M. (2005) 'Coherence and Conditionality in European Foreign Policy: Negotiating the EU–Mexico Global Agreement', *Journal of Common Market Studies* 43, 1: 171–92.

Taiwo, O. (1999) 'The Rule of Law: The New Leviathan?', *Canadian Journal of Law and Jurisprudence* 12, 1: 151–68.

Tamanaha, B. (2004) *On the Rule of Law: History, Politics, Theory*, Cambridge: Cambridge University Press.

Tanör, B. (1996) *Osmanli-Türk Anayasal Gelişmeleri, 1789–1980* (Developments in Ottoman-Turkish Constitutions, 1789–1980), in Turkish, Istanbul: AFA Publication.

Tarner, A. (2005) *The Roma of Eastern Europe: Still searching for inclusion,* Migration Policy Institute. Online. Available HTTP:<http://www.migrationinformation.org/Feature/print.cfm?ID=308> (5 November 2006).

Thier, A. (2007) 'The Missing Link: State-Building and the Rule-of-Law in Afghanistan', seminar presentation at the Center on Democracy, Development and the Rule-of-Law (CDDRL), Stanford University, March 28th, 2007.

Tilly, C. (ed.) (1975) *The Formation of Nation States in Western Europe*, Princeton, Princeton University Press.

Tilly, C. (1990) *Coercion, Capital and European States AD 990–1992*, Malden MA: Blackwell Publishers.

Tomiuc, E. (2004) 'Romania: Brussels' Tough Stance Sends Clear Signal to Other EU Hopefuls', Radio Free Europe, RFERL. Online. Available HTTP:<http://www.rferl.org/featuresarticle/2004/02/8caa9cb7-9efb-4145-9a72-9aaf186a2511.html> (accessed 27 October 2006).

Tsebelis, G. (2002) *Veto Players: How Political Institutions Work,* Princeton: Princeton University Press.

Ugur, M. (2003) 'Testing times in the EU–Turkey relations: the road to Copenhagen and Beyond', Journal of Southern Europe and the Balkans 5, 11: 165–83.

Ungar, R. (1976) *Law in Modern Society*, New York: Free Press.

Uygun, O. (2004) 'Freedom of Expression under the ECHR and Turkish Law', Paper presented at the Human Rights General Assembly: European Convention of Human Rights and Turkey, Istanbul, 17–19 May 2004.

Vachudova, M.A. (2005) *Europe Undivided: Democracy, Leverage, and Integration after Communism*, Oxford: Oxford University Press.

Valenzuela, A. (1997) 'The Coup That Didn't Happen', *Journal of Democracy* 8, 1: 43–55.

Van Rijckeghem, C. and Üçer, M. (2005) *Chronicle of the Turkish Financial Crises of 2000-2001*, Boğaziçi University Press.

Vejvoda, I. (1998) 'Democratic despotism. Federal Republic of Yugoslavia and Croatia', in A. Ágh, *Emerging democracies in East Central Europe and the Balkans*, Great Britain: Edward Elgar Publishing, 219–36.

Vejvoda, I. (2000) 'Democratic despotism: Federal Republic of Yugoslavia and Croatia' in G. Pridham and T. Gallagher (ed.), *Experimenting with Democracy: Regime Change in the Balkans*, London: Routledge, 219–36.

Vejvoda, I. (2004) 'Serbia after four years of transition', in J. Batt (ed.) *The Western Balkans: Moving On*, Chaillot Paper 70, Institute for Security Studies, Paris, 37–55.

Viorescu, R. (2004) 'The Professionalising of the Civil Service according to Public Administration Reform (Romanian Case)', paper presented at the 12th NISPAcee Annual Conference, Vilnius, Lithuania, May 13-15, 2004.

Von Hippel, K. (2000) 'Democracy by Force: A Renewed Commitment to Nation-Building', *The Washington Quarterly* 23, 1: 95–112.

VV.AA. (2005) *A Quest for Political Integrity. Romanian Coalition for a Clean Parliament*, Iasi: Polirom.

Wallerstein, I. (1979) *The Capitalist World Economy*, Cambridge: Cambridge University Press.

Waltz, K. (1967) *Foreign Policy and Democratic Politics, the American and British Experience*, Little Brown and Co.

Whitehead, L. (ed.) (1996a) The International Dimensions of Democratization: Europe and the Americas, Oxford: Oxford University Press.

Whitehead, L. (ed.) (1996b) 'Democracy by Convergence: Southern Europe', in L. Whitehead (ed.) *The International Dimensions of Democratization: Europe and the Americas*, Oxford: Oxford University Press, 261–84.

Whitehead, L. (ed.) (2001a) 'The Enlargement of the European Union: A 'Risky' Form of Democracy Promotion', in L. Whitehead (ed.) *The International Dimensions of Democratization: Europe and the Americas*, Oxford: Oxford University Press, 415–42.

Whitehead, L. (ed.) (2001b) 'Three International Dimensions of Democratization', in L. Whitehead (ed.) *The International Dimensions of Democratization: Europe and the Americas*, Oxford: Oxford University Press, 3–25.

Whitehaed, L. (2001c) *The International Dimensions of Democratization: Europe and the Americas*, Oxford: Oxford University Press.

Whitehaed, L. (2004) 'Democratization With the Benefit of Hindsight: The Changing International Components', in E. Newmann and R. Rich (eds.) *The UN Role in Promoting Democracy: Between Ideals and Reality*, Tokyo: United Nations University Press, 135–66.

Wilson A. (1996) *Ukrainian Nationalism in the 1990s: a Minority Faith*, Cambridge: Cambridge University Press, 318.

Wilson A. (2002) *The Ukrainians. Unexpected Nation*, New Haven and London: Yale University Press, 330.

Wimmer, A. and Glick Schiller, N. (2002) 'Methodological Nationalism and Beyond: Nation-State Building, Migration and Social Sciences, *Global Networks* 2, 4: 301–34.

Wippman, D. (2000) 'Pro-democratic intervention by invitation', in G. Fox and B. Roth (eds.) *Democratic Governance and International Law,* Cambridge: Cambridge University Press, 293--327.

Wolczuk K. (2002) *The Moulding of Ukraine: The Constitutional Politics of State Formation*, Budapest: Central European University Press, 311.

Wolczuk K. (2004) 'Integration without Europeanisation: Ukraine and its Policy towards the European Union', EUI Working Paper RSCAS 04/15.

Woods, N. (2005) 'The Shifting Politics of Foreign Aid', *International Affairs* 81, 2: 393–409.

Yilmaz, H. (2002) 'External-Internal Linkages in Democratization: Developing an Open Model of Democratic Change', *Democratization* 9, 2: 67–84.

Youngs, R. (2001) *The European Union and the Promotion of Democracy,* Oxford: Oxford University Press.

Youngs, R. (2004) *International Democracy and the West. The Role of Governments, Civil Society, and Multinational Business*, Oxford: Oxford University Press.

Youngs, R. (2005) 'Engagement: Sharpening European Influence', in R. Youngs (ed.) *New Terms of Engagement*, London: The Foreign Policy Centre.

Zakaria, F. (1997) 'The Rise of Illiberal Democracy', *Foreign Affairs* 76, 6: 22–43.

Zhukovska, O.L. (2004) *The European Convention on Human Rights: Main Provision and Practical Application, the Ukrainian Context.* Kyiv: BIPOL.

Zurn, M. and Joerges, C. (2005) (eds.) *Law and Governance in Postnational Europe: Compliance Beyond the Nation State,* Cambridge: Cambridge University Press.

Documents

ABA-Ceeli (2005) 'Judicial Reform Index for Serbia – Volume II'. Online. Available HTTP:<http://www.abanet.org/ceeli/publications/jri/jri_serbia_2005_eng.pdf> (accessed November 2007).

Amnesty International (2002) 'Report'. Online. Available HTTP: http://web.amnesty.org/web/ar2002.nsf /eur/romania> (accessed 31 October 2006).

Amnesty International (2005) 'Turkey: Memorandum on Amnesty International's Recommendations to the Government to Address Human Rights Violations'.

Anti-Corruption Council of the Government of the Republic of Serbia (2004) 'Annual Report 2004'. Online. Available HTTP:<http://www.antikorupcijasavet.sr.gov.yu/Attach/annualreport04.pdf> (accessed 10 July 2007).

APADOR (1994–2005) 'Annual Report of APADOR-Helsinki Committee'. Online. Available HTTP:<http://www.apador.org/en/index.htm> (accessed 31 October 2006).

Balkan Media and Policy Monitor (1998) 'News and analysis digest special issue. Media in Serbia', Vol. 5. Online. Available HTTP:<http://www.nettime.org/ListsArchives/nettime-l9812/msg00002.html> (accessed November 2007).

BBC News, May 11, 2007 '*Serbian parties in coalition deal*'. Online. Available HTTP:<http://news.bbc.co.uk/2/hi/europe/6646239.stm> (accessed October 2007).

The Belgrade Times (2006) 'New Serbian Constitution stuck in time-warp', 19 October.

CCPR (1999), *Concluding Observations of the Human Rights Committee: Romania,* UN Human Rights Committee, 28/07/99, CCPR/C/79/Add.111.

Census (2002). Online. Available HTTP:<www.recensamant.ro> (accessed 31 October 2006).

Constitution of Ukraine, 28.06.1996, No. 254k/96-BP.

Council of Europe (1995), 'Conclusion of the Parliamentary Assembly' No. 190.

Council of Europe (1999a) 'Resolution of the Parliamentary Assembly' No. 1179.

Council of Europe (1999b) 'Resolution of the Parliamentary Assembly' No. 1194.

Council of Europe (2001a) 'Resolution of the Parliamentary Assembly' No. 1239.

Council of Europe (2001b) 'Resolution of the Parliamentary Assembly' No. 1244.

Council of Europe (2001c) 'Resolution of the Parliamentary Assembly' No. 1513.

Council of Europe (2001d), Recommendation of the Parliamentary Assembly' No. 1513.

Council of Europe (2002a) 'Compatibility with Yugoslav Law with the requirements of the European Convention on Human Rights', HRCAD 2002/5.

Council of Europe (2002b) 'Council of Europe and OSCE Final Joint Report on Police Accountability in Serbia' Online. Available Online at http://polis.osce.org/library/f/2928/1165/OSCE-SRB-RPT-2928-EN-CoE%20and%20OSCE%20Joint%20Final%20Report%20on%20Police%20Accountability%20in%20Serbia.pdf (last access: 22 November 2007).

Council of Europe (2002c) 'Criminal Law Convention on Corruption on 1/07/2002', CETS No. 173.

Council of Europe (2003a) 'Resolution of the Parliamentary Assembly: Implementation of its Duties and Obligations by Ukraine on Acceding Council of Europe', No. 1346.

Council of Europe (2003b) 'Civil Law Convention on Corruption on 1/11/2003', CETS No. 174.

Council of Europe (2004), 'European Judicial Systems 2002: Facts and Figures on the basis of a survey conducted in 40 Council of Europe Member States', Belgium: Council of Europe Publishing.

Council of Europe (2005) 'Resolution of the Parliamentary Assembly 1466'.

'Expert Comment – Opinions on the concept paper on National Judicial Reform Strategy', PCRED/DGI/EXP(2005) 33.

Council of Europe (2006a) 'Serbia and Montenegro: compliance with obligations and commitments and implementation of the post-accession co-operation programme', SG/Inf(2006)01.

Council of Europe (2006b) 'Serbia and Montenegro: compliance with obligations and commitments and implementation of the post-accession co-operation programme', SG/Inf(2006)15final.

Council of Europe (2006c) 'Group of State Against Corruption (GRECO) – Rapport d'evaluation sur la République de Serbie' Greco Eval I-II Rep (2005) 1F Révisé.

Council of Europe (2007a) (provisional edition) 'Resolution of the Parliamentary Assembly on the Functioning of democratic institutions in Ukraine', No. 1549.

Council of Europe (2007b) 'Serbia and Montenegro: Compliance with obligations and commitments and implementation of the post-accession co-operation programme', SG/Inf (2007) 05 final.

Council of the European Union (1995) 'Decision No 1/95 of the EC–Turkey Association Council of 22 December 1995 on implementing the final phase of the Customs Union', *Official Journal of the European Union*.

Council of the European Union (1996) 'Regulation (EC) No 1488/96 on financial and technical measures to accompany (MEDA) the reform of economic and social structures in the framework of the Euro-Mediterranean partnership', *Official Journal of the European Union*, L 189, 30.7.1996.

Council of the European Union (1999a) 'Decision on the principles, priorities, intermediate objectives and conditions contained in the Accession Partnership with Romania', *Official Journal of the European Union*.

Council of the European Union (1999b) 'The European Council Common Strategy of 11 December 1999 on Ukraine', Official Journal of the European Union, L331/1.

Council of the European Union (2000) 'Regulation (EC, EURATOM) No 99/2000 of 29 December 1999 concerning the provision of assistance to the partner States in Eastern Europe and Central Asia', *Official Journal of the European Union*, L 12/1, 18.01.2000.

Council of the European Union (2001) 'Decision of 8 March 2001 on the principles, priorities, intermediate objectives and conditions contained in the Accession Partnership with the Republic of Turkey', *Official Journal of the European Union*, L 85/13, 24.03.2001.

Council of the European Union (2002) 'Decision on the principles, priorities, intermediate objectives and conditions contained in the Accession Partnership with Romania', *Official Journal of the European Union*, L 44/82, 14.02.2002.

Council of the European Union (2003a) 'Decision on the principles, priorities, intermediate objectives and conditions contained in the Accession Partnership with Romania', *Official Journal of the European Union.*

Council of the European Union (2003b) 'Decision of 19 May 2003 on the principles, priorities, intermediate objectives and conditions contained in the Accession Partnership with Turkey', *Official Journal of the European Union,* L 145/40, 12.06.2003.

Council of the European Union (2004a) 'General Affairs and External Relations Council Meeting', 14 June 2004.

Council of the European Union (2004b) 'Decision of 14 June 2004 on the principles, priorities and conditions contained in the European Partnership with Serbia and Montenegro including Kosovo as defined by the United Nations Security Council Resolution 1244 of 10 June 1999', *Official Journal of the European Union*, L 227/21, 26.06.2004.

Council of the European Union (2006a) 'Decision of 23 January 2006 on the principles, priorities and conditions contained in the Accession Partnership with Turkey', *Official Journal of the European Union*, L 22, 26.1.2006.

Council of the European Union (2006b) 'Decision of 30 January 2006 on the principles, priorities and conditions contained in the European Partnership with Serbia and Montenegro including Kosovo as defined by the United Nations Security Council Resolution 1244 of 10 June 1999 and repealing Decision 2004/520/EC', *Official Journal of the European Union*, L 35/32, 7.02.2006.

Council of the European Union (2006c) 'General Affairs and External Relations Council Meeting', 11 December 2006.

Council of the European Union and European Parliament (2006) 'Regulation (EC) No 1638/2006 of the European Parliament and of the Council of 24 October 2006 laying down general provisions establishing a European Neighborhood and Partnership Instrument', *Official Journal of the European Union*, L 310/1, 9.11.2006.

CURS (2005) 'Survey conducted for the Anti-Discrimination National Council',Online. Available HTTP:<http://www.curs.ro/uploads/raport%20sondaj%20discriminare.pdf> (accessed 31 October 2006).

Decree of Verkhova Rada of Ukraine (1992), 'Concept of judiciary legal reform in Ukraine', 28.04.92. No. 2296-XII.

EAR (2005) 'CARDS Project Fiche 2.1.1 to Action Programme 2005 for Serbia/Justice and Home Affair'. Online. Available HTTP:<http://www.ear.eu.int/serbia/main/documents/2005JHA.pdf> (accessed 10 July 2007).

Economist (2006) 'Serbia's new nationalism', *Economist*, 20 July 2006.

Economist (2007) 'Radical in name only', January 25. Online. Available HTTP:<http://www.economist.com/world/europe/PrinterFriendly.cfm?story_id=8593029> (accessed October 2007).

Edict of the President of Ukraine (1998) 'On Measures for Implementing the Concept of the Administrative Reform in Ukraine', 22 July 1998, No. 810/98.

Edict of the President of Ukraine (2006) 'On Plan of Measures on the Implementation of Duties and Engagements of Ukraine Resulting from its Membership in the Council of Europe', 20 January 2006, No. 39/2006.

Edict of the President of Ukraine (2007a) 'About pre-term termination of the Verkhovna Rada activities, 2 April 2007, No. 264.

Edict of the President of Ukraine (2007b) 'About pre-term termination of the Verkhovna Rada activities', 26 April 2007, No. 335.

Eurobarometrul (2006) 'Raport National Romania' [StandardEurobarometer 66/Autumn 2006 – TNS Opinion & Social]. Online. Available HTTP:<http://ec.europa.eu/public_opinion/archives/eb/eb66/eb66_ro_nat.pdf> (accessed 1 February 2007).

European Agency for Reconstruction (2006) 'Annual Report 2005', 12 June 2006.

European Commission (1997) 'Opinion on Romania's Application for Membership of the European Union'.

European Commission (1998 to 2005). 'Regular Reports on Romania'. Online. Available HTTP:<http://ec.europa. eu/enlargement/archives/pdf/key_documents/1998/romania_en.pdf> (accessed 24 April 2006).

European Commission (1999) 'Regular Report from the Commission on Turkey's Progress towards Accession'.

European Commission (2000) 'Regular Report from the Commission on Turkey's Progress towards Accession'.

European Commission (2001) 'Regular Report from the Commission on Turkey's Progress towards Accession'.

European Commission (2002a) 'Regular Report from the Commission on Turkey's Progress towards Accession'.

European Commission (2002b) 'Federal Republic of Yugoslavia Stabilisation and Association Report', 4 April 2002, SEC (2002) 343.

European Commission (2003a) 'Communication from the Commission to the Council and the European Parliament – Wider Europe – Neighborhood: A New Framework for Relations with our Eastern and Southern Neighbors, 11 March 2003', COM(2003) 104 final.

European Commission (2003b) 'Serbia and Montenegro Stabilization and Association Report', 23 March 2003 SEC(2003) 343.

European Commission (2003c) 'Project Fiche Turkey 0301.01: Strengthening Accountability of Police'. Online. Available HTTP:<http://ec.europa.eu/enlargement/fiche_projet/document/TR%200301.01%20Strengthening%20accountability%20of%20police.pdf> (accessed 17 May 2007).

European Commission (2003d) 'Regular Report from the Commission on Turkey's Progress towards Accession'.

European Commission (2003e) 'EU-Funded Programmes in Turkey: 2003–2004', Ankara: European Union Delegation of the European Commission.

European Commission (2004a) 'Serbia and Montenegro Stabilization and Association Report', 30 March 2004, SEC(2004) 376.

European Commission (2004b), 'Regular Report on Turkey's Progress towards Accession', Brussels, SEC (2004) 1201, COM (2004) 656 final.

European Commission (2004c) 'Communication from the Commission to the Council of the Commission proposals for Action Plans under the European Neighborhood Policy', 9 December 2004, COM(2004) 795 final.

European Commission (2005a) 'Communication on the preparedness of Serbia and Montenegro to negotiate a Stabilisation and Association Agreement with the EU', 12 April 2005, COM(2005) 476 final.

European Commission (2005b) 'Serbia and Montenegro Progress Report', 9 November 2005, SEC(2005) 1428.

European Commission (2005c) 'Turkey: 2005 Progress Report', Brussels, SEC (2005)1426, COM (2005) 561 final.

European Commission (2006a) 'Turkey Progress Report', 8 November 2006, SEC(2006) 1390.

European Commission (2006b) 'Commission presents its recommendation on the continuation of Turkey's accession negotiations', 29 November 2006, IP/06/1652.

European Commission (2006c) 'Serbia 2006 Progress Report', COM, 649 final.

European Commission (2007), 'Turkey 2007 Progress Report', COM (2007) 663 Final.

European Commission and OECD (2006) 'EU Donor Atlas 2006 Volume I. Mapping Official Development Assistance'. Online. Available HTTP:<http://ec.europa.eu/development/body/publications/docs/eu_donor_atlas_2006.pdf> (accessed 14 July 2007).

European Council (1993) 'Conclusions of the Presidency', Copenhagen, 21–22 June 1993.

European Council (1999) 'Common Strategy of 11 December 1999 on Ukraine', *Official Journal of the European Union*, L331/1.

European Council (2004) 'Presidency Conclusions', Brussels European Council 16/17 December 2004, 16238/4.

European Parliament (2006) 'Report on Turkey's Progress towards Accession', 13 September 2006, 2006/2118(INI), A6-0269/2006, 13 September 2006.

EU–Ukraine (2003) 'EU Action Plan on Justice and Home Affairs in Ukraine', *Official Journal of the European Union*, C 077.

EU–Ukraine Cooperation Council (2005) 'Recommendation No. 1/2005 of 21/02/2005 on the implementation of the EU/Ukraine Action Plan'.

FIDH – International Federation for Human Rights (2004) 'Serbia-Montenegro (excluding Kosovo): The failure of transition. Annual Report 2004'. Online. Available HTTP: <http://www.fidh.org/IMG/pdf/yu0704a.pdf> (accessed 13 July 2007).

Forum for Ethnic Relations (2006) 'Gender and minority overview in Serbia 2005', Online. Available HTTP:<http://www.fer.org.yu/eng/htmls/reportsanalysis.html> (accessed 10 July 2007).

Freedom House (2004) *Nations in Transit. Democratization in East Central Europe and Eurasia.*

Freedom House (2005a) *The Anticorruption Policy of the Romanian Government. Assessment Report* (commissioned by the Romanian Ministry of Justice), March 2005. Online. Available HTTP:<http://www.just. ro/files/lupta_anti_coruptie/FH_audit_EN_16_031.pdf> (last accessed 24 April 2006).

Freedom House (2005b) 'Freedom in the world. Country Report Serbia and Montenegro'. Online. Available HTTP:http://www.freedomhouse.org/template.cfm?page=22&country=6898&year=2005> (last accessed 13 July 2007).

Freedom House (2005c) 'Nation in Transit. Country Report Serbia-Montenegro'. Online. Available HTTP:<http://www.freedomhouse.org/template.cfm?page=47&nit=380&year=2005> (accessed 13 July 2007).

Freedom House (2006) 'Freedom in the world. Country Report Serbia and Montenegro'. Online. Available HTTP:<http://www.freedomhouse.org/template.cfm?page=22&year=2006> (accessed 13 July 2007).

Freedom House (2007) 'Nation in Transit. Country Report: Serbia'. Online. Available HTTP: <http:// www.freedomhouse.hu//images/fdh_galleries/NIT2007final/nit-serbia-web.pdf> (accessed November 2007).

Gallup Romania and Institute for Public Policies (2004) *Barometrul Functiei Publice in Romania,* October. Online. Available HTTP:<www.ipp.ro> (accessed September 2005).

Helsinki Committee for Human Rights in Serbia (2004) 'Annual Report 2004. National Minorities in Serbia: In Conflict With a State Ethnic Identity'. Online. Available HTPP: <http://www.osce.org/documents/eea/2005/05/14663_en.pdf> (accessed 13 July 2007).

Helsinki Committee for Human Rights in Serbia (2007) 'Human Rights: hostage to the state's regression – Annual Report: Serbia 2006'. Online. Available HTPP:<http://www.helsinki.org.yu/doc/reports/eng/Report2006.pdf> (accessed November 2007).

HRCAD (2001) 'Compatibility of Ukrainian Law and Practice with the Requirements of the European Conventions on Human Rights', 4, Strasbourg.

Human Rights Watch (1990) HRW World Report. Online. Available HTTP:<http://www.hrw.org/reports/1990/WR90/HELSINKI.BOU-02.htm> (accessed 25 October 2006).

Human Rights Watch (2000) HRW World Report. Online. Available HTTP:<http://www.hrw.org/wr2k1/europe/romania.html> (accessed 20 October 2006).

Human Rights Watch (2006a), 'Turkey: Human Rights Overview'. Online. Available HTTP:<http://hrw.org/english/docs/2006/01/18/turkey12220.htm> (last accessed 17 May 2007).

Human Rights Watch (2006b) 'Dangerous Indifference: Violence against Minorities in Serbia'. Online. Available HTPP: <http://hrw.org/english/docs/2006/01/18/serbia12242.htm> (last access: November 2007).

Human Rights Watch (2006c) 'Turkey: First Steps toward Independent Monitoring of Police Stations and Gendarmeries', Briefing Paper, 6 March.

Hürriyet (2004) 'Eğitim Bütçesi Savunmayi Ilk Kez Aşti' (The Budget for Education has for the First Time Exceeded the Defence Budget), 1 July 2004.

IMF (2001) 'Turkey Letter of Intent and Memorandum (to IMF) on Economic Policies', 3 May, http://imf.org/external/np/loi/2001/tur/02/index.htm#mep, last access: 14 December 2007.

IMF (2007) 'Turkey: Sixth Review and Inflation Consultation Under the Stand-By Arrangement and Request for Waiver of Non-observance and Applicability of Performance Criteria - Staff Report'; Country Report No. 07/363, 16 November.

Institute for Public Policy (2003) *Dynamics of Mayors' Political Affiliation: the Case of Romania – One Year Before the Local Elections in 2004*, Bucharest.

International Commission on the Balkans (2005) 'The Balkans in Europe's Future'. Online. Available HTTP:<http://www.balkan-commission.org> (accessed 13 July 2007).

International Helsinki Federation for Human Rights (2002) 'YU_Serbia Annual Report 2002'. Online. Available HTPP:<http://www.ihf-hr.org> (accessed 13 July 2007).

Judges Association of Serbia (2005) 'The Constitutional position of the judiciary'. Online. Available HTTP:<http://www.sudije.org.yu/Members/milos/publikacije/posebna_izdanja/constitutional_position_judiciary/attachment> (accessed 13 July 2007).

Law of Ukraine (1993) 'On Public Service', 16.12.1993, No. 3723-XII.

Law of Ukraine (1995a) 'On Fight Against Corruption', 05.10.1995, No. 356/95-BP.

Law of Ukraine (1995b) 'On Amendments and Additions to Some Legislative Acts of Ukraine in View of Adoption of Law of Ukraine "On Fight Against Corruption"', 05.10.1995, No. 358/95-BP.

Law of Ukraine (2003a) 'On Democratic Civil Control over Military Units and State Law-Enforcement Organs', 19.06.2003, No. 975-IV.

Law of Ukraine (2003b) 'On Basis of the State Regulatory Policy in the Sphere of Business Activity', 11.09.03, No. 1160-IV.

Law No. 4721 (2001), *Resmi Gazete*, No. 24607, 8 December 2001.

Law No. 5018 (2003), *Resmi Gazete*, No: 25326, 24 December 2003.

Law No. 5237 (2004), *Resmi Gazete*, No. 25611, 12 October 2004.

Law No. 5253 (2004), *Resmi Gazete*, No. 25649, 23 November 2004.

Minister of Justice (2007) 'Hukumetten TSK'nin Aciklamasina Yanit' (Response from the Government to Declaration by the Turkish Armed Forces'). Online. Available HTTP: <http://www.ntvmsnbc.com/news/406658.asp> (accessed 30 April 2007).

National Democratic Institute for International Affairs (2003) *Roma Political Participation in Romania*, February.

National Program for the Adoption of the Acquis Communautaire, Official Gazette Number 24352, March 24, 2001.

OECD (2006a) 'Romania Aid at a Glance Chart'. Online. Available HTTP:<http://www.oecd.org/countrylist/0,3349,en_2649_34447_25602317_1_1_1_1,00.html> (accessed 12 July 2007).

OECD (2006b) 'Serbia-Montenegro Aid at a Glance Chart'. Online. Available HTTP: <http://www.oecd.org/dataoecd/12/58/1883506.gif> (accessed 12 July 2007).

OECD (2006c) 'Turkey Aid at a Glance Chart'. Online. Available HTTP:<http://www.oecd.org/dataoecd/17/54/38054639.gif> (accessed 12 July 2007).

OECD (2006d) 'Ukraine Aid at Glance a Chart'. Online. Available HTTP:<http://www.oecd.org/dataoecd/12/33/1883309.gif> (accessed 12 July 2007).

Offical Gazette (2003a) Law No. 4928. Offical Gazette No. 25173, 19 July 2003.

Offical Gazette (2003b) Law No. 4963. Offical Gazette No. 25, 7 August 2003.

Offical Journal (2003) 'EU Action Plan on justice and Home Affairs in Ukraine' (text approved by the Council on 10 December 2001). *Offical Journal* C077, 29 March 2003:1–5.

Office of the Chief of Staff, Turkish Armed Forces (2007) Press Release on 'Son Gunlerde Meydana Gelen Gelismeler Hakkinda' (On Developments that Occurred over the Course of Last Days), No. BA-08/07, 27 April 2007. Online. Available HTTP:<http://www.tsk.mil.tr/10_ARSIV/10_1_Basin_Yayin_Faaliyetleri/10_1_Basin_Aciklamalari/2007/BA_08.html> (accessed 12 July 2007).

Open Society Foundation Romania (2004) *Public Opinion Barometer*.

OSCE (2003) 'Report on Judicial Reform in Serbia'. Rule of Law/Human Rights Department. Online. Available HTTP:<http://www.osce.org/documents/fry/2003/03/13_en.pdf> (accessed 13 July 2007).

OSCE (2006) 'Report of the Head of the OSCE Mission to Serbia and Montenegro', PC.FR/3/06/Rev.1. Online. Available HTTP:<http://www.osce.org/documents/fry/2006/03/18313 en.pdf> (accessed 13 July 2007).

Radikal (2005a) 'Vakiflardan Bu Kadar Artik Gözler Hükümette (The Foundations have done their part, now it is the Government's Turn)', 15 April 2005.

Radikal (2005b) 'Gerekirse Asker Yine Göreve (The Military on Duty if Needed)', 26 October 2005.

Radikal (2006a) 'Vakifta AB'ye Uyum (Harmonisation with the EU in Foundations)', 1 January 2006.

Radikal (2006b) 'Orhan Pamuk Davasi Düştü' (Orhan Pamuk Case has been Dropped), 23 January 2006.

ReliefWeb (2006) 'Serbia: Constitutional referendum results obtained only under severe government pressure', 31 October 2006. Online. HTTP:<http://www.reliefweb.int/rw/RWB.NSF/db900SID/TKAE-6V59UF? OpenDocument> (accessed 10 July 2007).

Resmi Gazete (2003a) No. 25173, 19 July 2003.

Resmi Gazete (2003b) No. 25192, 7 August 2003.

Romanian Association for Transparency (2005) *Studiu privind perceptia magistratilor asupra independentei sistemului judiciar 2005* [Study on the magistrates' perception on the independence of the judiciary] and *ibidem* 2006 (in Romanian). Online. Available HTTP:<http://www.transparency.ro/politici_si_studii/sondaje/2006/index.html> (accessed 2 February 2007).

Romanian Coalition for a Clean Parliament (2005) *A Quest for Political Integrity*, Polirom: Iasi.

Romanian EC Delegation (2004) *What do Romanians think about European Union funding and how do they perceive the EC Delegation to Romania*, survey conducted by IRSOP Market Research Ltd, Bucharest, August.

Romanian National Statistics Institute (2003), *Statistical Yearbook 2003*.

Romani Criss Report (2006) 'Overview of the Roma situation in Romania', 'Impreuna' Agency for Community Development & Romani Criss (Roma Center for Social Intervention and Studies). Online. Available HTTP:<http://www.romanicriss.org/ documente/DDO/noutati/

Alternative%20report%20on%20Romania%20aug%202006%20CRISS%20Impreuna%20FINAL.pdf > (accessed 10 October 2006).

Serbian European Integration Office (2005) 'National strategy of Serbia for the Serbia and Montenegro accession to the European Union'. Online. HTTP: <http://www.seio.sr.gov. yu/code/navigate.asp?Id=73> (accessed 13 July 2007).

Transparency International (2004) 'Global Corruption Report 2004. Country Report Serbia'. Online. Available HTTP:<http://www.transparency.org/publications/gcr/download_gcr/download_gcr_2004> (accessed 13 July 2007).

Turkish Daily News, *Article 301 new benchmark for EU*, 7th November 2007.

UNDP (2006) 'At Risk: Roma and the Displaced in Southeast Europe', UNDP Regional Bureau for Europe and CIS. Online. Available HTTP: http://europeandcis.undp.org/uploads/public/File/rbec_web/vgr/vuln_rep_all.pdf> (accessed 12 October 2006).

UNDP Romania (2006) *Evaluation of Programmes Targeting Roma Communities in Romania*, Cluj-Napoca: AMM Design.

US Department of State (2006) '*Romania. Country Reports on Human Rights Practices 2006*', Bureau of Democracy, Human Rights and Labor. Online. Available HTTP: <http://www.state.gov/g/drl/rls/hrrpt/2006/78834.htm> (accessed October 2007).

US Department of State - Bureau of Democracy, Human Rights, and Labor (2005) 'Serbia-Montenegro Country Reports on Human Rights Practices 2005'. Online. Available HTTP: <http://www.state.gov/g/drl/rls/hrrpt/2005/61673.htm> (last access: 10 July 2007).

World Bank (2001) World Bank Development Report 2000/2001.

World Bank (2003), 'Turkey: Poverty and Coping after Crises', Turkey Main Report No. 24185, 28 July.

World Bank (2004) *World Bank Development Report 2004*.

World Bank (2006) 'Turkey: Country Economic Memorandum: Promoting Sustained Growth and Convergence with the European Union', Report No. 33549, 23 February.

World Bank Office for South East Europe (2005) 'Serbia, EU integration and the State Union. Reforms – Updated Statement'. Online. Available HTTP:<http://www.seerecon.org/serbiamontenegro/documents/reforms_statement_serbia/annex4-1-serbia_eu_su.pdf> (accessed 13 July 2007).

Index

page references followed by f indicate an illustrative figure; n indicates a note; t indicates a table

For Product Safety Concerns and Information please contact our EU representative GPSR@taylorandfrancis.com
Taylor & Francis Verlag GmbH, Kaufingerstraße 24, 80331 München, Germany

www.ingramcontent.com/pod-product-compliance
Ingram Content Group UK Ltd.
Pitfield, Milton Keynes, MK11 3LW, UK
UKHW022022180926
475701UK00005B/993